The Concept of Genocide in International Criminal Law

This book presents a review of historical and emerging legal issues that concern the interpretation of the international crime of genocide.

The Polish legal expert Raphael Lemkin formulated the concept of genocide during the Nazi occupation of Europe, and it was then incorporated into the 1948 Convention on the Prevention and Punishment of the Crime of Genocide. This volume looks at the issues that are raised both by the existing international law definition of genocide and by the possible developments that continue to emerge under international criminal law. The authors consider how the concept of genocide might be used in different contexts, and see whether the definition in the 1948 convention may need some revision, also in the light of the original ideas that were expressed by Lemkin. The book focuses on specific themes that allow the reader to understand some of the problems related to the legal definition of genocide, in the context of historical and recent developments.

As a valuable contribution to the debate on the significance, meaning and application of the crime of genocide the book will be essential reading for students and academics working in the areas of Legal History, International Criminal Law, Human Rights, and Genocide Studies.

Marco Odello, PhD (Madrid), LLM (Nottingham), LLB (Rome), is Reader in Law at Aberystwyth University.

Piotr Łubiński, PhD, is Senior Lecturer at the Institute of Security and Civic Education, Pedagogical University, Krakow, Poland.

The Concept of Genocide in International Criminal Law

Developments after Lemkin

Edited by Marco Odello and Piotr Łubiński

Routledge
Taylor & Francis Group
LONDON AND NEW YORK

First published 2020
by Routledge
2 Park Square, Milton Park, Abingdon, Oxon OX14 4RN

and by Routledge
605 Third Avenue, New York, NY 10017

First issued in paperback 2022

Routledge is an imprint of the Taylor & Francis Group, an informa business

British Library Cataloguing-in-Publication Data
A catalogue record for this book is available from the British Library

Library of Congress Cataloging-in-Publication Data
A catalog record has been requested for this book

ISBN: 978-0-367-85819-3 (hbk)
ISBN: 978-0-367-50498-4 (pbk)
ISBN: 978-1-003-01522-2 (ebk)

DOI: 10.4324/9781003015222

Typeset in Galliard
by Swales & Willis, Exeter, Devon, UK

Dedicated to Ola, Zosia, Jurek and my Mum – Piotr

Contents

Editors and contributors

Marco Odello, PhD (Madrid), LLM (Nottingham), LLB (Rome), is Reader in Law at Aberystwyth University. He teaches International Law, International Humanitarian Law, Human Rights Law, and Comparative Public Law. He is a member of the International Institute of Humanitarian Law. He has been a guest lecturer at several institutions including the NATO School (Oberammergau); the International and European Doctoral Seminar at the University of Nice; the LLM in International Criminal Law, University of Turin and UNICRI; and the Summer University on Human Rights in Geneva. His publications include: 'The United Nations Declaration on the Rights of Indigenous Peoples' in D. Short and C. Lennox (eds), *Handbook of Indigenous Peoples' Rights*, 2016; (with F. Seatzu, eds) *Latin American and Caribbean International Institutional Law*, 2015; (with F. Seatzu, eds) *Armed Forces and International Jurisdictions*, 2013; (with F. Seatzu) *The UN Committee on Economic, Social and Cultural Rights*, 2012; (with S. Cavandoli, eds) *Emerging Human Rights in the XXI Century*, 2011; (with R. Piotrowicz, eds) *International Military Missions and International Law*, 2011.

Piotr Łubiński, PhD (Aberystwyth 2016, Krakow 2012), is a lawyer and senior lecturer (Institute of Security Studies, Pedagogical University) in Humanitarian Law, International Criminal Law, Human Rights, and International Public Law. He attended programs and courses run by international institutions, such as workshops on rules of engagement conducted by the International Institute of Humanitarian Law Sanremo (Italy), the Seminar in the Centre for Studies and Research in International Law and International Relations (The Hague Academy of International Law, Netherlands) and the Warsaw Summer School on Humanitarian Law in Poland. He was also legal adviser to the Polish military forces in Afghanistan in 2008. His publications include: 'Human rights and humanitarian law in EU military operations' in *European Union with Brexit Ahead* (ed. J. Barcik; in Polish), 2018; (editor) *International Humanitarian Law of Armed Conflicts: Selected Issues*, 2017; and four chapters in *The International Humanitarian Law of Armed Conflict Manual* (eds Z. Falkowski and M. Marcinko; in Polish), 2014.

Ruth Amir is Senior Lecturer at the Department of Political Science at Yezreel Valley College. Her research and publications focus on transitional justice, genocidal forcible child transfers, and forced migration. Among her recent books are: *Twentieth Century Forcible Child Transfers: Probing the Boundaries of the Genocide Convention*, *Who Is Afraid of Historical Redress: The Israeli Victim-Perpetrator Dichotomy*, *The Politics of Victimhood: Historical Redress in Israel?* (in Hebrew), and the co-edited volume *Critical Insights: Anne Frank, the Diary of a Young Girl*. Her two recent articles (2018) are 'Canada and the Genocide Question: It Did Happen Here' and 'Law Meets Literature: Raphael Lemkin and Genocide Studies'.

Tamas Vince Adany is Associate Professor of International Law and the Head of Department for International Law at the Pazmany Peter Catholic University in Budapest. He graduated as a lawyer (Doctor iuris) in 2000, and he holds a PhD in International Law and a master's degree in International Relations. He was a research assistant for the Hungarian Government in the Gabcikovo–Nagymaros Case. He has advised a number of legal practitioners and has also assisted Hungarian government experts as well as several non-governmental organisations. During the nearly two decades of his academic career he has been teaching courses on various aspects of international law in several universities in Hungary, Poland, the Netherlands, Lithuania, and the United States. He is a member of the International and European Law Sub-commission of the Hungarian Academy of Sciences and the Hungarian Branch of the International Law Association.

Agnieszka Bieńczyk-Missala is Dr hab. Assistant Professor at the Institute of International Relations, University of Warsaw. She is also Vice-Director for Academic Research and International Cooperation at the Institute of International Relations, University of Warsaw (since 2008), and has been an analyst at the Polish Institute of International Affairs (2006–2008), an expert at the European TUNING Programme (2009–2010), and a participant in the Network on Humanitarian Action (since 2006).

Kamil Boczek is a PhD student of the Faculty of Law in the Warsaw University. He specialises in international law, especially on the issues related to crimes against humanity, genocide, and human rights.

Michala Chadimová, JUDr., LLM, is Legal Advisor at La Strada Czech Republic, and a PhD candidate at Palacky University Olomouc with research on international criminal responsibility for special intent crimes. An LLM graduate at the Amsterdam University in International Public and European Law, she has legal experience in national and international prosecution. She spent six months at the International Criminal Court and participated in the prosecution of Bosco Ntaganda for war crimes and crimes against humanity. She also served at the Office of the Co-Prosecutor at the Extraordinary Chambers in the Courts of Cambodia. She is a member of the International Association of Genocide Scholars.

Łukasz Dawid Dąbrowski, PhD in law; attorney-at-law. Assistant professor of the Collegium of World Economy, Warsaw School of Economics. Lecturer in the Department of Human Rights Protection and International Humanitarian Law at University Cardinal Stefan Wyszyński in Warsaw. Member of the Legislative Commission of the Polish Bar Council, member of International Law Association Polish branch and member of European Society of International Law. Provides legal services to telecommunications companies and represents legal entities in administrative and civil procedures in all types of courts. Author of publications in the field of international criminal law, international protection of human rights law and telecommunications law.

Tamás Hoffmann holds a PhD in Law from the International Law Department, Eötvös Loránd University of Sciences, Budapest. He obtained a Diploma in International Humanitarian Law from the International Committee of the Red Cross, Geneva, in 2005 and an LLM in Public International Law (University of London, King's College). He is an associate professor at the Corvinus University of Budapest and a senior research fellow at the Institute for Legal Studies of the Centre for Social Studies of the Hungarian Academy of Sciences, and has served as an intern in the Office of the Prosecutor, Appeals Section, of the International Criminal Tribunal for the Former Yugoslavia, The Hague. He is the author of several publications in Hungarian and English.

Milena Ingelevič-Citak, PhD, is Junior Teaching and Research Assistant for the Chair of Public International Law at Jagiellonian University, and a member of the International Law Association – Polish Group and the Association of Polish Academics in Lithuania. Her research interests lie in the area of public international law, with a particular focus on state-building processes, international recognition of states and the issue of non-recognised entities, human rights, the Russian doctrine of international law, and terrorism in cyberspace. She is the author or co-author of 13 scientific articles, co-author of one monograph, and co-editor of two publications.

Marcin Marcinko, PhD, is Senior Teaching and Research Assistant for the Chair of Public International Law at Jagiellonian University in Krakow; Coordinator of the International Humanitarian Law and Human Rights Centre, Faculty of Law and Administration, Jagiellonian University; and Chairman of the National Commission on Dissemination of International Humanitarian Law, Polish Red Cross Main Board.

Hanna Schieve is Projects and Policy Manager at the Natural History Museum (London), focused particularly on due diligence, ethics, and data protection. She is an alumna, with an MSc in Conflict Studies, of the London School of Economics and Political Science, where she specialised in political violence in Sub-Saharan Africa. She has wide-ranging experience working in policy and politics across the US and the UK, including as an intern at the House of Commons, the United States Senate, and the Pacific Council on International

Policy in Los Angeles. She is a proud Badger alumna with a BA with Honors in Letters and Science and a double major in Political Science and French from the University of Wisconsin-Madison.

Olga Wasiuta is Director of the Institute of the Security Studies at the Pedagogical University KEN in Krakow. Currently her scientific interests focus on the problems of regional security, information security, and hybrid war led by Russia, and its impact on the perception of security by European countries. She conducts research on political and social challenges in Russia and Ukraine, showing the interdependence and contradiction of interests between Russia and the former USSR republics. She is the author of approximately 400 publications including monographs, edited books, and textbooks.

Introduction

The idea to celebrate the 70th anniversary of the Genocide Convention seemed to be not only appropriate but also necessary for international lawyers from this part of the Europe. Krakow is located in proximity to Auschwitz – the tragic reminder and cause of Lemkin's concerns and legal endeavours. In addition, Jagiellonian University is located in Krakow, which is where his colleagues, professors, and even opponents were often educated. However, this book is also a tribute and contribution from many other persons and scholars. Ten years ago, Warsaw University organised a conference commemorating the 60th anniversary of the convention. We are extremely proud to continue the research that for many Polish lawyers is often intermingled with personal experiences. This book is the result of a conference marking the 70th anniversary of the Genocide Convention, which was organised in Krakow jointly by the Pedagogical University and Jagiellonian University.

The contributors to this book have been asked to address and discuss, whenever possible, the legacy and ideas that were introduced by Raphael Lemkin in relation to the concept of genocide. Born in Poland, Lemkin formulated the concept of genocide during the Nazi occupation of different countries in Europe before and during the Second World War. Following the end of the war, and while the atrocities committed against millions of civilians were coming to light, the United Nations committed itself to adopting a legal document that would define certain types of crimes that could be prevented and punished under international law. The 1948 Convention on the Prevention and Punishment of the Crime of Genocide was the result of Lemkin's dedicated personal and intellectual efforts to provide a legal definition of the crime that he had already identified as an international crime in his writings. In many ways, it was the result of an almost one-person lobbying machine, including meetings with and letters sent to a variety of individuals, institutions, and politicians.

Lemkin's original definition of genocide – a word that he invented – included a variety of acts that would affect certain groups and that could lead to the destruction or annihilation of those targeted groups. Today, 70 years after the adoption of the Genocide Convention, there are still examples of massive violations of human rights that are directed against certain groups and sections of the population with the possible intention of exterminating them. The concept, and the convention, are still living works and ideas. The nature of the media, which can be used for the incitement to genocide, as well as the issue of cultural genocide, are theoretical issues that are very much debated nowadays. On practical side, the scale of ISIS's brutality again shocked the world in its genocide of the Yazidi population.

This living document is also debated thanks to Philippe Sands' excellent book *East West Street*,[1] which still raises questions whether Lemkin's original formulation and understanding of the concept of genocidal acts and intentions were, possibly, the right ones. In the past 70 years there has been an increasing international focus on crimes that might fit within the Genocide Convention's definition – in particular as a consequence of the developments in international human rights and international criminal law and the decisions of international courts. The present book looks at the issues that are raised by both the existing international law definition of genocide and the possible developments that are emerging under international criminal law. It provides an updated review of both the historical and emerging legal issues that concern the interpretation of the international crime of genocide.

The contributions to this book are organised into three sections. The first part covers the theoretical and historical framework. Agnieszka Bieńczyk-Missala deals with Rafał Lemkin's concept of genocide vs that encompassed in the Genocide Convention. She goes back to Lemkin's early Madrid paper and the evolution of the concept of 'genocide'. Lemkin's understanding and knowledge about the Soviet policy in Ukraine during the Great Holodomor (great famine) also had a great influence on his writing, and he openly called the Holodomor genocide. Professor Olga Wasiuta examines and describes this Ukrainian experience of genocide in 1932–1933, while Hanna Schieve provides a revised consideration of the Rwandan genocide and its actors to complete this first section of the book.

The second part of the book addresses the international and national legal dimensions. The prohibition of genocide has a significant influence on the domestic legal orders, as it is important to include a definition of the crime in national criminal law that would provide the necessary characterisation and procedures to make it possible to prosecute individuals who are considered responsible for such a crime. Tamás Hoffmann looks at the crime of genocide in its (nearly) infinite domestic varieties to show how the international definition may be integrated into states' national and international practice. In connection with this aspect of national prosecution, Kamil Boczek considers in detail the responsibility of members of the government and other public officials in relation to the application of Article 4 of the Genocide Convention. This section of the book concludes with a chapter written by Łukasz Dawid Dąbrowski on the liability of transnational corporations for genocide, with specific attention paid

1 P. Sands, *East West Street: On the Origins of Genocide and Crimes against Humanity* (Weidenfeld & Nicholson, London, 2017).

to contemporary international law. The increasing role of corporations and their complicity in many very serious violations of international law and human rights raises important questions about their potential responsibility, including in the context of the crime of genocide.

The third and final section of the book provides a discussion on topics and issues that show how the law on genocide remains a subject of both continuing interpretation and evolution, making the Genocide Convention a living instrument that could and should adapt to the evolving situations and events that threaten the survival of different groups of people. Ruth Amir argues in her chapter – entitled 'Probing the boundaries of the Genocide Convention: children as a protected group' – for an increased protection of children, especially in the context of forcible recruitment of child soldiers and forcible child transfers by non-state actors perpetrating genocide and mass atrocities. Michala Chadimová considers the interaction between genocide and the doctrine of superior responsibility. This is done by looking at the requirement of the 'special intent' for the crime of genocide and thus dealing with the very core of the Genocide Convention, while addressing the unique relationship between superior responsibility and the required special intent to commit the crime of genocide, which deserves a more complex analysis. Milena Ingelevič-Citak and Marcin Marcinko address the topic of the misinterpretation of religiously motivated terrorism in relation to the crime of genocide. They clarify that religiously motivated terrorism, although concerning a specific religious group, is guided by completely different assumptions based on the objective that terrorist groups intend to achieve.

Despite the International Criminal Tribunal for the Former Yugoslavia's decisions on the topic, 'ethnic cleansing' still lacks a clear and universally accepted legal definition. Tamas Vince Adany considers the possible interactions and distinctions between the crimes of ethnic cleansing and genocide, and argues that ethnic cleansing can be tantamount to genocide in certain cases.

Marco Odello considers some elements of the never-ending debate on cultural genocide. His chapter takes into consideration the evolution of the protection of culture, cultural heritage, and cultural goods, both material and immaterial, under the broader context of international law and international criminal law. He addresses the issue of whether there is a need for new forms of revised protection of different types of cultural expressions within the context of international criminal law, particularly in relation to genocide. This third section ends with Piotr Łubiński's chapter discussing the role of social media in the incitement to genocide, with a particular focus on the situation within countries that are parties to the European Convention on Human Rights. He analyses the extent to which the new media may serve as a platform for direct and public incitement to genocide.

In conclusion, the broad scope of this book should contribute to a revised consideration of a number of issues that raise concerns in relation to the crime of genocide, and that to some extent have been excluded, forgotten, or maybe even set aside on purpose, by those viewpoints that take a narrow interpretation of the crime of genocide. It seems that narrow interpretations are sometimes supported by states whose actions and policies have shown little sympathy for the victims of genocide, and sometimes might become forms of collusion with regimes that led to genocidal actions and that are based on different political, economic, and ideological motivations.

Every year, many states commemorate the millions of victims of the Nazis' genocidal policies with events that often take the name of Holocaust Remembrance Day. It is very important that these events take place to avoid the oblivion of the past and remember that these crimes may occur even within the most refined societies. However, it would be also important that those same states take adequate actions when these types of crimes manifest themselves and, even more importantly, work more closely together to prevent the manifestation of genocide wherever it may occur.

We hope that this collective work will contribute to the debate on the definition and the meaning of the crime of genocide[2] in light of the broader developments that occurred in international law since the adoption of the 1948 Genocide Convention.

The aim is not only to test, but also to provide, some ideas that might be used in different legal and non-legal contexts and that could support an evolutionary and updated interpretation of the 'crime of crimes' more in line with the ideas, aims, and purposes that were originally conceived by Lemkin more than 70 years ago.

Marco Odello and Piotr Łubiński
Aberystwyth and Krakow, July 2020

2 See, among others: S. Totten and H.C. Theriault, *The United Nations Genocide Convention: An Introduction* (University of Toronto Press, 2020); J.S. Bachman, *Cultural Genocide: Law, Politics, and Global Manifestations* (Routledge, 2019); L. Whitt, A.W. Clarke, *North American Genocides: Indigenous Nations, Settler Colonialism, and International Law* (CUP, 2019); S. Totten (ed), *Teaching about Genocide* (Rowman & Littlefield, 2018); B. Lang, *Genocide: The Act as Idea* (Pennsylvania Studies in Human Rights; University of Pennsylvania Press, 2017).

Acknowledgements

This publication is a result of the conference, marking 70 years of the Genocide Convention, which took place in Kraków 6–7 December 2018. This event wouldn't have been possible without the help and support of many people. I would particularly like to express my gratitude to Dr Alicja Bartuś and the Oswięcim Institute of Human Rights; Professor Adam Bodnar, Commissioner for Human Rights; Piotr Ćwik, the Małopolska Provincial Governor; Beata Machul-Telus and the Parliamentary Committee on Ethnic and National Minorities; Jerzy Marcinko and MPEC; Anna Pietrzykowska and Tygodnik Powszechny; Hanna Polak and the "Angel of Sinjar" movie crew as well as dear guests Hanifa, Saeed i Waddha, Joachim Rusek and the Judaica Foundation – Centre for Jewish Culture in Krakow; Magdalena Stefańska and the Polish Red Cross and Maciej Zabierowski – Auschwitz Jewish Centre.

On behalf of academic institutions: Professor Kazimierz Karolczak and the Pedagogical University; Professor Olga Wasiuta and the Institute of Security Studies; Joanna Bocheńska and the Jagiellonian University Department of Iranian Studies; Marcin Marcinko, Milena Ingelevič-Citak, Przemysław Roguski and the Jagiellonian University Department of Law and Administration; staff members of the Institute of Security Studies, especially Przemysław Mazur, Marek Pietrzyk, Przemysław Wywiał, Katarzyna Pabis, Cisowska, Justyna Rokitowska, Sylwia Fabiańska, Zuzanna Juszczyk and all contributors, participants and students of the Pedagogical University in Kraków.

Part I

Theoretical and historical framework

1 Raphael Lemkin's legacy in international law

Agnieszka Bieńczyk-Missala

It took many years to restore the memory of Raphael Lemkin, who coined the term "genocide." Currently he is a well-known figure, especially among lawyers and historians, who appreciate his massive contribution to the concept of genocide and to the Convention on the Prevention and Punishment of the Crime of Genocide of 9 December 1948 which, taking into account his personal engagement and the influence on the treaty, is often called Lemkin's Convention.

Lemkin's concept arose in a difficult period for humanity, during which the slaughter of Armenians, the Great Famine in Ukraine, mass exterminations in the Soviet Union, the Holocaust, and mass crimes against the population of Central and Eastern European countries occupied by Fascist Germany all took place. However, there was no prohibition of mass killings in international law, as well as no comprehensive rules to protect minorities and other vulnerable groups. In addition, sovereignty was understood as the full power of the state over its territory and population, which resulted in the lack of reaction on the part of other governments to the suffering of the people.[1] The dominant practice of non-interference in relations between a state and its citizens put the international community in the role of a passive observer of the tragedies experienced by individuals and entire groups as a result of government actions.

Raphael Lemkin was one of those engaged lawyers who lived at a turning point in history and influenced the development of international law. Before World War II, only selective initiatives were implemented regarding the protection of human rights in international law. These were related to, among other issues, the prohibition of slavery, the protection of religious and national minorities, the rights of employees or the protection of persons during armed conflicts. The drama of the mass crimes of World War II finally revealed the need to take greater responsibility for the individual and his/her dignity and to protect entire groups exposed to a violation of their

1 See: J. Bodin, *Six Books on Commonwealth* (Basil Blackwell 1955); E. Andrew, "Jean Bodin on Sovereignty" (2011) 2(2) *Republics of Letters: A Journal for the Study of Knowledge, Politics, and the Arts.*

rights.[2] Raphael Lemkin was one of the first to notice the threats arising from the deficit of legal protection for entire social groups exposed to persecution and extermination. He made his first legal proposals even before the outbreak of war. However, it was the cruelty of mass crimes after 1939 that brought about a change in international consciousness and enabled the implementation of his ideas. The purpose of this chapter is to present Raphael Lemkin's legacy in international law.

Personal context

Raphael Lemkin was born on 24 June 1900, in a Jewish family in Bezwodne, near Volkovysk.[3] These lands, known as the Eastern Borderlands, belonged to Russia at the time of the partitions of the multinational Commonwealth at the end of the eighteenth century. He was the son of Bella and Josef. His father was a farmer, and his well-educated mother took care of her son's upbringing and education, exerting a great influence on him. He spent his childhood in an extremely ethnically diverse part of the country, where for centuries Poles, Ukrainians, Jews, Belarusians, Lithuanians, and Karaites lived side by side. He witnessed various situations, both good and peaceful cooperation and serious tensions between ethnic groups, including discrimination against Jews. He graduated from middle school in Volkovysk, and then studied law at the Jan Kazimierz University in Lviv – one of the most important academic centers in the Second Polish Republic. He attended the courses of many outstanding Polish lawyers there, including Juliusz Makarewicz, Ludwik Ehrlih, and Stanisław Starzyński.[4] Lemkin obtained a doctoral degree in law from the University of Lviv in 1926.

Multiethnic and multicultural Lviv strongly influenced him and was intellectually inspiring. Although Lemkin was interested in the suffering of minorities already in childhood – he read about the situation of Christians in ancient Rome in Henryk Sienkiewicz's *Quo Vadis* – it was only during his student years that he seriously analyzed the tragedy of mass crimes committed on religious and ethnic communities. He was especially interested in the case of the massacre

2 D. Shelton, *An Introduction to the History of International Human Rights Law* (George Washington University Law School, Working Paper No. 346, August 2007) 1–13; R. Kuźniar, *Prawa człowieka, prawo, instytucje, stosunki międzynarodowe* (Wydawnictwo Naukowe Scholar 2000) 29–33.

3 R. Szawłowski, "Raphael Lemkin's Life Journey: From Creative Legal Scholar and Well-to-do Lawyer in Warsaw until 1939 to Pinnacle of International Achievements during the 1940s in the States, Ending Penniless Crusader in New York in the 1950s" in A. Bieńczyk-Missala and S. Dębski (eds.), *Rafał Lemkin: A Hero of Humankind* (Polish Institute of International Affairs 2010) 31–57.

4 A. Redzik and I. Zeman, "Masters of Rafał Lemkin: Lwów School of Law" in A. Bieńczyk-Missala (ed.), *Civilians in Contemporary Armed Conflicts* (Warsaw University Press 2017) 235–240.

of the Armenians, which he discussed with his professors.[5] Lemkin's interest in mass crimes was particularly influenced by two events: the murder of Talaat Pasha, who was responsible for the pogroms of the Armenians in Turkey; and the assassination of Symon Petliura in retaliation for the pogroms against Jews by the Ukrainian People's Republic in 1919.[6] These events prompted him to ask questions about international justice and the legal responsibility of units for the crimes they committed.

He moved to Warsaw in 1926, where as a Doctor of Law he began his career. Lemkin became the secretary of the Appellate Court in Warsaw, and then worked as a prosecutor and a secretary in criminal law sections and subcommissions of the Polish Codification Commission.

Lemkin also participated in the forensic seminar of Wacław Makowski at the University of Warsaw. In 1933, Lemkin became an assistant professor at the Law School of the Polish Open University in Warsaw, which was headed by Professor Emil Rappaport. He closely observed the contemporary tendencies in European criminal law, especially the legislation and new criminal law codifications in Fascist Italy and Soviet Russia. He published several papers in this field, including a translation of the Soviet Penal Code.[7] He also published several papers on the codification of Polish penal law.[8]

Lemkin was introduced to the International Bureau for the Unification of Penal Law in the 1930s. He became a permanent Polish delegate to numerous conferences and international congresses in the field of criminal law.[9] He prepared a famous lecture at the 5th International Conference for the Unification of Criminal Law in Madrid, in which he proposed new crimes against the law of nations – the crime of barbarity (exterminations by means of massacres, pogroms, or economic discrimination), and the crime of vandalism (the destruction of cultural and artistic works). His idea did not gain national or international support. At the beginning of 1934 Lemkin quit his service as a vice-prosecutor and joined the Bar of the District Chambers of Advocates in Warsaw.

After the outbreak of World War II on 1 September 1939 Lemkin made the decision, not understood by his immediate family, to escape from Poland. He

5 See: D.-L. Frieze (ed.), *Totally Unofficial: The Autobiography of Raphael Lemkin* (Yale University Press 2013).

6 M. Kornat, "Rafał Lemkin's Formative Years and the Beginning of his International Career in Inter-war Poland (1918–1939)" in Bieńczyk-Missala and Dębski (eds.), *Rafał Lemkin*, 61–62.

7 R. Lemkin, "Dzieje i charakter reformy prawa karnego we Włoszech" in *Kodeks karny faszystowski*, Warsaw 1929 7–89; *Kodeks Karny Republik Sowieckich* (1926) (R. Lemkin's translation in cooperation with T. Kochanowski); see also: *Kodeks karny Rosji Sowieckiej. 1927* (translation and introduction by R. Lemkin) (1928); R. Lemkin, *Ustawodawstwo karne Rosji Sowieckiej. Kodeks Karny. Procedura Karna* (1938).

8 For example, Lemkin edited the new Penal Code of the Republic of Poland in cooperation with J. Jamont and E.S. Rappaport: *Kodeks karny r. 1932 z dostosowanymi do kodeksu tezami z Orzeczeń Sądu Najwyższego* (1932).

9 A. Redzik, *Rafał Lemkin (1900–1959) Co-Creator of International Criminal Law* (Oficyna Allerhanda - Instytut Allerhanda 2017) 25–26.

went to Sweden through Lithuania, and as a polyglot he quickly began to give lectures in Swedish. Lemkin also cooperated with the Swedish government in collecting material on Nazi Germany's policy in Europe. After about a year, he was given the opportunity to go to the United States, where he taught law at Duke University.[10] His major life's work, entitled *Axis Rule in Occupied Europe*, was written there and published by the Carnegie Endowment for International Peace in 1944. This book was the first to explain the term "genocide."[11]

After World War II he served as an advisor on the staff of the chief prosecutor in the trials of Nazi war criminals in Nuremberg in 1946. He was disappointed that the term "genocide" was not included in the Nuremberg Charter and the final judgment.[12] It was also stated that murders committed before the war were not punishable offenses. Lemkin could not understand why governments' actions against their own citizens could not be the subject of international law.

While in Europe he visited the displaced persons' camps, met his friends, and found out that almost 50 members of his family were killed, including his parents.[13] He was shocked and depressed by how Europe was so affected by World War II. His personal experiences influenced his determination to propose the convention against genocide in the United Nations (UN), a new, universal organization founded in 1945. Lemkin devoted absolutely everything to the adoption of the convention. He gave up his scientific and professional work and he stopped writing and lecturing. He devoted his personal relations to the idea of outlawing genocide, and while lobbying for the convention was difficult and disruptive for him, still he succeeded. The Convention on the Prevention and the Punishment of the Crime of Genocide (Genocide Convention, or the Convention) was adopted by the General Assembly of the UN on 9 December 1945 and entered into force on 12 January 1951. Raphael Lemkin was personally involved in its ratification. He conducted hundreds of talks with diplomats and sent letters to politicians in which he urged the adoption of the Convention.[14]

Raphael Lemkin, who is called the father of the Genocide Convention, was nominated for the Nobel Peace Prize many times, although he never received it. He died in New York on 28 August 1959 in poverty and oblivion. The funeral was attended only by seven relatives and his closest friends. A few days after his death, a note appeared in the *New York Times*:

10 D.-L. Frieze (ed.), *Totally Unofficial* 60–78.

11 Lemkin R., *Axis Rule in Occupied Europe: Laws of Occupation – Analysis of Government – Proposals for Redress* (Carnegie Endowment for International Peace 1944).

12 P. Sands, *East West Street: On the Origins of "Genocide" and "Crimes Against Humanity"* (W&N 2016) 186–189, 297–299.

13 Ibid. 358–360.

14 See also: J. Cooper, *Raphael Lemkin and the Struggle for the Genocide Convention* (Palgrave Macmillan 2008).

> This devoted man did more than any other individual to win formal acceptance of the principle that it is criminal to injure or destroy any national, ethnical, racial or religious group. Raphael Lemkin, once a successful lawyer in Warsaw, had suffered the loss of his family at the hands of the Nazis, except for one brother. He had a distinguished carrier as a teacher, lecturer, and a writer in Poland, but the burden of his final years was his crusade against slavery, degradation, and killing. It was a heavy burden, and it killed him at the age of 58.[15]

Lemkin's concept of genocide and its penalization

Raphael Lemkin wrote – in the famous chapter 9 of *Axis Rule in Occupied Europe* – that "new conceptions require new terms." In his work he explained the concept of "genocide," which he created by combining the ancient Greek word *genos* (race, tribe) with the Latin *cide* (killing). He pointed out that wars were increasingly not waged against state sovereignty but against entire populations. By "genocide" he meant a coordinated plan of different actions directed at the destruction of a nation or of an ethnic group. He pointed to the disintegration of political and social institutions, of culture, language, national feelings, religion, and the economic existence of national groups, but also to the deprivation of individual lives, personal security, health, and property. The fact that his concern was about actions against individuals because of their belonging to a specific group, and not because of their individual capacity, was to distinguish genocide from human rights violations.[16] He wrote that:

> [A]s in the case of homicide, the natural right of existence for individuals is implied: by the formulation of genocide as a crime, the principle that every national, racial, and religious group has a natural right of existence is claimed.[17]

Lemkin distinguished two stages of genocide: "One, destruction of the national pattern of the oppressed group; the other, the imposition of the national pattern of the oppressor."[18] This probably resulted from the experience imposed by the powers ruling over neighboring Poland, which, having been for over 100 years under partitions, experienced Germanization and Russification. He broadly presented genocidal techniques: political, social, cultural, economic, biological,

15 *New York Times* (31 August 1959) 20.
16 Lemkin, *Axis Rule* 79.
17 R. Lemkin, "Genocide" (1946) 15 *American Scholar* 227.
18 Lemkin, *Axis Rule* op.cit., www.preventgenocide.org/lemkin/AxisRule1944-1.htm [accessed 5 January 2020].

physical, religious, and moral ones, referring to German practices in occupied Europe.

Lemkin believed that genocide should be banned during both war and peace. He expressed disappointment by the fact that the Nuremberg Tribunal judged the crimes committed only after the outbreak of World War II. This fact motivated him to submit a draft convention prohibiting genocidal practices regardless of the times of their application. As we know, the scope of crimes against humanity has evolved in this direction.[19]

A part of Lemkin's concept was penalization of the crime. Because he perceived genocide as an affront to the whole of humanity, he formulated that it should be introduced into the penal legislation of all states, and because of the consequences of the crime for international relations he also advocated for universal criminal jurisdiction.[20] He argued that genocides are organized by states or groups supported by states; therefore, the states are not usually interested in punishing perpetrators.[21] These rules should be accompanied by provisions on the protection of national, racial, and religious minority groups placed in national constitutions and international law. As we now know, plans to adopt a universal convention on national, ethnic, religious, and racial minorities have failed to date, and countries have different approaches to their minorities. The UN General Assembly adopted the Declaration on the Rights of Persons Belonging to National or Ethnic, Religious, and Linguistic Minorities only on 18 December 1992.[22]

Lemkin's first implementation of the ban on genocide was the UN General Assembly resolution of 11 December 1946, approved unanimously, which stated that genocide is a crime under international law.[23] It called for genocide to be considered as a crime with universal jurisdiction under the domestic law of all member states. The resolution called for domestic cooperation of all states to coordinate the international prosecution of genocide.

Two years later, the definition of genocide was found in the Convention on the Prevention and Punishment of the Crime of Genocide, adopted in Paris on 9 December 1948. Article I of the Convention declares that states party to it confirmed that genocide, whether committed in a time of peace or in a time of war, is a crime under international law, which they undertake to prevent and to punish. The adopted definition of genocide corresponded to Lemkin's main

19 M.Ch. Bassiouni, *Crimes Against Humanity: Historical Evolution and Contemporary Application* (Cambridge University Press 2011); N. Geras, *Crimes Against Humanity: Birth of a Concept* (Manchester University Press 2011); L.N. Sadat, "Crimes Against Humanity in the Modern Age" (2013) 107 *American Journal of International Law* 334.

20 Lemkin, *Axis Rule* 93–94.

21 A.F. Vrdoljak, "Human Rights and Genocide: The Work of Lauterpacht and Lemkin in Modern International Law" (2010) 20 *The European Journal of International Law* 1185.

22 UN General Assembly Resolution, No. 47/135.

23 UN General Assembly Resolution, 11 December 1946, A/RES/96-I.

assumptions,[24] although it was formulated in a slightly narrower way. According to it:

> Genocide means any of the following acts committed with intent to destroy, in whole or in part, a national, ethnical, racial or religious group, as such:
>
> a. Killing members of the group;
> b. Causing serious bodily or mental harm to members of the group;
> c. Deliberately inflicting on the group conditions of life calculated to bring about its physical destruction in whole or in part;
> d. Imposing measures intended to prevent births within the group;
> e. Forcibly transferring children of the group to another group.[25]

The above definition was the result of a negotiating process and reflected the compromise reached among the UN member states. In the end political groups were not included as protected groups, nor was the so-called "cultural genocide". The need to precisely distinguish genocide from the issue of protecting national and ethnic minorities, crimes against humanity, and human rights was not addressed. Political issues were also important. Serious doubts in this regard were raised by the major powers – the United States, France, and the Soviet Union. The Soviet Union and China sought to eliminate political groups from the concept as being difficult to define precisely. The goal of the USSR was to identify the crime of genocide as closely as possible with Nazi and racist policies. This policy was aimed at diverting attention from Soviet mass deportations, killings, and repression.[26] France feared the category of cultural genocide because of the possibility of its association with colonialism.

The issue of how to punish the crime of genocide was also controversial. The United States was skeptical about the idea of setting up an international criminal court, and France contested the proposal to criminalize genocide in national law. The argument of state sovereignty was invoked in both cases. The main

24 A.-D. Rotfeld, "Rafał Lemkin's Concept of Genocide" in A. Bieńczyk-Missala (ed.), *Civilians in Contemporary Armed Conflicts* 225–231.

25 Convention on the Prevention and Punishment of the Crime of Genocide, 9 December 1948, www.un.org/en/genocideprevention/documents/atrocity-crimes/Doc.1_Convention%20on%20the%20Prevention%20and%20Punishment%20of%20the%20Crime%20of%20Genocide.pdf [accessed 5 January 2020]. See also: M. Shaw, *What is Genocide?* (Polity Press 2007); W. Schabas, *Genocide in International Law: The Crime of Crimes* (Cambridge University Press 2003); A. Jones, *Genocide: A Comprehensive Introduction* (Routledge 2006); L. Kuper, *Genocide* (Yale University Press 1981); S.P. Rosenberg, "Genocide Is a Process, Not an Event" (2012) 7(1) *Genocide Studies and Prevention*, https://scholarcommons.usf.edu/gsp/vol7/iss1/4 [accessed 26 March 2020]; E. D. Weitz, *Century of Genocide: Critical Essays and Eyewitness Accounts* (Princeton University Press 2003); B. Valentino, *Final Solutions: Mass Killing and Genocide in the 20th Century* (Cornell University Press 2004).

26 A. Weiss-Wend, "The Soviet Union and the Genocide Convention: An Exercise in Cold War Politics" in Bieńczyk-Missala and Dębski (eds.), *Rafał Lemkin*, 179–194.

powers significantly contributed to narrowing the definition of genocide as well as the weakening of implementation mechanisms.

Given the limited utility of the Convention, especially during the Cold War, there were allegations that the conventional definition of genocide had many shortcomings. They referred mainly to the category of intent; the too-narrow scope of the groups mentioned in the definition; and the fact that the definition of genocide overlapped with the definition of crimes against humanity. It is easy to make such accusations from the perspective of the past decades and the evolution of the scope of crimes against humanity, especially their extension to times of peace. Raphael Lemkin was not satisfied with the Nuremberg trials and could not predict the evolution of international law.

Despite the difficulties in implementing the Genocide Convention, it was never decided to extend the scope of the crime. The same definition was included in the Rome Statute of the International Criminal Court (Article 6), and was also part of the jurisdiction of ad hoc and hybrid courts, including the International Criminal Tribunal for the Former Yugoslavia and the International Criminal Tribunal for Rwanda. The Convention has been ratified by 152 states,[27] and the International Court of Justice (ICJ) has repeatedly stated that the Convention embodies principles that are part of general customary international law. The ICJ has also stated that the prohibition of genocide is a *ius cogens* norm of international law (peremptory norm) and that no derogation from it is allowed.

Prevention of genocide

Raphael Lemkin's goal was that genocide would never be repeated. He believed that banning the annihilation of groups of people in international law because of their race, national and ethnic character, and religion would have a preventive effect. The day on which the Convention was adopted was the happiest day in his life. Researchers of genocide and Lemkin's ideas rarely refer to the idea of prevention, which is part of the title of the Convention, focusing mainly on elements of the definition of genocide and the effectiveness of international criminal justice. Meanwhile, the concept has *never again* primarily included the idea of prevention.[28]

27 This is the number of ratifications as of 31 December 2019, https://treaties.un.org/Pages/ViewDetails.aspx?src=TREATY&mtdsg_no=IV-1&chapter=4&clang=_en [accessed 5 January 2020].

28 S. Power: *"A Problem from Hell": America and the Age of Genocide* (Basic Books 2013); W. Schabas, "Preventing the 'Odious Scourge': The United Nations and the Prevention of Genocide" (2007) 14(2) *International Journal on Minority and Group Rights* 379; L. Kuper, *The Prevention of Genocide* (Yale University Press 1985); S. McLoughlin, *The Structural Prevention of Mass Atrocities* (Routledge 2014); A.J. Bellamy and A. Lupin, *Why We Fail: Obstacles to the Effective Prevention of Mass Atrocities* (International Peace Institute June 2015); A. Bieńczyk-Missala, "Early Warning and the Prevention of Atrocity Crimes: The Role of the United Nations" in K. Bachmann and D. Heidrich (eds.), *The Legacy of Crimes and Crises: Transitional Justice, Domestic Change and the Role of the International Community* (Peter Lang Edition 2016) 199–207.

Raphael Lemkin saw the obligation to prevent genocide in broad terms.[29] First, he believed that international law itself fulfills a preventive function. When he wrote about the need to adopt legal rules regarding the prohibition of barbarism in the 1930s or genocide in the 1940s, he was convinced that any future convention in this area would ensure the protection of entire groups. Even during World War II he claimed that the swift adoption of the convention would prevent the further genocidal policy of Nazi Germany and the changes which Adolf Hitler sought in the national and ethnic structure in Europe.

Second, Lemkin was convinced that criminal law has a powerful preventive influence. He postulated that the need to punish criminals would lead to the introduction of parallel criminal mechanisms in both domestic and international law. He believed that punishment would stop other perpetrators from committing crimes of genocide.

Third, he believed in institutions. In *Axis Rule in Occupied Europe*, he called for the establishment of institutions that would allow effective control of occupation practices, and he believed that in addition to law the relevant institutions could play a preventive role.

Lemkin's vision of prevention was largely included in the 1948 Convention. It acknowledged that genocide is a crime of international law and should be prevented. From the point of view of the use of UN organs, the most important provisions are contained in Article 8, which provides that any state party to the Convention may request the competent organs of the UN to take the measures provided for in the Charter which it deems appropriate to prevent and suppress acts of genocide or other acts mentioned in Article 3, such as collusion to commit genocide, direct and public incitement to commit crimes, complicity, and more.[30]

However, the Convention does not precisely set out the nature and extent of the prevention obligation. The focus was on the need to punish perpetrators. Thus, states were obliged to establish domestic law that would allow them to be found guilty of genocide, regardless of whether they are constitutionally responsible members of the government, public officials, or private individuals (Article 4).[31] It is not explained what other actions should be taken by states to prevent genocide.

This lack of precision also concerns the area of international cooperation. There were discussions about states, "competent" UN bodies, and "appropriate" instruments for preventing and suppressing genocide, and the source of these instruments was to be the UN Charter. It is not known in what exact situations a particular state was to turn, to which UN body, nor exactly what action should be taken. Nonetheless, this provision could prove sufficient in the event there is the political will to take an action.

29 Lemkin, *Axis Rule*, Chapter IX, ibid.
30 O. Ben-Naftali, "The Obligations to Prevent and to Punish Genocide" in P. Gaeta (ed.), *The UN Genocide Convention: A Commentary* (Oxford University Press 2009) 36–44.
31 Ibid.

The high level of generality of records and the imprecise language have certainly contributed to the overall abandonment of greater efforts to prevent genocide after the adoption of the Convention. In the times of inter-national rivalry during the Cold War period, in principle genocide was not discussed. Works on the establishment of an international criminal tribunal were blocked, and states and experts focused rather on matters related to the creation of an international human rights protection system. After the turn of 1989, however, it turned out that the international community did not have an adequate response to the threat of genocide. Efforts were not sufficient to stop the massacres in the Balkans, Somalia, or Rwanda. What is more, the international community was unable to respond effectively, often compromising – as in Srebrenica in 1995, where the crime took place of killing over 8,000 Bosnian Muslims who were counting on effective shelter in the UN security zone. The events of the 1990s changed the thinking about the reality of international crimes, and the inhumane displacement in Kosovo in 1999[32] motivated experts and state representatives to seek new solutions in the sphere of preventing and responding to international crimes. An important role in this respect was played by the UN Secretary-General Kofi Annan, who argued that the twenty-first century must be the century of prevention,[33] and proclaimed the need to adopt a "culture of prevention" and to look through a "prevention lens" when undertaking development activities.[34]

A broader approach to the idea of prevention can be found in the concept of the responsibility to protect (R2P), presented in the report of the International Commission on Intervention and State Sovereignty of 2001.[35] It proposed a new approach to the issue of state sovereignty and the obligation to prevent and respond to situations of mass suffering of the population. The UN General Assembly, which accepted the idea of the responsibility of states and the international community for civil protection, adopted the concept in a limited, mainly preventive, scope in the Final Document of the jubilee UN summit in 2005. It announced the provision of preventive support to states for civil protection, including construction of their internal potential in this field. The need to develop early-warning capabilities and UN prevention instruments was also recognized.[36] These provisions have been adopted by consensus by all member countries of the UN. It is worth adding that

32 A. Bieńczyk-Missala, "Kosovo: The First War for Human Rights" in M. Madej (ed.), *Western Military Interventions After the Cold War: Evaluation of the Wars of the West* (Routledge 2019).

33 Address by Secretary-General Kofi Annan at the opening of the 54th session of the Commission on Human Rights, 18.03.1998, SG/SM/6487 HR/4355.

34 UN Secretary-General Report, *Prevention of Armed Conflict*, A/55/985–S/2001/574, 07.06.2001.

35 Report of the International Commission on Intervention and State Sovereignty, The Responsibility to Protect, 12.2001, http://responsibilitytoprotect.org/ICISS%20Report.pdf [accessed 5 January 2020].

36 General Assembly, 2005 World Summit Outcome, par. 138–140, www.un.org/en/preventgenocide/adviser/pdf/World%20Summit%20Outcome%20Document.pdf#page=30 [accessed 5 January 2020].

regional organizations have also made efforts to build capacity in order to prevent mass crimes, including genocide. This applies especially to the African Union and the Economic Community of West African States, which have granted themselves the right to armed intervention in situations where there are threats of genocide. In 2006, the International Conference of the Great Lakes Region adopted the Protocol on the Prevention and Punishment of the Crime of Genocide, War Crimes and Crimes Against Humanity and All Forms of Discrimination.[37]

In 2007, the obligation to prevent was confirmed by the ICJ. It considered Bosnia and Herzegovina's request for interim measures against Former Yugoslavia (FRY, today the Republic of Serbia). It had to answer the question whether FRY was obliged to take action to prevent the genocide in Srebrenica in June 1995. In 2007, the ICJ ruled that FRY had not complied with its obligation to prevent genocide and had not imposed a penalty on perpetrators as provided for in Article 1 of the Convention. The ICJ noted that the prevention obligation applies to all parties, is not territorially limited, and refers to immediate and effective action using all necessary funds.

Sovereignty and humanitarian intervention

An important issue raised in the discussion about genocide and other mass crimes is the problem of admissible actions of the international community in situations of an oppressive policy by states towards their own population. In the past, discussions were held about a war of just, humanitarian intervention, until finally the concept of R2P was adopted.[38] Its creators proposed a new understanding of the sovereignty of the state as including a responsibility for civil protection,[39] and defined the responsibility of the international community in three dimensions – prevention, response, and reconstruction – understood as the restoration of a situation of respect for human rights.[40] This concept has evolved with its approval by UN General Assembly in its Summit Outcome Document in 2000[41]

37 See: A. Bieńczyk-Missala, *Zapobieganie masowym naruszeniom praw człowieka. Międzynarodowe instytucje i instrumenty* (WN Scholar 2018) 70–78.

38 A.J. Bellamy and T. Dunne, *The Oxford Handbook of the Responsibility to Protect* (Oxford University Press 2016); W.A. Knight and F. Egerton, *The Routledge Handbook of the Responsibility to Protect* (Routledge 2014); J. Genser and I. Cotler, *The Responsibility to Protect: The Promise of Stopping Mass Atrocities in our Time* (Oxford University Press 2012); R.H. Cooper and J. Voïnov Kohler (eds.), *Responsibility to Protect: The Global Moral Compact for the 21st Century* (Palgrave Macmillan 2009).

39 L. Axworthy, "RtoP and the Evolution of State Sovereignty" in Genser and Cotler (eds.), *The Responsibility to Protect* 3–16.

40 Report of the International Commission on Intervention and State Sovereignty, The Responsibility to Protect, December 2001, http://responsibilitytoprotect.org/ICISS%20Report.pdf [accessed 5 January 2020].

41 General Assembly, 2005 World Summit Outcome, par. 138–140, www.un.org/en/preventgenocide/adviser/pdf/World%20Summit%20Outcome%20Document.pdf#page=30 [accessed 5 January 2020].

as well as numerous reports of the UN Secretary-General. In the January 2009 Report Implementing the Responsibility to Protect, he proposed three dimensions of R2P, which included: responsibility of the state for civil protection; international assistance to states in carrying out their duties; and an international response.[42] At each stage of the discussion, armed intervention was indicated as the last possible international instrument, except that the right to use force has not changed since the adoption of the UN Charter of 1945. In light of international law therefore, only the Security Council can decide to intervene.[43]

Raphael Lemkin also referred to the issue of state sovereignty and humanitarian intervention. As a student, he asked professors why the community did not respond to the massacres of the Armenians. In reply he heard an anecdote about a farmer deciding to kill his own chickens.[44] However, he disagreed with the idea that the authorities could regulate their relations with citizens by resorting to inhumane instruments. He was an advocate of an innovative approach to the sovereignty of the state for those times, maintaining that it could not be a pass/excuse for criminal practices.

He also expressed a favorable attitude towards humanitarian intervention. He referred to it in his manuscript *The Introduction to the Study of Genocide*, written in the 1950s, in which he extensively referred to Professor of International Law Ellery C. Stowell[45] and his definition of a humanitarian intervention, according to which: "Justifiable use of force for the purpose of protecting the inhabitants of another state from treatment so arbitrary and persistently abusive as to exceed the limits within which the sovereign is presumed to act with reason and justice."[46]

Lemkin drew attention to the reluctance of states towards the concept of the legality of humanitarian interventions, and he advocated for its acceptance, citing the arguments of recognized philosophers and lawyers like Hugo Grotius, Johann Kaspar Bluntschli, Henry Wheaton, John Westlake, August Wilhelm Heffner, and Karl von Rotteck, as well as the American president Theodore Roosevelt. In light of Stowell's views, he questioned the belief that the independence of states and the principle of non-interference in internal affairs are "sacred" even in the event of serious violations of international law, when human life is at stake. He believed interventions to protect lives should be allowed.[47]

42 B. Ki-moon, Implementing the Responsibility to Protect, Report of the Secretary-General, A/63/677, 12 January 2009.
43 P. Grzebyk, "Miejsce interwencji zbrojnej w koncepcji odpowiedzialność za ochronę"(2015) 51 Stosunki Międzynarodowe. *International Relations* 61.
44 H. Yahraes, "He Gave a Name to the World's Most Horrible Crime" (3 March 1951) *Collier's*, www.unz.com/print/Colliers-1951mar03-00028 [accessed 5 January 2020]; Sands, *East West Street* 146–149; Frieze (ed.), *Totally Unofficial* 20.
45 E.C. Stowell, *International Law: A Restatement of Principles in Conformity with Actual Practice* (Henry Holt 1931).
46 S.L. Jacobs (ed.), *Lemkin on Genocide* (Lexington Books 2012) 47–48.
47 S.L. Jacobs, "The Human, the Humane, and the Humanitarian: Their Implications and Consequences in Raphael Lemkin's Work on Genocide" in Bieńczyk-Missala and Dębski (eds.), *Rafał Lemkin* 153–164.

The problem of interventions undertaken for humanitarian reasons remains one of the most controversial issues, and history has proven – especially in the interventions in Somalia in 1993, Kosovo in 1999, and Libya in 2011 – that there are no simple solutions to the complicated situations of genocide and other mass crimes. Lemkin's interest in the limits of state sovereignty and the idea of humanitarian intervention demonstrate that he, believing in the power of international law, did not limit his concepts to definitions and legal standards. He believed that the international community must have instruments for implementing the law and be able to provide practical assistance to victims. He believed that international law is an expression of moral feelings,[48] must have a social and human meaning, and must be a real instrument for human progress and justice, and certainly not an obstacle to them.[49]

***

Raphael Lemkin belonged to that small group of lawyers who were extremely involved in building a new international legal order after World War II, aimed at improving the situation of individuals and entire groups. Lemkin's greatest success was that despite the numerous difficulties, including a lack of understanding, a huge personal tragedy, and a struggle with the political will of states, he turned his personal idea into a universal standard: the Convention on the Prevention and Punishment of the Crime of Genocide. His concept and message have always been universal. He did not focus on any one particular case of genocide, but dealt with colonial crimes, Indian massacres, mass murders in Soviet Russia, the Great Famine in Ukraine, and many others. He extrapolated common ethnic, political, and genocidal patterns, which can be considered his personal contribution to comparative studies of genocide. The Holocaust was the massive tragedy that eventually pushed him to fight for the Convention in the UN.

Lemkin's merits go beyond the Genocide Convention. He consistently demonstrated his humanist attitude that international relations were about people. States are not entitled to decide on the existence of population groups, or effect their annihilation. Finally, Lemkin showed that one man can make a difference. He was not a passive observer of reality, but an example of positive activism for a better world.

48 Jacobs (ed.), *Lemkin on Genocide* 10–11.
49 R. Lemkin, "The Legal Case Against Hitler" (24 February 1945) *The Nation* 205.

2 The crime of genocide in Ukraine (1932–1933)

Olga Wasiuta

In the memory of the Ukrainians, as well as other nations, the Holodomor (Great Famine) in 1932–1933 in Ukraine will always be recalled as one of the cruellest, emotionally difficult to perceive, tragedies of the twentieth century. Yet at the same time the Holodomor is a historical occurrence that took place at a defined time and place and was the result of specific people's activity. However, 85 years after the "end" of famine/genocide in Ukraine we still do not know how many people died of unbelievable torture as a result of the homicidal, murderous, and atrocious policy of Joseph Stalin and other loyal leaders of the communist ideology: 5 million, 8 million, or even 12 million or more?[1]

Since 2018, 24 countries have officially declared the Holodomor as a genocide committed against the Ukrainian people. The fact is that a genocide is indisputable and approved by the international community – except, however, Russia, where the issue of the Holodomor does not exist and reminding people of Stalin's genocidal policy is regarded as hostile, anti-Russian propaganda. The Great Famine was recognized as a genocide by the United Nations (UN) General Assembly (November 2003), the European Parliament (23 October 2008) and the Parliamentary Assembly of the Council of Europe (28 April 2010). In 2016 the Parliament of Ukraine appealed to democratic states to recognize the Great Famine of 1932–1933 as a genocide against the Ukrainian people. At the 72nd session of the UN General Assembly in New York on 20 September 2017, the President of Ukraine Petro Poroszenko appealed for a common, global

1 In 1932–1933, as a result of an artificially-provoked famine, according to various sources and demographers' estimations between 7 and 10 million people died of famine and its effects (physical exhaustion, diseases, mass cannibalism). The same estimations are presented in the UN Resolution confirmed by more than 50 states (Address of the President of Ukraine Viktor Yushchenko to the Ukrainian people, to the people's deputies of Ukraine in connection with the consideration of the draft Law of Ukraine 'On the Holodomor of 1932–1933 in Ukraine', 16.11.2006, http://ww7.president.gov.ua/news/data/print/11832.html [Accessed 11.01.2019]; 'Joint Statement by the Delegations of the UN Member States on the 70th Anniversary of the Holodomor in Ukraine 1932–33', 7 November 2003, www.prezident.gov.ua/content/150_10.html [accessed 11.01.2019].

recognition of the Holodomor as a genocide committed against the Ukrainian people.[2]

At the 85th anniversary of the Great Famine in Ukraine, the US Senate recognized it as genocide in a resolution which marked the first legal act in the history of the US Congress devoted to this tragedy. The document includes the conclusions of the US government's Commission on the Ukraine Famine (of 22 April 1988), stating that Stalin and his regime committed genocide on the Ukrainian people in 1932–1933. In the accepted resolution they condemned the systemic violation of Ukrainians' human rights, including the right to self-determination and freedom of speech in Ukraine.[3]

On 24 November 2018, on the 85th anniversary of the Holodomor, Ukrainians all over the world lit candles as a symbol of collective memory of the most horrific tragedy in Ukrainian history; one which wreaked havoc on millions of innocent people, who were the victims of the Holodomor of 1932–1933 – a famine organized by human beings, planned and executed by the Russian communists and Stalin's regime. The Holodomor is recognized by the Ukrainian Parliament as a genocide against the Ukrainians. For decades the Soviet Union had tried to keep this atrocious act and national tragedy secret and the communist regime emphatically negated it. Millions of people, mainly farmers – the backbone of Ukrainian identity, culture and tradition – were literally starved to death within two years. Stalin's policy and regime carried out the genocide in order to make the Ukrainians surrender to the Soviet authority and to "resolve" the Ukrainian issue. The results of research conducted in Ukraine prove that 93 percent of all the victims were villagers. According to the available statistics, at the height of the Holodomor 25,000 Ukrainians died every day. At the same time, during these two years the Soviet Union sold 1.7 million tons of grain on the Western markets.[4]

During the USSR period three waves of famine swept over Ukraine: the first right after the October Revolution of 1921–1923; the Holodomor in

2 "Warsaw: The ecunemic service at the 85th anniversary of The Great Famine in Ukraine", 25.11.2018, https://ekai.pl/warszawa-ekumeniczne-nabozenstwo-w-85-rocznice-wielkiego-glodu-na-ukrainie/[accessed 12.01.2019].

3 "The US Senate: The famine is a genocide", 04.10.2018, www.istpravda.com.ua/short/2018/10/4/153037/[accessed 12.01.2019]; "The US Congress has recognized the Holodomor as genocide against the Ukrainian people", https://gordonua.com/eng/news/worldnews/-u-kongresi-ssha-viznali-golodomor-genotsidom-ukrainian-nation-575279.html [accessed 12.01.2019]; *Kijów: amerykańscy senatorowie uznali Wielki Głód za ludobójstwo*, 26.11.2018, www.tvn24.pl/wiadomosci-ze-swiata,2/kijow-senat-usa-uznal-wielki-glod-za-ludobojstwo,873661.html [accessed 12.01.2019].

4 "Statement on commemoration of victims of the Holodomor of 1932–1933 in Ukraine. As delivered by Ambassador Ihor Prokopchuk, Permanent Representative of Ukraine to the International Organizations in Vienna, to the 1203rd meeting of the Permanent Council", 22.11.2018, www.osce.org/permanent-council/404429?download=true [accessed 15.01.2019].

1932–1933; and the third after World War II, in 1946–1947.[5] The first famine in Ukraine in 1921–1923 was, similar to the two subsequent ones, the result of the Bolsheviks' political-ideological decisions. On one hand they wanted, as they say today with a beautiful word, to "pacify" the rebellious Ukrainians, and on the other, to gain money to install the "red plague" all over the world.[6] The "pacification" was nothing other than a policy of murderous terror, the aim of which was to nip the Ukrainian quest for independence in the bud. The Bolsheviks believed that imprisonment, forced labour, public executions and the "confiscation" of agricultural products would convince the Ukrainians to accept communism, to stop their resistance to the new power, and most importantly, eliminate the affluent people from the society.[7]

However, the famine in the 1930s – the most tragic in its effects[8] – was not discussed at all, because it was an act of genocide against the Ukrainian people. The compulsory collectivization of Ukrainian farming, food confiscation, and the repressions which accompanied the introduction of the new agricultural system caused large-scale starvation in one of the most fertile areas of Europe.

For a long time, the Great Famine of 1932–1933 remained one of the *terrae incognita* in Soviet and Ukrainian history. This disaster was not, however, similar to the other cases of famine. It was the direct consequence of a new system of exploitation of farmers. In the period 1921–1922 the Soviet regime admitted that people suffered from starvation, and openly asked for international aid, while in the disaster of 1932–1933 it used propaganda to silence the voices of foreign public opinion drawing attention to the tragedy.

For a deeper insight into what the Holodomor was actually like, the following facts should be highlighted: when researchers talk about the Holodomor of 1932–1933, they refer to the period from April 1932 to November 1933. Within just those 17 months, i.e. about 500 days, millions of people died in Ukraine. It is not possible to accurately count the number of direct and indirect

5 A. Dubynanska, "The Truth about Three Cases of the Famine". "Дзеркало тижня", nr 44 (419), 16–22 Листопада 2002 року.

6 Cz. Rajca and M. Łesiów, *The Famine in Ukraine/Głód w Ukrainie*. Wydawnictwo Werset, Lublin 2005, p. 41; O. Veselova, V. Marochko, and O. Movchan, *Holodomor in Ukraine, 1921–1923, 1932–1933, 1946–1947: Crimes against the People*. M.П. Cat, Kyiv 2000; A.Kulish, *Holodomor of 1921–1923 in Rus-Ukraine as a Continuation of the Ethnic War of 1917–1921*. Association of Holodomor Researchers in Ukraine, Kyiv 2003.

7 "The citizen-guillotine and the citizen-famine. Three scenes of genocide in Ukraine"/*Obywatelka gilotyna i obywatel głód. Trzy odsłony ludobójstwa w Ukrainie*, www.pch24.pl/obywatelka-gilotyna-i-obywatel-glod–trzy-odslony-ludobojstwa-na-ukrainie,64342,i.html [accessed 15.01.2019].

8 *The National Trial in Ukraine: Past and Present Times – Documents and Materials*. У 2 ч. Ч.2, Kyiv 1997; International Commission on the Investigation of Hunger in Ukraine 1932–1933. "Final Report 1990". Kyiv 1992; "The Holodomor of 1932–1933 in Ukraine: Causes and Consequences". International Scientific Conference. Kyiv, September 9–10, 1993. Materials, Kyiv 1995.

victims.[9] Among historians there is still a debate on how many victims died: 5, 7, 9, or 10 million or maybe more? Nevertheless it is unquestionable that there were *millions* of innocent victims. And if indirect losses, i.e. children unborn due to the Holodomor, are taken into account the number of victims reaches as high as 14 million.[10]

The Great Famine occurred in one of the most fertile soils in Europe and during a time of peace, during which the USSR exported huge amounts of grain from the area. In Ukraine the grain, and later all food, was seized by the communist authorities. In 1932 in the USSR a state property-protection law was introduced, under which a man could be shot even for taking one ear of grain from the field of a kolkhoz (collective farm).[11] The decree imposed a complete blockade of a village due to the alleged sabotaging of the compulsory delivery of grain. Many farmers broke the law in order to survive, and escaped to the cities, where food allocations for working people were enforced. Farmers attempted to escape to Russia, but the administrative borders of Ukraine were controlled by the USSR army. Most historians claim that the famine was generated artificially to break farmers' resistance to collective agriculture, a resistance which was the greatest in Ukraine.[12]

The Soviet authorities scrupulously cleaned up the traces of genocide. The GPU (State Political Directorate – the Soviet political police, a successor of the "Cheka" created by Feliks Dzierżyński and a predecessor of the NKVD, or People's Commissariat for Internal Affairs), forbade public officials from reporting famine as a cause of death. When in the spring of 1933 the death toll reached a massive scale, the administration refrained from issuing death certificates and the dead were simply buried. At the height of the Great Famine, 25,000 people died every day; i.e. 1,000 every hour or 17 people every minute.[13] The famine wreaked havoc on all villages. Numerous cases of cannibalism were reported. Children suffered most: it is estimated that one-third of all children in the region lost their lives. Very often parents could not stand the emotional strain of dealing with starvation, and killed themselves and their children. The most honest and hard-working died. Human relations changed.

9 S. Kulchytsky, *Holodomor 1932–1933 as Genocide: Difficulties of Awareness.* Nash chas., Kyiv 2008.

10 E. Shnore and I. Pavle, "The Famine in Ukraine"/"Український історичний журнал", 2012, nr 6, pp. 85–95.

11 K. Laskowska, "Crime in Russia from the Crime Science and Crime Code Perspectives"/ *Przestępczość w Rosji z perspektywy kryminologii i prawa karnego.* Wydawnictwo Temida 2, 2016, p. 66; *Studia z dziejów Rosji i Europy Środkowo-Wschodniej*, Tom 43. Zakład Narodowy im. Ossolińskich, 2008, p. 277.

12 "The President of the Institute of National Remembrance: the victims of the Great Famine in Ukraine included also the Polish people", https://dzieje.pl/aktualnosci/prezes-ipn-ofiarami-wielkiego-glodu-na-ukrainie-byli-tez-polacy [accessed 14.01.2019].

13 V. Yushchenko, "Telling about the tragedy", www.belarus.mfa.gov.ua/belarus/ua/1229.htm [accessed 11.01.2019].

When the famine first started, farmers helped one another, but as it spread and grew in strength everyone thought only about themselves and how to survive.[14]

The arsenal of repressive measures included the above-mentioned famous state property-protection (this is the full name of the law: *state property-protection law*) law, which played a decisive role and was published on 7 August 1932, at the height of the war between farmers and the regime. This law specifically provided for ten years in prison camps or the death penalty for "any theft or waste of socialistic property". The issue date of the decree was not accidental. It was aimed at preventing attempts by starving farmers' families to illegally gather grain during the harvest. In the face of the approaching winter, people watched all the crops being transported to the central warehouses, so under cover of night they attempted to gather even stray ears in the fields. The law permitted the shooting of a person taking an ear of grain from a kolkhoz field. People dubbed this law as "the law on ears", as the people were most often punished for stealing a few ears of wheat or rye from kolkhoz fields.[15] The waves of famine migration started at this time, and the authorities reacted to it by introducing passports and a ban on travelling by train.[16]

A consecutive step taken by the authorities was to isolate the rural areas affected by starvation from the rest of the country. The decree of 22 January 1933, signed by Stalin and Vyacheslav Molotov, Chairman of the Council of People's Commissars of the Soviet Union, was the legal basis for this action. It stated that local authorities and the GPU "under no condition shall allow villagers to leave their place of living" due to the alleged sabotaging of the compulsory delivery of grain. In order to fulfil the unrealistic production norms imposed, grain was callously impressed and taken from farmers without leaving them an ear of grain for planting or making flour. Under this law, a ban on selling train tickets in the affected areas was introduced, and the roads were blocked and controlled by organized military inspection posts. Scrupulous controls seized food transported to the affected areas. The whole region was patrolled by special military and police units so that farmers could not escape from the villages where they and their families were dying. At the same time, the authorities denied that people in Ukraine ware starving, and refused any aid from abroad.[17]

The human suffering and atrocities underlying these facts and data are heightened by the fact that, as mentioned above, in 1933 – at the very time when

14 *The National Tragedy: The Documents and Materials about the Famine 1932–1933 in Dnipropetrovsk Oblast.* Compiled by O.V. Kasvanov. Dnipropetrovsk, 1993, p. 67, 72, 73; *33rd: Hunger. People's Book Memorial.* Compiled by L.B. Kovalenko and V.A. Maniak. Soviet Writer Publishing House, Kyiv, 1991, p. 71.

15 S. Kulchytsky, "The causes of the 1933 Famine in Ukraine: One page of a forgotten book". Mirror of the Week, 16–22 August 2003, nr 31 (456).

16 *The Famine 1932–1933 in Ukraine: Seen with the Historian's Eyes, My Document.* Compiled by R.Y. Pyrig. Politwydaw Ukrainy, Kyiv 1990, p. 308.

17 *The Famine 1932–1933 in Ukraine*, p. 254, 257, 284.

millions of Ukrainian citizens were dying of starvation – the Soviet Union exported about 1 billion tons of grain to Western markets. According to Russian historian Roy Medvedev, the grain was sold almost for a song due to the economic crisis in Western Europe. At the same time, even half of the grain exported by the USSR during this 1932–1933 period would have been enough to save the Ukrainian people from famine.[18]

The victory of the Bolsheviks in the civil war and their seizure of power in 1917 would not have been possible without the use of media. During the time of the first famine, 75 Bolshevik newspapers were established, with a total circulation of 600,000, with money from the German General Staff. These were distributed among soldiers and workers. "Our most important weapon is print" claimed Stalin in 1921.[19] According to most archive documents, "The Great Book of Recollections", and historical research, the famine in Ukraine was aimed first of all at the intelligentsia and farmers, which were – quite logically and legitimately – considered the base of the Ukrainian independence movement, and the first famine was not a consequence of natural actions but a direct consequence of Stalin's policy. It was necessary to destroy national values in the Ukrainian people in the villages and stultify their quest for independence. Besides terror by hunger committed on the Ukrainians, mass deportations of the intelligentsia and individual persecutions were also applied. Abandoned villages were inhabited by newcomers from Russia.

The 1932–1933 famine was also the effect of the remodelling of villages, i.e. the destruction of the kulaks[20] and individual farmers, who were usually the backbone of the local society and thanks to whom a village held together. The newly developed kolkhozes had low productivity as farmers were not willing to work well in fields owned by Soviets. At the same time, according to the political party's plans overall productivity was supposed to grow as the USSR bought everything necessary to boost heavy industry from the money obtained from selling grain. This hyper-industrialization was thus clearly implemented at the cost of rural villages. Stalin extracted everything from a farmer, to the last kernel of grain. He also began implementing his programme against kulaks, i.e. their culture and spirit, and these most important values suffered the greatest consequences over time.

So why was starvation targeted only at farmers? At that time, around 90 percent of villagers were Ukrainians; they were the representatives of Ukrainian tradition and national spirit. The Holodomor broke the backbone of their ethos and strongly influenced the mentality of the nation. It clipped the wings of the

18 *The Famine and Repression of Polish People in Ukraine.* (ed.) R. Dzwonkowski SAC (Society of the Catholic Apostolate), Towarzystwo Naukowe KUL, Lublin 2005.

19 K. Raszyński. "Serving a lie", www.polskieradio.pl/media/print.aspx?id=35 [accessed 18.01.2019].

20 "Kulaks" was the term used to describe peasants with over 8 acres (3.2 hectares) of land towards the end of the Russian Empire.

Ukrainian people – exterminating farmers and destroying villages meant eliminating that social class upon which Ukraine's social development rested.

To condemn millions of people to death in the very area known for its fertility involved a series of legal and organizational actions. It was not that easy to starve people in the area where farmers could harvest several times a better crop than anywhere else. Russia had always perceived Ukraine as a colony which could be continually robbed under various pretences, and famine was for Russians the best method to destroy the Ukrainians' quest for independence. The totalitarian regime of the USSR subordinated all spheres of social life to the state. This system simply did not allow for different interpretations of history than those in line with the Communist Party's official documentation and version of events. The party was interested in destroying, keeping secret, or falsifying facts which were not in accordance with its official version of history and which could threaten the existence of the USSR itself.[21]

Preventive measures taken by the Kremlin a day before the mass genocide began prove that Stalin had been preparing for this tragedy and trying to preclude dissemination of information about it.[22] In a letter to Lazar Kaganovich, First Secretary of the Communist Party of Moscow City, on 11 August 1932, Stalin warned that if no steps were taken "we can lose Ukraine".[23] The letter shows Stalin's fear, and organizing the artificial famine was his reaction to the threat. Stalin's motive to subordinate Ukraine at any cost led to millions of deaths from starvation, and his firm decision to achieve his intention was not a mystery in the Kremlin. The hidden goal of genocide in Ukraine was to reduce the Ukrainian population and replace it with people from other parts of the USSR, and in this way quench any movements for independence.[24]

At that time the international situation was advantageous for the USSR, as some democratic states were establishing closer ties with the communist empire in the face of the Nazi threat. It is crucial to note that their relations improved in 1932, before the Great Famine happened. In order to organize the Holodomor, Moscow needed peace on the international stage and changed its policy early enough to achieve its goals.[25]

21 O. Vasyuta and S. Vasyuta, *Russian Hybrid War against Ukraine*. Arcana, Kraków 2017.

22 'The conspiracy of silence: how the West reacts to the Famine in Ukraine 1932–1933', 2018.11.24, http://argumentua.com/stati/zmova-movchannya-yak-zakh-d-reaguvav-na-golodomor-ukra-nts-v-1932-1933-rok-v

23 *Stalin to Kaganovich: Correspondence, 1931–1936*. Compiled by O.V. Khlevnyuk, R.W. Davis, L.P. Kosheleva, E.A. Ris, and L.A. Horn. Federal Archive Service of Russia; The Russian State Archive of Socio-Political History. ROSSPEN, Moscow 2001, p. 274.

24 A. Bierielovich (ed.), *Russian Village with the Eyes of Joint State Political Directorate: The People's Commissariat for Internal Affairs, 1918–1939*. Documents and materials, 4 vols. Vol. 3: 1930–1934, Book 2. Moscow 2005, p. 572; A. Bierielovich (ed.), *Soviet Village in the Eyes of the Cheka-OGPU-NKVD, 1918–1939*. Documents and materials, 4 volumes. Vol. 3, 1930–1934. Book 2. Russian Political Encyclopedia (ROSSPEN), Moscow 2005.

25 A. Papuga, *The Conspiracy of Silence: How the West Reacts to the Famine in Ukraine 1932–1933*. Видавець Олег Філюк, Kyiv 2018.

The issue of international recognition of the Great Famine of 1932–1933 in Ukraine as genocide on the Ukrainian people was important during this time. Starting in 1934, when the US Congress decided to condemn this act of extermination of Ukrainians, many countries, institutions, and researchers supported recognition of the Holodomor as an atrocity targeted at the Ukrainian people.[26]

As emphasized by Professor Roman Serbyn:

> the historicity of the Ukrainian famine of 1932–1933 is no longer challenged. What is still disputed is the number of victims, the reasons for the catastrophe, and its nature. Estimates of loss of life from starvation and related diseases vary from three to ten million.[27]

Raphael Lemkin is the author of the term "genocide", one of the initiators of its definition, and co-author of the legal definition of genocide.[28] He considered the famine in 1932–1933 in Ukraine as a typical example of Soviet genocide, the longest and most widespread Russification and destruction of the Ukrainian people.[29] He was the first Western scientist who analysed the famine in the context of the 1948 Convention on the Prevention and Punishment of the Crime of Genocide. As Professor Serbyn said, in 1953 Lemkin called on the UN to say

> that the USSR and its satellites were guilty of breaking the Convention on Genocide because [of] their planned campaigns to destroy minorities behind the 'iron curtain'.[30] That same year in his article 'Investigation of Soviet Genocide by the U.N.', Lemkin claims that it is an irony of history that eight million Ukrainians had to die of genocidal starvation, that a thousand Ukrainians had to be destroyed in Vinnytsia, and that countless numbers of Ukrainian women and children had to be buried in salt mines before the world conscience was shocked.[31]

26 M. Doroshko and W. Golovchenko, "Holodomor of 1932–33 in Ukraine as genocide: the problem of international recognition". *Current Issues in International Relations*, 1 (46), 2017, pp. 5–10.

27 R. Serbyn, "The Ukrainian famine of 1932–1933 as genocide in the light of the UN Convention of 1948". *Ukrainian Quarterly*, 2008, 2, p. 181.

28 R. Serbyn, "Lemkin on the Ukrainian genocide". *Journal of International Criminal Justice*, 2009, 7 (1), pp. 123–130.

29 R. Lemkin, *Papers*, New York Public Library, Manuscripts and Archives Division, Astor, Lenox and Tilden Foundation, Raphael Lemkin ZL-273. Reel 3. 1953; L.Y. Luciuk, *Holodomor: Reflections on the Great Famine of 1932–1933 in Soviet Ukraine*. Kashtan Press, Kingston 2008; R. Lemkin, "Soviet Genocide in Ukraine: New York 1953", Holodomor Studies Journal, 1 (1), Winter–Spring 2009, pp. 3–8; R. Serbyn and S.Grabovsky, "Rafael Lemkin and the Holodomor as genocide of the Ukrainian people", http://shron1.chtyvo.org.ua/Lemkin_Rafal/Radianskyi_henotsyd_v_Ukraini.pdf [accessed 18.01.2019].

30 R. Serbyn, "Raphael Lemkin's conceptualization of the crime of genocide and his analysis of the Ukrainian genocide" in R. Lemkin, *Soviet Genocide in Ukraine*. Article was published in 28 languages. R. Serbyn (ed.), O. Stasiuk (compiler). Maisternia Knyhy, Kyiv 2009, p. 16.

31 D. Irvin-Erickso, *Raphael Lemkin and the Concept of Genocide*. University of Pennsylvania Press, 2016, p. 207.

While the Ukrainian population was too large to be completely destroyed, the religious, intellectual, and political elites were rather small and easy to eliminate. Therefore the Russian authorities applied a common set of tools: massive extermination, deportation, forced labour, exile, and famine.

Lemkin believed that for as long as Ukraine preserved its unity, language and culture, and Ukrainians recognized their identity and strove for independence, it would constitute a serious threat to Soviets. It is not surprising that the communist leaders paid utmost attention to the Russification of this independent nation and decided to remake it to match the model of the uniform "Russian nation". Ukraine is not and never was Russian. Their culture, temper, language and religion – in all these aspects Ukrainians are different. They rejected Moscow's collectivization, and accepted deportation and even death in their efforts to fight it.[32]

According to Professor Serbyn:

> Lemkin's views on the Ukrainian tragedy are virtually unknown and hardly ever figure in scholarly exchanges on the Ukrainian famine of 1932–1933, or on genocides in general. Yet his holistic approach to the Soviet regime's gradual destruction of the Ukrainian nation is enlightening and makes a valuable, if belated, addition to the scholarly literature.[33]

Lemkin claimed the issue of genocide was wider than the later-accepted UN definition indicates.[34] In his article "Soviet Genocide in Ukraine", Lemkin presented the Ukrainian genocide as the Soviet regime's intention to destroy the Ukrainian people on four levels, in four stages:[35]

1 Destroying the national elite, i.e. destroying the brain of the nation to paralyze the body. The most serious attacks were organized in 1920, 1926 and 1932–1933, when teachers, writers, artists, thinkers, and political leaders were executed, imprisoned, or deported. In 1931, 51,713 intellectuals were sent to Siberia. At least 114 of the most prominent poets, writers and artists, and cultural leaders suffered the same fate. It is cautiously estimated that at least 75 percent of Ukrainian intellectuals from Western Ukraine, the Carpathian Mountains, and Bukovina were cruelly exterminated by the Soviets;[36]

32 Lemkin, "Soviet Genocide in Ukraine", pp. 3–8.

33 Serbyn, *Lemkin on the Ukrainian Genocide*, pp. 123–124.

34 R. Lemkin, *Axis Rule in Occupied Europe: Laws of Occupation* – Analysis of Government – Proposals for Redress. Washington, DC, Carnegie Endowment for International Peace 1944, p. 80.

35 R. Lemkin. *Soviet Genocide in the Ukraine*; R. Lemkin, "Soviet Genocide in Ukraine", Journal of International Criminal Justice, 2009, 7, pp. 125–130; R. Lemkin, *Papers*; Luciuk, *Holodomor.*

36 Lemkin. "Soviet Genocide in Ukraine", *Journal of International Criminal Justice*, 2009, 7, pp. 126–127.

2 Destroying the national Church, i.e. carrying out a campaign against churches, priests and the Church hierarchy, and closing the Ukrainian Autocephalous Church – "the soul of Ukraine". Between 1926 and 1932 the Ukrainian Autocephalous Orthodox Church was closed, and its metropolitan bishop and 10,000 priests were eliminated. In 1945, when the Soviets seized Western Ukraine, the Ukrainian Greek Catholic Church shared the same fate. The thesis that Russification was the only issue is clearly supported by the fact that the Church, before it was closed, was offered the opportunity to join the Russian patriarch in Moscow, a political tool of the Kremlin;
3 Extermination of a large part of Ukrainian farmers – the guardians of Ukrainian culture, language and tradition. Ukrainian farmers were sacrificed for establishing a unified Soviet nation. There were also attempts to justify the Holodomor simply as a consequence of collectivization and expropriation;
4 Colonizing Ukraine with alien elements, mixing Ukrainians with other nations and dispersing the Ukrainian people all over Eastern Europe.[37]

As Lemkin said, at all stages of the Ukrainian genocide the national character of the operation was important, and he presented the main victims of genocide – the Ukrainian farmers who starved to death – as the repository of the national spirit and all those values that made them "a culture and a nation". Roman Serbyn indicates that Lemkin's analysis of the four-staged destruction of the Ukrainian people is the main contribution to the research on the Ukrainian genocide.[38] According to Lemkin, the Soviet Union applied similar measures against other minorities.

Under the UN Genocide Convention of 9 December 1948, the 1932–1933 Holodomor in Ukraine bears all the characteristics of genocide, which is defined as acts committed with the intent to destroy, in whole or in part, a national, ethnical, racial or religious group[39].

At the International Conference on the Holocaust and Genocide in Israel in 1982, a then-unknown researcher of the Ukrainian Research Institute of Harvard University, James E. Mace, was the first among Western historians who characterized the Great Famine of 1932–1933 in Ukraine as an act of genocide, the goal or which was "extermination of the Ukrainian people as a political factor and social organism".[40] Thereafter, in 1983 Americans broke their silence about the Great Famine and established a special US Congress committee to

37 Lemkin, *Papers*; Luciuk, *Holodomor*.
38 Serbyn, "Rafael Lemkin".
39 S. Mahun, *Crucified Village*, www.zn.Kyiv.ua/nn/show/625/55216/[accessed 12.01.2019].
40 A. Cidoruk, "American democracy sometimes ends where the Ukrainian question begins". *Mirror of the Week*, 19 (547), May 21–27, 2005.

examine the acts of genocide and reasons why the famine in Ukraine in 1932–1933 was organized by the Soviet government.[41]

Under a special declaration of the US President, 4 November 1984 was officially the Day of Commemoration of the Great Famine in Ukraine in 1932–1933.

As regards international acts concerning the Great Famine of 1932–1933, one of the first was the Report of the International Commission of Inquiry on the Famine of 1932–1933 in Ukraine,[42] published on 14 February 1988 as an initiative of the World Congress of Free Ukrainians, made up of leading international lawyers.

The committee was established as a completely independent nongovernmental body.[43] It analysed the time, reasons, geography, number of victims of the Holodomor, and its consequences. The famine in Ukraine in 1932–1933 was brought intentionally and indisputably accepted. The Soviet authorities were fully aware of the famine and its consequences as they intentionally caused the deaths of millions of people.[44] The committee came to the conclusion that Ukraine was undoubtedly cruelly and intentionally starved in 1932–1933, and that the authorities of the USSR and its allies knew about the shortage of food among the people. There is no doubt that although Soviet authorities knew about the dramatic conditions in Ukraine, they refrained from providing aid until the summer of 1933. The committee concluded also that the Soviet authorities took various legal steps which deepened the tragic consequences of the famine, such as preventing people from searching for any food and depriving them of any possibility to leave the affected regions. It was determined that the Soviet authorities denied the famine at that time and, in spite of overwhelming evidence to the contrary, continued denying the famine for over 50 years, except for Khrushchev's private evidence.[45] The committee stressed that the Soviet authorities deliberately used the famine to implement their new policy of denationalization.[46]

John Sopinka, the proxy of the World Congress of Free Ukrainians, said in his speech that in the period of 1932–1933 about 5–10 million Ukrainians were starved to death as a result of the brutal and excessive elimination of grain by the Soviet government. Sopinka asked the committee to draw conclusions on the famine as a planned action and political tool of the state; the famine as an act of genocide; and whether Stalin, Molotov, Kaganovich, Pavel Postyshev

41 International Commission on the Investigation of Hunger in Ukraine 1932–1933. "Final Report 1990". Kyiv 1992.

42 International Commission of Inquiry into the 1932–33 Famine in Ukraine. "The Final Report". 1990, p. 1, www.ukrainianworldcongress.org/UserFiles/File/Holodomor-Commission.pdf [accessed: 17.01.2019].

43 Ibid.

44 International Commission on the Investigation of Hunger, pp. 53, 56.

45 International Commission of Inquiry, pp. 45–48.

46 International Commission of Inquiry, p. 5.

(Head of the Organizational-Instruction Department of the Central Committee), and others were responsible for it.[47]

In 1988 the report of the US Congress committee was published in Washington. It said that in accordance with international legal standards the Holodomor in Ukraine of 1932–1933 is recognized as an act of genocide. Moreover, the committee approved 19 points which condemned the lack of any actions and the deliberate silence on the part of the then US government, and confirmed that the famine in Ukraine was a planned action of Moscow targeted at Ukrainians.[48] The report was also to disseminate the information about the famine worldwide in order to give US citizens a better insight into the Soviet system and present the negative role of the Soviet government in planning the famine in Ukraine. The Ukrainian diaspora's activities aimed at paying tribute to the victims of the Great Famine were supported by the representatives of US political circles, and as a result paying tribute to victims was transformed into a political action which won worldwide publicity.

Among other international acts on the Great Famine is the common statement on the 70th anniversary of the 1932–1933 Holodomor in Ukraine, accepted at the 58th session of the UN General Assembly in 2003 and signed by 64 states. In this statement the famine is defined as a national tragedy for the Ukrainian people that claimed from seven to 10 million innocent lives.[49] On 1 November 2007, at the 34th session of the UNESCO General Assembly, 193 countries unanimously accepted the Resolution on Commemorating Holodomor Victims on the 75th anniversary of the Great Famine. The resolution declared that the Great Famine, which was the result of Stalin's totalitarian political regime, should be a warning for present and future generations to preserve democratic values, human rights, and the rule of law.

In the Soviet Union itself, the Great Famine in the Ukrainian Soviet Socialist Republic was mentioned for the first time by Volodymyr Shcherbytsky, a member of the Central Committee of the Communist Party of the Soviet Union, in his speech in December 1987.[50] It consisted of only a few sentences, but the impact of the mention gave rise to the beginning of historical research and the publication of archive materials in Ukraine. Almost immediately, in January 1988, an article appeared in the central journal of Ukrainian historians ("Український історичний журнал").[51] And in 1990 a collection of documents

47 Ibid., p. 2.

48 Ya. Dubinyanska, "The Truth about Three Famine Holodomors". *Mirror of the Week*, 44 (419), 16–22 November 2002.

49 Great Famine in Ukraine in 1932–1933, http://holodomorct.org [accessed 15.01.2019].

50 S. Kulchytsky, *Holodomor 1932–1933*; S. Kulchytsky, *Holodomor 1932–1933 in Ukraine as Genocide*, http://history.org.ua/JournALL/pro/14/14.pdf [accessed 01.17.2019]; O. Veselova, "Book on Ukrainian Calvary: The Key to Knowledge and Research". *Mirror of the Week*, 26 (401), July 13–19, 2002.

51 S. Kulchytskyy, "Towards an Assessment of the Situation in Agriculture of the Ukrainian SSR in 1931–1933", *Ukrainian Historical Journal*, 1988, 3, pp. 15–27.

was released: *Famine of 1932–1933 in Ukraine: Through the Eyes of Historians, in the Language of Documents.*[52]

In March 1993, on the 60th anniversary of the Holodomor genocide of 1932–1933, the president of the then-independent Ukraine, Leonid Kravchuk, signed a resolution on respect for those people who were starved to death, establishing mass funerals, erecting crosses, cleaning cemeteries and organizing prayer and mourning services in *tserkovs* (a type of an Eastern Orthodox church in Ukraine) and churches. As a result of this resolution, crosses and monuments were erected in most Ukrainian cities to commemorate the Holodomor victims. And in September 1993, at the international conference on the occasion of the 60th anniversary of Holodomor, Kravchuk said that during the artificial famine some regions of Ukraine, including the Kyiv Oblast, lost almost one-third of their population, and every fifth person died of starvation.[53]

In November 1998 Ukrainian President Leonid Kuchma signed a resolution on establishing a day of commemoration for the Holodomor victims. At the same time a number of documents were published. These confirmed that the Holodomor of Ukrainian farmers in 1932–1933 was a deliberately planned murder of millions of innocent people, mostly children and the elderly.[54]

The 70th anniversary of the 1932–1933 Holodomor in Ukraine was an event held on a global scale. On 10 November 2003 at the UN assembly on the occasion of the 70th anniversary, the Joint Statement on the Great Famine of 1932–1933 in Ukraine (Holodomor) was announced by 36 states. In that statement, for the first time in the history of the UN the Holodomor 1932–1933 in Ukraine was referred to as a tragedy of the Ukrainian people. Slightly earlier, on 20 October, the US Congress accepted a short resolution which said that the "Holodomor was planned and implemented by the Soviet regime as a planned act of terror and mass murder targeted at the Ukrainian people". However, due to the Russian position neither the Joint Statement of 36 states nor the US Congress resolution defined the 1932–1933 Great Famine as genocide.[55]

52 *Famine of 1932–1933 in Ukraine: Through the Eyes of Historians, in the Language of Documents.* Compiled by R.Y. Pyrig. Politvydav Ukrainy, Kyiv 1990.

53 "The Holodomor of 1932–1933 in Ukraine: Causes and Consequences". International Scientific Conference. Kyiv, September 9–10, 1993. Materials, Kyiv 1995, p. 9.

54 *Collectivization and Famine in Ukraine 1928–1933: Collection of Documents and Materials.* Edited by S.V. Kulchyckiy. Naukova Dumka, Kyiv 1992; *Famine of 1921–1923 in Ukraine: Collection of Documents and Materials.* Edited by S.V. Kulchyckiy. Naukova Dumka, Kyiv 1993; V. Sergiychuk, *How We Were Starved.* 3rd ed. Taras Shevchenko National University of Kyiv, Center for Ukrainian Studies, Kyiv 2006; *Black Book of Ukraine.* Collection of documents, archival materials, letters, reports, articles, studies, essays. Compiled by F. Zubanych. Prosvita Publishing Center, Kyiv 1998; P.P. Yashchuk, *Portrait of Darkness.* Testimonies, documents, and materials in 2 books. Book I. MP Kotz, Kyiv and New York 1999; S. Bilokin, *Mass Terror as a Person of Public Administration in the USSR, 1917–1941.* Instytut Istorii Ukrainy NAN Ukrainy, Kyiv 1999; A. Kulish, *Genocide, Famine 1932–1933: Causes, Victims, Criminals.* Association of Holodomor Researchers in Ukraine, Kyiv 2001.

Professor James E. Mace, an author of the special US Congress committee report of 1988, has unequivocally stated that 16 items of evidence collected have, in the light of international law, qualified the Great Famine in Ukraine in 1932–1933 as genocide. The documents published after the fall of the USSR only added details to the already-outlined procedures employed to carry out the crime. In analysing the results of the famine in Ukraine, Mace claims that they can be observed even today and, together with other disasters the Ukrainian people suffered in the twentieth century, have created a post-genocidal society, i.e. a society unable to undergo the transformation which is so expected by the people.[56]

In May 2003 the Ukrainian Parliament called the events of 1932–1933 acts of genocide against the Ukrainian people, although it should be noted that only 226 deputies out of 450 voted for the statement. The special statement emphasised that for the first time in history the method of food confiscation was applied by a state as a tool for extermination of its own people to achieve some political goals. According to the deputies who voted for the statement, the aim of the extermination in 1932–1933 was to destroy the Ukrainians' national spirit, the elite and farmers as an element of economic independence of the country.

On 26 November 2005 for the first time the whole of Ukraine took part in a day of commemoration of the artificially-provoked famine in 1932–1933 and the political repressions of Soviet totalitarianism. Various events and mass meetings were organized to commemorate these historical events, and candles were lit to pay tribute to the millions of innocent victims.[57] The Holodomors in 1921–1923, 1932–1933 and 1946–1947 were declared to be acts of genocide, and Ukrainian president Viktor Yushchenko signed Resolution No. 1544 of 4 November 2005 "On respect for Holodomor victims in Ukraine". Additionally, the president put forward a project for an act to the Parliament in which the famine of 1932–1933 was qualified as an act of genocide against the Ukrainian people.

On 16 March 2006, Poland accepted the Resolution of the Senate of the Republic of Poland on the anniversary of the Great Famine, which said that:

> The Senate of the Republic of Poland wishes to remind people about the Great Famine 'Holodomor', which was deliberately provoked by the despotic Bolshevik regime in the Soviet Union and was planned and realized to weaken and destroy the Ukrainian people and at the same time strangle

55 "Was the 1933 Holodomor a genocide?" www.golodomor.org.ua/pub.php?sp [accessed 15.01.2019].

56 E. Rybałt, *Wielki Głód i śmierć ziemi w Ukrainie w latach 1932–33*, "Great Famine and death in Ukraine, Conference report, Vicenza, Italy". Kultura i Historia, 5, 2003.

57 Odzyskiwanie pamięci Wielkiego Głodu, "Getting the Great Famine memory back", http://norymberga.blox.pl/html/1310721,262146,169.html?4 [accessed: 11.01.2019].

> their desire for independence and to rebuild their own independent country (...) The Senate of the Republic of Poland shares the Ukrainian point of view that the Great Famine of 1932–1933 should be recognized as an act of genocide as well as to list the people responsible for this crime. The states that at that time bought food from the Soviet Union, and journalists, politicians and intellectuals who visited Ukraine and did not notice the genocidal activities and even proclaimed that these kinds of accusations were groundless, are also responsible for that crime. ... Some journalists received some prestigious international awards for propagating this lie. This dismal chapter of cynicism and servility should be carefully examined and the described awards nullified.[58]

In August 2006 the Security Service of Ukraine published on the Internet 5,000 pages of documents of the Soviet GPU which had been available only for historians[59]. According to published NKVD documents, the Great Famine was a planned policy of the Soviet authorities against Ukrainian desires for independence and against the "class enemy", as the communist regime regarded the farmers/owners of fields who fought against compulsory collective farming. The director of the Security Service of Ukraine, Ihor Driżczanyj, said that diminishing the scale of the Holodomor in Ukraine not only makes no sense, but is also dishonest and unjust from the historical point of view. The documents were collected over several years, and earlier they were kept by the KGB (Committee for State Security) and classified as "top secret", hidden from society in special warehouses.[60]

On 28 November 2006 the Verkhovna Rada (Supreme Council) of Ukraine voted, as requested by President Yushchenko, for the act of law recognizing the Great Famine in 1932–1933 as an act of genocide.[61] On 29 November 2006 the president signed the act recognizing the Holodomor in 1932–1933 as a genocide against the Ukrainian people.[62] Yushchenko thanked all countries

58 "Resolution of the Senate of the Republic of Poland of 16 March 2006 regarding the anniversary of the Great Famine in Ukraine"/ *Uchwała Senatu Rzeczypospolitej Polskiej z dnia 16 marca 2006 r.* w sprawie rocznicy Wielkiego Głodu w Ukrainie, www.senat.gov.pl/k6/dok/uch/007/090uch.htm [accessed:12.01.2019].

59 http://www.sbu.gov.ua/sbu/control/uk/publish/article?art_id=49757&cat_id=53076 [accessed: 14.01.2019]; "The Verkhovna Rada recognized the Holodomor as genocide", www.unian.net/eng/news/news-174851.html [Accessed 14.01.2019].

60 "The Security Service of Ukraine collected 5000 documents on The Great Famine kept by KGB USSR (Committee for State Security", www.unian.net/ukr/news/news-174361.html [accessed: 14.01.2019].

61 "The Supreme Council of Ukraine accepted the Great Famine as a genocide"/*Верховна Рада визнала Голодомор геноцидом*, www.unian.net/ukr/news/news-174851.html [accessed: 14.01.2019]; J. Junko. *Ukraina- Parlament uznał Wielki Głód za ludobójstwo*. www.dziennik.pap.pl/index [accessed: 14.01.2019].

62 "The president signed the act recognizing the Holodomor as a genocide against the Ukrainian people", www.unian.net/ukr/news/news-174944.html [accessed: 14.01.2019].

which recognized the Great Famine as a crime, adding that: "I believe that the United Nations will do the same on the 75th anniversary."[63]

Conclusions

Following the Great Famine, practically the whole of Western Ukraine was inhabited by settlers from the Soviet Union, for whom the language of communication was Russian, and – over the course of time – their only identity became the Soviet identity. The cities of Eastern Ukraine had been previously Russified. Today, the post-Soviet populations of Eastern Ukraine, the Black Sea, and Taurida – not to mention Crimea, annexed by the Kremlin – are strongholds of pro-Russian parties in Ukraine. The Russians shamelessly use these territories as a tool to put pressure on Kyiv to come back to the sphere of Russian influence. These particular regions are not interested in the main steps taken to create genuine Ukrainian governance. According to the local and Russian press, a major part of the population promotes completely different ideas: Slavic Brotherhood, the True Orthodox Church, Great Russia, fighting against American imperialism, and the followers of Stepan Bandera, a hero of Ukraine for defending national ideas and battling for an independent Ukrainian state, who came to power in Kyiv. These ideas are accompanied by a quite interesting set of historical symbols: the cap of Monomakh (the Grand Prince of Rus in the eleventh century) is placed next to the red flag, an eagle with two heads and the five-sided star and the icon of the Emperor of Russia, Nicholas Romanov – to finish with the portrait of the Bolshevik leader Stalin. What is interesting is that a citizen is expected to believe that this mosaic is just and accept it without any criticism towards the symbols, which belong to the past. A similar situation occurs in Russia, where at Red Square there are the White Emperor (the Tsar) and the Red Emperor's murderer, representatives of the White and Red Army, Nicholas in the icons, and mummified Lenin, and people pay tribute to the remains of General Denikin, against whom Lenin called on them to fight.[64]

The Great Famine is one of the main symbols which should connect the historical awareness of all the Ukrainian people. This happens when every Ukrainian family commemorates the famine: about 80 percent of Ukrainians consider the Great Famine in 1932–1933 an act of genocide against the Ukrainian people. Almost half of respondents point to Joseph Stalin as personally responsible for organizing the Great Famine. One-third of respondents point to the USSR law enforcement authorities, such as the NKVD, and every fourth respondent to the highest management of the Ukrainian SSR.[65]

63 Ibid.

64 O. Wasiuta, "Is the crime of genocide in Ukraine in 1932 a myth?"/*Czy zbrodnia ludobójstwa w Ukrainie w latach 1932–1933 to mit?* "Forum Politologiczne", Odmiany dyskursu politycznego, 2007, nr 6, s.29–30.

The Soviet regime has consistently denied the famine in Ukraine. For over half a century the whole world was silent about this horrific crime, as none of the influential states were willing to put themselves in conflict with a superpower. The issue of the Holodomor was considered closed, and any attempt to raise it was considered to be an attempt to destroy the Soviet authority. In addition, researchers were repressed in a variety of ways. In the USSR everyone knew about the Great Famine, but nobody talked about it. Any mention of the famine in mass media was treated as anti-Soviet propaganda. At the time the Great Famine was carried out, none of the countries offered help to the dying, and there was no humanitarian aid. The scale and the degree of cruelty exceeded anything man had invented and implemented to that date. The number of victims is estimated by researchers in approximate terms because all statistics and the truth were hidden and falsified by the Stalin regime. Because of this silence and the ban by the USSR (e.g. the Ukrainian Communist Party still denies the Holodomor), the truth about the Great Famine began to reach European public opinion only after the fall of the USSR. Previously any mention of it in the USSR was punished as commission of the crime of spreading "anti-Soviet propaganda".

Moreover, even after Stalin's death there remained a deeply rooted fear in the society: everyone knew what they could talk about and what they should not even mention. Under Article 62 of the Criminal Code of the Soviet Ukraine (anti-Soviet campaigning and propaganda), people could be sent to prison or committed to a psychiatric hospital for doing so. The totalitarian system even tried to erase this tragedy from the memory of the Ukrainian people. Only thanks to the Ukrainian diaspora and researchers was it eventually revealed. Until then the truth was concealed by 'experts' – historians who diminished the effects of the Great Famine.

The research into the causes and results of the Great Famine in Ukraine in 1932–1933, which was one of the most tragic events of the twentieth century, has jolted the Ukrainian public conscience for years. As Stalin grew in power at the top of Kremlin, he ruled the USSR implementing his repressive policies. This policy was marked by a return to the mass terror and methods of "war communism" tried and tested by the communists ten years earlier. However, in Ukraine the famine was the most powerful method of repression (although one of many), and a special social tool for subjugating farmers who were ruthlessly exploited by the totalitarian regime.

Around 15 volumes of works on the genocide against the Ukrainian people in 1932–1933 have been published. The authors of these works express their objective scientific opinions. Canadian researcher Marco Carynnyk published over 10,000 books and articles at the beginning of the 1990s.[66] The books by

65 "How many Ukrainians claim the Great Famine is a genocide and how this opinion has been changing in a course of time"/*Ilu Ukraińców uznało Wielki Głód za ludobójstwo i jak z biegiem lat zmieniała się ta tendencja*, https://wschodnik.pl/spoleczenstwo/item/19149-ilu-ukraincow-uznalo-wielki-glod-za-ludobojstwo-i-jak-z-biegiem-lat-zmieniala-sie-ta-tendencja.html [accessed 15.01.2019].

Larysa Burian and Inna Rikun in 2014 include over 12,000 papers.[67] All these works were an attempt to determine whether there was or was not (as claimed) a famine in Ukraine, and to recognize the Holodomor genocide as the Ukrainian tragedy of the twentieth century. Certainly, there were other stimuli and motives for such huge intellectual energy of many generations of historians, writers, artists and social activists in Ukraine and abroad. The truth about the famine was always alive, and remains so among the Ukrainian people. This is a historical fact, which after the political and legal analyses in 2006 gained the status of legal acts.

Even today – 87 years after the famine – the mortality rate in Ukraine is higher in the regions which were affected, and the birth rate is higher in the regions which were not.[68]

Fighting the trauma from the past is not just a question of security, but of the existence of the Ukrainian people. Trauma influences values, and the value of surviving in these regions won over values of self-actualization. This is the key trauma, which much like gravity influences the Ukrainian people from that time.

The total losses in Ukraine in the twentieth century from wars, revolutions, repressions, and famine are estimated by researchers at 15–16 million.[69] The year 1933 marks the bitter anniversary of the year in which the greatest number of people died in the whole history of Ukraine.

Bibliography

33rd: Hunger. People's Book Memorial. Compiled by L.B. Kovalenko and V.A. Maniak. Soviet Writer Publishing House, Kyiv, 1991.

85. rocznica „Wielkiego Głodu" w Ukrainie. „W interesie Polski zawsze była i zawsze będzie wolna Ukraina", 27.11.2018, https://wpolityce.pl/historia/423039-85-rocznica-wielkiego-glodu-na-ukrainie [Accessed 12.01.2019].

"Address of the President of Ukraine Viktor Yushchenko to the Ukrainian people, to the people's deputies of Ukraine in connection with the consideration of the draft Law of Ukraine", "On the Holodomor of 1932–1933 in Ukraine", 16.11.2006, http://ww7.president.gov.ua/news/data/print/11832.html [Accessed 11.01.2019].

66 *Collectivization and Famine in Ukraine 1928–1933: Collection of Documents and Materials.* Edited by S.V. Kulchytskyi. Instytut Istorii Ukrainy NAN Ukrainy, Kyiv 1992, p. 14.

67 *The Genocide by Famine in Ukraine 1932–1933.* Compiled by L.M. Burian and I.E. Rikun; ed. board: O.F. Botushanska (execut. ed.), S.V. Kulchytskyi (ed.), W. Motyka, I.S. Shelestovych; Odesa National Research M. Gorky Library, Institute of the History of Ukraine of the National Academy of Sciences of Ukraine, Odessa 2014.

68 B. Golovchenko, "Holodomor of 1932–1933 in historical and national memory". *Gilea: The Scientific Bulletin*, 82, 2014, pp. 46–53.

69 "The Holodomor of 1932–1933: The Loss of the Ukrainian Nation". *Proceedings of the International Scientific and Practical Conference* (Kyiv, 4 October 2016). National Museum of Holodomor Victims Memorial, Kyiv 2017.

Bilokin, C. *Mass Terror as a Person of Public Administration in the USSR*. Instytut Istorii Ukrainy NAN Ukrainy, Kyiv 1999.

Black Book of Ukraine. Collection of documents, archival materials, letters, reports, articles, studies, essays. Compiled by F. Zubanych. Prosvita Publishing Center, Kyiv 1998.

Cidoruk, A. "American Democracy Sometimes Ends Where the Ukrainian Question Begins". *Mirror of the Week*, 19 (547), May 21–27, 2005, 21–23.

Collectivization and Famine in Ukraine 1928–1933: Collection of Documents and Materials. Edited by S.V. Kulchytskyi. Instytut Istorii Ukrainy NAN Ukrainy, Kyiv 1992.

Doroshko, M., and V. Golovchenko. "Holodomor of 1932–33 in Ukraine as Genocide: The Problem of International Recognition". *Current Issues in International Relations*, 1 (46), 2017, 5–11.

Dubinyanska, Ya. "The Truth about Three Famine Holodomors". *Mirror of the Week*, 44 (419), 16–22 November 2002, 15–17.

Famine of 1921–1923 in Ukraine: Collection of Documents and Materials. Edited by S. V. Kulchytskyi. Instytut Istorii Ukrainy NAN Ukrainy, Kyiv 1993.

Famine of 1932–1933 in Ukraine: Through the Eyes of Historians, in the Language of Documents. Compiled by R.Y. Pyrig. Polityvdav Ukrainy, Kyiv 1990.

Folk tragedy. Documents and materials on the famine of 1932–1933 in Dnipropetrovsk. Compiled by O.V. Kasyanov. Dniproknyha, Dnipropetrovsk, 1993.

Głód i represje wobec ludności polskiej w Ukrainie 1932–1947. Relacje, red. R.Dzwonkowski SAC, Towarzystwo Naukowe KUL. Lublin 2005.

Golovchenko, B. "Holodomor of 1932–1933 in historical and national memory". *Gilea: The Scientific Bulletin*, 82, 2014, 46–53.

"Great Famine in Ukraine in 1932–1933", http://holodomorct.org [Accessed 15.01.2019].

https://gordonua.com/eng/news/worldnews/-u-kongresi-ssha-viznali-golodomor-genotsidom-ukrainian-nation-575279.html [Accessed 12.01.2019].

Ilu Ukraińców uznało Wielki Głód za ludobójstwo i jak z biegiem lat zmieniała się ta tendencja, https://wschodnik.pl/spoleczenstwo/item/19149-ilu-ukraincow-uznalo-wielki-glod-za-ludobojstwo-i-jak-z-biegiem-lat-zmieniala-sie-ta-tendencja.html [Accessed 15.01.2019].

International Commission of Inquiry into the 1932–1933 Famine in Ukraine. "The Final Report". 1990, www.ukrainianworldcongress.org/UserFiles/File/Holodomor-Commission.pdf [Accessed 17.01.2019].

International Commission on the Investigation of Hunger in Ukraine 1932–1933. "Final Report 1990". Kyiv 1992.

Irvin-Erickso, D. *Raphael Lemkin and the Concept of Genocide*. University of Pennsylvania Press, Philadelphia 2016.

"Joint Statement by the Delegations of the UN Member States on the 70th Anniversary of the Holodomor in Ukraine 1932–1933", November 7, 2003, www.prezident.gov.ua/content/150_10.html [Accessed 11.01.2019].

Junko, J. *Ukraina - Parlament uznał Wielki Głód za ludobójstwo*, www.dziennik.pap.pl/index [Accessed 14.01.2019].

Kijów: amerykańscy senatorowie uznali Wielki Głód za ludobójstwo, 26.11.2018, www.tvn24.pl/wiadomosci-ze-swiata,2/kijow-senat-usa-uznal-wielki-glod-za-ludobojstwo,873661.html [Accessed 12.01.2019].

Kulchytsky, S. *Holodomor 1932–1933 as Genocide: Difficulties of Awareness*. Nash chas., Kyiv 2008.

Kulchytsky, S. "Holodomor 1932–1933 in Ukraine as genocide", http://history.org.ua/JournALL/pro/14/14.pdf [Accessed 01. 17.2019].
Kulchytsky, S. "The causes of the 1933 famine in Ukraine: One page of a forgotten book". *Mirror of the Week*, 31 (456), 16–22 August 2003, 19–21.
Kulchytsky, S. "Towards an assessment of the situation in agriculture of the Ukrainian SSR in 1931–1933". *Ukrainian Historical Journal*, 3, 1988, 15–27.
Kulish, A. *Genocide, Famine 1932–1933: Causes, Victims, Criminals*. Association of Holodomor Researchers in Ukraine, Kyiv 2001.
Kulish, A. *Holodomor of 1921–1923 in Rus-Ukraine as a Continuation of the Ethnic War of 1917–1921*. Association of Holodomor Researchers in Ukraine, Kyiv 2003.
Lemkin, R. *Axis Rule in Occupied Europe: Laws of Occupation – Analysis of Government – Proposals for Redress*. Carnegie Endowment for International Peace, Washington, DC 1944.
Lemkin, R. "Soviet Genocide in the Ukraine" "Societ. Document from the Raphael Lemkin Papers, the New York Public Library, Manuscripts and Archives Division, Astor, Lenox, and Tilden Foundation, Raphael Lemkin ZL-273. Reel 3. (1953). Published in L.Y. Luciuk (ed), *Holodomor: Reflections on the Great Famine of 1932–1933 in Soviet Ukraine*. Kashtan Press, Kingston 2008.
Lemkin, R. "Soviet Genocide in Ukraine: New York, 1953". *Holodomor Studies Journal*, 1 (1), 2009, 36–37.
Lemkin, R. *Soviet Genocide in the Ukraine*. Kashtan Press, Kingston 2014.
Mahun, S. "Crucified village", www.zn.Kyiv.ua/nn/show/625/55216/ [Accessed 12.01.2019].
National Processes in Ukraine: History and Modernity. Documents and Materials. Part 2. Edited by V.F. Panibud'laska. Vyshcha Shkola, Kyiv 1997.
Obywatelka gilotyna i obywatel głód. Trzy odsłony ludobójstwa w Ukrainie, www.pch24.pl/obywatelka-gilotyna-i-obywatel-glod–trzy-odslony-ludobojstwa-na-ukrainie,64342,i.htmln [Accessed 15.01.2019].
Odzyskiwanie pamięci Wielkiego Głodu, http://norymberga.blox.pl/html/1310721,262146,169.html?4 [Accessed 11.01.2019].
Parrot, Ya. *"Conspiracy of Silence": How the West Responded to the Holodomor of Ukrainians in 1932–1933*. Oleg Filyuk, Kyiv 2018.
"President signs law recognizing Holodomor as genocide", www.unian.net/eng/news/news-174944.html [Accessed 14.01.2019].
Prezes IPN: ofiarami Wielkiego Głodu w Ukrainie byli też Polacy, https://dzieje.pl/aktualnosci/prezes-ipn-ofiarami-wielkiego-glodu-na-ukrainie-byli-tez-polacy [Accessed 14.01.2019].
Proceedings of the International Scientific and Practical Conference. "The Holodomor of 1932–1933: The Loss of the Ukrainian Nation" (Kyiv, October 4, 2016). National Museum of Holodomor Victims Memorial, Kyiv 2017.
Rajca, Cz., and M. Łesiów. *Głód w Ukrainie*. Wydawnictwo Werset, Lublin 2005.
Raszyński, K. *W służbie kłamstwu*, www.polskieradio.pl/media/print.aspx?id=35 [Accessed 18.01.2019].
Rybałt, E. *Wielki Głód i śmierć ziemi w Ukrainie w latach 1932–33*. Sprawozdanie z konferencji w Vicenzy (Włochy). 'Kultura i Historia' nr 5, 2003, 172–174.
"SBU has collected 5000 KGB documents on the Holodomor in Ukraine", www.unian.net/eng/news/news-174361.html [Accessed 14.01.2019].
"SBU presents declassified archival documents on the Holodomor in Ukraine", www.unian.net/eng/news/news-174216.html [Accessed 14.01.2019].

Schnore, E., and I. Paavle. "Holodomor in Ukraine". *Ukrainian Historical Journal*, 6, 2012, 85–95.
Serbyn, R. "Lemkin on Genocide of Nations", *Journal of International Criminal Justice*, 2009a, 7 (1).
Serbyn, R. "Rafael Lemkin on the Ukrainian Genocide". *Holodomor Studies*, 1, 2009b, 123–130.
Serbyn, R. "Raphael Lemkin's conceptualization of the crime of genocide and his analysis of the Ukrainian genocide" in R. Lemkin, *Soviet Genocide in Ukraine*. Ed. R. Serbyn, compiler O. Stasiuk. Maisternia Knyhy, Kyiv 2009c.
Serbyn, R. "The Ukrainian famine of 1932–1933 as genocide in the light of the UN Convention of 1948". *Ukrainian Quarterly*, 2, 2008, 181–194.
Serbyn, R., and S. Grabovsky.. "Rafael Lemkin and the Holodomor as genocide of the Ukrainian people", http://shron1.chtyvo.org.ua/Lemkin_Rafal/Radianskyi_henotsyd_v_Ukraini.pdf [Accessed 18.01.2019].
Sergeyuk, V. *How We Were Starved*. 3rd ed. Taras Shevchenko National University of Kyiv, Center for Ukrainian Studies, Kyiv 2006.
Soviet Village in the Eyes of the Cheka-OGPU-NKVD, 1918–1939. Documents and materials in 4 volumes. Vol. 3, 1930–1934. Book 2. Ed. A. Berelovich. Russian Political Encyclopedia (ROSSPEN), Moscow 2005.
Stalin to Kaganovich: Correspondence, 1931–1936. Compiled by O.V. Khlevnyuk, R.W. Davis, L.P. Kosheleva, E.A. Ris, and L.A. Horn. Federal Archive Service of Russia; the Russian State Archive of Socio-Political History. ROSSPEN, Moscow 2001.
"Statement on commemoration of victims of the Holodomor of 1932–1933 in Ukraine". As delivered by Ambassador Ihor Prokopchuk, Permanent Representative of Ukraine to the International Organizations in Vienna, to the 1203rd meeting of the Permanent Council, 22.11.2018, www.osce.org/permanent-council/404429?download=true [Accessed 15.01.2019].
"Stalinskaja 'riewolucyja swierchu' posle 'wielikogo pieriełoma' 1930-1939. Politika, osuszczestwlenije, riezultaty", Ilja Jewgienijewicz Zielenin, Moskwa 2006 : [recenzja] Studia z Dziejów Rosji i Europy Środkowo-Wschodniej, Tom 43 (2008) s. 275-280 Romuald Wojna, Ilja Jewgienijewicz Zielenin (aut. dzieła rec.).
The Genocide by Famine in Ukraine 1932–1933. Compiled by L.M. Burian and I.E. Rikun; ed. board: O.F. Botushanska (execut. ed.), S.V. Kulchytskyi (sci. ed.), W. Motyka, I.S. Shelestovych. Odesa National Research M. Gorky Library, Institute of the History of Ukraine of the National Academy of Sciences of Ukraine. Odessa 2014.
"The Holodomor of 1932–1933 in Ukraine: Causes and Consequences". International Scientific Conference. Kyiv, September 9–10, 1993. Materials, Kyiv 1995.
"The US Congress has recognized the Holodomor as genocide against the Ukrainian people", https://gordonua.com/eng/news/worldnews/-u-kongresi-ssha-viznali-golodomor-genotsidom-ukrainian-nation-575279.html [accessed 12.01.2019].
"The Verkhovna Rada recognized the Holodomor as genocide", www.unian.net/eng/news/news-174851.html [Accessed 14.01.2019].
Uchwała Senatu Rzeczypospolitej Polskiej z dnia 16 marca 2006 r. w sprawie rocznicy Wielkiego Głodu w Ukrainie, www.senat.gov.pl/k6/dok/uch/007/090uch.htm [Accessed 12.01.2019].
"US Senate: Famine is genocide", 10/04/2018, www.istpravda.com.ua/short/2018/10/4/153037/[Accessed 12/01/2019].
Vasyuta, O., and S. Vasyuta. *Russian Hybrid War against Ukraine*. Arcana, Kraków 2017.

Veselova, O. "Book on Ukrainian Calvary: The Key to Knowledge and Research". *Mirror of the Week*, 26 (401), July 13–19, 2002, https://dt.ua/CULTURE/kniga_pro_ukrayinsku_golgofu_klyuch_do_piznannya_y_doslidzhennya.html [Accessed 16.04.2020].

Veselova, O., V. Marochko, and O. Movchan. *Holodomor in Ukraine, 1921–1923, 1932–1933, 1946–1947: Crimes against the People*. M.П. Cat, Kyiv 2000.

Warszawa: ekumeniczne nabożeństwo w 85. rocznicę Wielkiego Głodu w Ukrainie, 25.11.2018, https://ekai.pl/warszawa-ekumeniczne-nabozenstwo-w-85-rocznice-wielkiego-glodu-na-ukrainie/ [Accessed 12.01.2019].

"Was the 1933 Holodomor a genocide?", www.golodomor.org.ua/pub.php?sp [Accessed 15.01.2019].

Wasiuta, O. *Czy zbrodnia ludobójstwa w Ukrainie w latach 1932–1933 to mit?* "Forum Politologiczne", Odmiany dyskursu politycznego, 2007, nr 6, 29–62.

Wasiuta, O., and S. Wasiuta. *Wojna hybrydowa Rosji przeciwko Ukrainie*. Wydawnictwo Arcana, Kraków 2017.

Yashchuk, P.P. *Portrait of Darkness*. Testimonies, documents, and materials in 2 books. Book I. MP Kotz, Kyiv and New York 1999.

Yushchenko, V. "Tell the truth", www.belarus.mfa.gov.ua/belarus/en/1229.htm [Accessed 11.01.2019].

3 Kingpins of contention

Local-level dynamics of mobilization in the Rwandan genocide

Hanna Schieve

Introduction

Genocide: the crime of all crimes; a "problem from hell."[1] Enter Jean-Baptiste: civil servant, Rwandan villager, Hutu, perpetrator of genocide (Hatzfeld, 2005: chapter 3). An ordinary man who participated in an extraordinary offense. The vulgarity and sheer unimaginable barbarity of the Rwandan genocide—wrought with images of machetes tainted red and rivers teeming with corpses—entices we observers from afar to ask *why*? In turn, we are spoon-fed half-tales of ancient hate, of leaders gone mad, and of individuals born evil. Conflict studies at large is susceptible to sensationalizing the very events it seeks to delineate, particularly when it comes to genocide, in all their infamy. Yet, atrocious as genocide is, genocide is political violence all the same. If we focus our lens a little closer and start asking Jean-Baptiste *how* he came to murder his Tutsi neighbors, instead of *why*, we will start to see that what we once saw as a cataclysmic event of gargantuan proportion is but one episode among many, with recognizable and predictable patterns. In this study, the lens will focus in just enough—to the local level—to observe what happens in communities. In asking *how* communities collectively mobilized to commit political violence in Rwanda in 1994, I will examine genocide through a more pragmatic lens and garner insights on social mobilization processes and explanations of the temporal variation of its onset along the way.

Jean-Baptiste's account of the days following April 6, 1994 mirror the dynamics seen throughout many communes in rural Rwanda. In Rwandan communes, a burgomaster is akin to a local mayor. The role is the most powerful position of authority in the commune and is charged with controlling the state's security apparatus in the community (Straus, 2006: 68). History matters, context matters, and community-specific nuances matter, but the burgomasters' role as kingpins of contention is undeniable in explaining the variation in timing of the onset of genocide across communes. This study operationalizes a framework derived from the social movement literature to demonstrate the instrumental role local authority figures played in activating mechanisms of collective mobilization in a transgressive

1 In reference to Nicole Rafter's *The Crime of All Crimes: Toward a Criminology of Genocide* (2016) and Samantha Power's *A Problem from Hell: America and the Age of Genocide* (2007).

episode of contention. I begin by defining key terms pertinent to the analysis. Next, I highlight some of the key literature from the field of genocide, mobilization, and social movement studies. I then explain the theoretical framework and associated mechanisms employed throughout the study, followed by a description of my methodology and justification of my case selection, as well as a definition of the scope conditions of the micro-comparative case analysis. Following that, I move on to the study itself, which analyzes two communes separately before discussing their commonalities, differences, and the significance of each. Finally, I address alternative explanations before concluding with a discussion of policy implications and avenues for further research.

Definitions

Genocide

Article II of the United Nations Convention on the Prevention and Punishment of the Crime of Genocide defines genocide as such: "acts committed with intent to destroy, in whole or in part, a national, ethnical, racial, or religious group, as such" (1948). The intentional vagueness in the official definition has at times hindered its utility. Almost all cases of genocide are contested and the implications associated with labeling a conflict as genocide are often riddled with politics. The case of Rwanda, though, is indisputably accepted as genocide throughout the academic, public, and political spheres. Therefore, I use the word "genocide" to describe the episode rather than use alternative monikers such as "ethnic cleansing," "mass killing," "crimes against humanity," or any other labels commonly used in its stead.

Onset

In this study I refer to the "onset" of genocide as defined by Scott Straus: "public and generalized attacks against Tutsi" (Straus, 2006: 12). While private, specific acts of violence were sometimes committed in the communes I analyze, I will not mark those acts as points of onset. Related to this, there are many ways in which civilians participated in the genocide. Lee Ann Fujii created a spectrum of responses to illustrate the range of acts that participants committed throughout the course of the genocide, ranging from "rescuing," "resisting," "witnessing," "evading," "pillaging," and "denouncing," to "killing" (2009: 30). For the purposes of this study I accept that there is variation at the individual level in methods of participation, but as my analysis is concerned with community-based action, *mobilization* will broadly refer to active, collective support for the genocide.

Meso-level

According to Evgeny Finkel and Scott Straus, the *meso-level* refers to "the space between national—or international—level factors and individual-level ones"

(2012: 58). In this analysis, I refer to the meso-level synonymously with the local or community level. Units of evaluation include political parties, civil society, social or patronage networks, economic organizations, local military units, etc. (58–59). Despite being the least-researched branch of genocide studies, analysis at this level is well-suited to provide valuable insight regarding variation in the dynamics of violence through cross-case comparisons (56). This study in particular will demonstrate how local-level actors play an instrumental role in explaining variation in the onset of genocide.

Explanations of genocide

From the convention that named the crime in the wake of the Holocaust up until the 1990s, scholars of genocide have provided primarily macro-level theoretical and historical explanations of ethno-national sentiments run tragically amok. Public understanding traditionally followed the sensationalist accounts from journalists of brute tribalism beyond Western comprehension, and scholars were primarily historians who focused on explaining particular cases of genocide rather than searching for broader explanations (Valentino, 2014: 90). For example, Leo Kuper posited that genocides occurred in divided or plural societies with deep ethnic cleavages (1982: 57). Other scholars, particularly R.J. Rummel, contended that authoritative regimes where power was concentrated in the hands of a few powerful individuals were more likely to commit genocide (1995). The characterization of genocide as a purely modern phenomenon was popularized by Zygmunt Bauman, who pointed to the degree of bureaucratic, technological, and logistical capacities necessary to carry out the destruction of a group (1989). Alternatively, Eric Weitz described that the crime was ideological in nature and the result of leaders' desire to transform society into "utopias" (2005). Barry Posen offers an additional explanation in his "Ethnic Security Dilemma." In his theory, ethnic groups overestimate the security threat posed by the other and thereby take action and unnecessarily, albeit rational in intent, instigate and escalate ethnic conflict (1993). These macro-historical theories provide frameworks for understanding *why* genocide occurs, but they fall short of explaining *how*.

The Rwandan genocide of 1994, while publicly interpreted as a product of the ancient hatred model, in conjunction with the genocide in the Balkans around the same time, sparked new efforts by scholars seeking to debunk the explanations of old and provide more robust, less superficial insights into what drives such violence (Straus, 2006: 40, Valentino, 2014: 93). As Charles King points out, there has been a recent turn in social violence research toward micropolitics (2004: 32). To expand on the gaps in understanding of causal mechanisms at a micro-level, socio-psychological research has been used to explain participation in the Rwandan genocide. For example, Christopher R. Browning's analysis of Police Battalion 101 during the Holocaust highlights the role of group pressure and conformity (1998). Experiments like the Stanford Prison Experiment and research conducted by Stanley Milgram illustrate how obedience to authority leads perpetrators to partake in violence, which Prunier argues was a prevalent factor in Rwandese society (Milgram, 1963; Prunier, 1998: 245; Zimbardo, 2007). Additionally, research has found that social networks are important factors in explaining the mobilization of participants in the Rwandan genocide on an individual level (Fujii, 2009; McDoom, 2011a). Such socio-psychological models are useful in explaining genocide at the micro, individual level; just as macro-political and structural models are helpful in describing genocide at the national level. However, to date, research on the dynamics of the genocide at the meso-level remains underdeveloped (Finkel & Straus, 2012: 58–59). Conflict scholars such as Stathis Kalyvas argue that local dynamics of political violence operate distinctively from the national level, and therefore increased consideration should be given to understanding meso-level processes (2003). Scott Straus's empirical finding that genocidal violence did not radiate from the capital of Kigali supports Kalyvas' supposition that the periphery ought not be assumed to mimic dynamics at the center (2003; Straus, 2006: 60). Further development within this level of research will generate insight into the variations of the dynamics of violence (Finkel & Straus, 2012: 59). This study in particular offers an explanatory model of timing variation across an episode of genocide.

Given the massive civilian participation level inherent to the conflict, the Rwandan genocide also generated a scholarly interest in understanding processes of civilian mobilization in episodes of mass political violence. At the same time, scholars from the field of research on social movements transitioned from thinking of episodes of collective action as the result of rational, rather than irrational, politics. As such, theories were developed to answer not *why* episodes happen, but *how*. Doug McAdam, Sidney Tarrow, and Charles Tilly developed a unified framework to theorize processes of social mobilization (McAdam et al., 2001). Several scholars of conflict studies have called attention to the potential benefit of considering these ideas in episodes of political violence. For example, Elisabeth Wood contends that mobilization patterns in conflict can benefit from lessons presented by scholars of social movements and collective action (Della Porta & Diani, 2015: 457). Like war, genocide is best understood as a process (Shaw, 2003). I contend that the process-centric models from the social movement literature could help genocide researchers, who are also increasingly concerned with understanding the *how* side of the conflict. Drawing on these existing theories of genocide and social mobilization, and the demand for further research in the area, this study utilizes a framework from contentious politics to identify mobilizing mechanisms at the meso-level of the Rwandan genocide to explain cross-commune variations in timing of the onset.

Theoretical framework

Contentious politics

Social movement theory lends a useful framework for explaining processes of collective violence at the local level. The Rwandan genocide was remarkable in that an estimated 14–17 percent of adult male Hutu civilians were collectively mobilized to participate in the violence (Straus, 2006: 118). Indisputably, the genocide was a wildly successful social movement. Therefore, it follows that the collective action in this context can be analyzed by borrowing from social movement theory. In discussing the escalation of violence in civil wars, Elisabeth Wood contends that given their shared concern with understanding the dynamics of social mobilization scholars of civil wars ought not to work in isolation from scholars of social movements (Wood, 2015: 457). The same can be said for scholars of genocide.

As the literature on genocide continues to search for theories of mobilization and participation processes, I posit that the collective action frameworks offer a useful lens through which to conduct analysis. McAdam, Tarrow, and Tilly put forward a unified framework of contentious politics that I will employ in my micro-comparative case study of the Rwandan genocide. *Contentious politics* is defined by McAdam et al. as:

> episodic, public, collective interaction among makers of claims and their objects when a.) At least one government is a claimant, and object of claims, or a party to the claims and b.) The claims would, if realized, affect the interests of at least one of the claimants
>
> (2001: 5)

This chapter draws on insights from collective action theorists' attempts to describe the mobilization of communities into transgressive collective action. By transgressive action, McAdam et al. add additional criteria to their definition as follows: "c.) At least some parties to the conflict are newly self-identified political actors or d.) At least some parties employ innovative collective action" (8). Episodes are defined by McAdam et al. as "continuous streams of contention including collective claims making that bears on other parties' interests" (28). Using this framework, I trace the dynamics of the contentious episode—community-level mobilization into genocidal violence in the Rwandan genocide—and explain how meso-level mobilization mechanisms of competition for power, framing, and diffusion operated at the commune level.

This framework allows for the identification of recurrent sequences of causal mechanisms in episodes of contention, thus providing an explanation of the variations in outcomes within and across cases. Mobilization processes concatenate mechanisms, starting with environmental factors and passing through framing and diffusion mechanisms (McAdam et al., 2001: 28). McAdam et al.'s framework places such mechanisms in a dynamic mobilization model, where mechanisms continuously interact (45). In this study, I identify three causal mechanisms most relevant to community mobilization in the Rwandan genocide: competition for power, framing, and diffusion. While these mechanisms concatenated in predictable ways in each commune, variation in the initial political affiliation of the burgomaster accounted for a protracted period of mobilization prior to the onset of genocide in Taba. I will first summarize the theory behind these mechanisms before identifying the environmental factors pertinent to the micro-comparative case study.

Mechanisms

Competition for power

McAdam et al.'s framework for contentious politics contends that "nearly all protracted episodes of contention produce a mechanism of competition for power" (2001: 67). Filip Reyntjens contends that struggles over power are conducive to genocide (1996: 242). The competition mechanism operates when environmental factors create a "space of opportunity" (Straus, 2006: 88). Structural changes, as argued by Charles Tilly, create windows in which elites may jockey for power and consolidate their power through the elimination of competition (Krain, 1997: 335). According to Tarrow, such factors could include: "the opening up of the access to participation, shifts in ruling alignments, the availability of influential allies, and cleavages within and among elites" (1994: 86).

Framing

Analyses of framing processes in collective action have proliferated in studies of social movements and have come to be understood as one of the central dynamics in the literature (Benford & Snow, 2000: 612). Robert D. Benford and David A. Snow define collective action frames as such: "action-oriented sets of beliefs and meanings that inspire and legitimate the activities and campaigns of a social movement organization" (614). Framing can take various forms, including: adversarial framing, which involves drawing the distinction between "good" and "evil"; prognostic framing, which presents the frame as a solution to a problem; and motivational framing, which inspires mobilization and action (616–617). Other framing theories relevant to this study includes the creation of "us–them boundaries," where intergroup distinctions are drawn and acted upon, as well as the implementation of "crisis frames," which manipulate the pervasive insecurities of wartime environments (Hunt et al., 1994: 192). Through written and spoken acts, the frames are then disseminated through discursive processes (Benford & Snow, 2000: 623). This micro-comparative study will show how the Hutu hardliners appropriated existing differences between Hutu and Tutsi into collective action frames conducive to genocidal mobilization. In the sequence of collective mobilization mechanisms, what follows next is diffusion.

Diffusion

Diffusion includes, but is not limited to, the dissemination of the collective action frames described above. As defined by McAdam et al., diffusion is "any transfer of information across existing lines of communication" (2001: 69). According to Sarah A. Soule, the mechanism can occur through "a transmitter, an adopter, an innovation that is being diffused, and a channel along which the item may be diffused" (2007: 29). Examples of diffusion include the broadcasting of propaganda through media or the diffusion of the threat of coercion to nonparticipants in the episode (Luft, 2015b: 159–160). Diffusion can also operate through social networks and patronage or kinship ties (Diani & McAdam, 2003). In this case study I illustrate that within the repertoires of diffusion, the burgomaster played the role of transmitter in the processes of mobilization toward genocide at the commune level.

Situating the episode

Before zooming in on the local-level dynamics and mobilization processes of the Rwandan genocide, some context-specific theory must be defined. Macro-theories of genocide, as well as studies of conflict in general, hypothesize on the significance of state capacity, wartime environments, ethnicity, democratic reform, "triggering" events, and their relationship to political violence and the collective action mechanisms described above. The explanatory variables and the theories surrounding their relationship to genocide addressed in this section are all important to any analysis of the Rwandan case. Taken on their own, however, they cannot fully explain why the transgressive episode occurred. My micro-comparative case analysis does not seek to prove or disprove the significance of any of these national-level variables, but because the communes and sequence of events examined herein were influenced by the environmental national context, it is therefore necessary to identify and address them before proceeding to a meso-level analysis.

State administration

First, in the historical theories developed to analyze the Rwandan genocide, scholars have pointed to the precolonial and colonial legacy of Rwanda's strong state institutions as a key factor in sustaining a "socially conformist" population capable of mobilizing into genocidal violence (Reyntjens, 1996: 242–243). This contention hinges on the theories regarding state strength and its relationship to genocide. Indeed, the Rwandan state is remarkably efficient and pervasive throughout society. This sets it apart from most other African nations. In fact, Rwanda is unique in several ways that contribute to its state strength. For one, it is the most densely populated country on the continent (McDoom, 2014: 25). Thus it does not suffer from the governance challenges caused by the center-–periphery divide observed by Jeff Herbst in most other African states (2000: 20–21). Second, Rwanda's geography is dotted by thousands of rolling hills and (over)cultivated fields, with little uninhabited territory, rendering the land relatively easily surveilled and traversed (Straus, 2006: 215). In addition, well-developed Rwandan institutions date back to the precolonial era and have existed ever since with a degree of continuity uncommon for contemporary African states. In this sense, Rwanda as a nation did not suffer from arbitrariness and its creation was uncharacteristically neither new nor foreign (Straus, 2006: 207). As such, the five levels of state administration[2] that operated in the country prior to the genocide were meaningful to a high degree (203). While state power is not sufficient in explaining genocide, it does help to illuminate dynamics at the local level (McDoom, 2014: 23). For example, as the following case study will demonstrate, the salience of the Rwandan state—whereby the burgomaster[3] identified with the national order—was indeed critical to the operation of mobilizing mechanisms at the local level.

Ethnicity

It would be impossible to conduct an analysis of the Rwandan genocide without discussing ethnicity. After all, the violence was primarily interethnic. Kanchan Chandra defines ethnic identities as "a subset of identity categories in which eligibility for membership is determined by attributes associated with, or believed to be associated with, descent" (2006: 398). However, the very concept of ethnicity is notoriously contested, with academics divided between primordialist, instrumentalist, and constructionist views (Oberschall, 2000: 982–983). Juan J. Linz and Alfred Stepan, speaking as constructionists, highlight the dynamic nature of ethnic identity, which varies in meaning across time and space and is amenable to change in response to political influences (1996: 366). The debates surrounding ethnicity in conflict hinge on how ethnicity is defined and on what it is based. This analysis will not seek to provide an explanation for these questions, but instead will illustrate how constructions of ethnicity are appropriated during collective mobilization.

During the Rwandan genocide, the Hutu majority (consisting of 14–17 percent of the total population) attempted, and to a large degree succeeded, to eliminate the Tutsi based on their ethnic membership (Straus, 2006: 118). However, there are deep flaws in the literature on ethnic violence, especially as it is applied to the Rwandan genocide. James D. Fearon and David D. Laitin are right to point out that the accounts based on "ancient hatred" suffer from gross over-prediction. Ethnic differences and even tensions are present in societies throughout most of the world, yet genocide remains a rare event (Fearon & Laitin, 1996: 715). Also, Rwanda has never even had tribes (Straus, 2006: 40). Furthermore, Tutsis were not the only targets: Hutu moderates were among the first groups to be eliminated, and non-participant Hutus

2 For the purposes of this study, I refer to the three highest levels of the bureaucratic hierarchy: the national government, prefectures, and communes (Straus, 2006: 204).

3 The burgomaster can be equated with the role of a mayor. The role is the most powerful position of authority in the commune and is charged with controlling the state's security apparatus in the community (Straus, 2006: 68).

were deemed "accomplices" and targeted for murder (Straus, 2006: 49). To that end, there is little evidence to assert that the tensions between Hutus and Tutsis were even particularly severe (Valentino, 2014: 93). The categorical distinction between the Hutu and Tutsi ethnic groups existed before colonial occupation, though the distinctions between the two grew more salient during such occupation. Before, the differences were generally related more to occupation or social hierarchy, or even region, rather than to steadfast physiological features (Clapham, 1998: 197). The meaning of the terms "Hutu" and "Tutsi" was not static, but instead varied across time and space in Rwanda (Fujii, 2009: 60). However, awareness of the categories was widespread and salient. By the time of the genocide, Rwandan identification cards listed an individual's ethnicity (Straus, 2006: 234).

If there was not always a consensus about what the differences between the Hutus and Tutsis were, it was at least understood that the difference existed (Fujii, 2009: 121). It is important to point out that much of the racial propaganda and appropriation of ethnic identities that the Hutus spread in their genocidal campaign equated all Tutsis with the *inkotanyi*.[4] The hardliners explicitly linked all Tutsis with the Rwandan Patriotic Front (RPF). They were labeled as either "enemies" or at least "accomplices" of the rebel group (Straus, 2006: 25). Historically speaking, precolonial and colonial control of Rwanda was placed in the hands of the Tutsi minority. Hutus later took power in the independence period, yet the omnipresent threat of a Tutsi reprisal became an important part of Hutu myth-building (McDoom, 2005: 18). By linking an ethnic category with a rebel group which did pose a legitimate threat to the majority Hutu parties' control over power, the hardliners succeeded in appropriating existing ethnic categories in a genocidal construct. Given this, as Charles King aptly notes, if ethnicity is but a tool of mobilization, then ethnic conflict itself may well be a misnomer (2004: 451). This study will show how this occurred during the mobilization process.

Introduction of multipartyism

While I contend that the violence was primarily interethnic, it is necessary to acknowledge the role that intra-Hutu politics played in instigating the genocide. As Benjamin Valentino points out, intra-ethnic violence, usually committed by extremists against moderates, is commonplace in ethnic conflict (Valentino, 2014: 94). Post-independence Rwandan politics pitted Hutus in conflict with one another based on longstanding regional rivalries (Fujii, 2009: 10). There is ample scholarship to suggest that the political infighting and maneuvering rampant in the wake of the introduction of multipartyism in Rwanda played a significant role in the run-up to the genocide. Fujii contends that the historical narrative reveals not a culture of ethnic hatreds, but rather a sometimes-violent

4 *Inkotanyi* became synonymous with the RPF rebels, or "enemies" (Straus, 2006, p. 172).

process of state-building and competition for power (73). Michael Mann's *The Dark Side of Democracy* describes how states in the midst of democratic transition are susceptible to genocidal violence as the ethnos (ethnic group) becomes conflated with the demos (democracy), and the majority ethnic group justifies its targeting of the minority as justified by majoritarian, democratic rule (1999). The argument suffers from frequency mismatch, but parallels could well be drawn from Mann's theory to the political instability experienced by Rwanda in its attempt to reform away from authoritarian rule.

The introduction of multi-party politics in 1991 in Rwanda legitimized and emboldened parties that were previously dormant (McDoom, 2014: 42). The resounding significance of intra-Hutu political rivalries leading up to and during the 1994 genocide takes credence away from the explanatory models that emphasize ethnic fear and ancient tribal hatreds. The shift to multi-party politics exposed that the major cleavages in Rwandan society were not inherently ethnic, but rather had important political and regional characteristics, with President Juvenal Habyarimana's northern Hutu faction pitted against the Republican Democratic Movement (MDR) and MDR-Power Hutus[5] of the center-south (Fujii, 2009: 56). Therefore, the Rwandan genocide was not an example of African tribalism and ancient ethnic hatreds run amok. Instead, as is illustrated in my analysis below, it was an example of contentious politics gone transgressive.

War and genocide

The relationship between war and genocide is often emphasized in the conflict studies literature. One can safely say that war does not *cause* genocide, because if it were the case there would be many more genocides. Genocide is (thankfully) a rare event—much more so than war. However, war can act as a proximate factor to genocidal violence in several important ways. In a psychological sense, war serves to desensitize the population to violence and mass death (Bartrop, 2002: 520). War can also create an environment of mass hysteria (Fettweis, 2003: 228). From a rational-actor perspective, the prevalence of violence already present in war makes it easier for leaders to take extraordinary measures. In a sense, war acts as a stepping stone to acts that would otherwise require a great leap. Genocide becomes entangled in the strategy of war, far from operating in distinction from it (Valentino, 2014: 95). As Valentino and his colleagues conclude, sometimes mass killing is simply war by other means (Valentino et al., 2004: 401–402). Indeed, Barabra Harff's quantitative study found that all episodes of genocide in recent history occurred in the context of a war (2003: 70). However, due to definitional inconsistencies, this finding can be disputed. For

5 After the assassination of Burundi president Melchior Ndadaye in 1993, opposition parties split into "Power" factions, which expounded extremist Hutu ideology and agendas (Fujii, 2009: 53).

example, Bartrop points out that the Ukrainian famine, which he asserts constituted genocide, occurred during peacetime (2002: 527). As regards social movements, McAdam et al. state that episodes of contention develop from environmental uncertainty (2001: 97). War by all measures contributes to a great environmental uncertainty. Rwanda's genocide was no exception.

Since 1990, Rwanda had been enveloped in a civil war between the RPF and the ruling government led by President Habyarimana. The national army was expanded during this time of civil war, and a youth militia known as the Interaham we was created (Straus, 2006: 26). These factors, made possible by the war, would later aid the genocide efforts. The war continued until peace was negotiated in the form of the Arusha Accords in the Fall of 1993 (24). The peace lasted until the assassination of President Habyarimana, which led to a resumption of the civil war and later genocide. Hypotheses supporting the causal relationship between the civil war and genocide are supported by Scott Straus's bivariate regression analysis, which found a statistically significant relationship between the date of onset within a prefecture and proximity to the RPF (the front) (62). Martin Shaw, too, postulates the connection between Rwanda's civil war and its genocide, stating that the episode was political and militaristic, not tribal (2003: 211).

Environmental trigger: assassination

President Habyarimana was assassinated just outside the capital, Kigali, on April 6, 1994, when two missiles shot down the plane carrying him, several of his key advisors, and the Burundian president (Straus, 2006: 44). The significance of this event cannot be understated. While the genocide might well have taken place without the assassination, the intense crisis and period of acute insecurity that followed the assassination had an undeniable, direct influence on the contentious episode that followed. Who was responsible for the assassination remains unknown to this day. The most likely suspects were the hardliners within Habyarimana's National Republican Movement for Democracy and Development (MRND), who viewed the president as a political corpse. Habyarimana was deemed to be too soft because of his acceptance of the Arusha Accords and the opening of political space, which led to competition through the introduction of multipartyism. It is less plausible to believe that the attack was executed by the RPF, who had come out of the peace agreement in a strong position. After all, the result was the genocide of hundreds of thousands of Tutsis (Prunier, 1998: 220). Nonetheless, whoever was responsible for the assassination was successful in creating an immediate explosion of chaos that rattled the country, down to the furthest communes. McAdam et al. note that processes of mobilization are triggered by environmental changes. Seen in this light, the assassination of President Habyarimana was the trigger (McAdam et al., 2001: 70). The hardliners immediately went to work on eliminating all competition, including the moderate Hutu leaders. At the macro-level, genocide had begun. How it would continue to spread throughout the country, however, varied in temporal terms.

Methodology

Process tracing

Using process tracing, I will draw on evidence from the Taba and Nyakizu communes to conduct a micro-comparative case study. This method will allow me to analyze the processes within each case and identify and demonstrate how three causal mechanisms—competition for power, framing, and diffusion—explain the dependent variable: the date of the onset of collective mobilization into genocide in the commune. *Process tracing* is defined as "the use of evidence from within a case to make inferences about causal explanation of that case" (Bennett & Checkel, 2015: 4). Therefore, by comparing a timeline of events from the period of President Habyarimana's assassination to the onset of genocidal violence in Taba and Nyakizu, this study will identify a concatenation of causal mechanisms within the episode to explain how the communes were mobilized into committing genocide. The process-tracing method will enable me to identify the concatenation of mechanisms, as derived from McAdam et al.'s social movement theory on the dynamics of contentious politics, which accounted for the temporal variation in mobilization (2001: 6). Critically, this analysis will illustrate the central role of the local authority figure in facilitating the mobilization process.

Process tracing at the meso-level is particularly conducive to explaining temporal variations in individual cases. Research at this level is empirically advantageous because the units of analysis, which involve subnational institutions, local leaders, and events, offer the potential to uncover variation within a single-case analysis (McDoom, 2014: 7). Meso-level quantitative data is sometimes difficult to obtain, so social movement theory offers a useful framework suitable for analyzing the available evidence. Aside from merely linking micro processes to the macro-level, the meso-level dynamics often do not operate in the same fashion at all. Therefore, the locally-based unit of analysis warrants attention on its own accord (Kalyvas, 2003: 487). Moreover, because national-level variables remain constant, it is possible to identify elements that explain variation independently from macro-level features (Finkel & Straus, 2012: 64). In this analysis, the variation I seek to explain is the difference in timing of the onset of genocide within each commune.

Case selection

Comparison at the commune level affords the opportunity to compare distinct repertoires of mobilization that share most environmental factors and result in distinct dependent variables. The relative homogeneity allows a greater certainty in identifying the causal mechanisms responsible for the timing of the onset (McDoom, 2014: 12). In accordance with this assertion, I have chosen the communes of Taba and Nyakizu for several important reasons. The aim of this study is to identify the factors that were responsible for the temporal discrepancies in the onset of genocide across Rwandan communes. Therefore, I have chosen two communes located in Central and South Rwanda which, despite sharing most characteristics prior to the genocide, experienced the onset of violence at different times. In Taba, the onset was three days later than expected,[6] and in Nyakizu the violence erupted seven days earlier than expected. Both communes experienced strong interethnic relations prior to the onset of violence and both were under the political control of the same political party, albeit of different factions of that party—a critical distinction that is addressed below. Consequently, the recent history of struggle within each of the communes was political, not ethnic, in nature (Des Forges, 1999: 353–357; McDoom, 2014: 42). In addition, their respective prefectures were densely populated, experienced similar rates of population growth, and were located far from the front of the civil war (Straus, 2006: 259–260). Wealth, education rank, and levels of unemployment were also comparable between the two prefectures (Straus, 2006: 259). Only Nyakizu was host to Burundi refugees, but both communes would experience an influx of Tutsi refugees from neighboring regions throughout the course of the genocide (Des Forges, 1999: 394; McDoom, 2014: 42). Given the relative homogeneity of these factors, the variation is considerable.

It must also be noted that the selection of Taba and Nyakizu was highly contingent on the availability of data. Much evidence from Taba during the time of the genocide is available due to the high-profile nature of the burgomaster Jean-Paul Akayesu's case in the International Criminal Tribunal for Rwanda (ICTR). Witness reports and documentation abound to offer a well-triangulated and corroborated account of events within the commune (*Prosecutor v. Akayesu*, 1998). The rich qualitative data available on Nyakizu can be attributed to the incredibly thorough work and careful documentation of the renowned historian and Rwanda expert Alison Des Forges in her book *"Leave None to Tell the Story"* (1999). Through these sources, I was able to glean sufficient information to conduct my research through the method of process tracing. This study hypothesizes that the independent variable is the political affiliation of the burgomaster, which through a process of mobilizing mechanisms explains the variation in the dependent variable—the date of the onset of genocide within the commune—in each case.

Scope conditions

The scope of this study is constricted on several fronts. First, the claims made in the previous section concerning the homogeneity between Taba and Nyakizu were based on a combination of data, some of which is not available at the commune level. There is a chance that either of the communes in question could be statistical outliers for any of the categories. To be certain of the cross-case

6 Expected onset is the regional average (see Table 3.1).

similarities, further disaggregation of the data would be necessary. Furthermore, the selection of the communes itself is susceptible to a degree of arbitrariness, given that I selected them based on the nature of their dependent variables. Indeed, there is a possibility that completely different communes, both with a similar degree of homogeneity but with different onset dates, could operate under different mobilization dynamics than in Taba and Nyakizu. While I intend to avoid this potential pitfall by emphasizing the mechanisms within the process rather than testing my hypothesis a priori, it is necessary to consider the constraints that a micro-comparative case study presents in regard to arbitrariness. Second, the micro-comparative case study that I conduct spans temporally from President Habyarimana's assassination on April 6, 1994 until the onset of genocide in each respective commune. The study is limited in that the history of pre-genocide Rwanda is inextricably linked to the dynamics of the genocide at large, yet my analysis spans only several weeks. I have chosen this time period because I find that while the events leading up to April 6 are indeed relevant to the dynamics of the genocide at every level, they are *most* critical for explanations at the macro national level. Nonetheless, I attempt to ameliorate some of the issues associated with this by highlighting several key contextual factors below. Ultimately though, this analysis of local-level mobilization processes need only begin with the triggering event—in this case the assassination that occurred on April6. Finally, it must be noted that a potential for bias exists in some of the sources from which my data has been drawn. Much of the consensus on what happened at the local level during the genocide is based on testimony, which can be problematic in terms of reliability.

Micro-comparative case analysis

The Nyakizu Commune

The southern prefecture of Butare was widely seen as a safe haven for Tutsis during the first weeks of the genocide, as the sole Tutsi prefect in the country preached resistance and protection. The commune of Nyakizu, however, was an anomaly. Led by an MDR-Power hardliner, the onset of genocide occurred a full week earlier than the average Butare commune (Des Forges, 1999: 353; Straus, 2006: 250–255). The mobilization of Nyakizu residents to participate in the genocide was swift at the behest of the burgomaster. After consolidating what remaining power he did not already possess circa April 6, the leader instigated and sustained the collective mobilization through framing and diffusion mechanisms.

At the outset of the genocide, the Tutsi population in Nyakizu comprised 18 percent of the total population—far higher than the national average of 8 percent, but consistent with the demographics in Butare (Des Forges, 1999: 355). The intermarriage rates, which are commonly used to assess levels of social cohesion, were thus predictably high and Butare had a reputation as an intellectual center and bastion of tolerance (353). Like most of rural Rwanda, Nyakizu was poor and densely populated. Its shared border with Burundi was, however, a distinguishing factor as 15,000 Burundi refugees flowed into the commune following the assassination of President Ndadaye in 1993 (363). Although intuition would suggest that the influx of refugees would exacerbate insecurities and the potential for violence, Straus's bivariate regression analysis does not find this to have had a statistically significant relationship with the onset of genocide (Straus, 2006: 60). The administrative and bureaucratic institutions of the state operated with as much saliency as elsewhere in the country, as exemplified by the fact that the commune was the largest employer of salaried workers (Des Forges, 1999: 355). The local politics in Nyakizu, however, were atypical of the region. The prefect of Butare was the only Tutsi and Liberal Party member in the country to hold the prefectural title (354). In marked contrast, Nyakizu's burgomaster, Ladislas Ntaganzwa—a member of the extremist Power wing of the MDR, which had not historically had a presence in Butare—had ascended to power through the forceful removal of opposition (357). Through adoption of the radical ethnic Hutu Power ideology and a swift consolidation of power, Ntaganzwa became the unquestioned local leader and by early 1994 had fostered a well-developed personal and professional inner network of backers within the commune, and received significant support from national MDR-Power leaders (361). Residents reported that military training sessions had begun in the fall of 1993 and that Ntaganzwa controlled a stockpile of weaponry (365). These were the demographic and political conditions under which Nyakizu residents found themselves when news of President Habyarimana's assassination reached the commune.

News of the plane crash on April 6 reached most residents by radio (Des Forges, 1999: 368). An acute sense of uncertainty descended upon Nyakizu immediately, as people fleeing violence in neighboring prefectures began to arrive. At this point, the exact nature of the reported violence remained unclear and confusion and uncertainty plagued the community as normal activities were disrupted (368). During these first few days, burgomaster Ntaganzwa made public reassurances of the safety of Tutsis in his commune, while simultaneously holding private meetings with his inner circle. Facing no competition for power from within Nyakizu, the burgomaster was the supreme authority figure through which information and instructions were diffused and disseminated. Ntaganzwa took keen advantage of the "space of opportunity" that the assassination and ensuing period of acute insecurity provided. There were few challengers to the burgomaster in the competition for power. Thus began the direction, at the behest of Ntaganzwa, that Tutsis were to gather in Cyahinda Church "for their safety" (370). At the same time, the inner circle was spreading an anti-Tutsi propaganda campaign throughout the commune. By appropriating existing ethno-social cleavages—which were particularly vulnerable to manipulation by the acute insecurity following the events of April 6—Ntaganzwa and his cronies began referring to all Tutsis as *inkotanyi* and attributed grave levels of threat to Hutus by the Tutsi "enemy." On April 13, broadcasts on Radio Télévision Libre des Mille Collines (RTLM) falsely reported that *inkotanyi* were hiding among the people in Gitarama and Butare, lending further credence and certification to the framing efforts of Ntaganzwa and his supporters (372–373). That night, the first Nyakizu Tutsis were killed (373).

The next morning, Ntaganzwa and members of his inner circle held public meetings throughout the commune encouraging participation in patrols. From this point on, reports of violent repercussions against nonparticipants proliferated (Des Forges, 1999: 374). The threat of intra-Hutu coercion was diffused via incitements at the public meetings and rallies, as well as by rumors and hearsay among residents. Ntaganzwa reportedly drove around the commune with a loudspeaker, exhorting residents to gather the "rebels" at Cyahinda to prevent them from attacking, and ordered the killers to "get to work" and "leave no one alive" (377). The repertoires of diffusion—of the appropriation of Tutsis as "enemies" posing an imminent mortal danger to Hutus and of the threat of punishment for nonparticipating Hutus—were repeated by the burgomaster as he traversed the commune in his pick-up truck on his mobilization tour. By April 15, an estimated 20,000 people had been gathered at Cyahinda (395). Accompanied by up to 2,000 others, Ntaganzwa arrived at the church and, over the loudspeaker, issued a countdown: "One, two, three" (383). Genocide had reached Nyakizu.

Framing and diffusion efforts continued throughout the commune during the massacres. The burgomaster emerged from Cyahinda with a fake bandage tied around his head and proceeded to drive throughout the commune spreading wild claims of Tutsi brutality that nearly killed him. Such claims were rampantly employed to inspire more recruits as the genocide continued (Des Forges, 1999: 386). It is of course important to note that not all *génocidaires* are created equal. That is, the levels of participation varied widely within the perpetrator community (Straus, 2006: 110). The burgomaster in Nyakizu made concerted efforts to mobilize bona fide killers, not just looters (who far outnumbered the former). To do so, Ntaganzwa had the remaining influential Hutu moderates in the commune killed. In an effort to further distort identity frames, the murders were reported over the radio as having been committed by Tutsi (Des Forges, 1999: 388–389).

On April 17, the prefect of Butare was removed from his post, having lost control (391). Following the orders of national MDR-Power leaders announced on Radio Rwanda, the burgomaster and his group went door-to-door to weed out any remaining dissenters and incite more joiners (392). Another notable event occurred when Interim President Théodore Sindikubwabo stopped in Nyakizu as part of his mobilization tour. He gave a speech endorsing the ongoing violence, providing further certification of the burgomaster's words and actions (393). Soldiers armed with heavy weaponry arrived the next day to finish the genocide at Cyahinda. By April 22, the killers had completed the ten-day massacre. The dead at the church alone numbered at least 5,500, and perhaps as many as 15,000 (395).

Despite the fact that the prefect of Butare was Tutsi and discernibly worked rigorously to resist the violence from breaking out in the region, Ntaganzwa was able to carry out his own genocidal agenda in direct violation of the administratively superior orders of the prefect (Des Forges, 1999: 402). This provides further evidence that the role of the burgomaster is deeply resonant in the local-level dynamics of social movements in Rwanda. In a region characterized by a delayed onset of violence, the anomaly of Nyakizu can be primarily attributed to the one factor that set it apart from the outset: Ntaganzwa's affiliation with the MDR-Power party and ruling hardliners. The initial competition for (or rather, consolidation of) power in the wake of Habyarimana's assassination was swift—practically nonexistent were it not for the Tutsi prefect and several of the moderates mentioned above that Ntaganzwa ordered murdered. From there, the mobilization mechanisms of framing and diffusion flowed through the burgomaster's unchallenged command. The result was the swift commencement of genocide in a region otherwise characterized as a bastion of resistance.

Taba Commune

Taba is located in the Gitarama prefecture of central Rwanda. Historically, the region had been home of the Parmehutu party,[7] whose agenda had reemerged with the introduction of multipartyism in 1991 as the MDR. The genocide was late in reaching Gitarama, and Taba was no exception. In fact, the onset of genocide occurred three days later than the two-week average (from the date of Habyarimana's assassination) observed in the rest of the commune (Straus, 2006: 83). The burgomaster, Jean-Paul Akayesu, gained worldwide infamy as he became the first individual to become a convicted criminal at the ICTR (*The Prosecutor v. Jean-Paul Akayesu (Trial Judgement)*, 1998) for his acts committed during the genocide (Straus, 2006: 87). What is less known is that the delay in violence in Taba was made possible by the moderate MDR leader, even though his eventual and sudden political reversal of position instigated genocide in the commune all the same (83).

In the run-up to the genocide, political maneuvering was a more salient feature of tensions within the community than were ethnic cleavages. Approximately 4,680 Tutsi comprised 8 percent of the population of the Taba commune just before the genocide in 1994, which was around the average countrywide composition. Social cohesion within the community, as evidenced by no reported incidents of ethnic violence prior to the genocide, was notably strong (McDoom, 2014: 42). Political tensions between the recently ousted MRND and the MDR (led by Akayesu), were seemingly more relevant than ethnic ones. The divide between MRND members primarily composed of northern Hutus, and the southern and centrally based Hutus of the MDR, was contentious from the time of the democratic openings in 1991. Gitarama was the

7 The Parmehutu party ruled Rwanda in the period immediately following independence. Its strength emanated from the south and central regions. The MDR, created with the introduction of multipartyism, was a reincarnation of the party (McDoom, 2014: 42).

birthplace of the Parmehutu party of old and was consequently a stronghold for the MDR in the early 1990s. Intra-Hutu political infighting in the wake of RPF advances and the disintegrating authority of Habyarimana resonated in Taba, where tensions followed party lines (42).

Immediately following the plane crash on April 6, Jean-Paul Akayesu preached resistance to the extremist hardliners and went to significant lengths to prevent violence from fomenting in Taba. For example, he arranged for the commune offices to provide safe sanctuary for Tutsis and he dispatched three of the commune policemen to protect them. In public meetings, he insisted on solidarity (McDoom, 2014: 42). Interahamwe forces repeatedly attempted to disrupt the commune, but witnesses from the ICTR testified to Akayesu's efforts to maintain peace (Straus, 2014: 339). As burgomaster and therefore the preeminent figure of power in the commune, Akayesu was deemed by the ICTR as being responsible and authoritatively capable of maintaining order (*The Prosecutor v. Jean-Paul Akayesu (Trial Judgement)*, 1998). Thus, when the burgomaster held meetings in the days following the assassination and instructed the residents to act against the violence, his words were widely observed. Residents even went so far as to kill Interahamwe attempting an incursion at the behest of Akayesu. The pattern of resistance led by the burgomaster followed this trajectory for the first ten days following April 6 (Straus, 2014: 339). However, competition for power in the region began to infiltrate Taba and destabilize the status quo.

On April 12, the interim national government moved its capital from Kigali to Gitarama (McDoom, 2014: 42). With this move, accompanied by an estimated 1,000 Interahamwe, pressure from above mounted against Akayesu's monopoly on authority (Melvern, 2006: 195). The competition for power culminated in a meeting in Gitarama on April 18 between the extremist interim prime minister Jean Kambanda and noncompliant burgomasters (McDoom, 2014: 42). The diffusion of an intra-Hutu coercion threat from the national hardliner leaders forced Akayesu to determine that switching sides was either his only, or his best, option for maintaining authority (Straus, 2006: 84). On the morning of April 19, he broadcast a new message at a meeting of over 100 people, in which he urged the residents to eliminate the RPF and its accomplices. This message was framed in such a way that the people widely understood that the RPF was synonymous with all Tutsis (*The Prosecutor v. Jean-Paul Akayesu (Trial Judgement)*, 1998). Appearing alongside an Interahamwe member waving a document, Akayesu announced that the *inkotanyi* and local "accomplices" planned to murder the Hutus and take supreme control of Rwanda (Straus, 2006: 84). In response, he gave orders for specific Tutsi to be murdered. At his command, shortly after the meeting the residents of Taba obeyed and began killings. Genocide had come to Taba. By the end of June, an estimated 2,000 Tutsis were murdered under the command of Jean-Paul Akayesu (*The Prosecutor v. Jean-Paul Akayesu (Trial Judgement)*, 1998).

While the maintenance of peace in the days in the immediate aftermath of the assassination can be largely attributed to the efforts of burgomaster Akayesu, so too can the eventual genocide which took place. The decision of the ICTR supported this claim and convicted Jean-Paul Akayesu for direct and public incitement to commit genocide (*The Prosecutor v. Jean-Paul Akayesu (Trial Judgement)*, 1998). Interim Prime Minister Kambanda confirmed the significance of local authority figures in the mobilization process by remarking that in areas where the MRND was not as strong, the population did not kill until it was endorsed as policy by the local authority (Melvern, 2006: 196). Diffusion of identity frames that conflated all Tutsis with the RPF thus operated through the command of the burgomaster. At least 2,000 Tutsis were killed in the commune (*The Prosecutor v. Jean-Paul Akayesu (Trial Judgement)*, 1998). Despite having initially led a resistance to the hardliners, Akayesu acquiesced to their agenda during the period of political competition following April 6and thereby instantaneously enlisted his dense network of authority in Taba to diffuse the genocidal mobilization orders, threats of noncompliance, and propaganda framing the Tutsi synonymously with the *inkotanyi*. During the public meetings, he disseminated the appropriated identity frames and diffused threats of coercion for nonparticipants. Like in Nyakizu, these mobilization mechanisms of framing and diffusion flowed through the burgomaster following the resolution of the competition for power.

Attributing the difference

My findings support the work of scholars from both of the fields with which this study is concerned. In terms of social movement studies, my conclusions are consistent with one of the central tenets of McAdams's political process model: that social movements are political phenomena (1999). Nyakizu and Taba provide clear examples of how differences in the political affiliation of the burgomasters of otherwise reasonably similar communes exhibiting the same sequence of mobilization mechanisms led to a significant difference in the timing of the onset of genocide. Table 3.1 shows that Nyakizu was "tipped" into genocide seven days earlier than the regional average, while Taba did so later by three days. The combined difference relative to the expected onset date (the average of all onset dates within the respective prefecture) was thus a spread of ten days. My analysis attributes the difference to the initial (as of April 6, 1994) political preferences of the burgomasters, Ladislas Ntaganzwa and Jean-Paul Akayesu. In terms of the literature on the Rwandan genocide, my argument is consistent with Straus's findings from his bivariate regression analyses of explanatory variables to describe regional variations in the onset of violence, in which the strongest statistical relationship was with the degree of support for the ruling MRND party[8] within the commune. In these areas, Straus found the violence was more likely to foment earlier. Conversely, in areas where there was opposition to the hardliners, the genocide took longer to occur (Straus, 2006: 61).

8 The MRND consisted of Hutu hardliners, as did MDR-Power. For the purposes of this analysis, I assume mutual support for the genocide between these factions.

Table 3.1 Comparing the communes before April 6, 1994

	Taba (Gitarama)	*Nyakizu (Butare)*
Onset date of relative to regional average	+3	-7
Party affiliation of burgomaster	MDR	MDR-Power
Party affiliation of prefect	MDR	Liberal Party
% of Tutsi population in the commune	8	18
# of Tutsi killed	2000	5,500–15,000
Recent history of ethnic violence	No, but political struggles	No, but political struggles
Military presence	Not initially, but 1,000 Interahamwe followed the interim government's move to Gitarama	Yes, as early as September 1993
Distance from the "front" (RPF position)	Considerable	Considerable
Burundi refugees	No	Yes
Interethnic cohesion	Strong	Strong

As illustrated in Table 3.1, Taba and Nyakizu experienced comparatively similar environmental factors in the days leading up to the genocide. The ways in which they diverge—for example, the presence of Burundi refugees and the high Tutsi population in Nyakizu—have not been found to have a statistically significant relationship to the onset of genocide (Straus, 2006: 60). The most salient difference between the communes was the affiliation of Ntaganzwa with the "Power," or hardliner branch of the MDR. Akayesu's active status as an MDR of the non-hardliner brand blocked the mobilization mechanisms of framing and diffusion until he switched sides during the competition for power following the government's move to Gitarama and the diffusion of coercion threats for noncompliance (Straus, 2006: 84). It should also be reiterated that the prefect—a post of administrative authority higher than the burgomaster—in Butare (Nyakizu's prefecture) was the exact opposite of a hardliner. In fact, it was the only Liberal Party prefect in the country (Des Forges, 1999: 384). This fact supports my contention that it was the burgomaster's affiliation that mattered most in terms of local mobilization, because intuition would suggest that a moderate presence at the prefect level should have trumped the power of the burgomaster, but such was not the case. Therefore, it was the burgomaster's politics that mattered most in community mobilization. I do not argue that the onset of genocide was contingent on the agency of the authority figures, nor do I mean to overstate the role of individuals in a complex, complicated episode. Rather, my analysis shows that mobilization mechanisms of framing and diffusion flowed through the burgomasters after the competition for power was complete. The concatenation of mechanisms was the same in each commune—an initial competition for power, followed by framing and diffusion orchestrated by the burgomasters through public meetings; dissemination of frames through RTLM broadcasts; propagandizing and rumor-spreading through informal networks; signaling of pro-genocide positions; certification of authority, etc. Yet the length of time it took each repertoire to culminate in collective action and mass violence was not the same. I argue that the difference, then, is attributable to the burgomasters' relationship with the ruling hardliner party. Framing and diffusion mechanisms operated *through* the command of the local authority, and the manner of their command was determined during the competition for power. The burgomasters were not the kings, but rather the kingpins in the genocidal episode of transgressive contention.

Alternative explanations

In this study, I have given little attention to theories of the impact of social networks in the episodes of collective action. Studies by Lee Ann Fujii and Omar McDoom have found that social networks are critical for understanding who did the killing and how the violence spread (Fujii, 2009; McDoom, 2011a). While networks of influence are endogenous to my argument that mechanisms of collective action operated through the burgomaster, I chose to avoid delving deeply into these theories because the principal focus of this study is to answer how mobilization occurs at the meso-level, and to date social network data is primarily concentrated on the individual, micro-level, as exemplified by Fujii's comprehensive interviewing of selected *génocidaires* (2009).

Another alternative explanation that I have not fully disproven in my findings includes the role of the militia in influencing the onset date. I have shown that the existence of military training programs in Nyakizu in late 1993 was an important environmental factor, as was the arrival of 1,000 Interahamwe with the interim government's move to Gitarama on April 12, 1994. I contend that the nexus of tensions within the commune hinged first and foremost along political lines, and that military power emanated from political power and not vice versa. However, alternative explanations could attribute greater importance to these factors where I have instead featured the role of the burgomaster.

Finally, the mechanisms I have identified in this study are susceptible to a degree of selection bias and arbitrariness. McAdam et al.'s theoretical framework of contentious politics identifies far more interactive causal mechanisms than the constraints of this study allowed to be considered. For example, mechanisms of brokerage, radicalization, and convergence are relevant to the episode, yet I chose to examine the competition for power, framing, and diffusion because through my method of process tracing I found these mechanisms to feature most prominently. While more comprehensive research could benefit from analyzing as many mechanisms as feasible, nonetheless the mechanisms selected for this study are sufficient to support my findings.

Discussion

As this study confirms, local political dynamics matter. Nyakizu and Taba experienced the onset of the 1994 genocide at different times because their respective burgomasters significantly influenced the course of the mobilization mechanisms. The communities "tipped" into violence at the behest of these men, who instigated a sequence of mobilizing mechanisms. The difference in their political affiliations accounted for the temporal difference in the onset dates.

The difference in relative averages of the onset of genocide has significant policy implications. Policymakers have long struggled to predict and prevent genocide. There are, of course, significant political, legal, and logistical obstacles to these efforts. Furthermore, models of genocide prediction are plagued by over-prediction (Verdeja, 2016: 22). By looking at local-level dynamics of violence rather than macro-level indicators, scholars are more reasonably able to make predictions on where and when violence will occur within a given conflict (McDoom, 2014: 25). For example, in light of my findings if a mandate were acquired to dispatch a certain number of peacekeeping forces, my findings could provide useful insights into which locales offer the largest window of opportunity for effective deployment. In Nyakizu, any dispatch of aid would have been unlikely to arrive in time to quell the violence. In Taba, however, a peacekeeping force could feasibly have dispatched and arrived prior to the onset.

The ultimate goal for scholars of genocide is generally to prevent such violence from occurring in the future. However, there remains no unified theory of genocide and even the best calculations are subject to false positives (Verdeja, 2016: 22). Politically, this reduces the will and capital of international actors to take preventive action against the crime to almost nil. The recent trend in conflict studies calling for further analysis into meso-level processes in mobilization could offer policymakers more realistic agendas in mitigating violence. Local-level assessments provide an empirical ability to account for variation within and across conflicts, and social movement theory offers a framework that is conducive to extrapolating from meso-level analyses (McDoom, 2014: 12). While stopping violence before it starts is often an impossible task or too tall an order, this new research could provide roadmaps for the efficient, targeted allocation of resources to curb conflicts as they unfold. As social movement theory has shown, collective mobilization processes consist of a concatenation of mechanisms that repeat themselves across and within contentious episodes. By understanding how they operate and what accounts for the differences in their outcomes, we can make better predictions about how, where, and when future episodes of genocide might occur. In the case of Rwanda, as proven by this analysis, it was the burgomasters who held the keys of contention. They were not the kings, but the *kingpins* of contention.

Appendix Timeline of events

Taba:

1. April 6 Habyarimana assassinated
2. April 12 Interim government moves its capital from Kigali to Gitarama
3. April 13 RTLM announces that *inyenzi*, or "cockroaches," are hiding among refugees fleeing to Butare and Gitarama
4. April 18 Meeting ordered by Prime Minister Jean Kambanda in Gitarama to address the prefecture's resistant burgomasters
5. April 19 Akayesu addresses several hundred Taba residents and urges them to unite and hunt down the enemy
6. April 19–20 Mass killing
7. June 27 Akayesu flees the commune ahead of RPF arrival

Nyakizu:

1. April 6 Habyarimana assassinated
2. April 6 Witnesses see smoke from houses burning in Gikongoro
3. April 8 Tutsi begin to gather at Cyahinda Church
4. April 12 News that the Interahamwe are targeting Tutsi reaches Nyakizu. Ntaganzwa holds a meeting with his inner circle at the communal office
5. April 13 RTLM announces that *inyenzi* are hiding among refugees fleeing to Butare and Gitarama
6. Night of April 13 First Tutsis are killed in Nyakizu. Ntaganzwa holds a meeting at Cyahinda and orders residents to carry out patrols and stay away from the church
7. April 15 Preliminary attack on Cyahinda
8. April 16 National police obtain pick-up trucks
9. April 17 Prefect Habyarimana arrives with other officials and killing briefly stops
10. April 17 National radio announces the removal of Habyarimana
11. April 18 Interim prime minister makes a speech at the communal office
12. April 20 Killing at Cyahinda is complete. At least 5,500 Tutsi are estimated dead

Bibliography

Bartrop, P. (2002) The Relationship between War and Genocide in the Twentieth Century: A Consideration. *Journal of Genocide Research*, 4(4), pp. 519–532.

Bauman, Z. (1989) *Modernity and the Holocaust*. Cambridge: Polity Press.

Benford, R.D., & Snow, D.A. (2000) Framing Processes and Social Movements: An Overview and Assessment. *Annual Review of Sociology*, 26(1), pp. 611–39.

Bennett, A., & Checkel, J.T. (2015) *Process Tracing: From Metaphor to Analytic Tool*. Cambridge: Cambridge University Press.

Bhavnani, R., & Backer, D. (2000) Localized Ethnic Conflict and Genocide. *Journal of Conflict Resolution*, 44(3), pp. 283–306.

Browning, C.R. (1998) *Ordinary Men: Reserve Police Battalion 101 and the Final Solution in Poland*. New York, NY: Harper Perennial.

Chandra, K. (2006) What Is Ethnic Identity and Does It Matter? *Annual Review of Political Science*, 9, pp. 397–424.

Clapham, C. (1998) Rwanda: The Perils of Peacemaking. *Journal of Peace Research*, 35(2), pp. 193–210.

Convention on the Prevention and Punishment of the Crime of Genocide, *adopted* 9 Dec. 1948, G.A. Res. 260 (III), U.N. GAOR, 3d Sess., U.N. Doc. A/RES/3/260 (1948), 78 U.N.T.S. 277.

Della Porta, D., & Diani, M. (2015) *The Oxford Handbook of Social Movements*. Oxford: Oxford University Press.

Des Forges, A.L. (1999) "Human Rights Watch & Fédération Internationale Des Droits De L'homme" in *"Leave None to Tell the Story": Genocide in Rwanda*, pp. 353–402. New York, NY, and Paris: Human Rights Watch; International Federation of Human Rights.

Diani, M., & McAdam, D. (2003) *Social Movements and Networks: Relational Approaches to Collective Action*. Oxford: Oxford University Press.

Fearon, J., & Laitin, D. (1996) Explaining Interethnic Cooperation. *American Political Science Review*, 90(4), p. 715.

Fettweis, C. (2003) War as Catalyst: Moving World War II to the Center of Holocaust Scholarship. *Journal of Genocide Research*, 5(2), pp. 225–236.

Finkel, E., & Straus, S. (2012) Macro, Meso, and Micro Research on Genocide: Gains, Shortcomings, and Future Areas of Inquiry. *Genocide Studies and Prevention*, 7(1), pp. 56–67.

Fujii, L.A. (2009) *Killing Neighbors: Webs of Violence in Rwanda*. Ithaca, NY: Cornell University Press.

Harff, B. (2003) No Lessons Learned from the Holocaust? Assessing Risks of Genocide and Political Mass Murder since 1955. *American Political Science Review*, 97(1), pp. 57–73.

Hatzfeld, J. (2005). *Machete Season: The Killers in Rwanda Speak: A Report*. New York, NY: Farrar, Straus and Giroux.

Herbst, J.I. (2000) *States and Power in Africa: Comparative Lessons in Authority and Control*. Princeton, NJ: Princeton University Press.

Hunt, S.A., Benford, R.D., & Snow, D.A. (1994) "Identity Fields: Framing Processes and the Social Construction of Movement Identities" in Larana, E., Johnston, H., and Gusfield, J.R. (Eds.), *New Social Movements: From Ideology to Identity*, pp. 185–208. Philadelphia, PA: Temple University Press.

Kalyvas, S.N. (2003) The Ontology of "Political Violence": Action and Identity in Civil Wars. *Perspectives on Politics*, 1(3), pp. 475–494.

King, C. (2004) The Micropolitics of Social Violence. *World Politics*, 56(3), pp. 431–455.

Krain, M. (1997) State-Sponsored Mass Murder. *Journal of Conflict Resolution*, 41(3), pp. 331–60.

Kuper, L. (1982) *Genocide: Its Political Use in the Twentieth Century*. New Haven, CT: Yale University Press.

Linz, J.J., & Stepan, A. (1996) *Problems of Democratic Transition and Consolidation: Southern Europe, South America, and Post-Communist Europe*. Baltimore, MD: Johns Hopkins University Press.

Luft, A. (2015a) Genocide as Contentious Politics. *Sociology Compass*, 9(10), pp. 897–909.

Luft, A. (2015b) Toward a Dynamic Theory of Action at the Micro Level of Genocide. *Sociological Theory*, 33(2), pp. 148–172.

Mann, M. (1999) The Dark Side of Democracy: The Modern Tradition of Ethnic and Political Cleansing. *New Left Review*, Vol. I/235, p. 18.

McAdam, D. (1999) *Political Process and the Development of Black Insurgency, 1930–1970* (2nd ed.). Chicago, IL: University of Chicago Press.

McAdam, D., Tarrow, S., & Tilly, C.S. Tarr (2001) *Dynamics of Contention*. Cambridge: Cambridge University Press.

McDoom, O. (2011a) Who Kills? Social Influence, Spatial Opportunity, and Participation in Inter-Group Violence, available at: http://eprints.lse.ac.uk/36294 [accessed 27 March 2020].

McDoom, O. (2005) *Rwanda's Ordinary Killers: Interpreting Popular Participation in the Rwandan Genocide*. London: Crisis States Research Centre, London School of Economics and Political Science.

McDoom, O.S. (2014) Predicting Violence within Genocide: A Model of Elite Competition and Ethnic Segregation from Rwanda. *Political Geography*, 42, pp. 34–45.

McDoom, O.S. (2011b) LSE Research: The Psychology of Security Threats – Evidence from Rwanda, available at: https://blogs.lse.ac.uk/africaatlse/2011/12/05/new-lse-research-the-psychology-of-security-threats-evidence-from-rwanda/ [accessed 27 March 2020].

Melvern, L. (2006) *Conspiracy to Murder: The Rwandan Genocide* (Rev. ed.). London and New York, NY: Verso.

Milgram, S. (1963) Behavioral Study of Obedience. *Journal of Abnormal Psychology*, 67, pp. 371–78.

Oberschall, A. (2000) The Manipulation of Ethnicity: From Ethnic Cooperation to Violence and War in Yugoslavia. *Ethnic and Racial Studies*, 23(6), pp. 982–1001.

Posen, B.R. (1993) The Security Dilemma and Ethnic Conflict. *Survival*, 35(1), pp. 27–47.

Power, S. (2007) *A Problem From Hell: America and the Age of Genocide*. New York: Harper Perennial.

Prunier, G. (1998) *The Rwanda Crisis: History of a Genocide* (Rev. ed.). London: Hurst.

Rafter, N. (2016). *The Crime of All Crimes: Toward a Criminology of Genocide*. New York, NY: NYU Press.

Reyntjens, F. (1996) Rwanda: Genocide and Beyond. *Journal of Refugee Studies*, 9(3), pp. 240–51.

Rummel, R.J. (1995) Democracy, Power, Genocide, and Mass Murder. *Journal of Conflict Resolution*, 39(1), pp. 3–26.

Shaw, M. (2003) *War and Genocide: Organized Killing in Modern Society*. Cambridge: Polity Press.

Soule, S.A. (2007) "Diffusion Processes within and across Movements" in Soule, S.A., Snow, D.A., & Kriesi, H. (Eds.), *The Blackwell Companion to Social Movements* (pp. 294–311). London: Blackwell.

Straus, S. (2006) *The Order of Genocide: Race, Power, and War in Rwanda*. Ithaca, NY: Cornell University Press.

Straus, S. (2014) "From 'Rescue' to Violence: Overcoming Local Opposition to Genocide in Rwanda" in *Resisting Genocide* (Chapter 21). Oxford: Oxford University Press.

Tarrow, S.G. (1994) *Power in Movement: Social Movements, Collective Action and Politics*. Cambridge: Cambridge University Press.

The Prosecutor v. Jean-Paul Akayesu (*Trial Judgement*), ICTR-96-4-T, International Criminal Tribunal for Rwanda (ICTR), 2 September 1998, available at: www.refworld.org/cases,ICTR,40278fbb4.html [accessed 17 August 2017].

Tilly, C. (2003) *The Politics of Collective Violence*. Cambridge: Cambridge University Press.

Valentino, B., Huth, P., & Balch-Lindsay, D. (2004) Draining the Sea: Mass Killing and Guerrilla Warfare. *International Organization*, 58(2), pp. 375–407.

Valentino, B.A. (2004) *Final Solutions: Mass Killing and Genocide in the Twentieth Century*. Ithaca, NY: Cornell University Press.

Valentino, B.A. (2014) Why We Kill: The Political Science of Political Violence against Civilians. *Annual Review of Political Science*, 17, pp. 89–103.

Verdeja, E. (2016) Predicting Genocide and Mass Atrocities. *Genocide Studies and Prevention: An International Journal*, 9(3), pp. 13–32.

Weitz, E.D. (2005) *A Century of Genocide: Utopias of Race and Nation*. Princeton, NJ: Woodstock and Princeton University Press.

Wood, E.J. (2003) *Insurgent Collective Action and Civil War in El Salvador*. Cambridge: Cambridge University Press.

Wood, Elisabeth J. (2015). "Social Mobilization and Violence in Civil War and their Social Legacies", in Porta, Donatella Della and Diani, Mario, eds., *The Oxford Handbook of Social Movements*. (pp. 452–466). Oxford: Oxford University Press.

Zimbardo, P.G. (2007) *The Lucifer Effect: How Good People Turn Evil*. London: Rider.

Part II

International and national legal dimensions

4 The crime of genocide in its (nearly) infinite domestic variety

Tamás Hoffmann[1]

International unity and domestic fragmentation of the definition of the crime of genocide

Since the adoption of the Genocide Convention by the United Nations General Assembly on 9 December 1948, the crime of genocide has been universally regarded as the "crime of crimes"[2] in international criminal law.[3] Article II of the Convention defined genocide as:

> [a]ny of the following acts committed with intent to destroy, in whole or in part, a national, ethnical, racial or religious group, as such:
>
> (a) Killing members of the group;
> (b) Causing serious bodily or mental harm to members of the group;
> (c) Deliberately inflicting on the group conditions of life calculated to bring about its physical destruction in whole or in part;
> (d) Imposing measures intended to prevent births within the group;
> (e) Forcibly transferring children of the group to another group.

In contrast to all other international crimes, the legal concept of genocide has remained unchanged ever since on the international plane. The Genocide Convention's definition was adopted and reiterated verbatim in the statutes of all international and internationalized criminal fora whose material jurisdiction extended to genocide – thus it was followed by the International Criminal

1 This publication is based on research supported by the Corvinus Institute for Advanced Studies. I would like to thank and acknowledge the assistance of Mirwais Janan with the translation of the relevant section of the Criminal Code of Afghanistan, and Guido Acquaviva and Kevin Jon Heller for their comments on the draft. The usual caveats apply.

2 *Prosecutor v. Kambanda* (Case No. ICTR-97-23-S), Judgment and Sentence, 4 September 1998, para. 16.

3 Convention on the Prevention and Punishment of the Crime of Genocide (1951) 78 UNTS 277.

Tribunal for the Former Yugoslavia (ICTY),[4] the International Criminal Tribunal for Rwanda (ICTR),[5] the International Criminal Court (ICC),[6] the Iraq High Tribunal,[7] and the Extraordinary Chambers of the Courts of Cambodia.[8] Such consensus and consistency might seem obvious since, after all, the prohibition of genocide has achieved *jus cogens* status,[9] and as a peremptory norm of general international law it can only be modified by "the international community of States as a whole."[10]

Given the general acceptance of this construction and the widespread ratification of the Genocide Convention[11] and the Rome Statute of the ICC,[12] one could reasonably expect that the domestic definitions of the crime of genocide would be identical to the international one. Until now, the scholarly literature only focused on a select number of jurisdictions and generally held that even though there are a few notable examples of changes in domestic criminal legislation, these can be seen as aberrations. However, after conducting for the first time a comprehensive review of the domestic criminal laws of 196 countries (all 193 UN member states and the Holy See, Kosovo, and Palestine) and the Special Administrative Region of Macao, I have found that the differences are actually much more significant than hitherto assumed, since 100 countries and the Special Administrative Region of Macao have opted to change – through their national implementations – at least some aspects of the internationally recognized definition of genocide, often significantly expanding or limiting the scope of application of the crime.[13]

4 Art. 4 of the Statute of the International Criminal Tribunal for the Former Yugoslavia. UN Doc. S/RES/827 (1993).

5 Art. 2 of the Statute of the International Criminal Tribunal for Rwanda. UN Doc. S/RES/955 (1994).

6 Art. 6 of the Rome Statute of the International Criminal Court, (2002) 2187 UNTS 90.

7 Art. 11 of Law No. (10) 2005 of the Iraqi Higher Criminal Court, 18 October 2005.

8 Art. 9 of the Agreement between the United Nations and the Royal Government of Cambodia concerning the Prosecution under Cambodian Law of Crimes Committed during the Period of Democratic Kampuchea of 2003.

9 *Case Concerning Armed Activities on the Territory of the Congo* (New Application: 2002) (*Democratic Republic of the Congo v. Rwanda*), Jurisdiction of the Court and Admissibility of the Application, 3 February 2006, para. 64. International Law Commission, Peremptory norms of general international law (*jus cogens*). Text of the draft conclusions and draft annex provisionally adopted by the Drafting Committee on first reading, 29 May 2009. Annex (b). UN Doc. A/CN.4/L.936.

10 Art. 53 of the Vienna Convention on the Law of Treaties (1980) 1155 U.N.T.S. 331.

11 The Genocide Convention currently has 152 States Parties. See https://treaties.un.org/pages/ViewDetails.aspx?src=TREATY&mtdsg_no=IV-1&chapter=4 [downloaded on 8 September 2019].

12 A total of 122 countries are currently States Parties to the Rome Statute. See https://asp.icc-cpi.int/en_menus/asp/states%20parties/pages/the%20states%20parties%20to%20the%20rome%20statute.aspx [downloaded on 8 September 2019].

13 During the research I have always used the original language of the domestic criminal law if it was in English, German, French, Hungarian, Italian, Spanish, or Portuguese. In all other

This chapter first classifies the different ways domestic criminal legislation can restrict or expand the scope of application of the crime of genocide, and then explains the potential reasons for these changes. Finally, I speculate on the potential ramifications of the existence of these domestic varieties on the development of the international law of genocide.

Changing the scope of application of the crime of genocide through national implementation

Art. 5 of the Genocide Convention requires that states adopt "the necessary legislation to give full effect to [its] provisions," but it does not create an international obligation to incorporate the precise definition of genocide in the member states' criminal legislation. Similarly, Members of the Rome Statute undertake an obligation to avoid "the culture of impunity" by prosecuting the international crimes within the material jurisdiction of the ICC, but this does not include codifying the exact same terms. Even though the principle of complementarity promotes national implementation since states want to avoid being declared "unable to prosecute"[14] and thus have to take measures to make their domestic legal systems compatible with the Statute, in practice states have often retained older and different definitions of international crimes.[15]

The application of international legal norms in domestic legal systems is dependent on the respective national constitutional framework, which is traditionally classified either as monist (if domestic law and international law constitute a single system) or dualist (if the domestic legal order is separate from international law).[16] Even though theoretically courts could directly apply customary law norms and consequently prosecute international crimes in monist and even in some dualist countries, in practice most countries prefer to enact implementing legislation to avoid potential complications during domestic criminal proceedings. However, national implementation might result in either limiting or expanding the scope of application of the crime of genocide.

instances I had to rely on the available English translations, which could potentially result in mistakes.

14 Jan K. Kleffner, "The Impact of Complementarity on National Implementation of Substantive International Criminal Law" 1 (2003) *Journal of International Criminal Justice* 86–113, at 88.

15 Julio Bacio Terracino, "National Implementation of ICC Crimes Impact on National Jurisdictions and the ICC" 5 (2007) *Journal of International Criminal Justice* 421–440, at 423.

16 For a thorough examination of the relationship between domestic and international law, see Dinah Shelton (ed.) *International Law and Domestic Legal Systems – Incorporation, Transformation, and Persuasion* (Oxford: Oxford University Press, 2011).

Limiting the scope of application of the crime of genocide

Limiting the scope of application of the crime of genocide by excluding specific protected groups

Currently nine states have chosen to omit specific protected groups from their domestic criminal legislation. Racial groups are not included in the definition of genocide in Bolivia,[17] Ecuador,[18] Guatemala,[19] Paraguay,[20] and Peru[21]; and national groups are missing from the criminal code of Nicaragua,[22] while ethnic groups are excluded from the criminal law frameworks of Costa Rica,[23] El Salvador,[24] and Oman.[25] It must be emphasized, however, that none of these states opted to exclude more than one protected group. This is potentially significant as the exact definition of protected groups is far from obvious. Even though the ICTR attempted to define them based on objective criteria and clearly delineated them,[26] that approach is not generally accepted. Raphael Lemkin himself originally described genocide as "the destruction of a nation or of an ethnic group,"[27] and Schabas convincingly argues that in practice it is often virtually impossible to differentiate between protected groups since these terms "not only overlap, they also help to define each other, operating much as four corner posts that delimit an area within which a myriad of groups covered by the Convention find protection."[28] Consequently, the absence of reference to a national, ethnic, or racial group from the domestic definition of genocide might not necessarily result in excluding a targeted group from protection. Moreover, most of these countries added social or political groups to their lists of protected groups, which counterbalances this omission.[29]

17 Art. 138 of the Criminal Code of the Plurinational State of Bolivia of 1972.
18 Art. 79 of the Criminal Code of the Republic of Ecuador of 2014.
19 Art. 376 of the Criminal Code of the Republic of Guatemala of 1973.
20 Art. 319 of the Criminal Code of the Republic of Paraguay of 1997.
21 Art. 319 of the Criminal Code of the Republic of Peru of 1991.
22 Art. 484 of the Criminal Code of the Republic of Nicaragua of 2007.
23 Art. 382 of the Criminal Code of Costa Rica of 1998.
24 Art. 361 of the Criminal Code of the Republic of El Salvador of 1997.
25 Art. 88 of the Royal Decree No. 110 on the Military Jurisdiction Law of the Sultanate of Oman of 2011.
26 In the *Akayesu* case, the ICTR defined national groups as a collection of people sharing the same citizenship (para. 512), ethnic groups as people sharing a common language and culture (para. 513), and racial groups as people sharing "hereditary physical traits often identified with a geographical region" (para. 514), while religious groups were characterized by "the same religion, denomination or mode of worship" (para. 515). *Prosecutor v. Akayesu*, Case No. ICTR-96-4-T, Judgment of 2 September 1998.
27 Raphael Lemkin, *Axis Rule in Occupied Europe* (Washington: Carnegie Endowment for International Peace, 1944) 79.
28 William A. Schabas, *Genocide in International Law: The Crime of Crimes* (Cambridge: Cambridge University Press, 2010) 129.
29 See "'Over-definition' of protected groups," below.

On the other hand, the Latvian approach is somewhat different as it did not specifically exclude religious groups but instead only included a smaller subset by protecting "defined religions."[30] This is potentially problematic as it might not extend to smaller religious groups[31] or people sharing common spiritual ideas.[32] Similarly, the Dari language version of the Criminal Code of Afghanistan replaces *ethnic groups* with *tribal groups*. However, this seems to be a translation error as the Pashto language version retains the original international definition.[33]

Limiting the scope of application of the crime of genocide by including the requirement of a genocidal plan

There has been a recurring debate in international scholarship concerning the necessity of including a "contextual element" to the definition of genocide; i.e. whether an individual genocidal act has to be committed in a broader context forming part of other similar acts against the protected groups, or can be committed without any cooperation with other perpetrators, possibly even by a "lone *génocidaire*."

Lemkin's original conception required "a coordinated plan of different actions aiming at the destruction of essential foundations of the life of national groups, with the aim of annihilating the groups themselves."[34] The ICTY, however, rejected this notion. In the Jelisić Appeals Judgment the Tribunal emphasized that "the existence of a plan or policy is not a legal ingredient of the crime" although the existence of such a plan or policy may be important to proving the crime.[35] This view was also supported by the International Court of Justice in the Bosnia Genocide case.[36]

Nevertheless, that authoritative statement failed to settle the debate. Though some scholars support the idea that even an isolated individual acting alone can

30 Art. 71 of the Criminal Code of the Republic of Latvia of 1998.

31 Daniel D. Ntanda Nsereko, "Genocide: A Crime against Mankind" in Gabrielle Kirk McDonald and Olivia Swaak-Goldman (eds.) *Substantive and Procedural Aspects of International Criminal Law – The Experience of International and National Courts*, Vol. 1. (The Hague: Kluwer, 2000) 115–140, at 117.

32 Antonio Planzer, *Le Crime de Génocide* (St. Gallen: Schwald, 1956) 98.

33 Art. 333 of the Criminal Code of the Islamic Republic of Afghanistan of 2017.

34 Raphael Lemkin, *Axis Rule in Occupied Europe* (Washington: Carnegie Endowment for International Peace, 1944) 79.

35 *Prosecutor v. Jelisić*, Case No. IT-95-10-A, Judgement of 5 July 2005, para. 48.

36 "The specific intent to destroy the group in whole or in part, has to be convincingly shown by reference to particular circumstances, unless a general plan to that end can be convincingly demonstrated to exist; and for a pattern of conduct to be accepted as evidence of its existence, it would have to be such that it could only point to the existence of such intent." ICJ, *Case Concerning Application of the Convention on the Prevention and Punishment of the Crime of Genocide (Bosnia And Herzegovina v. Serbia And Montenegro)*, Judgment of 26 February 2007, para. 373.

commit genocide,[37] others have vehemently rejected this thesis.[38] The ICC Elements of Crimes tried to take a middle position by requiring that "the conduct took place in the context of a manifest pattern of similar conduct directed against that group or was conduct that could itself effect such destruction."[39] While the ICTY held that this definition "was not mandated by customary international law,"[40] this approach was upheld in the Al Bashir arrest warrant decision, which did "not observe any irreconcilable contradiction between the definition of the crime of genocide provided for in article 6 of the Statute and the contextual element provided for in the Elements of Crimes with regard to the crime of genocide."[41]

While the domestic criminal legislation of the majority of states does not explicitly require the existence of contextual elements, there are some notable exceptions. The existence of a "concerted plan" is explicitly spelt out in the criminal codes of Cabo Verde,[42] the Central African Republic,[43] the Republic of Congo,[44] France,[45] and Niger.[46] Albania prosecutes the execution of a "premeditated plan,"[47] Andorra of a "preconceived plan,"[48] and Georgia of an "agreed plan,"[49] while Turkey punishes following a plan.[50] Other countries also allude to the necessity of following a plan – thus Angola prescribes the existence of a "concerted operation"[51] and Ecuador criminalizes the commission of acts "in a systematic and generalized manner."[52]

37 See, for example, Antonio Casse, *International Criminal Law* (Oxford: Oxford University Press, 2008) 140–141; Gerhard Werle, *Principles of International Criminal Law* (The Hague: TMC Asser, 2009) 271–273.

38 Schabas, for instance, acerbically stated that "The theory that an individual, acting alone, may commit genocide is little more than a sophomoric hypothèse d'école, and a distraction for judicial institutions." William Schabas, "Darfur and the 'Odious Scourge': The Commission of Inquiry's Findings on Genocide," 18 Leiden Journal of International Law (2005) 871–885, at 877.

39 Art. 6(a)(4), (b)(4), (c)(5), (d)(5), (e)(7), ICC Elements of Crimes.

40 *Prosecutor v. Krstić*, Case No. IT-98-33-A, Judgment of 19 April 2004, para. 224.

41 *Al Bashir (Decision on Arrest Warrant)*, Case No. ICC-02/05-01/09, Decision of 4 March 2009, para. 132.

42 Art. 268 of the Criminal Code of the Republic of Cabo Verde of 2003 (*plano concertado*).

43 Art. 152 of the Criminal Code of the Central African Republic of 2007 (*plan concerté*).

44 Art. 1 of the Law 8/98 of 31 October 1998 on the Definition and Repression of Genocide, War Crimes, and Crimes against Humanity of the Republic of Congo (*plan concerté*).

45 Art. 211(1) of the Criminal Code of the Republic of France of 1992 (*plan concerté*).

46 Art. 208 of the Criminal Code of the Republic of Niger of 2003 (*plan concerté*).

47 Art. 73 of Criminal Code of the Republic of Albania of 1995.

48 Art. 456 of the Criminal Code of the Principality of Andorra of 2005 (*plan préconçu*).

49 Art. 407 of the Criminal Code of the Republic of Georgia of 1999.

50 Art. 76(1) Criminal Code of Turkey of 2004.

51 Art 367 of the Criminal Code of Angola of 2019 (*actuação concertada*).

52 Art. 79 of the Criminal Code of the Republic of Ecuador of 2014 (*de manera sistemática y generalizada*).

These 11 countries clearly go beyond even the arguably more expansive interpretation of the ICC by clearly excluding the prosecution of "lone *génocidaires*," or potentially refusing to try a perpetrator who committed the underlying offences with others who lacked genocidal intent.[53]

Limiting the scope of application of the crime of genocide by omitting or restricting underlying offences

The overwhelming majority of states that have implemented the crime of genocide have criminalized all the five prohibited acts listed in the Genocide Convention. According to the survey of domestic criminal legislations, there are only nine countries and the Special Administrative Region of Macao that omitted or restricted underlying offences. Instead of prohibiting serious mental harm as set out in Art. II(b) of the Genocide Convention, Bulgaria criminalizes causing "permanent derangement of the consciousness of a person,"[54] which explicitly contravenes the established jurisprudence of the ad hoc tribunals.[55] In a similar fashion, the United States prohibits causing "the permanent impairment of the mental faculties of members of the group."[56] On the other hand, the Czech Republic,[57] Georgia,[58] Guinea-Bissau,[59] Poland,[60] and the Special Administrative Region of Macao[61] have completely omitted the mental harm requirement by only criminalizing "serious bodily injury."

Mexico changed the crime of "imposing measures intended to prevent births within the group" – specified in Art. II(d) of the Genocide Convention – to "imposing massive sterilizations with the aim to prevent the reproduction of the group."[62] Italy restricted the scope of application of Art. II(e) of the Convention ("Forcibly transferring children of the group to another group") by

53 Valerie Oosterveld and Charles Garraway, "The Elements of Genocide" in Roy S.K. Lee and Hakan Friman (eds.) *The International Criminal Court: Elements of Crimes and Rules of Procedure and Evidence* (Ardsley: Transnational, 2001) 41–57, at 47–8.

54 Art. 416 of the Criminal Code of the Republic of Bulgaria of 1968.

55 *Prosecutor v. Krstić*, Case No. IT-97-24-T, Judgment of 31 July 2003, para. 513. In the Seromba case the ICTR declared that "to support a conviction for genocide, the bodily or the mental harm inflicted on members of a group must be of such a serious nature as to threaten its destruction in whole or in part." *Prosecutor v Seromba*, Case No. ICTR-2001-66-A, Judgment of 12 March 2008, para. 46.

56 Section 1091(a)(3) of the US Code – 18. Crimes and Criminal Procedure of 1948.

57 Art. 400(1)(c) of the Criminal Code of the Czech Republic of 2009.

58 Art. 407 of the Criminal Code of Georgia of 1999.

59 Art. 101(1)(a) of the Criminal Code of Guinea-Bissau of 1993 (*Homicídio ou ofensa à integridade física grave de elementos do grupo*).

60 Art. 118(1) of the Criminal Code of the Republic of Poland of 1997.

61 Art. 230(b) of the Criminal Code of the Special Administrative Region of Macao of 1995 (*praticar ofensa grave à integridade física de membros do grupo*).

62 Art. 149-Bis of the Federal Criminal Code of the Republic of Mexico of 1931 (*impusiese la esterilización masiva*).

specifying that it applies only to "minors until the age of 14."[63] Finally, Mozambique defined genocide as "deliberate killing motivated by ethnic, national, racial or religious differences,"[64] which excludes every other underlying offence besides killing members of the group.

Alterations that do not necessarily expand or restrict the scope of application of the crime of genocide

'Over-definition' of protected groups

Some countries seemingly expand the list of protected groups, but these additions do not actually result in a different scope of application. The Austrian Criminal Code defines genocide as acts committed against a "group determined by belonging to a church or religious community, to a race, an ethnic group, a tribe or a state."[65] Even though in this definition – and the identical definition in the Criminal Code of Liechtenstein[66] – the terms "church" and especially "tribe" seem to be expansive, they only serve to further specify the protected religious and ethnic groups.[67] Similarly, the terms "colour" and "nationality" in Ethiopian legislation only further emphasize the protection of racial and ethnic groups.[68]

Finally, the US federal criminal law definition prosecuting perpetrators for committing acts "with the specific intent to destroy, in whole or in substantial part" conforms to customary international law standards.[69]

63 Art. 5 of the Law No. 962 on the Prevention and Punishment of the Crime of Genocide of 9 October 1967 of the Republic of Italy (*minori degli anni quattordici*).

64 Art. 160(2)(j) of the Criminal Code of the Republic of Mozambique of 2014 (*genocídio, quando o agente pratica assassinato deliberado a pessoas motivada por diferenças étnicas, nacionalidades, raciais ou religiosas*).

65 Art. 321 of the Criminal Code of the Republic of Austria of 1974 (*Zugehörigkeit zu einer Kirche oder Religionsgesellschaft, zu einer Rasse, einem Volk, einem Volksstamm oder einem Staat*).

66 Art. 321 of the Criminal Code of the Principality of Liechtenstein of 1987.

67 Ferdinandusse, however, interpreted the inclusion of the term "tribe" as extending the category of protected groups. See Walt Ferdinandusse, *Direct Application of International Criminal Law in National Courts* (The Hague: TMC Asser, 2006) 24, fn. 118.

68 Art. 269 of the Criminal Code of the Federal Democratic Republic of Ethiopia of 2004.

69 See, for example, Benjamin Whitaker, *Revised and Updated Report on the Question of the Prevention and Punishment of the Crime of Genocide*, UN Doc. E/CN.4/Sub.2/1985/6, 16, para. 29; *Prosecutor v. Kayishema and Ruzindana*, Case No. ICTR-95-1-T, Judgment of 21 May 1999, para. 97; *Prosecutor v. Bagilishema*, Case No. ICTR-95-1A-T, Judgment of 7 June 2001, para. 64. Nevertheless, the actual determination of whether the intent was to destroy a "substantial" or "significant" part of the protected group inevitably depends on the circumstances as "the perpetrator's genocidal intent will always be limited by the opportunity presented to him." *Prosecutor v. Krstić*, Case No. IT-98-33-A, Judgment of 19 April 2004., para. 13.

Specifying the underlying offences

KILLING MEMBERS OF THE GROUP

Killing members of a protected group is the most obvious modality of genocide, which can be committed by intentionally causing death.[70] However, the plural form could potentially imply that the perpetrator has to kill at least two members of the protected group to be found responsible. This could theoretically result in the absurd outcome of genocide without *génocidaires*; i.e. if every killer takes only the life of a single victim. Accordingly, the consistent jurisprudence of the ICTR clearly proves that the requirement is fulfilled if a single member of the group is killed,[71] and that view enjoys scholarly consensus.[72] This approach is further reinforced by the ICC Elements of Crimes, which requires that "[T]he perpetrator (killed etc) one or more persons."[73]

Consequently, defining the prohibited act as the killing of even one individual – which can be found in the domestic legislation of the Dominican Republic,[74] Fiji,[75] Germany,[76] Italy,[77] and Uruguay[78] – is in line with the internationally supported interpretation of the offence. Moreover, Albania,[79] France,[80] and Uruguay[81] prohibit "intentional killing." This is also in conformity with the jurisprudence of the ICTY establishing that the act of killing has to be intentional, albeit not necessarily premeditated.[82]

70 Art. 6(a)(1), fn. 2., ICC Elements of Crimes. The Kayishema Appeals Chamber emphasized that it is "intentional but not necessarily premeditated murder." *Prosecutor v. Kayishema*, Case No. ICTR-95-A, Judgment of 1 June 2001, para. 151.

71 *Prosecutor v. Akayesu*, Case No. ICTR-96-4-T, Judgment, 2 September 1998, para. 588.

72 See, for example, Werle, *supra* note 37, 265; Schabas, *Genocide in International Law*, *supra* note 28, 179. However, Ambos argues that the *lex stricta* rule of interpretation enshrined in Art. 22(2) of the ICC Statute calls for at least two victims. Kai Ambos, *Treatise on International Criminal Law – Vol. II: The Crimes and Sentencing* (Oxford: Oxford University Press, 2014) 10.

73 Art. 6(a)(1), ICC Elements of Crimes.

74 Art. 89(1) of the Criminal Code of the Dominican Republic of 2014 (killing of one or more members of the group).

75 Art. 77(a) of Crimes Decree of 2009 of the Republic of Fiji Islands (the perpetrator causes the death of one or more persons).

76 German Code of Crimes against International Law of 2002 (*ein Mitglied der Gruppe tötet*).

77 Art. 3 of Law No. 962 on the Prevention and Punishment of the Crime of Genocide of 9 October 1967 of the Republic of Italy (*la morte di una o piu' persone*).

78 Art. 16(A) of the Law on Cooperation with the International Criminal Court in the Fight against Genocide, War Crimes and Crimes against Humanity of the Republic of Uruguay of 2006 (*homicidio intencional de una o más personas del grupo*).

79 Criminal Code of the Republic of Albania of 1995.

80 Art. 211(1) of the Criminal Code of the Republic of France of 1992 (*atteinte volontaire à la vie*).

81 Art. 16(A) of the Law on Cooperation with the International Criminal Court in the Fight against Genocide, War Crimes and Crimes against Humanity of the Republic of Uruguay of 2006 (*homicidio intencional de una o más personas del grupo*).

82 See, for example, *Prosecutor v. Stakić*, Case No. IT-97-24-T, Judgment of 31 July 2003, para. 515.

CAUSING SERIOUS BODILY OR MENTAL HARM TO MEMBERS OF THE GROUP

While genocide is clearly not confined only to killing members of a protected group, the exact acts which constitute the underlying offence of "causing serious bodily or mental harm" cannot be determined easily, even though the jurisprudence of the ad hoc tribunals has provided certain yardsticks. The ad hoc tribunals emphasized that the harm must go "beyond temporary unhappiness, embarrassment or humiliation," and result "in a grave and long-term disadvantage to a person's ability to lead a normal and constructive life."[83] While the harm "must be of such serious nature as to threaten [the group's] destruction in whole or in part," "it does not necessarily have to be permanent or irremediable, and … it includes non-mortal."[84]

Consequently, a wide range of acts could potentially fall under this category. Even though these acts could also constitute crimes against humanity and war crimes, if committed with genocidal intent against members of a protected group they would constitute genocide. The District Court of Jerusalem thus listed

> enslavement, starvation, deportation and persecution, confinement to ghettos, to transit camps and to concentration camps – all this under conditions intended to humiliate the Jews, to deny their rights as human beings, to suppress and torment them by inhuman suffering and torture.[85]

The Karadžić Trial Chamber specified similar conduct, although emphasizing that the determination of these acts is context-dependent. It included

> torture, inhumane or degrading treatment, sexual violence including rape, interrogations combined with beatings, threats of death, and harm that damages health or causes disfigurement or serious injury to the external or internal organs of members of the group. While forcible transfer does not of itself constitute an act of genocide, depending on the circumstances of a given case it may cause such serious bodily or mental harm as to constitute an act of genocide under Article 4(2) (b).[86]

83 *Prosecutor v. Krstić*, Case No. IT-97-24-T, Judgment of 31 July 2003, para. 513.

84 *Prosecutor v. Kamuhanda*, Case No. ICTR-95-54A-T, Judgment of 22 January 2004, paras. 633–634.

85 *Israeli Government Prosecutor General v. Adolph Eichmann*, Jerusalem District Court, Criminal Case No. 40/61, Judgment of 12 December 1961, para. 199.

86 *Prosecutor v. Radovan Karadžić*, Case No. IT-95-5/18-T, Judgment of 24 March 2016, para. 545. The Stakić Trial Chamber underlined, however, that mere deportation cannot automatically qualify as genocide since "[A] clear distinction must be drawn between physical destruction and mere dissolution of a group." *Prosecutor v. Stakić*, Case No. IT-97-24-T, Judgment of 31 July 2003, para. 519.

This approach was reaffirmed in the ICC Elements of Crimes, stating that "[T]his conduct may include, but is not necessarily restricted to, acts of torture, rape, sexual violence or inhuman or degrading treatment,"[87] as well as the Bosnia Genocide Judgment of the International Court of Justice, which found that acts of sexual violence committed with the requisite specific intent could constitute serious bodily or mental harm.[88]

In light of the above it is hardly surprising that national implementation of this particular *actus reus* displays remarkable variety. Three countries only made slight changes in the terminology. The Criminal Code of Russia[89] and Turkmenistan[90] contain identical provisions which criminalize "grave injury to health" but do not mention mental health specifically, while Mexican legislation prohibits "attacks against the bodily integrity or health."[91] On the other hand, 17 countries have introduced specific prohibited acts falling within the scope of "causing serious bodily and mental harm."

Fourteen countries criminalize the forced removal of protected groups, including Andorra ("forced deportation"),[92] Cabo Verde[93] and Italy[94] ("deportation"), Côte d'Ivoire ("displacement or forced dispersion of the population or children"),[95] Nicaragua[96] and Spain[97] ("forcible displacement"), the Dominican Republic[98] and Panama[99] ("forcible displacement and forcible transfer"), El Salvador ("violent displacement"),[100] Ethiopia ("compulsory movement or dispersion of people"),[101]

87 Art. 6(b)(1), fn. 3, ICC Elements of Crimes.

88 *Case concerning the Application of the Convention on the Prevention and Punishment of the Crime of Genocide (Bosnia and Herzegovina v. Yugoslavia [Serbia and Montenegro*]), Judgment of 26 February 2007, para. 319.

89 Art. 357 of the Criminal Code of the Russian Federation of 1996.

90 Art. 168(1) of the Criminal Code of Turkmenistan of 1997.

91 Art. 149-Bis of the Federal Criminal Code of the Republic of Mexico of 1931 (*ataques a la integridad corporal o a la salud*).

92 Art. 456(1)(c) of the Criminal Code of the Principality of Andorra of 2005 (*déportation forcée de tous ou d'une partie des membres du groupe en question*).

93 Art. 268(b) of the Criminal Code of the Republic of Cabo Verde of 2003 (*deportação*).

94 Art. 2 of the Law No. 962 on the Prevention and Punishment of the Crime of Genocide of 9 October 1967 (*deporta persone*).

95 Art. 137(3) of the Criminal Code of Côte d'Ivoire of 1981 (*le déplacement ou la dispersion forcés de populations ou d'enfants*).

96 Art. 484(d) of the Criminal Code of the Republic of Nicaragua of 2007 (*desplazamientos forzosos*).

97 Art. 607(1)(4) of the Criminal Code of the Kingdom of Spain of 1995 (*desplazamientos forzosos*).

98 Art. 89(6) of the Criminal Code of the Dominican Republic of 2004 (*llevar a cabo desplazamientos forzosos del grupo o de sus miembros, o trasladar por la fuerza a miembros de un grupo a otro*).

99 Art. 440(6–7) of the Criminal Code of the Republic of Panama of 2007 (*trasladar por la fuerza a los miembros de un grupo a otro; desplazar forzosamente al grupo o a sus miembros*).

100 Art. 361 of the Criminal Code of the Republic of El Salvador of 1997 (*realizare el desplazamiento violento de personas hacia otros grupos*).

101 Art. 269(c) of the Criminal Code of the Federal Democratic Republic Ethiopia of 2004.

Guinea-Bissau ("violent separation of members of the group to another group"),[102] Paraguay ("forcing the dispersion of the community"),[103] Russia ("forcible resettlement"),[104] and Timor-Leste ("Violent separation of members of the group to another group"; "Acts that violently prevent a group to settle down or remain in a geographical area which it traditionally recognized as its own").[105]

Different forms of sexual violence are included in the criminal legislation of nine states: Andorra ("sexual aggression"),[106] the Dominican Republic[107] and Spain[108] ("sexual assault"), Colombia ("forced pregnancy"),[109] Fiji ("rape and sexual violence"),[110] Nicaragua ("attack against sexual integrity"),[111] Panama ("abuse against sexual freedom"),[112] Timor-Leste ("Rape, sexual slavery, enforced prostitution, forced pregnancy, forced sterilization or any other form of sexual violence of a comparable gravity"),[113] and Uruguay ("sexual aggression and forced pregnancy").[114]

Torture, inhuman and degrading treatment is criminalized by five countries: Cabo Verde,[115] Andorra,[116] Fiji,[117] Lithuania,[118] and Uruguay.[119] Different

102 Art. 101(1)(c) of the Criminal Code of Guinea-Bissau of 1993 (*separação por meios violentos de elementos do grupo para outro grupo*).
103 Art. 319(6) of the Criminal Code of the Republic of Paraguay of 1997 (*forzara a la dispersión de la comunidad*).
104 Art. 357 of the Criminal Code of the Russian Federation of 1996.
105 Art. 123(1)(d-e) of the Criminal Code of the Republic of Timor-Leste of 2009 (*separação por meios violentos de elementos do grupo para outro grupo; Actos que por forma violenta impeçam o grupo de se instalar ou manter em espaço geográfico que por tradição ou historicamente lhe sejam reconhecidos*).
106 Art. 456(1)(g) of the Criminal Code of the Principality of Andorra of 2005 (*agression sexuelle*).
107 Art. 89(6) of the Criminal Code of the Dominican Republic of 2004 (*agredir sexualmente a cualquiera de los miembros del grupo*).
108 Art. 607(1)(2) of the Criminal Code of the Kingdom of Spain of 1995 (*agredieran sexualmente*).
109 Art. 101(2) of the Criminal Code of Colombia of 2000 (*embarazo forzado*).
110 Art. 78(2) of the Crimes Decree of 2009 of the Republic of Fiji Islands.
111 Art. 484(a) of the Criminal Code of the Republic of Nicaragua of 2007 (*attentar contra la integridad sexual*).
112 Art. 440(4) of the Criminal Code of the Republic of Panama of 2007 (*abuso contra la libertad sexual*).
113 Art. 123(1)(c) of the Criminal Code of the Republic of Timor-Leste of 2009 (*violação, escravidão sexual, prostituição forçada, gravidez forçada, esterilização forçada ou qualquer outra forma de violência sexual de gravidade comparável*).
114 Art. 16(B) of the Law on Cooperation with the International Criminal Court in the Fight against Genocide, War Crimes and Crimes against Humanity of the Republic of Uruguay of 2006 (*agresión sexual, embarazo forzoso*).
115 Art. 268(c) of the Criminal Code of the Republic of Cabo Verde of 2003 (*maciças de tortura ou tratamentos cruéis, degradantes e desumanos*).
116 Art. 456(1)(f) of the Criminal Code of the Principality of Andorra of 2005 (*traitements inhumains ou dégradants*).
117 Art. 78(2) of the Crimes Decree of 2009 of the Republic of Fiji Islands.
118 Art. 99 of the Criminal Code of the Republic of Lithuania of 2000.
119 Art. 16(B) of the Law on Cooperation with the International Criminal Court in the Fight against Genocide, War Crimes and Crimes against Humanity of the Republic of Uruguay of 2006.

forms of deprivation of liberty are criminalized by Andorra ("enslavement of the group in whole or in part"),[120] Cabo Verde (enslavement),[121] Nicaragua ("attack against liberty"),[122] and Uruguay ("deprivation of liberty").[123]

"Enforced disappearance" is listed in the criminal codes of Cabo Verde[124] and Andorra.[125] Guinea-Bissau[126] and Timor-Leste[127] criminalize "[D]issemination of an epidemic likely to cause death or serious harm to the physical integrity of the members of the group." Finally, the Commonwealth of Dominica punishes "the use of any biological or microbial agent or toxin, or of any weapon, equipment or means of delivery designed to use biological or microbial agents, which has no justification for prophylactic protective or other peaceful purposes."[128]

DELIBERATELY INFLICTING ON THE GROUP CONDITIONS OF LIFE CALCULATED TO BRING ABOUT ITS PHYSICAL DESTRUCTION IN WHOLE OR IN PART

The Akayesu Trial Chamber construed measures which aim to inflict on the group conditions of life calculated to bring about its physical destruction in whole or part as "methods of destruction by which the perpetrator does not immediately kill the members of the group, but which, ultimately, seek their physical destruction."[129] Such acts can

> include, but are not limited to, subjecting the group to a subsistence diet; failing to provide adequate medical care; systematically expelling members of the group from their homes; and generally creating circumstances that would lead to a slow death, such as the lack of proper food, water, shelter, clothing, sanitation, or subjecting members of the group to excessive work or physical exertion.[130]

120 Art. 456(1)(f) of the Criminal Code of the Principality of Andorra of 2005 (*réduction de la totalité ou de partie du groupe à l'esclavage*).
121 Art. 268(b) of the Criminal Code of the Republic of Cabo Verde of 2003 (*redução à escravidão*).
122 Art. 484(b) of the Criminal Code of the Republic of Nicaragua of 2007 (*atentar contra la libertad*).
123 Art. 16 of the Law on Cooperation with the International Criminal Court in the Fight against Genocide, War Crimes and Crimes against Humanity of the Republic of Uruguay of 2006 (*privación de libertad*).
124 Art. 268(b) of the Criminal Code of the Republic of Cabo Verde of 2003 (*sequestro seguido de desaparecimento*).
125 Art. 456(1)(b) (*séquestration de membres du groupe en question, suivie de leur disparition*).
126 Art. 101(1)(g) of the Criminal Code of Guinea-Bissau of 1993 (*difusão de epidemia susceptível de causar a morte ou ofensas graves à integridade física de elementos do grupo*).
127 Art. 123(1)(i) of the Criminal Code of the Republic of Timor-Leste of 2009 (*difusão de epidemia susceptível de causar a morte ou ofensas a integridade física de elementos do grupo*).
128 Act 20 of 1969 to Give Effect to the Convention on the Prevention and Punishment of the Crime of Genocide.
129 *Prosecutor v. Akayesu*, Case No. ICTR-96-4-T, Judgment of 2 September 1998, para. 518.
130 *Prosecutor v. Radovan Karadžić*, Case No. IT-95-5/18-T, Judgement of 24 March 2016, para. 547.

Depending on the circumstances, deportation[131] or forcible transfer of civilians could also fall into this category.[132] The ICC Elements of Crimes restates this approach by stating that the "term 'conditions of life' may include, but is not necessarily restricted to, deliberate deprivation of resources indispensable for survival, such as food or medical services, or systematic expulsion from homes."[133]

Numerous countries follow this approach. Fiji implemented almost verbatim the ICC Elements of Crimes definition ("'conditions of life' includes, but is not limited to, intentional deprivation of resources indispensable for survival, such as deprivation of food or medical services, or systematic expulsion from homes.");[134] Panama,[135] Spain,[136] and Uruguay[137] include conditions that "seriously affect health"; Bolivia includes "inhuman survival conditions";[138] and Uruguay also includes "systematic expulsion from their homes."[139] Finally, Guinea-Bissau[140] and Timor-Leste[141] add the "[p]rohibition, omission or impediment by any means of the provision of humanitarian assistance to the members of the group required to combat situations of epidemic or serious food shortage."

IMPOSING MEASURES INTENDED TO PREVENT BIRTHS WITHIN THE GROUP

The aim of measures intended to prevent birth within the protected group is "denying the group the means of self-propagation."[142] Such measures might include "sexual mutilation, the practice of sterilization, forced birth control, separation of the sexes and prohibition of marriages" or forced impregnation "in

131 International Law Commission, Code of Crimes against the Peace and Security of Mankind, UN Doc. A/51/332 (1996), 126.
132 *Prosecutor v. Tolimir*, IT-05–88/2-A, Judgment of 6 April 2015, para. 209.
133 Art. 6(c), fn. 4, ICC Elements of Crimes.
134 Art. 79(2) of the Crimes Decree of 2009 of the Republic of Fiji Islands.
135 Art. 440 of the Criminal Code of the Republic of Panama of 2007 (*perturben gravemente la salud*).
136 Art. 607(1)(3) of the Criminal Code of the Kingdom of Spain of 1995 (*perturben gravemente su salud*).
137 Art. 16(C) of the Law on Cooperation with the International Criminal Court in the Fight against Genocide, War Crimes and Crimes against Humanity of the Republic of Uruguay of 2006 (*una perturbación grave de salud*).
138 Art. 138 of the Criminal Code of the Plurinational State of Bolivia of 1972 (*condiciones de inhumana subsistencia*).
139 Art. 16(C) of the Law on Cooperation with the International Criminal Court in the Fight against Genocide, War Crimes and Crimes against Humanity of the Republic of Uruguay of 2006 (*la expulsión sistemática de sus hogares*).
140 Art. 101(1)(h) of the Criminal Code of Guinea-Bissau of 1993 (*proibição, omissão ou impedimento por qualquer meio a que seja prestada assistência humanitária aos elementos do grupo, adequada a combater situações de epidemia ou de grave carência alimentar*).
141 Art. 123(1)(j) of the Criminal Code of the Republic of Timor-Leste of 2009 (*proibição, omissão ou impedimento por qualquer meio a que seja prestada aos elementos do grupo assistęncia humanitária adequada a combater situações de epidemia ou de grave caręncia alimentar*).
142 Ambos, *Treatise on International Criminal Law – Vol. II*, *supra* note 72, 14.

patriarchal societies, where membership of a group is determined by the identity of the father."[143] Other measures which prevent birth through their psychological effects could also fall into this category. The Akayesu judgment stressed that

> rape can be a measure intended to prevent births when the person raped refuses subsequently to procreate, in the same way that members of a group can be led, through threats or trauma, not to procreate.[144]

Based on the above, depending on the circumstances most acts causing the serious bodily or mental harm specified in the section "Causing serious bodily or mental harm to members of the group" above could potentially be classified as measures intended to prevent birth, especially forms of sexual violence and torture, and inhuman and degrading treatment. Still, the Criminal Code of Afghanistan specifically complements the underlying offence with measures preventing procreation, which does not seem to change the scope of application of the *actus reus.*[145]

FORCIBLY TRANSFERRING CHILDREN OF THE GROUP TO ANOTHER GROUP

The aim of the crime of forcibly transferring children of a protected group to another group is to eradicate the children's attachment to their original group and thus the long-term destruction of the group in a non-physical form. The ICC Elements of Crimes defines the term "children" as persons under the age of 18 years[146] and indicates that the term "forcibly" is

> not restricted to physical force, but may include threat of force or coercion, such as that caused by fear of violence, duress, detention, psychological oppression or abuse of power, against such person or persons or another person, or by taking advantage of a coercive environment.[147]

Accordingly, the Criminal Code of Austria[148] and Liechtenstein[149] both stipulate that this form of genocide can be committed "with violence or with threat of violence."

143 *Prosecutor v. Akayesu*, Case No. ICTR-96-4-T, Judgment of 2 September 1998, para. 507–508. As regards sterilization and castration as forms of genocide, see *Poland v. Hoess* (Supreme National Tribunal of Poland), 7 *Law Reports of Trials of War Criminals* 11 (1948) 25.
144 Ibid.
145 Afghanistan, Art. 333 of the Criminal Code of the Islamic Republic of Afghanistan of 2017. In both the Dari and Pashto language versions.
146 Art. 6(e)(5), ICC Elements of Crimes.
147 Art. 6(e)(1), fn. 5, ICC Elements of Crimes.
148 Art. 321(1) of the Criminal Code of the Republic of Austria of 1974 (*mit Gewalt oder durch Drohung mit Gewalt*).
149 Art. 321(1) of the Criminal Code of the Principality of Liechtenstein of 1987.

In their domestic legislation, Mexico[150] and Chile[151] explicitly stipulate that the crime can be committed against "minors under the age of 18," with Chile adding also the crime of "preventing them from returning."[152] Nicaragua implemented in its act "displacing with violence the boys, girls and adolescents of the group."[153]

Bolivia,[154] Ecuador,[155] Guatemala,[156] and Paraguay[157] all prohibit the forcible transfer of both "children and adults," and Paraguay also criminalizes transferring children and adults "to places different from their habitual residence,"[158] while Uruguay punishes "displacement of the group from the place it is located."[159] These latter regulations clearly go beyond the scope of the underlying offence of forcibly transferring children of a group to another group. However, depending on the circumstances they can still constitute "causing serious bodily or mental harm to members of the group" or "deliberately inflicting on the group conditions of life calculated to bring about its physical destruction in whole or in part," so these regulations do not necessarily have to be viewed as expanding the scope of application of the crime of genocide in domestic law.

Expanding the scope of application of the crime of genocide

Expanding the scope of application of the crime of genocide by including additional protected groups

The closed list of groups of people protected by the Genocide Convention has been a source of contention ever since the adoption of the Convention. Already during the drafting process numerous countries suggested the inclusion of other groups, especially political and social ones, but these proposals were ultimately

150 Art. 149-Bis of the Federal Criminal Code of the Republic of Mexico of 1931 (*se trasladaren de ellas a otros grupos menores de dieciocho años*).
151 Art. 11 (5) of the Law No. 20.357 of 18 July 2009 (*trasladar por fuerza a menores de 18 años del grupo a otro grupo*).
152 Ibid. (*se les impida regresar a aquél*).
153 Art. 484(d) of the Criminal Code of the Republic of Nicaragua of 2007 (*desplazar con violencia a los niños, niñas o adolescentes del grupo*).
154 Art. 138 of the Criminal Code of the Plurinational State of Bolivia of 1972 (*realizare con violencia el desplazamiento de niños o adultos hacia otros grupos*).
155 Art. 79(5) of the Criminal Code of the Republic of Ecuador of 2014 (*traslado forzado de niñas, niños o adolescentes, de un grupo a otro*).
156 Art. 376(4) of the Criminal Code of the Republic of Guatemala of 1973 (*desplazamiento compulsivo de niños o adultos del grupo, a otro grupo*).
157 Art. 319(3) of the Criminal Code of the Republic of Paraguay of 1997 (*trasladara, por fuerza o intimidación a niños o adultos hacia otros grupos*).
158 Ibid. (*lugares ajenos a los de su domicilio habitual*).
159 Art. 16(e) of the Law on Cooperation with the International Criminal Court in the Fight against Genocide, War Crimes and Crimes against Humanity of the Republic of Uruguay of 2006 (*el desplazamiento del grupo del lugar donde está asentado*).

rejected.[160] Nevertheless, the expansion of the list of protected groups enjoys considerable academic support.[161]

A significant part of the international community – i.e. 34 countries – have decided to expand the scope of their domestic genocide legislation beyond the enumerated groups by incorporating specific groups beyond the closed enumeration of the Genocide Convention. The most common addition is to include political groups, with 13 countries belonging to this category, including: Colombia,[162] Bangladesh,[163] Costa Rica,[164] Côte d'Ivoire,[165] Ecuador,[166] Ethiopia,[167] Lithuania,[168] Nicaragua,[169] Panama,[170] Poland,[171] Switzerland,[172] Togo,[173] and Uruguay.[174] Social groups are included in the criminal legislation of Paraguay,[175] Estonia,[176] São Tomé and Príncipe,[177] Switzerland,[178] Peru,[179] and the Philippines.[180]

Besides political and social groups, some states have opted to introduce other specific protected groups as well. Thus the Czech Republic criminalizes underlying offences against people belonging to a class,[181] Estonia prosecutes crimes

160 See Schabas, *Genocide in International Law*, *supra* note 28, 153–171.
161 See, for example, Pieter N. Drost, *The Crime of State: Genocide* (The Hague: A.W. Sythoff, 1950) 62; Beth van Schaack, "The Crime of Political Genocide: Repairing the Genocide Convention's Blind Spot" 106 (1997) *The Yale Law Journal* 2259–2291; Elisa Novic, *The Concept of Cultural Genocide: An International Law Perspective* (Oxford: Oxford University Press, 2016).
162 Art. 101 of the Criminal Code of the Republic of Colombia of 2000.
163 Art. 3(2)(c) of International Crimes (Tribunals) Act 1973 (Bangladesh).
164 Art. 382 of the Criminal Code of Costa Rica of 1998.
165 Art. 137 of the Criminal Code of Côte d'Ivoire of 1981.
166 Art. 79 of the Criminal Code of the Republic of Ecuador of 2014.
167 Art. 269 of the Criminal Code of the Federal Democratic Republic of Ethiopia of 2004.
168 Art. 99 of the Criminal Code of the Republic of Lithuania.
169 Art. 484 of the Criminal Code of the Republic of Nicaragua of 2007.
170 Art. 440 of the Criminal Code of the Republic of Panama of 2007. Interestingly, the Code simply lists it as one of the Crimes against the International Law of Human Rights (*Delitos contra el Derecho Internacional de los Derechos Humanos*) without specifying the term "genocide."
171 Art. 118 of the Criminal Code of the Republic of Poland of 1997.
172 Art. 264 of the Criminal Code of the Swiss Confederation of 1937.
173 Art. 143 of the Criminal Code of the Togolese Republic of 2015.
174 Art. 16 of the Law on Cooperation with the International Criminal Court in the Fight against Genocide, War Crimes and Crimes against Humanity of the Republic of Uruguay of 2006.
175 Art. 319 of the Criminal Code of the Republic of Paraguay of 1997.
176 Art. 90 of the Criminal Code of the Republic of Estonia of 2001.
177 Art. 210 of the Criminal Code of 2012 of the Democratic Republic of São Tomé and Principe.
178 Art. 264 of the Criminal Code of the Swiss Confederation of 1937.
179 Art. 319 of the Criminal Code of the Republic of Peru of 1991.
180 Art. 5 of the Act on Crimes against International Humanitarian Law, Genocide, and Other Crimes against Humanity of 2009.
181 Art. 400 of the Criminal Code of the Czech Republic of 2009.

committed against "a group resisting occupation,"[182] Honduras criminalizes offences against "ideological groups,"[183] and Poland extends protection to groups with "a different perspective on life,"[184] while both Spain[185] and the Dominican Republic[186] regard as genocide the commission of acts committed against "a specific group determined by the disability of its members." The most expansive definition, however, can be found in the Criminal Code of Uruguay, which protects "political, syndical, and any other group identified by reasons of gender, sexual orientation, cultural or social background, age, disability or health."[187]

The criminal legislation of 16 countries has adopted an all-encompassing approach that potentially extends to any identifiable group. Nine countries – Andorra,[188] Belarus,[189] Burkina Faso,[190] Cabo Verde,[191] the Central African Republic,[192] Chad,[193] Comoros,[194] France[195] and Niger[196] – use the wording "group determined by any arbitrary criterion." Canada includes "an identifiable group of persons,"[197]

182 Art. 90 of the Criminal Code of the Republic of Estonia of 2001.
183 Art. 143 of the Criminal Code of the Republic of Honduras of 2019.
184 Art. 118 of the Criminal Code of the Republic of Poland of 1997.
185 Art. 607 of the Criminal Code of the Kingdom of Spain of 1995.
186 Art. 89 of the Criminal Code of the Dominican Republic of 2014.
187 Art. 16 of the Law on Cooperation with the International Criminal Court in the Fight against Genocide, War Crimes and Crimes against Humanity of the Republic of Uruguay of 2006.
188 Art. 456 of the Criminal Code of the Principality of Andorra of 2005 (*groupe déterminé à partir de tout autre critère arbitraire*).
189 Art. 127 of the Criminal Code of the Republic of Belarus of 1999.
190 Art. 421-1 of the Criminal Code of Burkina Faso of 2019 (*groupe déterminé à partir de tout autre critère arbitraire*).
191 Art. 268 of the Criminal Code of the Republic of Cabo Verde of 2003 (*outro, determinado a partir de qualquer critério arbitrário*).
192 Art. 152 of the Criminal Code of the Central African Republic of 2010 (*groupe déterminé à partir de tout autre critère arbitraire*).
193 Art. 296 of the Penal Code of the Republic of Chad of 2017 (*groupe déterminé à partir de tout autre critère arbitraire*).
194 Art. 17 of Decree N° 12-022/PR, promulgating law No. 11–022 of 2011 on the Implementation of the Rome Statute (*groupe déterminé à partir de tout autre critère arbitraire*).
195 Art. 211(1) of the Criminal Code of the Republic of France of 1992 (*groupe déterminé à partir de tout autre critère arbitraire*).
196 Art. 208(1) of the Criminal Code of the Republic of Niger of 2003 (*groupe déterminé à partir de tout autre critère arbitraire*).
197 Section 4(3) of the Crimes against Humanity and War Crimes Act of 2000. However, the law proceeds by defining the crime as which "at the time and in the place of its commission, constitutes genocide according to customary international law or conventional international law or by virtue of its being criminal according to the general principles of law recognized by the community of nations." Consequently, it seems that despite the confusing language, the Canadian legislator did not intend to expand the scope of protected groups. Still, the Canadian Criminal Code for the purpose of prosecuting incitement to genocide also defines genocide as a crime that can be committed against "an identifiable group of persons." Art. 318 of the Criminal Code of Canada of 1985.

the Czech Republic "other similar groups of people,"[198] Finland "another comparable group,"[199] Georgia "members of which are united … by any other signs,"[200] Lesotho "any other identifiable group,"[201] the Philippines "any other similar stable group,"[202] and Senegal groups "determined by any other criterion."[203]

Finally, the Ethiopian Criminal Code not only protects groups but also nations,[204] so presumably a military action threatening the existence of another state could qualify as genocide.

Expanding the scope of application of the crime of genocide by abolishing the special-intent requirement

The special- or specific-intent requirement for the crime of genocide is one of its defining features. In the words of the Kirstić Trial Chamber, it is a crime "characterised and distinguished by a 'surplus' of intent."[205] Unsurprisingly, the survey only found one country – Mozambique – that categorically dispensed with the *mens rea* requirement.[206] The Mozambique Criminal Code regulates genocide as one of the specific forms of "heinous crimes," along with extermination, terrorism, and the rape of minors under the age of 12, and defines it as "deliberate killing motivated by ethnic, national, racial or religious differences."[207] Consequently, this legislation only requires a discriminatory intent, but not an intent to destroy the protected group, on the part of the perpetrator.

Expanding the scope of application of the crime of genocide by the omission of "as such"

The words "as such" do not seem to have an important role in the definition of genocide and indeed it has been suggested that they could be omitted without entailing any consequences for the interpretation of the crime.[208] However,

198 Art. 400(1)(c) of the Criminal Code of the Czech Republic of 2009.
199 Chapter 11, Section 1 of the Criminal Code of the Republic of Finland of 1889.
200 Art. 407 of the Criminal Code of Georgia of 1999.
201 Art. 93 of the Criminal Code of the Kingdom of Lesotho of 2012.
202 Art. 5 of the Act on Crimes against International Humanitarian Law, Genocide, and Other Crimes against Humanity of 2009.
203 Art. 431 (1) of the Criminal Code of 1965 (*déterminé à partir de tout autre critère*).
204 Art. 269 of the Criminal Code of the Federal Democratic Republic Ethiopia of 2004.
205 *Prosecutor v. Krstić*, Case No. IT-97-24-T, Judgment of 31 July 2003, para. 520.
206 Bekou claims that the genocide definitions in French and Burkina Faso criminal law abolished the special-intent requirement but that seems unfounded as both legislations specifically require the intent to destroy. Olympia Bekou, "Crimes at Crossroads – Incorporating International Crimes at the National Level" 10 (2012) *Journal of International Criminal Justice* 677–691, at 683.
207 Art. 160 (2) (j) of the Criminal Code of the Republic of Mozambique of 2014.
208 Dino Carlos Caro Coria, "Prosecuting International Crimes in Peru" 10 (2010) *International Criminal Law Review* 583–600, at 587.

a perusal of the *travaux préparatoires* of the Genocide Convention reveals that the term "as such" was originally intended by Venezuela to serve as a reference to a racist or discriminatory intent.[209] Even though the perpetrator does not necessarily have to be driven by racist motivations, this requirement ensures that genocide can only be committed when "it is the group that has been targeted, and not merely specific individuals within that group."[210]

Nevertheless, 66 countries – out of the total 138 countries that have implemented the crime of genocide – have omitted the term "as such."[211]

209 Schabas, *Genocide in International Law*, *supra* note 28, 294–305. Schabas even submits that "The organizers and planners must necessarily have a racist or discriminatory motive, that is, a genocidal motive, taken as a whole. Where this is lacking, the crime cannot be genocide." Ibid., at 305.

210 *Prosecutor v. Sikirica et al.*, Case No. IT-95-8-I, Judgment on Defence Motions to Acquit, 3 September 2001, para. 89. Ultimately, the ICTR emphasized that "the term 'as such' clarifies the specific intent requirement. It does not prohibit a conviction for genocide in a case in which the perpetrator was also driven by other motivations that are legally irrelevant in this context." *Prosecutor v. Niyitegeka*, Case No. ICTR-96-14-A, Judgment of 9 July 2004, para. 49.

211 *Afghanistan*, Art. 333 of the Criminal Code of the Islamic Republic of Afghanistan of 2017; *Albania*, Art. 73 of the Criminal Code of the Republic of Albania of 1995; *Andorra*, Art. 456 of the Criminal Code of the Principality of Andorra of 2005; *Angola*, Art 367 of the Criminal Code of Angola of 2019; *Armenia*, Art. 393 of the Criminal Code of the Republic of Armenia of 2003; *Azerbaijan*, Art. 103 of the Criminal Code of the Republic of Azerbaijan of 2000; *Bangladesh*, Section 3(2) (c) of the International Crimes (Tribunals) Act 1973 of the People's Republic of Bangladesh; *Belarus*, Art. 127 of the Criminal Code of the Republic of Belarus of 1999; *Benin*, Art. 463 of the Criminal Code of 2018; *Bolivia*, Art. 138 of the Criminal Code of the Plurinational State of Bolivia of 1972; *Bosnia and Herzegovina*, Art. 171 of the Criminal Code of the Federation of Bosnia and Herzegovina of 2003; *Bulgaria*, Art. 416 of Criminal Code of the Republic of Bulgaria of 1968; *Burkina Faso*, Art. 16 of Law No. 2009-52/AN of 3 December 2009, Implementing the Rome Statute of the International Criminal Court at Domestic Level; *Cabo Verde*, Criminal Code of the Republic of Cabo Verde of 2003; *Cambodia*, Art. 183 of the Criminal Code of the Kingdom of Cambodia of 2009; *Canada*, Section 4(3) of the Crimes against Humanity and War Crimes Act of Canada of 2000 (French version); *Central African Republic*, Art. 152 of the Criminal Code of the Central African Republic of 2010; *Chad*, Art. 296 of the Criminal Code of the Republic of Chad of 2017; *Republic of Congo*, Art. 1 of the Law 8/98 of 31 October 1998 on the Definition and Repression of Genocide, War Crimes, and Crimes against Humanity; *Costa Rica*, Art. 382 of the Criminal Code of Costa Rica of 1998; *Côte d'Ivoire*, Art. 137 of the Criminal Code of Côte d'Ivoire of 1981; *Czech Republic*, Art. 400 of the Criminal Code of the Czech Republic of 2009; *Dominican Republic*, Art. 89 of the Criminal Code of the Dominican Republic of 2004; *Ecuador*, Art. 79 of the Criminal Code of the Republic of Ecuador of 2014; *El Salvador*, Art. 361 of the Criminal Code of the Republic of El Salvador of 1997; *Estonia*, Art. 90 of the Criminal Code of the Republic of Estonia of 2001; *Ethiopia*, Art. 269 of the Criminal Code of the Federal Democratic Republic of Ethiopia of 2004; *Finland*, Chapter 11, Section 1 of the Criminal Code of the Republic of Finland of 1889; *France*, Art. 211(1) of the Criminal Code of the Republic of France of 1992; Georgia, Art. 407 of the Criminal Code of the Republic of Georgia of 1999; *Guatemala*, Art. 376 of the Criminal Code of the Republic of Guatemala of 1973; *Guinea-Bissau*, Art. 101 of the Criminal Code of Guinea-Bissau of 1993; *Holy See*, Art. 14 of

Interestingly, 21 of these countries have otherwise completely identical national definitions to the internationally recognized definition of the crime.[212] This potentially suggests that a considerable number of states might indeed regard the term "as such" to be irrelevant for the application of the crime of genocide.

Expanding the scope of application of the crime of genocide by altering the wording of underlying offences

The internationally recognized interpretation of certain forms of genocide is significantly broader than borne out by a simple textual interpretation; therefore, a simple change in the wording does not necessarily result in expanding the

Vatican City State Law No. VIII, of 11 July 2013: Supplementary Norms on Criminal Law Matters; *Honduras*, Art. 143 of the Criminal Code of the Republic of Honduras of 2019; *Hungary*, Art. 142 of the Criminal Code of Hungary of 2012; *Kazakhstan*, Art. 168 of the Criminal Code of the Republic of Kazakhstan of 2014; *Kosovo*, Art. 148 of the Criminal Code of the Republic of Kosovo of 2012; *Kyrgyzstan*, Art. 383 of the 2017 Criminal Code of the Kyrgyz Republic; *Lesotho*, Art. 93 of the Penal Code of the Kingdom of Lesotho of 2010; *Lithuania*, Art. 99 of the Criminal Code of the Republic of Lithuania of 2000; *Mexico*, Art. 149-Bis of the Federal Criminal Code of the Republic of Mexico of 1931; *Moldova*, Art. 135 of the Criminal Code of the Republic of Moldova of 2002; *Montenegro*, Art. 426 of the Criminal Code of Montenegro of 2003; *Mozambique*, Art. 160 of the Criminal Code of the Republic of Mozambique of 2014; *Nicaragua*, Art. 484 of the Criminal Code of the Republic of Nicaragua of 2007; *Niger*, Art. 208(1) of the Criminal Code of the Republic of Niger of 2003; *North Macedonia*, Art. 403 of the Criminal Code of the Republic of Macedonia of 1996; *Norway*, Art. 101 of the Criminal Code of the Kingdom of Norway of 2005; *Panama*, Art. 440 of the Criminal Code of the Republic of Panama of 2007; *Paraguay*, Art. 319 of the Criminal Code of the Republic of Paraguay of 1997; *Peru*, Art. 319 of the Criminal Code of the Republic of Peru of 1991; *Poland*, Art. 118 of the Criminal Code of the Republic of Poland of 1997; *Republic of Korea*, Art. 8 of Act No. 8719 of 2007 on the Punishment of Crimes Within the Jurisdiction of the International Criminal Court; *São Tomé and Príncipe*, Art. 210 of the Criminal Code of the Democratic Republic of São Tomé and Principe of 2012; *Senegal*, Art. 431(1) of the Criminal Code of the Republic of Senegal of 1965; *Slovakia*, Art. 418 of the Criminal Code of the Slovak Republic of 2005; *Slovenia*, Art. 100 of the Criminal Code of the Republic of Slovenia of 2008; *Spain*, Art. 607 of the Criminal Code of the Kingdom of Spain of 1995; *Switzerland*, Art. 264 of the Criminal Code of the Swiss Federation of 1937; *Tajikistan*, Art. 398 of the Criminal Code of the Republic of Tajikistan of 1998; *Timor-Leste*, Art. 123 of the Criminal Code of the Republic of Timor-Leste of 2009; *Togo*, Art. 143 of the Criminal Code of the Togolese Republic of 2015; *Turkey*, Art. 76 of the Criminal Code of the Republic of Turkey of 2004; *Ukraine*, Art. 442 of the Criminal Code of Ukraine of 2001; *Uruguay*, Art. 16 of the Law on Cooperation with the International Criminal Court in the Fight against Genocide, War Crimes and Crimes against Humanity of the Republic of Uruguay of 2006; *Uzbekistan*, Art. 153 of the Criminal Code of the Republic of Uzbekistan of 1994; *Vietnam*, Art. 422 Criminal Code of the Socialist Republic of Viet Nam of 2015; *Zimbabwe*, Chapter 9:20 of the Genocide Act of the Republic of Zimbabwe of 2000.

212 Armenia, Azerbaijan, Benin, Bosnia and Herzegovina, Cambodia, Canada, Holy See, Kazakhstan, Kosovo, Kirgizstan, Moldova, Montenegro, Northern Macedonia, Norway, Republic of Korea, Singapore, Slovakia, Slovenia, Tajikistan, Ukraine, and Zimbabwe.

scope of application of the crime of genocide. Thus, the modality of "killing members of the group" is fulfilled even by the intentional killing of only one member of the group, and consequently most domestic changes only further specify but do not actually change the scope of application.[213] The only real change to this effect is the provision in the Criminal Code of Panama prohibiting the "inducing of suicide."[214] Correspondingly, due to the broad international interpretation of the crime of "causing serious bodily or mental harm to members of the group," there is no national provision actually extending its application.[215]

On the other hand, many states have substantially extended the *actus reus* of "deliberately inflicting on the group conditions of life calculated to bring about its physical destruction in whole or in part." Thirty-one countries – Andorra,[216] Angola,[217] Austria,[218] Costa Rica,[219] Côte d'Ivoire,[220] Czech Republic,[221] the Dominican Republic,[222] El Salvador,[223] Estonia,[224] Ethiopia,[225] Finland,[226] France,[227] Germany,[228] Guinea-Bissau,[229] Hungary,[230] Italy,[231] Liechtenstein,[232] Lithuania,[233] Macao,[234] Nicaragua,[235] Niger,[236] Panama,[237] Paraguay,[238] Peru,[239] Poland,[240] Russia,[241] São Tomé and

213 See "Killing members of the group," above.
214 Art. 440(2) of the Criminal Code of the Republic of Panama of 2007 (*inducir al suicidio*).
215 See above Section 2.2.2.2.
216 Art. 456(1)(d) of the Criminal Code of the Principality of Andorra of 2005.
217 Art 367(b) of the Criminal Code of Angola of 2019.
218 Art. 321(1) of the Criminal Code of the Republic of Austria of 1974.
219 Art. 382(2) of the Criminal Code of Costa Rica of 1998.
220 Art. 137(3) of the Criminal Code of Côte d'Ivoire of 1981.
221 Art. 400(1)(c) of the Criminal Code of the Czech Republic of 2009.
222 Art. 89(3) of the Criminal Code of the Dominican Republic of 2004.
223 Art. 361 of the Criminal Code of the Republic of El Salvador of 1997.
224 Art. 90(1) of the Criminal Code of the Republic of Estonia of 2001.
225 Art. 269(c) of the Criminal Code of the Federal Democratic Republic Ethiopia of 2004.
226 Chapter 11, Section 1(1)(3) of the Criminal Code of the Republic of Finland of 1889.
227 Art. 211(1) of the Criminal Code of the Republic of France of 1992.
228 Art. 6(3) of the German Code of Crimes against International Law of 2002.
229 Art. 101(d) of the Criminal Code of Guinea-Bissau of 1993 (*sujeição do grupo a condições de existência ou a tratamentos cruéis, degradantes ou desumanos, susceptíveis de virem a provocar a sua destruição, total ou parcial*).
230 Art. 142(1)(c) of the Criminal Code of Hungary of 2012.
231 Art. 4 of the Law No. 962 on the Prevention and Punishment of the Crime of Genocide of 9 October 1967 of the Republic of Italy.
232 Art. 321(1) of the Criminal Code of the Principality of Liechtenstein of 1987.
233 Art. 99 of the Criminal Code of the Republic of Lithuania of 2000.
234 Art. 230(c) of the Criminal Code of the Special Administrative Region of Macao of 1995.
235 Art. 484(c) of the Criminal Code of the Republic of Nicaragua of 2007.
236 Art. 208(1) of the Criminal Code of the Republic of Niger of 2003.
237 Art. 440(5) of the Criminal Code of the Republic of Panama of 2007.
238 Art. 319(2) of the Criminal Code of the Republic of Paraguay of 1997.
239 Art. 319(3) of the Criminal Code of the Republic of Peru of 1991.
240 Art. 118(2) of the Criminal Code of the Republic of Poland of 1997.
241 Art. 357 of the Criminal Code of the Russian Federation of 1996.

Príncipe,[242] Spain,[243] Switzerland,[244] Timor-Leste,[245] and the United States[246] – have completely removed the term "deliberately" during their national implementation and thus potentially expanded the applicability of the underlying offence to acts that are not calculated or intentional.[247] Germany also changed the requirement of "calculated to bring about" to "apt to bring about."[248] Moreover, El Salvador changed the wording to "subjecting to conditions which make subsistence difficult,"[249] and Georgia to "hard living conditions."[250] None of these definitions require the intention to physically destroy the protected group.

The underlying offence of "imposing measures intended to prevent births within the group" has also been altered by certain countries. Andorra included the act of "making births difficult"[251] and Lithuania "restricting the birth of the persons belonging to those groups."[252] The Cambodian definition requires "imposing forceful measures or voluntary means intended to prevent births within the group."[253] The addition of the words "'voluntary means'" extends the underlying act of genocide beyond its original construction.[254]

242 Art. 210(1)(c) of the Criminal Code of the Democratic Republic of São Tomé and Principe of 2012.
243 Art. 607(1)(3) of the Criminal Code of the Kingdom of Spain of 1995.
244 Art. 264(1)(b) of the Criminal Code of the Swiss Federation of 1937.
245 Art. 123(1)(f) of the Criminal Code of the Republic of Timor-Leste of 2009.
246 Section 1091(a)(4) of the US Code – 18. Crimes and Criminal Procedure of 1948.
247 See Kai Ambos, *Treatise on International Criminal Law – Vol. I.: Foundations and General Part* (Oxford: Oxford University Press, 2013) 294–295.
248 Art. 6(3) of the German Code of Crimes against International Law of 2002 (*die geeignet sind*).
249 Art. 361 of the Criminal Code of the Republic of El Salvador of 1997 (*difícil su subsistencia*).
250 Art. 407 of the Criminal Code of the Republic of Georgia of 1999.
251 Art. 456 of the Criminal Code of the Principality of Andorra of 2005 (*rendre les naissances difficiles*).
252 Art. 99 of the Criminal Code of the Republic of Lithuania of 2000.
253 Art. 183(4) of the Criminal Code of the Kingdom of Cambodia. This is based on the unofficial translation provided in Cheung Bunleng, *Criminal Code, Khmer – English Translation* (Phnom Penh: Edition Angkor, 2011). Another available online unofficial translation, however, translates the same provision as "submitting the members of the group to conditions that entail total or partial destruction of the group." www.unodc.org/res/cld/document/khm/criminal_code_of_the_kingdom_of_cambodia_html/Cambodia_Criminal-Code-of-the-Kingdom-of-Cambodia-30-Nov-2009-Eng.pdf [accessed on 12 September 2019]. If this is the correct translation then the Cambodian legislation did not change the scope of application of the underlying offence.
254 See Simon M. Meisenberg, "Complying with Complementarity? The Cambodian Implementation of the Rome Statute of the International Criminal Court" (2015) 5 *Asian Journal of International Law* 123–142, at 127.

Expanding the scope of application of the crime of genocide to additional modalities

Ten countries have introduced new forms of genocide in their domestic legislation that significantly expand the scope of application of the internationally accepted definition. Panama,[255] Spain,[256] and Uruguay[257] created the underlying offence of "preventing a group's way of life" to complement preventing birth; Italy criminalized as genocide "forcing members of the protected group to wear distinctive signs or emblems";[258] and Bolivia included committing "bloody massacres in the country";[259] while Paraguay prosecutes "making it impossible for [members of protected groups] to worship or practice their customs."[260]

Guinea-Bissau[261] and Timor-Leste[262] prohibit in identical terms "[G]eneral confiscation or seizure of goods owned by the members of the group" and "the prohibition of certain commercial, industrial or professional activities to the members of the group." The Criminal Code of Vietnam includes "destroying sources of living, cultural or spiritual life of a nation or sovereign territory, upsetting the foundation of a society in order to sabotage it."[263]

All these new underlying acts are obviously an extension of certain forms of crimes against humanity to genocide,[264] but the criminal legislation of São Tomé and Príncipe elevates its hate crime legislation by including persons who publicly "[d]efame or injure a person or a group of persons or expose them to public contempt for reasons of race, colour or ethnic origin" or who "[p]rovoke acts of violence against persons or group of persons of other races, colour or ethnic origin."[265]

255 Art. 440(8) of the Criminal Code of the Republic of Panama of 2007 (*imponer medidas destinadas a impeder … el género de vida de ese grupo*).

256 Art. 607(1)(4) of the Criminal Code of the Kingdom of Spain of 1995 (*adoptaran cualquier medida que tienda a impedir su género de vida*).

257 Art. 16(C) of the Law on Cooperation with the International Criminal Court in the Fight against Genocide, War Crimes and Crimes against Humanity of the Republic of Uruguay of 2006 (*condiciones de existencia que puedan impedir su género de vida*).

258 Art. 6 of Law No. 962 on the Prevention and Punishment of the Crime of Genocide of 9 October 1967 of the Republic of Italy (*imposizione di marchi o segni distintivi*).

259 Art. 138 of the Criminal Code of the Plurinational State of Bolivia of 1972 (*masacres sangrientas en el país*).

260 Art. 319(4) of the Criminal Code of the Republic of Paraguay of 1997 (*imposibilitara el ejercicio de sus cultos o la práctica de sus costumbres*).

261 Art. 101(1)(e)-(f) of the Criminal Code of the Republic of Guinea-Bissau of 1993 (*confisco ou apreensão generalizada dos bens propriedade dos elementos do grupo; proibição de determinadas actividades comerciais, industriais ou profissionais aos elementos do grupo*).

262 Art. 123(1)(g)-(h) of the Criminal Code of the Republic of Timor-Leste of 2009 (*confisco ou apreensão generalizada dos bens propriedade dos elementos do grupo; proibição de determinadas actividades comerciais, industriais ou profissionais aos elementos do grupo*).

263 Art. 422(1) of the Criminal Code of the Socialist Republic of Viet Nam of 2015.

264 This is especially clear with regard to the Criminal Code of Vietnam, which lists genocide as a crime against humanity. Ibid.

265 Art. 210(2)(a)-(b) of the Criminal Code of the Democratic Republic of São Tomé and Principe of 2012 (*difamar ou injuriar uma pessoa ou um grupo de pessoas ou expuser as mesmas*

Reasons for changing the crime of genocide in the domestic legal environment

This comprehensive review of national legislations has revealed a remarkable divergence from the internationally accepted definition of the crime of genocide. Admittedly, focusing solely on domestic legal regulations inevitably gives an incomplete picture, as domestic legal doctrine and ultimately domestic courts might (re)interpret the diverging criminal provisions to better align them with the international standard(s),[266] choose between plausible contradictory interpretations,[267] or even significantly expand their application.[268] Nevertheless, the compiled data makes it possible to draw certain preliminary conclusions about the reasons and possible ramifications of this phenomenon.

Domestic version of genocide as a means to ensure historical justice

A transition from authoritarianism to democracy almost inevitably brings about a reflection on the past and a need to reaffirm the fundamental values of the new political establishment in opposition to the legacy of oppression. In such periods, legal regulations are "both backward-looking and forward-looking, retrospective and prospective, continuous and discontinuous,"[269] essentially being a tool to assist in the transformation of the society. It is to be expected that under such circumstances many states may opt to expand the international definition of genocide to encompass specific victim groups or specific underlying offences.

a desprezo público por causa da raça, da sua cor ou da sua origem étnica; Provocar actos de violência contra pessoa ou grupos de pessoas de outra raça, de outra cor ou de outra origem étnica).

266 See, for example, the 1999 decision of the Estonian Supreme Court holding that the killing of three partisans in 1946 did not constitute an act of genocide but a crime against humanity. Eva-Clarita Pettai, "Prosecuting Soviet Genocide: Comparing the Politics of Criminal Justice in the Baltic States" (2016) *European Politics and Society* 1–14, at 6.

267 In the Ethiopian "Red Terror Trials," for instance, the Ethiopian Supreme Court held that political groups belonged to the protected groups in Art. 281 of the Penal Code of the Empire of Ethiopia of 1957, even though the authoritative Amharic version did not categorically list it, relying on the English version of the Code and the original French draft. Marshet Tadesse Tessema, *Prosecution of Politicide in Ethiopia – The Red Terror Trials* (Springer, 2018) 190–191.

268 See, for example, the decision of the German Federal Constitutional Court in the Jorgić case affirming lower German court judgments that held that genocidal intent can be established even if the perpetrator had not attempted to destroy the group physically or biologically but "in its social existence, as a social unit with its particularities and its self-perception as a group." Geltung deutschen Strafrechts für im Ausland begangenen Völkermord, German Federal Constitutional Court (BVerfG), Judgment of 12 December 2000 – 2 BvR 1290/99, at III. 4 a).

269 Ruti Teitel, *Transitional Justice* (Oxford: Oxford University Press, 2000) 215.

In the Baltic states, for instance, after regaining their independence following decades of brutal repression against political groups during the Soviet era,[270] Estonia included "a group resisting occupation or any other social group,"[271] Latvia "persons identifiable by social class,"[272] and Lithuania "social and political group."[273] Similarly, the atrocities committed by repressive regimes plausibly explain why most Latin American countries expanded the definition of genocide in their domestic criminal legislation.[274]

It is understandable that states with particular experiences of repression and human rights violations may seek to adapt the internationally agreed-upon definition to their particular contexts,[275] since "genocide," as the "crime of crimes," bears a special stigma and the term conveys an extraordinary sense of gravity and evil.[276] Indeed, in many countries debating the qualification of national tragedies as genocide could very well trigger public outrage since the general public might regard it as a denial of their historic grievances.[277] Moreover, many countries have opted to fuse the category of genocide with crimes against humanity, or simply employ the crime of genocide in the absence of a national definition of crimes against humanity. An interesting example of such an approach was the adoption of the law "On Genocide and Crimes against Humanity Committed in Albania during the Communist Regime for Political, Ideological and Religious Motives" in 1995.[278] While the title ostensibly claimed the law served to prosecute genocide, the text itself was focused on

270 For more detail see Eva-Clarita Pettai and Vello Pettai, *Transitional and Retrospective Justice in the Baltic States* (Cambridge: Cambridge University Press, 2014) 43–64.

271 Art. 61(1) of the Criminal Code of the Republic of Estonia of 1991 (as amended in 1994). The new Criminal Code retained this terminology. See Art. 90 of the Criminal Code of the Republic of Estonia of 2001.

272 Art. 68(1) of the Criminal Code of the Republic of Latvia of 1991 (as amended in 1993). This provision was changed with the adoption of the new Criminal Code in 1998 and this reference was omitted. See Art. 71 of the Criminal Code of the Republic of Latvia of 1998.

273 Art. 2 of the Law on the Liability for Genocide against the People of Lithuania of 1992 declared as genocide "the killing and torturing and deportation of Lithuanian inhabitants committed during the occupation and annexation of Lithuania by Nazi Germany and the USSR." The 1998 Amendment of the Criminal Code of 1991 introduced Art. 71, which defined "annihilation of people on social and political grounds" as genocide. The current formulation was adopted in 2000. See Art. 99 of the Criminal Code of the Republic of Lithuania of 2000.

274 Elizabeth Santalla Vargas, "An Overview of the Crime of Genocide in Latin American Jurisdictions" 10 (2010) *International Criminal Law Review* 441–452, at 442.

275 Cristina Fernández-Pacheco Estrada, "Domestic Prosecution of Genocide: Fragmentation or Natural Diversity?" in Larissa van den Herik and Carsten Stahn (eds.) *The Diversification and Fragmentation of International Criminal Law* (Leiden: Martinus Nijhof, 2012) 429–459, at 454.

276 For more on the tension between the socially and legally accepted meaning of the term, see David Luban, "Calling Genocide by its Rightful Name: Lemkin's Word, Darfur, and the UN Report" 7 (2006) *Chicago Journal of International Law* 303–320.

277 Estrada, *supra* note 275, 456.

278 Nr. 8001, 22 September 1995.

crimes against humanity, thus trying to draw on the moral stigma of genocide but still complying with international standards.[279]

Change through the "domestication" of international criminal law

International law norms are seldom automatically incorporated into the domestic legal framework, but instead become part of domestic law through "a process of translation from international to national."[280] Domestic lawyers have their own system of practices, "a body of internal protocols and assumptions, characteristic behaviors and self-sustaining values,"[281] which might be significantly different from the international law scholars' modus operandi. Domestic lawyers are usually not well acquainted with international law methodology and thus international norms have to be adapted so that they fit into the national legal system.[282] This creates a "double life" – a simultaneous co-existence of international and domesticated norms at one and the same time.[283] This is exacerbated by the fact that domestic lawmakers generally have very little political incentive to ensure the consistency of domestic law with international law, and sometimes might even be motivated to push for a diverging implementation.[284]

Such domestication is often explicitly endorsed by local courts. For instance, the Colombian Constitutional Court in 2005 emphasized that the domestic definition of genocide is not confined to international law, but rather finds its justification in the very protections afforded by the Constitution.[285] Similarly, in 2014 the Lithuanian Constitutional Court reaffirmed that states can broaden the concept of genocide and that the differences of the Lithuanian national definition of genocide were justified given "the concrete legal and historical context."[286]

279 For more on this law and the subsequent prosecutions, see Robert C. Austin and Jonathan Ellison, "Post-Communist Transitional Justice in Albania" 22 (2008) *East European Politics and Societies* 373–401.

280 Karen Knop, "Here and There: International Law in Domestic Courts" 32 (1999–2000) *New York University Journal of International Law and Politics* 501–535, at 506.

281 Pierre Bourdieu, "The Force of Law: Toward a Sociology of the Juridical Field" 38 (1987) *The Hastings Law Journal* 805–853, at 806.

282 André Nollkaemper, *National Courts and the International Rule of Law* (Oxford: Oxford University Press, 2011) 219.

283 Carsten Stahn and Larissa van den Herik, "'Fragmentation', Diversification and '3D' Legal Pluralism: International Criminal Law as the Jack-in-the-Box?" in Larissa van den Herik and Carsten Stahn (eds.) *The Diversification and Fragmentation of International Criminal Law* (The Hague: Martinus Nijhof, 2012) at 40.

284 See Kevin L. Cope and Hooman Movassagh, "National Legislatures – The Foundations of Comparative International Law" in Anthea Roberts et al. (eds.) *Comparative International Law* (Oxford: Oxford University Press, 2018) 271–294, at 272.

285 Colombian Constitutional Court, Sentence C-148/05 of 22 February 2005. See Vargas, *supra* note 275, at 448.

286 "On the Compliance of Certain Provisions of the Criminal Code of the Republic of Lithuania that are Related to Criminal Responsibility for Genocide with the Constitution of the Republic of Lithuania," Lithuanian Constitutional Court, Decision No. KT11-N4/2014,

Consequently, diverging national definitions of genocide might often be the result of different legal socialization processes and the necessity to adapt international norms into the domestic legal environment.

Path dependency

Legal regulation, and especially criminal law legislation, is inherently conservative and usually characterized by gradual change; hence states often retain preexisting definitions of international crimes even if they otherwise implement the provisions of the Rome Statute.[287] This, however, indicates that idiosyncratic versions of the crime of genocide often remain unaltered and can even spread to other jurisdictions, which adopt them due to existing historical/cultural/linguistic ties between the countries. For instance, the crime of genocide is identically defined in Austria[288] and Liechtenstein,[289] and in Guinea-Bissau[290] and Timor-Leste.[291] São Tomé and Principe[292] adopted the definition of genocide of the previous Portuguese Criminal Code.[293]

Even without a full-scale transplantation of a national definition, certain elements of the domestic approach can cross-pollinate. The French definition – which extended protected groups to groups "determined by any other arbitrary criterion"[294] – was adopted by Andorra,[295] Burkina Faso,[296] the Central African Republic,[297] Chad,[298] Comoros,[299] and Niger.[300] Similarly,

18 March 2014. For a contrary example, see the Hungarian Constitutional Court decision that declares that the content of international crimes are defined by the international community. Hungarian Constitutional Court, Decision No 53/1993, 13 October 1993, Section IV(1).

287 Terracino, *supra* note 15, at 423.

288 Art. 321 of the Criminal Code of the Republic of Austria of 1974.

289 Art. 321 of the Criminal Code of the Principality of Liechtenstein of 1987.

290 Art. 101 of the Criminal Code of Guinea-Bissau of 1993.

291 Art. 123 of the Criminal Code of the Republic of Timor-Leste of 2009.

292 Art. 210 of the Criminal Code of the Democratic Republic of São Tomé and Principe of 2012. However, the Portuguese provision was entitled "genocide and racial discrimination," while Art. 210 is only called "genocide"; thus, the legislation of São Tomé and Principe eliminated the difference between the two categories.

293 Art. 189 of the Criminal Code of the Republic of Portugal of 1982.

294 Art. 211(1) of the Criminal Code of the Republic of France of 1992 (*groupe déterminé à partir de tout autre critère arbitraire*).

295 Art. 456 of the Criminal Code of the Principality of Andorra of 2005 (*groupe déterminé à partir de tout autre critère arbitraire*).

296 Art. 421-1 of the Criminal Code of Burkina Faso of 2019 (*groupe déterminé à partir de tout autre critère arbitraire*).

297 Art. 152 of the Criminal Code of the Central African Republic of 2010 (*groupe déterminé à partir de tout autre critère arbitraire*).

298 Art. 296 of the Penal Code of the Republic of Chad of 2017 (*groupe déterminé à partir de tout autre critère arbitraire*).

299 Art. 17 of Decree N° 12-022/PR, promulgating law No. 11–022 of 2011 on the Implementation of the Rome Statute (*groupe déterminé à partir de tout autre critère arbitraire*).

300 Art. 208(1) of the Criminal Code of the Republic of Niger of 2003 (*groupe déterminé à partir de tout autre critère arbitraire*).

Panama[301] and Uruguay[302] borrowed the *actus reus* of "preventing a group's way of life" from the Spanish Criminal Code.[303]

Translation and drafting errors

In certain instances, differences between the international and domestic definitions of genocide might be the result of bad translation or sloppy drafting. This seems to be fairly common with regard to the term "as such." Even though 65 countries omitted the term from their domestic definition,[304] there is no evidence that this omission was deliberate on the part of these states, so the most plausible explanation is that they simply did not recognize its potential significance. Two countries, Bangladesh[305] and Cambodia[306], on the other hand reversed the words by implementing them "such as," which clearly can be attributed to a drafting error.[307]

In addition, the German definition of genocide prohibits "conditions of life imposed on the group that are apt to bring about its physical destruction."[308] Even though changing the term from "deliberately" to "apt to" arguably lowers the threshold of applicability of the crime, it is the result of a mistranslation.[309]

Conclusions: *e pluribus unum* or resurrection of the Lemkian ideal?

While legal scholarship concerning the domestic definitions of the crime of genocide has not been uncommon, until now these studies only focused on

301 Art. 440(8) of the Criminal Code of the Republic of Panama of 2007 (*imponer medidas destinadas a impeder ... el género de vida de ese grupo*).

302 Art. 16(C) of the Law on Cooperation with the International Criminal Court in the Fight against Genocide, War Crimes and Crimes against Humanity of the Republic of Uruguay of 2006 (*condiciones de existencia que puedan impedir su género de vida*).

303 Art. 607(1)(4) of the Criminal Code of the Kingdom of Spain of 1995 (*adoptaran cualquier medida que tienda a impedir su género de vida*).

304 See "Expanding the scope of application of the crime of genocide by the omission of 'as such'," above.

305 Section 3(2)(c) of the International Crimes (Tribunals) Act 1973 of the People's Republic of Bangladesh.

306 Art. 4 of the Law on the Establishment of the Extraordinary Chambers, with Inclusion of Amendments as Promulgated on 27 October 2004.

307 This is especially evident in the Cambodian case, as the law specifies that it should be interpreted in accordance with the Genocide Convention. Art. 4 of Law on the Establishment of the Extraordinary Chambers, with inclusion of amendments as promulgated on 27 October 2004 (NS/RKM/1004/006).

308 Art. 6(1)(3) of the German Code of Crimes against International Law of 2002.

309 Kai Ambos and Stephan Wirth, "Genocide and War Crimes in the Former Yugoslavia Before German Criminal Code" in Horst Fischer, Claus Kress, and Sascha Rolf Lüder (eds.) *International and National Prosecution of Crimes Under International Law* (Berlin: Berlin Verlag, 2001) 769, at 785.

a limited number of states and often failed to recognize changes in national legislation.[310] The hitherto-prevailing view held that, with a few limited exceptions, states generally followed the international definition of genocide.[311]

My research clearly disproves this view. Out of the 196 countries examined (193 UN member states and the Holy See, Kosovo, and Palestine) and the Special Administrative Zone of Macao, I found that only 39 countries have completely identical definitions,[312] while 100 countries and the Special Administrative Region of Macao have varying degrees of differences and 57

310 See Schabas, *supra* note 28, 405–409; Ferdinandusse, *supra* note 67, 26–39; Estrada, *supra* note 275, 429–459.

311 Bekou, *supra* note 206, at 680.

312 *Antigua and Barbados*, the Genocide Act of Antigua and Barbuda of 1975; *Argentina*, Art. 8 of Law No. 26.200 of 2007; *Australia*, Division 268 of the Criminal Code Act 1995 of the Commonwealth of Australia; *Bahamas*, the Genocide Act of 1969 of the Commonwealth of the Bahamas; *Belgium*, Articles 136ter of the Criminal Code of the Kingdom of Belgium of 1867; *Belize*, the Genocide Act of 1971 of Belize; *Brazil*, Art. 83.V of the Criminal Code of the Federative Republic of Brasil of 1940; *Burundi*, Art. 195 of the Criminal Code of the Republic of Burundi of 2009; *Croatia*, Art. 88 of the Criminal Code of the Republic of Croatia of 2011; *Cuba*, Art. 116(1) of the Penal Code of the Republic of Cuba; *Cyprus*, Section 2 of the 2006 Law Amending the Rome Statute for the Establishment of the International Criminal Court (Ratification) Law of 2002; *Democratic Republic of Congo*, Art. 221 of the Criminal Code of the Democratic Republic of Congo of 1940; *Eritrea*, Art. 107 of the Criminal Code of the State of Eritrea of 2015; *Fiji*, Crimes Decree of 2009 of the Republic of Fiji Islands; *Ghana*, Art. 49(A) of the Criminal Code of the Republic of Ghana of 1960; *Greece*, Law No. 3948/2011, on Compliance with the Provisions of the Statute of the International Criminal Court; *Grenada*, Grenada Genocide Act of 1972; *Guinea*, Art. 192 of the Criminal Code of the Republic of Guinea of 2016; *Iceland*, Law on the Punishment of Genocide, Crimes against Humanity, War Crimes and Crimes against Peace of 2018; *Indonesia*, Art. 8 of the Law No. 26 (2000) establishing the Ad Hoc Human Rights Court; *Iraq*, Art. 11 of the Statute of the Iraqi Special Tribunal; *Ireland*, Section 6 of the International Criminal Court Act 2006; *Israel*, the Crime Of Genocide (Prevention And Punishment) Law of 1950; *Kenya*, Art. 6(4) of the International Crimes Act of 2008; *Kiribati*, Art. 6(4) of the International Crimes Act of 2008; *Netherlands*, Section 3 of the International Crimes Act of 2003 Containing Rules Concerning Serious Violations of International Humanitarian Law; *Rwanda*, Art. 91 of the Criminal Code of the Republic of Rwanda of 2018; *Saint Vincent and the Grenadines*, Art. 157 of the Criminal Code of Saint Vincent and the Grenadines of 1988; *Samoa*, Section 5 of the International Criminal Court Act 2007; *Serbia*, Art. 370 of the Criminal Code of the Republic of Serbia of 2005; *Seychelles*, the Genocide Act of 1969; *Solomon Islands*, Art. 52 of the Criminal Code of the Solomon Islands of 1963; *South Africa*, Part 1 of Schedule 1 of the Implementation of the Rome Statute of the International Criminal Court Act (2002); *Sweden*, Section 1 of the Act on Criminal Responsibility for Genocide, Crimes against Humanity and War Crimes of 2014; *Tonga*, Section 2 of the Genocide Act of Tonga of 1969; *Trinidad and Tobago*, Art. 9 of the International Criminal Court Act of 2006; *Tuvalu*, Art. 62 of the Penal Code of Tuvalu of 1985; *United Kingdom*, Art. 50(1) of the International Criminal Court Act 2001 (four territories, however, have separate implementing legislation with identical text. *Scotland*, International Criminal Court (Scotland) Act 2001; *Isle of Man*, International Criminal Court Act 2003; *Bailiwick of Jersey*, the International Criminal Court (Jersey) Law 2014; *Bailiwick of Guernsey*, the International Criminal Court (Bailwick of Guernsey) Law, 2019).

countries have not even implemented the crime of genocide in their domestic criminal law.[313] These results clearly demonstrate that domestic divergences are not simply flukes or aberrations, but actually extend to the majority of states.

However, this does not necessarily mean that these changes should have an impact on the content or interpretation of the international definition of genocide. It has been suggested that these differences can be interpreted as a sign of the dissatisfaction of states with the international definition,[314] or that they can be evidence that the customary definition of the crime of genocide is much broader, even including political groups.[315] However, my research suggests that these changes are largely idiosyncratic modifications that are often based on considerations of historical justice, adaptation to the domestic legal system, path dependency, or simple errors; i.e. they are not modifications undertaken with the intention of creating a new *opinio juris* and state practice. As Kleffner aptly put it, they are simply "domestic crimes in 'international disguise'."[316]

As a result, states should be extremely cautious about how they apply these domestic definitions. Unless the prosecuted act constitutes a crime against humanity or genocide, expansive definitions of genocide should not be applied retroactively as that would violate the principle of legality. Exercise of universal jurisdiction based on such definitions could even result in international disputes. The existence of restrictive definitions, on the other hand, does not seem to be reconcilable with the international obligation to prevent and suppress the crime of genocide, and thus could be regarded as an internationally wrongful act.

313 Algeria, Bhutan, Botswana, Brunei, Cameroon, China, Egypt, Equatorial Guinea, Eswatini, Gabon, Gambia, Guyana, Haiti, India, Iran, Japan, Democratic People's Republic of Korea, Kuwait, Lao People's Republic, Lebanon, Liberia, Libya, Madagascar, Malaysia, Maldives, Marshall Islands, Micronesia, Monaco, Myanmar, Namibia, Nauru, Nepal, Nigeria, Pakistan, Palau, Palestine, Papua New Guinea, Qatar, Saint Kitts and Nevis, Saint Lucia, San Marino, Saudi Arabia, Sierra Leone, Somalia, South Sudan, Sri Lanka, Sudan, Suriname, Syria, Tanzania, Thailand, Tunisia, United Arab Emirates, Vanuatu, Venezuela, Yemen, and Zambia.

314 Coria, *supra* note 208, 457.

315 Schaack, *supra* note 161, at 2282–2283.

316 Kleffner, *supra* note 14, 100.

5 Responsibility of members of the government and other public officials pursuant to Article IV of the 1948 UN Convention on the Prevention and Punishment of the Crime of Genocide

Kamil Boczek

Convention provision and its definition

The concept of accountability of public officials

The rule setting out the legal accountability of public officials in international criminal law is older than the term "genocide" itself. It was expressed directly for the first time in Article 7 of the Charter of the International Military Tribunal in Nuremberg (IMT).[1] What needs to be underlined is that at the time when the IMT and its Charter were created there was no legal definition of genocide, and there are no provisions concerning genocide in the Charter. Despite Raphael Lemkin's struggles to include this term, it was deliberately omitted because of the lack of both a legal and customary definition.[2] However, the doctrine is nearly unanimous that the crime of genocide stems from the crimes against humanity while at the same time being the most heinous crime,[3] and thus we could apply the rules of the Charter to the crime of genocide. In its final judgment the IMT endeavoured to address the claims that both the Charter and the IMT were "*ex post facto* legal institutions", and that the IMT is solely "victors' justice", stating that both the individual responsibility of natural

1 Nuremberg Charter (Charter of the International Military Tribunal) (1945), United Nations Treaty Series, Volume 82, 279.

2 S. Power, *A Problem from Hell: America and the Age of Genocide*, London: Flamingo 2003, p. 50.

3 See H.T. King, Jr., "Genocide and Nuremberg" in *The Criminal Law of Genocide: International Comparative and Contextual Aspects*, edited by R.J. Henham and P. Behrens, Aldershot: Ashgate 2007, pp. 30–31, W.A. Schabas, Origins of the Genocide Convention: From Nuremberg to Paris, 40 *Case Western Reserve Journal of International Law*, 2008, p. 38; D. Drożdż, *Zbrodnia ludobójstwa w międzynarodowym prawie karnym*, Warsaw: Wolters Kluwer Polska - Oficyna 2010, pp. 40–41.

persons and the accountability of public officials in cases of war crimes were established, citing the *Ex parte Quirin* case from 1942[4] (the case of German submarine soldiers caught and sentenced in the USA), and the struggles of the international justice system to judge Kaiser William II after the atrocities of the First World War, struggles which turned out to be fruitless since Belgium denied his extradition. However, the treaty of Versailles[5] in Article 227 created an obligation to try him, and this legal act created a rule to try natural persons under Article 228.[6] More importantly, the IMT judgment presented an explanation of this rule, stating that "he who violates the laws of war cannot obtain immunity while acting in pursuance of the authority of the State if the State in authorizing action moves outside its competence under International Law".[7]

This reasoning is yet another illustration of Gustav Radbruch's famous formula of Statutory Lawlessness and the Supra-Statutory Law.[8] Thus in understanding this provision, we should not consider it as a refusal to provide for a defence by public officials to legal actions commenced against them, but as a formulation of their illegal act and granting the competence to undertake such actions against the state that exceeded its authority. This line of thinking is strongly expressed in the judgment of the District Court (then repeated in the Appellant Court) in Eichmann's case: "The very contention that the systematic extermination of masses of helpless human beings by a government or regime could constitute an 'Act of State,' appears to be an insult to reason and a mockery of law and justice."[9]

Also, the father of the term "genocide", Raphael Lemkin, provided an interesting view on the construction of relations between states and individuals who commit genocide. In his opinion, contrary to being an act relating to a public officer fulfilling an act of state through his or her service as a public officer, genocide is an act of individuals, carried out through the institutions and offices of a state.[10]

When the Convention on the Prevention and Punishment of the Crime of Genocide (hereinafter referred to as the "Convention")[11] was created, the rule regarding the accountability of public officers seemed to be, after the

4 *Ex parte Quirin*, 317 U.S. 1 (1942).

5 Treaty of Versailles (28 June 1919) available at www.loc.gov/law/help/us-treaties/bevans/m-ust000002-0043.pdf (accessed: November 2018).

6 *France et al. v. Goring et al.*, (1946) 22 IMT 203, 13 ILR 203, (1946) 41 *American Journal of International Law* 172, pp. 446–447.

7 Ibid., p. 447.

8 G. Radbruch, Gesetzliches Unrecht und übergesetzliches Recht, Süddeutsche Juristenzeitung (1946), p. 107.

9 *Attorney General v. Adolf Eichmann*, District Court of Jerusalem, Israel, Criminal Case No. 40/61, 11 December 1961.

10 D. Irvin-Erickson, *Raphael Lemkin and the Concept of Genocide*, Philadelphia: University of Pennsylvania Press 2017, p. 245.

11 Convention on the Prevention and Punishment of the Crime of Genocide (1948) 78 UNTS 277.

Nuremberg precedent was established, an essential but also an obvious element of the legal act under international criminal law. This rule is placed in the Article IV of the Convention:

> Persons committing genocide or any of the other acts enumerated in Article III shall be punished, whether they are constitutionally responsible rulers, public officials, or private individuals.

After the Convention was adopted, this rule was not only repeated but also developed in many other legal acts, including (to name the most important ones): the Rome Statute establishing the International Criminal Court of Justice (ICC), in Article 27;[12] and the statutes of interim international criminal courts – i.e. the International Criminal Court for the Former Yugoslavia (ICTY), in Article 7,[13] and the International Criminal Court for Rwanda (ICTR), in Article 6.[14]

Contemporarily, the accountability of a person despite his or her official capacity is not only a commonly recognized rule *expressis verbis* in the above-mentioned legal acts (as well as in multiple others), but is also considered to be a norm of customary international law and thus capable of being enforced even in the case of an absence of a binding written act. This interpretation was established in the judgment of the IMT in Nuremberg[15] and has been confirmed during numerous subsequent trials.[16] This norm was also included in the so-called Nuremberg Principles.[17] What is more, "official capacity" may be treated even as an exacerbating factor against the accused, as was stated by the ICTR in its *Jean Kambanda* judgment, which concerned a prime minister during the civil war in Rwanda, as his power and responsibility towards society were made much more immense by this office.[18]

Dual definition

The issue of the accountability of public officials is a twofold problem. On one hand, the basic understanding of this rule has been presented above and was

12 Rome Statute of the International Criminal Court, UN Doc. A/CONF.183/9.

13 Statute of the International Criminal Tribunal for the Former Yugoslavia, Annex of Report S/25704 of the UN Secretary-General.

14 Statute of the International Criminal Tribunal for Rwanda, Annex of Resolution 955, S/RES/955 (1994) of the UN Secretary-General.

15 T. Cyprian and J. Sawicki, *Ludzie i sprawy Norymbergi*, Poznań: Wydawn 1967, p. 457.

16 For example, *Milošević* (IT-02-54-PT), Decision on Preliminary Motions, 8 November 2001, paras. 26–34; *Taylor* (SCSL-03-01-I), Special Court of Sierra Leone, Decision on Immunity from Jurisdiction, 31 May 2004, para. 43–53.

17 Principle III, Principles of International Law Recognized in the Charter of the Nürnberg Tribunal and in the Judgment of the Tribunal, 1950.

18 *Jean Kambanda* (ICTR 97-23-S), Judgment and Sentence, 4 September 1998, para. 44.

explained in the Nuremberg and Eichmann trials. It consists of the prohibition of an "official capacity" defense; i.e. that a defendant cannot avoid accountability by claiming that his actions were solely acts of state and reflected not his own actions but those of the state. On the other hand, it could be viewed as a case of abolishing the legal immunities granted by states to their representatives. According to William A. Schabas, only the first part of the definition constitutes the rejection of the "official capacity" defense, and the issues concerning immunities are a completely separate topic.[19] Others claim that the abolishment of immunities is implicit in the above-mentioned provisions.[20] In spite of this interpretation, many rulings treat Article IV of the Convention (and its equivalents in other legal acts) as a boundary to the exercise of one's immunity.[21]

Nonetheless the issue of immunity is strictly connected to the accountability of public officials, especially heads of state and other important public figures. However, while rejection of the "act of state" defense is not controversial, the case of immunities and its impact on Article IV raises serious questions in the legal doctrine and in both international and national judicial systems. The desire to sentence the most important people collides with the issue of immunities and a country's sovereignty – which are also parts of customary international law. This distinction is exhibited in Article 27 of the Rome Statute, which treats both of these situations separately:

> 1 This Statute shall apply equally to all persons without any distinction based on official capacity. In particular, official capacity as a Head of State or Government, a member of a Government or parliament, an elected representative or a government official shall in no case exempt a person from criminal responsibility under this Statute, nor shall it, in and of itself, constitute a ground for reduction of sentence.
> 2 Immunities or special procedural rules which may attach to the official capacity of a person, whether under national or international law, shall not bar the Court from exercising its jurisdiction over such a person.

The Statute creates a clear distinction between a defence based on the merits ("act of state") and one based on procedural grounds.[22] Certainly, the latter is restricted to a much narrower group, because states grant immunities only to their most important representatives (e.g. prime minister, minister of foreign affairs, or head of state) and it is limited to only procedural aspects.

19 W.A.Schabas, *Genocide in International Law*, Cambridge: Cambridge University Press 2009, pp. 370–371.
20 E. David, "Official Capacity and Immunity of an Accused before the International Criminal Court" in *The Legal Regime of the International Criminal Court*, edited by J. Doria, H.P. Gasser, and M. Cherif Bassoiouni, Leiden and Boston: Marinus Nijhoff 2009, p. 743.
21 For example, in the case Special Court For Sierra Leone *Taylor* (SCSL-03-01-I), Decision on Immunity from Jurisdiction, 31 May 2004, paras. 43–53.
22 David, *Official Capacity*, p. 743.

In my opinion, restricting the meaning of Article IV of the Convention only to the "act of state" defence and excluding immunities from its scope is not only dangerous but also a contradiction in terms. The above-mentioned logic behind the rejection of the "official capacity" defence is that a state exceeds its competence according to the international law by allowing or ordering a perpetrator to commit genocide. On the other hand, if we stipulate that immunities are located outside the scope of Article IV, a state would be authorized to grant immunity for committing crimes that are outside its competence.

The issue of immunity was widely argued in the *Arrest Warrant* case (*Yerodia*).[23] Belgium had issued an arrest warrant against Abdoulaye Yerodia Ndombasi – who at the time was an incumbent minister of foreign affairs of the Congo – based on the fact that he had committed war crimes and crimes against humanity. The *Arrest Warrant* case and its judgment are discussed more thoroughly below.

Also, during the *Saddam Hussein Dujail Trial* the defendant's attorneys tried to invoke immunity, stating that the dictator was, during the trial, an incumbent head of state and that the coalition forces were just an "occupying authority".[24] The same defence was used during the *Anfal Trial*, which was limited strictly to genocide committed on the Kurds.[25] Not surprisingly, this strategy was dismissed in both cases – it would be highly unprecedented if the courts would have denied the legality of the administration that had established them.

Jurisprudence on immunity and the official capacity defence

The Eichmann case

Adolf Eichmann was one of the most significant Nazi perpetrators. He was hiding in Argentina after the war and was captured by the Israeli special forces and subsequently transferred to Israel in 1960, where he was later judged and sentenced to death.[26]

The defendant tried to undermine the legality of the trial, stating that none of the actions he was accused of took place in the state of Israel (which did not even exist during the Second World War); that he was not an Israeli citizen; that the legal basis of the trial was enacted after the actions in question (the act under which he was tried was passed in 1950); and that the court, together with all the judges, were Jewish, which raised the issue of their neutrality. Nevertheless, the court dismissed his motion for extradition to the Federal

23 *Arrest Warrant of 11 April 2000* (*Democratic Republic of Congo v. Belgium*), Judgment, 14 February 2002.

24 Judgment of the Dujail Trial at the Iraqi High Tribunal, English Translation, Case No. 1/C 1/2005.

25 M.J. Kelly, *Ghosts of Halabia*, London: Praeger Security International 2008, pp. 80–82.

26 Supreme Court of Israel judgment from 29 May 1962, *Attorney General v. Adolf Eichmann*, Criminal Appeal 336/61.

Republic of Germany. Eichmann then endeavoured to apply the "act of state" defence, claiming that every action he undertook was performed as a state official, and thus that the state was solely responsible for his actions. This defence was dismissed on the grounds that the defence of official capacity stemming from the sovereignty of the state was limited in cases of extreme violations of international and criminal law, while also underlining that a limitless sovereignty would deprive international law of the sense of its existence. According to international law, the state does not have a competence to order its representatives to violate international criminal law. What is more, the court contended that the extent of the sovereignty of a state had to be established taking into consideration the specific circumstances of each case. The court thus indicated the strong moral grounds for the conviction that justified the potential lack of authority in this case.

Arrest Warrant case

As mentioned above, Belgium issued an arrest warrant for the incumbent minister of foreign affairs of the Congo. In doing so it argued that the atrocities that he had committed had taken place before he was appointed as a minister and without any connection whatsoever to his function as minister of foreign affairs (the atrocities he was indicted for were connected to the Rwandan genocide and had taken place before he was appointed to his office). Furthermore, the arrest warrant did not include situations in which he had acted as a legal representative (e.g. during the time of his delegation). Belgium tried to prove that the arrest warrant was strictly linked to Yerodia personally, not as a minister, and that any immunity attached solely to acts undertaken as a minister of foreign affairs.

The International Court of Justice (ICJ) declared, however, that the arrest warrant was issued in breach of international law. The ICJ contended that, despite Article 27 of the Rome Statute, the exception of immunity in international humanitarian law crimes did not exist in customary international law, and thus the immunities of officials of states not bound by the Rome Statute was opposable. It was underlined that the foreign minister represented his country only by the virtue of his position, and thus any exception to his immunity as an incumbent representative would pose a threat to the interests of the represented state. The ICJ maintained that there is no distinction between the actions of an incumbent minister of foreign affairs and his personal acts, and that in the event of his arrest he would not be capable of serving his position as a public official, which would pose a threat to the wellbeing of the state. Furthermore, the ICJ asserted that a significant part of performing this particular official position consisted of travels and delegations, and that such an arrest warrant may restrain a minister of foreign affairs from leaving the borders of his country. In opposition to the international criminal tribunals (like the ICTY or ICTR), Belgium was not granted the authority to sentence incumbent officials. At the same time, the ICJ stated that the immunity of officials did not constitute a bar in the situations listed below:

- When such public officials are tried in their own country according to the domestic law;
- When a state decides to waive the immunity of its representative (which did not happen in this situation);
- When a public official ceases to hold office;
- When an international tribunal is expressly provided with jurisdiction over such a person (in practice if such jurisdiction is granted by the state, the best example being the *Milosevic* trial, when he was indicted while he was still in office).

The Pinochet trials

There were actually several trials of the former dictator of Chile – in Belgium, Spain, Great Britain, and Chile, most of which were conducted with Pinochet *in absentia*. I focus here on the case in Great Britain, since it was the one which garnered the most publicity.[27]

In October 1998 Augusto Pinochet was arrested in London (where he was staying in hospital) based on the Extradition Act from 1989.[28] This was a consequence of the arrest warrant issued by Spain, and it resulted in a judgment for his temporary arrest for 40 days.[29] In a final judgment concerning the former dictator, the court agreed to commence the extradition procedure in spite of his immunity.[30] In its judgment it stated that the immunity of a former head of state (who was in office while the atrocities were committed) did not protect him in cases of crimes against international humanitarian law, noting that it was the first time "a local domestic court has refused to afford immunity to a head of state or former head of state on the grounds that there can be no immunity against prosecution for certain international crimes".

The judgment differentiated two types of immunity. The first, *ratione personae*, asserts immunity for incumbent public officials and is absolute irrespective of the character of the process or allegations. The second, *ratione materiae*, is a logical consequence of the first – it pertains only to actions undertaken within the scope of the office and during service in the office. The court contended that crimes violating international humanitarian law could not under any circumstances be considered as acting within the scope of office, and thus the immunity of Augusto Pinochet did not protect him from legal procedures relating to such acts.

27 M. Komosa, *Sprawa Pinocheta*, Warsaw: Oficyna Wydawnicza 2005, p. 131.
28 Extradition Act 1989 (repealed) 1989 c. 33.
29 M. Komosa, *Sprawa Pinocheta*, pp. 122–123.
30 Judgment of House of Lords (2000), *R (Pinochet Ugarte) v Bow St Metropolitan Stipendiary Magistrate*, 1 AC 61, 119 and 147.

The first proceedings undertaken by the ICC

Despite the ICC's brief history (the Court began to operate on 1 July 2002), it has conducted a couple of proceedings that have been directly and/or indirectly connected to the scope of Article IV of the Convention. In particular, the issue of immunities was raised in front of the ICC in the cases of the arrest warrants for Colonel Gaddafi of Libya and Sudanese president Omar Al Bashir. Here I focus on the latter since it has garnered the most publicity, while the arrest warrant against Gaddafi did not raise many controversies since the dictator was assassinated (October 2011) just a few months after the issuance of said warrant in June 2011.[31]

The proceedings concerning President Omar Al Bashir are related to possible atrocities (namely war crimes, crimes against humanity, and genocide) that were conducted during the crisis in Darfur between March 2003 to, at least, 14 July 2008, and which were carried out against the Fur, Masalit, and Zaghawa tribes. The situation in Darfur was referred to the ICC's Prosecutor by the United Nations Security Council (UNSC) in 2005 in UNSC Resolution 1593.[32] In the resolution the UN urged that "the Government of Sudan and all other parties to the conflict in Darfur, shall cooperate fully with and provide any necessary assistance to the Court and the Prosecutor". The referral of the Security Council was based on Chapter VII of the UN Charter and such referral could constitute grounds to initiate proceedings based on Article 13 of the Rome Statute. The fact that it was the Security Council that referred the case to the ICC is very important because Sudan is not a party to the Rome Statute and the jurisdiction to initiate a proceeding was vested in the ICC by the UN.

After a few years of futile cooperation with the Sudanese government, the ICC decided that the atrocities were committed (at least in cooperation with and/or tolerated by) in fact by the highest-ranking public officers, and thus their will to carry out the actions was apparent. The Court decided to issue arrest warrants against the most important public figures, including the incumbent president at that time, Omar Al Bashir. The Pre-Trial Chamber issued, on 4 March 2009 and 12 July 2010, two warrants of arrest against Al Bashir for war crimes, crimes against humanity, and genocide allegedly committed in the Darfur region.[33] This action on the part of the ICC has contributed to a heated debate both in the doctrine and in political terms. Many jurists claims that the ICC has overreached its competence because the referral did not explicitly deal with the case of immunities, and that the application of Article 27 of the Rome

31 Warrant of Arrest for Muammar Mohammed Abu Minyar Gaddafi, 27 June 2011 (ICC-01/11-13).

32 S/RES/1593 (2005).

33 Warrant of Arrest for Omar Hassan Ahmad Al Bashir, 4 March 2009, ICC-02/05-01/09-1; Second Warrant of Arrest for Omar Hassan Ahmad Al Bashir, 12 July 2010, ICC-02/05-01/09-95.

Statute was unlawful because Sudan was a state non-party.[34] It has also been argued that that these kinds of actions could deteriorate the situation in the region, which over time has gained a fragile stability.

What is important is that the arrest warrant was issued also for the crime of genocide, and thus the Convention was directly applicable in this case. This is a paradox because throughout the history of the Convention almost every prosecutor has deliberately avoided a genocide indictment, since it is much more difficult to prove and to sentence a person for this crime due to the *dolus specialis*. However, in this case it was a way to facilitate the proceeding because Sudan is a signatory of the Convention and is bound by the Convention to punish and prevent genocide, which also includes the obligation to turn over a suspect to the international court based on Article VI.

Although the arrest warrants are still outstanding and the Sudanese president has visited numerous countries (e.g. Kenya, Chad, Djibouti, and Malawi) who are parties to the Rome Statute, so far he has never been arrested and turned over the ICC.

Prospects for the future

The accountability of states

It is clearly stated, both in the Convention and in numerous different international treaties, that public officers are accountable for genocide and they are not protected either by immunity or the "act of state" defence. There is another side of the coin, though, and that is the accountability of states. According to the famous Judge Jackson rule stated in the Nuremberg judgment, the crime is committed by men, not abstract entities, but also it is not just the sum of acts of many people that makes genocide such a heinous crime. It usually also uses all of the instruments that states are equipped with.

It may seem odd that the Convention does not explicitly forbid states from committing genocide, although one could deduce such a rule through other articles (e.g. Article IX or Article I). This peculiar omission is not accidental, however, but is a result of meticulous negotiations at the time the Convention was being created.[35] In my view, only a synergy of personal and state accountability can guarantee real justice for victims of genocide and for the history of humankind. We could dismiss the "act of state" defence by recalling Judge Jackson's quote, and by holding a state accountable we could dismiss another popular

34 W.A. Schabas, *The International Criminal Court: A Commentary on the Rome Statute*, Oxford: Oxford University Press 2010 p. 451; P. Gaeta, "Immunities and Genocide" in *The UN Genocide Convention: A Commentary*, edited by Paola Gaeta, Oxford: Oxford University Press 2009, pp. 323–325.

35 J. Quigley, *The Genocide Convention: An International Law Analysis*, Farnham: Ashgate, 2006, pp. 222–226.

defence of "margin or margins" or "it was just a few black sheep in a family". By proving that it was actually a state and that the genocide was committed at the highest level of the machinery of power, or at least tolerated, we could also enable victims to receive at least material compensation. The same issues were raised by the United Kingdom during a debate about the Convention at the time it was being created.[36] The United Kingdom strongly opted for the view that the responsibility of states should be imposed, and thus states would be accountable not only for punishing perpetrators of genocide and prevent it, but also for the genocide itself. The United Kingdom's efforts to support this view have partly succeeded, since the responsibility of states was expressed more explicitly in Article IX of the Convention. However, there are serious doubts whether the responsibility of a state under Article IX is considered to be a penal or civil sanction.[37] The fact that states could not be sued under the Convention was relied upon by Yugoslavia during its trial in a case filed by Bosnia and Herzegovina.[38] In the end, however, the Yugoslavian motion was dismissed by the ICJ, and thus a precedent was created.[39]

American practice and doctrine is traditionally against prohibition of the "official capacity" defence. The American judicial system also opposes the deprivation of immunity even for former heads of state and even in genocide trials – an observation that is a consequence of the judgments of Robert Mugabe of Zimbabwe[40] and Jiang Zemin of China.[41] During the voting over Article IV, the American representatives abstained, arguing that this kind of provision must not be applied to heads of states, and especially not to the president of the United States.[42] It is stated in the doctrine that usually a trial of a head of state is also a trial of the country's politics (as heads of states emanate it) as a whole, and thus it impacts substantially upon the country's sovereignty[43] and is a de

36 UN GAOR, Summary Records of Meetings 21 September – 10 December 1948, pp. 342–344, UN doc A/C/.6/SR.95.

37 N. Robinson, *The Genocide Convention: A Commentary*, New York: Institute of Jewish Affairs 1960, pp. 101–102.

38 Application of the Convention on the Prevention and Punishment of the Crime of Genocide (*Bosnia and Herzegovina v. Yugoslavia*), preliminary objections, Memorial of Yugoslavia, June 1995, p. 130.

39 Application of the Convention on the Prevention and Punishment of the Crime of Genocide (*Bosnia and Herzegovina v. Yugoslavia*), preliminary objections, Judgment, 1996, ICJ Rep., p. 595, p. 616.

40 United States Court of Appeals, Second Circuit, *Tachiona v. United States*, No. 03–6033(L), 03–6043(XAP), 6 October 2004.

41 United States Court of Appeals, Seventh Circuit, *Wei YE v. Jiang ZEMIN*, No. 03–8 September 3989, 2004.

42 UN DOC. A/C.6/SR.93.

43 G. Conso, USA, and ICC (Part II), Are There Hopes of Reconciliation? The basic reasons for US Hostility to the ICC in Light of the Negotiating History of the Rome Statute, 3 *Journal of International Criminal Justice*, 2005, p. 315.

facto trial between countries, not individuals,[44] and finally that the Rome Statute *expressis verbis* declares that the ICC possesses jurisdiction only over natural persons.[45] The American delegation has proposed to change the prohibition of the "official capacity" defence to direct accountability of a state provided that two conditions are fulfilled: the perpetrator would have to have acted within the scope of his/her office, and the state would consider and acknowledge this act as its own.[46] I suspect that such an alteration would be highly detrimental to holding perpetrators accountable, and also restrict potential legal procedures under such an article – which would be highly unjust. One can easily imagine that in numerous cases such a consent would not be granted since the administration that is charged with the genocide has not changed; while in other cases the situation would be rather different (i.e. if administration has changed and the new administration is more willing to condemn the members of the former one). This proposal, and its negative attitude towards holding public officials responsible, is even more alarming taking into account the active participation of the USA in many armed conflicts all over the world. Such proposals suggest an American will to evade its accountability or at least limit it, especially taking into consideration its history and infamous enhanced interrogation techniques from the so-called "Torture Memos".[47] Also, the American government has separate agreements with multiple states that assert that they will not surrender their citizens to the ICC but to the American national courts, and the USA made a reservation to Article IX of Convention (which concerns submission of cases to the ICJ), stating that the USA must give a specific consent each time a party wants to file a suit against them.[48] In addition the USA is not a party to the Rome Statute.

Furthermore, in my opinion the view that the accountability of a state and the personal accountability of perpetrators are interchangeable is greatly mistaken. These two notions have substantially different functions. Only individual accountability guarantees that persons responsible would feel threatened that they could be held accountable. It is easy to observe the consequences of a lack of personal criminal responsibility in the actions of vast international companies. The lack of such personal responsibility leads *de facto* to an overall lack of responsibility. Even when companies are sentenced with enormous fines or compensations for the victims, the profits they gain from such breaches often outweigh the costs.[49]

44 M. Morris, *Stany Zjednoczone i Międzynarodowy Trybunał Karny*, Warsaw: Instytut Spraw Publicznych 2004.

45 Article 25 of the Rome Statute.

46 UN DOC, A/CONF.183/C.1/L.90 from 16 July 1998.

47 Memorandum for William J. Haynes, II General Counsel, Department of Defense, March 13.2002, Washington, DC 20520.

48 Multilateral Treaties deposited with the Secretary-General, pp. 131–132, UN DOC. ST/LEG/SER.E/22. https://treaties.un.org/pages/Content.aspx?path=Publication/MTDSG/Volume_en.xml (accessed November 2018).

49 See, for example, R. Waters, GlaxoSmithKline's $3 Billion Hit: Deterrent or Business Expense, *Forbes*, 12 July 2012. www.forbes.com/sites/robwaters/2012/07/12/glaxosmithklines-3-billion-hit-deterrent-or-business-expense/#7f33347228ef (accessed November 2018).

Accountability of incumbent officials in light of the *Arrest Warrant case* and the recent proceedings of the ICC

During the Pinochet trial the British House of Lords declared that the state immunity of a former head of state does not cover heinous international crimes (in this case, torture).[50] While the end result of the extradition proceeding was ultimately not to extradite, this was only due to the health condition of the former dictator.[51] This is proof the traditional concept of laws is constantly changing. During the discussion over the Pinochet case another autocratic ruler who participated in the Rwandan genocide, the president of the Congo, Laurent Kabila, was a guest of the French government, and during his visit he became anxious about his immunity.[52] Also in the *Arrest Warrant* judgment, the court stipulated that while the arrest warrant in question was issued, Abdoulaye Yerodia Ndombasi was deliberately avoiding certain routes while travelling to different countries with the express purpose of avoiding arrest. One may presume that these cases contribute to the reducing the sense of impunity, especially of dictators, and prove that these kinds of measures are effective.

In this light, I disagree with the ICJ judgment in the *Arrest Warrant Case* and consider it a lost opportunity. In international criminal law there is a concept that there are obligations which cover every state, even if such a state is not connected to a certain case, which are sometimes referred to as obligations *erga omnes partes.*[53] Provisions already exist granting a party not suffering an injury the right to file a complaint on behalf of another party.[54] Furthermore, with reference to human rights this rule has already been espoused by the European Court of Human Rights.[55] Taking into consideration that genocide is tantamount to violating numerous human rights (the right to live being just number one on this list) and is considered as the "crime of crimes", we should recognize its prevention and punishment as an obligation *erga omnes partes.* In this light, it is difficult for me to understand why the fact that arresting an incumbent minister of foreign affairs results in consequent problems for the functioning of a country should overweigh (according to ICJ) the gravity of violations of international humanitarian law. If we take into consideration how rapidly countries nowadays exchange their ministers or other representatives, it

50 C.L. Blakesley, Autumn of the Patriarch: The Pinochet Extradition Debacle and Beyond–Human Rights Clauses Compared to Traditional Derivative Protections Such as Double Criminality, 91 *Journal of Criminal Law and Criminology*, 2000, p. 15.

51 Ibid, p. 16.

52 M.J. Kelly, *Nowhere to Hide: Defeat of the Sovereign Immunity Defense for Crimes of Genocide and the Trials of Slobodan Milosevic and Saddam Hussein*, New York: Lang 2005, p. 81.

53 A. de Hoogh, *Obligations* Erga Omnes *and International Crimes: A Theoretical Inquiry into the Implementation and Enforcement of the International Responsibility of States*, The Hague and Boston: Kluwer 1996, pp. 53–54.

54 International Covenant on Civil and Political Rights, art. 41, UNTS 999, p. 171.

55 Judgment of the European Court of Human Rights, in case *Ireland v. Great Britain*, ECHR, series A, no. 25, p. 239.

seem that when the absolute nature of the immunities was established the situation was quite different – the lack of absolute immunity respected by all the states would result in many assassinations during international visits (while nowadays in the worst-case scenario they may result in a legal trial). In addition, states without all the modern tools and solutions could not adapt as quickly as nowadays. If such a prominent figure as the American secretary of state (in this case Rex Tillerson) could find out that he was fired by the American president (Donald Trump) via a tweet,[56] I seriously doubt that the arrest of a significant public officer could result in the collapse of a state as a whole.

What is more, in Article I of the Convention the contracting parties confirm that genocide is a crime under international law and that they are obligated to prevent it and punish the perpetrators (even if the genocide took place during peacetime). The sense of this provision is to assert that genocide should be combated in every possible way by the contractual parties. While Lemkin has acknowledged that the annihilation of protected groups is always a last resort to destroy the group, and that genocide in fact is rational and the reasons behind it are perceivable, it is nevertheless possible to prevent it without a war.[57] However, this cannot be achieved if the states are deprived of instruments to influence potential perpetrators. The right of any country to address a breach of an obligation *erga omnes partes* – even if the country addressing it is not directly connected to such a breach – is inseparably related to this concept.[58]

The institutions of international criminal justice play a pivotal role in the prevention of violations of international humanitarian law. Lemkin has underlined that without a set of concrete sanctions, the matter of the genocide and its prevention is not a matter of international law but of international courtesy, or as a precept of morality.[59] By confirming the absolute rule of the immunity of incumbent public officials, the ICJ has enhanced the impunity of many perpetrators. Taking into consideration the situations listed by ICJ when officials could be held accountable (when tried in the country of origin, after the official ceases to hold the position, when the country of origin agrees to waive immunity, or if jurisdiction is specifically granted to an international tribunal), it can be easily seen that they do not cover all the situations in which a potential genocide could in fact be carried out. Such a regime would not be willing to be bound by any international treaty concerning humanitarian law, and even more it would not be willing to waive the immunities of its representatives, and only after the regime falls (when in most cases the damage is already done) will the representatives cease to perform their positions and international criminal

56 D. Mangan, Rex Tillerson Found Out He Was Fired as Secretary of State from President Donald Trump's Tweet, CNBC, 13 March 2018. www.cnbc.com/2018/03/13/tillerson-learned-he-was-fired-from-trumps-tweet.html (accessed December 2018).

57 Irvin-Erickson, *Raphael Lemkin*, p. 223

58 M. Królikowski, *Odpowiedzialność karna jednostki za sprawstwo zbrodni międzynarodowej*, Warsaw: Wydawnictwo Sejmowe 2011, p. 49.

59 Irvin-Erickson, *Raphael Lemkin*, pp. 224–225.

tribunals be established. For example, the Special Court for Sierra Leone has made use of the arguments presented in the *Arrest Warrant Case* and because of its international character (it was established by the UN and Sierra Leone) it has claimed that the immunities *ratione materiae* could not guarantee impunity for the former head of state Charles Taylor.

The importance of non-military methods of preventing genocide was underlined by Lemkin, which resulted in his struggles to include a provision in Article VIII of the Convention granting the right of a party to turn to the UN's General Assembly to undertake actions preventing a genocide.[60] He was aware that if this right to intervene would be granted to the Security Council, the rule could be rendered *de facto* inapplicable due to the veto of a single permanent member of the Security Council, and in fact it is very difficult to imagine an international conflict in which none of the states which are permanent members on the Security Council would not have an opposing interest which would or could justify a veto. This proves Lemkin's awareness of the importance of non-military, but concrete, tools to prevent the crime of genocide on the one hand, and also his awareness and profound knowledge of international relations and the inability of states to act unanimously on the other. This is why such subtle yet substantial instruments are crucial.

Especially taking into account genocide and its *dolus specialis*, granting absolute immunity can result in irreparable losses. If the perpetrators (which are usually state representatives and the state itself) possess this special intent of destroying a group in whole or in part, the chances that they would intentionally resign from the destruction of such protected groups is illusory. Also, these groups are usually minorities without their own states and they have almost no instruments to significantly influence public opinion. This is why there should be an instrument to prevent genocide and other violations of humanitarian law which is very specific, in contrast to vague declarations or resolutions, while at the same time not being a "nuclear" option (which military intervention clearly is, and which Lemkin called a "morally and legally fraught enterprise".[61])

I am aware of the risks concerning the establishment of such a precedent, and I suspect that shortly after it was created the most important states would try to mitigate these risks and try to create new rules that would address their own interests. Furthermore, international affairs are never ruled just by the law – the strongest actors will impose their interests nevertheless. Taking into account that even such a stable and long-established democracy as the USA struggles sometimes to avoid its responsibility, a failure to include this subtle instrument seems to be an overprotection of the ICJ's ruling. In my opinion, international criminal tribunals (especially the ICC) should act as the "conscience of humankind" and only by such ground-breaking verdicts could either the ICJ or ICC

60 Irvin-Erickson, *Raphael Lemkin*, p. 192.
61 Irvin-Erickson, *Raphael Lemkin*, p. 385.

reinforce their authority. Due to their inability to enforce their verdicts,[62] the only way that international criminal tribunals would actually matter is if they possessed an authority that states could not ignore.

As we have frequently observed in the history of international criminal law, various institutions begin to operate only after the damage is done, and even then they sometimes have to establish very far-fetched justifications for the legality of their actions, like in the Eichmann case (which does not mean that the trial was not just). In the case of genocide, I consider it likely that an arrest of a dictator or another important public figure that is an incumbent head of state could actually happen (by a state which is very influential or moral or has its own interest in such actions) in the future, and due to the viciousness of the crimes (i.e. using a moral rather than a legal justification) the rule of an absolute immunity could be broken.

We can observe, however, a lack of political will to impose such legal decisions considering incumbent heads of states or other important political figures. Even the ICC denied in the first instance issuing an arrest warrant considering a genocide allegation,[63] and only after the Appeals Chamber's judgment was the arrest warrant based on this allegation issued.[64] I suspect that the reluctance on the part of the lower-instance body was motivated by an awareness of the gravity of the charges as well as the new instruments that the prosecutor would be equipped with, considering the possibility to use the Convention, which is binding on many states that are not parties to the Rome Statute. Even when a state is willing to execute such a warrant, its actions are usually mostly verbal and pre-emptive – it declares such a will publicly, which results in warning the possible perpetrator not to enter such a state.[65] Even though there were declarations on the part of South Africa to enforce the arrest warrant and consultations between the ICC and South African representatives wherein the ICC urged South Africa to capture Omar Al Bashir during his declared stay in 2015, he arrived and left the country intact.[66] There are some minor inconveniences in becoming such a *persona non grata*, like the impossibility to visit such declaring states (which certainly impedes performing one's public office) or the necessity to verify whether such a public official could cross intervening borders

62 See, for example, G.P. Barnes, The International Criminal Court's Ineffective Enforcement Mechanisms: The Indictment of President Omar Al Bashir, 34(6) *Fordham International Law Journal*, 2011, p. 1585; N. Ali, Bringing the Guilty to Justice: Can the ICC be Self-Enforcing?, 14(2) *Chicago Journal of International Law*, 2014, p. 441.

63 Decision on the Prosecution's Application for a Warrant of Arrest against Omar Hassan Ahmad Al Bashir of 4 March 2009 (ICC-02/05-01/09-2-Conf).

64 Judgment on the appeal of the Prosecutor against the "Decision on the Prosecution's Application for a Warrant of Arrest against Omar Hassan Ahmad Al Bashir" of 3 February 2010 (ICC-02/05-01/09 OA).

65 This concerns, for example, South Africa. Available at: www.sanews.gov.za/south-africa/sa-obliged-arrest-al-bashir-says-ntsaluba (accessed: December 2018).

66 Pre-Trial Chamber II, Decision under Article 87(7) of the Rome Statute on the non-compliance by South Africa with the request by the Court for the arrest and surrender of Omar Al Bashir of No. ICC-02/05-01/091/536 July 2017of 6 July 2017(ICC-02/05-01/09).

without the risk of being captured, but this still does not approach the goal of capturing and potentially convicting perpetrators. Therefore, even the complying states will usually do their best not to jeopardize their political situations, which can be the result of capturing such an incumbent public official.

The issues concerning the Al Bashir arrest warrants are very complex. There are doubts about purely legal factors, like whether the very non-specific referral by the Security Council was sufficient to overcome the legal immunity of the incumbent head of state, or whether the ICC could be considered in this case to be, due to the said referral, an international criminal court with the power to pierce the immunity shield (one of the exceptions mentioned in the *Arrest Warrant Case* and in Article VI of the Convention).[67] In my opinion there are ample legal arguments to adjudicate either way, thus they actually do not matter and could be left to the scholars. What is really important is the political background of this situation – the fact that the arrest of the incumbent head of state of Sudan could destabilize the region and the interests that some other countries and organizations (especially the African Union[68]) represent. Also none of the most important states (including the democratic USA) are even parties to the Rome Statute. This does not create an atmosphere of compliance with the ICC's decisions, and these are the real reasons why the arrest warrants are not executed, even by parties to the Rome Statute. These concerns were also expressed by Lemkin himself. He did not want to establish a standing international criminal court because he believed that the primary agents of power were states, not international law. However, he considered that the acts of states were shaped by individuals and the values they and the society that they represent share in common, which is something international law and rulings can influence.[69]

De lege ferenda, the best solution would be for states to agree to capture incumbent public officials if they are suspected of committing genocide or other violations of international humanitarian law, while at the same time creating a special procedure for verifying such allegations, which could be created to give the ICC a very limited amount of time to adjudicate – counted in days rather than weeks, similar to rulings in contested elections. I doubt, however, that states would agree to this solution.

Conclusions

As has been mentioned, the ICJ finally dismissed Yugoslavia's motion and it may seem that adding provisions concerning the responsibility of states would be superfluous, but in my opinion *de lege ferenda* this rule should be declared

67 These concerns are expressed by, for example, S. Zappala, "International Criminal Jurisdiction over Genocide" in *The UN Genocide Convention: A Commentary*, edited by P. Gaeta, Oxford: Oxford University Press 2009, pp. 264–265.

68 AU Assembly Decision 366(XVII) § 5. Similarly in AU Assembly Decision 334(XVI) § 5.

69 Irvin-Erickson, *Raphael Lemkin*, p. 223.

more explicitly. In the current legal state of affairs, victims have instruments to receive compensation (which is the most significant issue), but the other *ratio legis* for such proclamations are rather symbolic. Such trials (against states *in corpore*) are trials before history; i.e. if the court acknowledges the responsibility of the state it will be strongly asserted that a specific country committed genocide. Responding to the debate over the character of such a finding of responsibility, I would say that it is civil in nature and *quasi* penal. It is civil because following a guilty verdict the victims have a simplified route to receive compensation, and *sui generis* penal because the fact that a given allegation of genocide is found to be true is unambiguously expressed, but certainly no punishment of a criminal nature (apart from the compensation) can be imposed on a state. That kind of verdict would be immensely grave and controversial. One could say that we do not need this symbolism, but I suspect that such a verdict would have concrete consequences. Even with respect to Hitlerism and the Third Reich there still appears every once in a while a book calling Hitler "a great leader",[70] or a politician claiming that Hitler did not know about the Holocaust,[71] or a mass-movement of negationism (of the Holocaust). A verdict by an international tribunal could be transmitted worldwide and would undermine such claims (if not criminalize them), and also make atrocities committed by a state a widely discussed and disputed topic in heated public debates. This would have a slightly smaller but similar impact as the commanders of the Allied countries showing the concentration camps to local German people. These kinds of trials are currently possible, but separate legal acts and proper procedures could give them substantial importance. Furthermore, it would become a standard to judge not only specific perpetrators but also a state, and the amount of such verdicts would increase. However, there is also a risk that these trials would be counter-productive, as happened during the Slobodan Milosevic trial, whereby his popularity actually increased, with only 33 percent of society believing in his guilt after one year of the trial. He was even elected to the parliament.[72]

Taking into consideration all the cases and provisions connected with the matter of immunities, the actual accountability of the highest public officials for the most heinous crimes (genocide, war crimes, and crimes against humanity) is still in my opinion more apparent than real. I would argue that that there are only two situations wherein the perpetrators are actually punished. The first is when the "justice" is handed out on the basis of the emotions of the society after the regime has collapsed, in proceedings the legality of which is highly controversial or even without any trial whatsoever. Such were the cases of Romanian

70 Information accessible at: www.theguardian.com/books/2018/mar/26/childrens-book-praising-hitler-as-amazing-leader-pulled-by-indian-publisher (accessed November 2018).

71 For example, Janusz Korwin-Mikke, a Polish Member of the European Parliament, in May 2014 – see https://histmag.org/Korwin-Mikke-i-historia.-Czy-Hitler-nie-wiedzial-o-Holokauscie-9553 (accessed November 2018).

72 Kelly, *Nowhere to Hide*, p. 117.

dictator Nicolae Ceausescu (and his wife), Italian fascist Benito Mussolini, and Colonel Gaddafi. The other cases are when a regime is so compromised that there are no supporters left – this was the case of all the Nazi trials, the Tokyo war crimes trial, the ICTR, or the Saddam Hussein case. Frequently in the latter situation trials are preceded by a military intervention which has effectively destroyed the regime and its apparatus.

Therefore, one could argue that the only situations whereby the perpetrators do not enjoy impunity are those without any political controversies whatsoever. What is highly ironic is in these cases usually the courts and tribunals show no remorse about bending the law at their will – *vide* the case of Adolf Eichmann, who was charged by a court of a country which did not exist when the atrocities were committed and by judges whose impartiality was at least questionable. On the other hand, if a case is politically controversial (for example, the *Arrest Warrant Case*), courts will either refuse to undertake legal steps (even if there are grounds for doing so), or states will not comply with the judicial decision or even do their best to avoid having to actually execute it (as in the Omar Al Bashir case). Frequently, even if a precedential decision is issued the case is dismissed because of other matters – here we should recall that eventually Pinochet was not extradited due to his health conditions and he was sent back to Chile in 2000, where he lived for six more years and faced a few other accusations, all of which were dismissed because of either his health condition or a lack of evidence. Another example is that of the former Polish communist leader General Wojciech Jaruzelski, who faced numerous trials, and even though he died more than 20 years after the communist system had collapsed he in fact did not suffer any severe consequences. In all of these cases the accused were incumbent public officials and/or preserved some political base, or at least had a substantial number of supporters. Frequently, the dictators live in infamy and in exile, but safely and without legal proceedings, like Kaiser William II after the First World War in Belgium and Mengistu Haile Mariam, the Ethiopian president responsible for thousands or even millions of deaths in his country, who now lives in Zimbabwe.[73]

In evaluating those cases where the perpetrators were actually punished, I must note that in each case the punishment occurred after the damage was done, and the trials did not impede or limit the violations of human rights. Therefore, in assessing the objectives of the Convention in the light of Article IV, one can conclude that it partially punishes the crime of genocide, but in no way prevents it. The only concrete means to stop such a violation of human rights remains a humanitarian intervention.

It seems as though there are enough rulings on this matter and now we are approaching a turning point – if the struggles of ICC eventually become fruitless (as they have been until now), the authority of the Court in this matter will collapse, but if the situation would somehow alter and the ICC's decisions become enforced,

73 B. Baker, Twilight of Impunity for Africa's Presidential Criminals, 25 *Third World Quarterly*, 2004, pp. 1492–1493.

the overall outcome could be completely different. If in fact an incumbent head of state is captured by one of the states and sent to The Hague for a trial, the international situation might well deteriorate, which would probably result in a substantial number of victims and possibly in a civil or regional war. At the same time, however, the precedent would be established – every dictator would fear the ICC's indictment and eventually this court would be able to resolve crises (at least partially) all over the world. No doubt this would be a long and drawn-out process, but the impact of such a situation would be vast. Certainly I am not contending that such a sacrifice of real people's lives is worth such a change. However, sooner or later this kind of cruel precedent would need to be established, as that is the only way to vest the authority to the ICC that the Court desperately needs. In the Omar Al Bashir case the situation has changed – the dictator has lost his power and has been under arrest in Sudan since April 2019. On the one hand that definitely ends the opportunity to try an incumbent head of state by the ICC, but on the other it is better for the authority of the ICC that he lost his power and is captured (based on other allegations, and he will probably be tried in Sudan) than if he had maintained his position and the ICC's arrest warrant was ignored for a number of subsequent years. Notwithstanding this, there is another solution: not to prosecute the perpetrators but to change the Court itself, which would require the decision makers to resign from setting such ambitious goals for the permanent ICC.

6 Transnational corporations' liability for genocide under international law

Łukasz Dawid Dąbrowski

Introduction

Activities of business enterprises affect the human rights of employees, consumers, and the communities in which they operate. This influence can be both positive and negative. A positive impact can be displayed, for example, by increasing access to employment or improving public services, or more generally by delivering products, innovation, and services that can improve the living standards for people across the globe. In turn, corporations can have a negative impact by, for example, destroying people's livelihoods, exploiting workers, polluting the environment,[1] displacing communities (especially in the extractive industries which require access to land for mining or other business activities), by taking a part in the torture of prisoners in the custody of private military companies, or by funding and supplying armed conflicts through various avenues and business networks.[2] Given this variety of relationships, businesses can be linked not only with domestic crimes, but also with international crimes, and consequently businesses can have a profound impact on human rights. In the literature it is frequently postulated that corporations cannot avoid responsibility for the most egregious violations of law.[3]

Crimes against humanity and genocide were included as a category of international crimes in response to the horrors of the Holocaust committed by Nazi Germany. Since then the law has come a long way. When Raphael Lemkin worked on the Convention on the Prevention and Punishment of the Crime of Genocide of 1948 (hereinafter the "Genocide Convention"), the number,

1 Ł.D. Dąbrowski, Human Rights Obligations of Enterprises under Public International Law, in M. Sitek, A.F. Uricchio and I. Florek (eds.), *Human Rights: Betweenness and Possibilities* (Józefów 2017), pp. 73–89.

2 J. Kyriakakis, Developments in International Criminal Law and the Case of Business Involvement in International Crimes, *International Review of the Red Cross* (Autumn 2012), Vol. 94, No. 887, p. 984.

3 See R.C. Slye, Corporations, Veils, and International Criminal Liability, *Brook. J. Int'l L.* (2008), Vol. 33, p. 959.

position,[4] and importance of companies were not as significant as they are today. Nevertheless

> Lemkin's belief that genocide was based on social processes led him to conclude that the best way to successfully prosecute the crime was through the doctrine of joint criminal enterprise – or criminal conspiracy laws – that were normally used to prosecute corporations and organized crimes.[5]

Nowadays it is widely accepted that crimes under both national law and international criminal law can be committed not only by perpetrators linked to a state, but also by non-state actors,[6] including corporations. It appears possible to attribute any conduct of a natural person to a legal person,[7] such as torture; cruel, inhuman, or degrading treatment; war crimes; crimes against humanity; summary executions; prolonged arbitrary detention; and forced disappearances. Some scholars have even postulated that corporations may be prosecuted for any crime which they are capable of committing, even aiding and abetting rape or murder.[8] However, the significant issue posed in this chapter is not about defining the scope of rights and freedoms which may be infringed by corporations, but whether corporations can be found responsible specifically for the crime of genocide, and the ways in which corporations can be held liable for that crime. In this respect the chapter is aimed at finding answers to two main issues. First, are corporations capable of committing the crime of genocide, and if so, in which way? Second, are corporations subject to the Genocide Convention? And if so, can they be held liable under international law?

The main method used in the chapter is formal-dogmatic. The chapter focuses on the analyses, first of all, of the provisions of the Genocide Convention, the Rome Statute of the ICC, and some regional human right regulations. Beyond the analyses of binding documents, the chapter also focuses on basic *soft law* regulations in the area of business and human rights, specifically the United Nations Guiding Principles on Business and Human Rights.

4 See. W.H.A.M. van den Muijsenbergh and S. Rezai, Corporations and the European Convention on Human Rights, *Pacific McGeorge Global Business & Development Law Journal* (2012), Vol. 43, p. 50.

5 D. Irvin-Erickson, Sixty Years of Failing to Prosecute Sexual Crimes: From Raphaël Lemkin at Nuremberg to Lubanga at the International Criminal Court, in M.M. Connellan and C. Fröhlich (eds.), *A Gendered Lens for Genocide Prevention* (Palgrave, 2017), p. 92.

6 V. Nerlich, Core Crimes and Transnational Business Corporations, *Journal of International Criminal Justice* (2010), 8, p. 903.

7 See N. Naffine, International Legal Personality, Collective Entities, and International Crimes, in N. Gal-Or, C. Ryngaert, and M. Noortmann (eds.), *Responsibilities of the Non-State Actor in Armed Conflict and the Market Place: Theoretical Considerations and Empirical Findings* (Boston 2015), pp. 79–104.

8 M.J. Kelly, Prosecuting Corporations for Genocide Under International Law, *Harvard Law & Policy Review* (2012), Vol. 6, p. 346; Nerlich, Core Crimes, p. 901.

Corporate responsibility

In considering whether corporations can commit genocide, and in what way, we should take into account not only the regulations stipulated in the Genocide Convention. Since the adoption of the Convention in 1948 the approach to many issues related to human rights has been changed and further developed and refined. States are still under an obligation to regulate relations between the state and individuals and groups, and are obliged to protect the people residing on their territory.[9] However, with the increased role of corporate entities in wide-ranging global affairs, the issue of businesses' impact on the enjoyment of human rights has also come to the fore. This is particularly visible in in area of *soft law* regulations. All international and national actions, condemnations, sanctions, prosecutions, interventions, and regulations, including *soft law* regulations, are important prevention tools and can deter individuals who may be the agents of genocide.[10] *Soft law* regulations may support the Genocide Convention, as in the words of Lemkin "the Convention is not only to punish genocide but also to prevent it. (...). Only a combination of punishment and prevention can lead to the proper result."[11] There are a number of non-binding international guidelines addressing businesses and human rights. Over the past decade, different organizations and institutions undertook many activities in the area of businesses and human rights. Specific actions have been undertaken by the Organisation for Economic Cooperation and Development (OECD), the International Labour Organization (ILO), and the United Nations (UN).

In 1976, the OECD adopted the Guidelines for Multinational Enterprises (updated 25 May 2011) to promote responsible business conduct consistent with applicable laws. In 1977, the ILO developed its Tripartite Declaration of Principles Concerning Multinational Enterprises (last updated in March 2017), which calls upon businesses to follow the relevant labour conventions and recommendations.[12] The Declaration provides direct guidance to enterprises on social policy and inclusive, responsible, and sustainable workplace practices. The next initiative was the UN Global Compact, which was proposed in January 1999 by the UN Secretary-General Kofi Annan.[13] The Global Compact is the leading global voluntary initiative for corporate social responsibility, and

9 D. Irvin-Erickson, Protection from Whom? Tensions, Contradictions, and Potential in the Responsibility to Protect, in E.D. Jacob (ed.), *Rethinking Security in the Twenty-First Century* (Palgrave, 2017), pp. 105–119.

10 See D. Irvin-Erickson, Understanding Culture and Conflict in Preventing Genocide, in M. Natarajan (ed.), *International and Transnational Crime and Justice* (Cambridge University Press, 2019), p. 336.

11 R. Lemkin, *Totally Unofficial: The Autobiography of Raphael Lemkin*, ed. by D.-L. Frieze (Polish edition 2018), p. 281.

12 Tripartite Declaration of Principles Concerning Multinational Enterprises 16.11.1977, revised 17.11.2000, 28.03.2006 and 24.03.2017.

13 The UN Global Compact's ten principles, www.unglobalcompact.org/what-is-gc/mission/principles [accessed 21.05.2017].

addresses the issue of business and human rights. In August 2003, the UN Sub-Commission on the Promotion and Protection of Human Rights approved the Norms on the Responsibilities of Transnational Corporations and Other Business Enterprises with Regard to Human Rights.[14] The norms reaffirm and reinforce the declarations that have been made so far with regard to the human rights responsibilities of business enterprises (e.g. the OECD guidelines and the UN Global Compact), and the core guidelines and standards are contained in this concise new document.[15] The UN Commission on Human Rights did not act on the draft norms. Instead, it appointed, in July 2005 Professor John Ruggie as the Special Representative of the Secretary-General on the issue of human rights and transnational corporations and other business enterprises, charged with the task of undertaking further study in the area of business and human rights.[16] Ruggie's work led to the development of a business and human rights framework, which the Human Rights Council welcomed in June 2008.[17] The resulting guiding principles were submitted in March 2011 and endorsed by the Human Rights Council in its resolution 17/4 of 16 June 2011. While the Guiding Principles on Business and Human Rights are not binding international law,[18] they are widely viewed as the most authoritative global standards in the area of business and human rights, and have an impact on other relevant international frameworks that guide or direct business behaviour under national laws and policies.[19] These *soft law* regulations reflect the global social expectation that businesses should avoid harming people not only through their own operations, but also through relationships with other entities such as suppliers, joint venture partners, or governments.[20] These are only *soft law* regulations but "non-binding standards are often invoked to show an evolution in acceptance of the international responsibility of transnational corporations for human rights

14 Norms on the Responsibilities of Transnational Corporations and other Business Enterprises with regard to Human Rights, Sub-Commission resolution 2003/16, U.N. Doc. E/CN.4/Sub.2/2003/L.11 at 52 (2003).

15 K-H. Moder, Norms on the Responsibilities of Transnational Corporations and other Business Enterprises with regard to Human Rights. Background paper to the FES side event at the 60th session of the UN Commission on Human Rights on 25 March 2005, www.fes-globalization.org/geneva/documents/UN_Norms/25March04_UN-Norms_Background.pdf, p. 1.

16 Dąbrowski, Human Rights Obligations, p. 76.

17 H. Clayton, Business and Human Rights: Businesses Doing More Than Domestic Law Requires, *Human Rights Research Journal* (2011), Vol. 2, p. 1.

18 Guiding Principles on Business and Human Rights Implementing the UN "Protect, Respect and Remedy" Framework, Human Rights Council resolution 17/4, 16 June 2011.

19 S. Jerbi, Assessing the Roles of Multi-Stakeholder Initiatives in Advancing the Business and Human Rights Agenda, *International Review of the Red Cross* (2012), Vol. 94, No. 887, p. 1043.

20 R. Davis, Preventing Corporate Involvement in Mass Atrocity Crimes: Implementing the UN Guiding Principles on Business and Human Rights, Global Centre for the Responsibility to Protect. Policy Brief (2016), www.globalr2p.org/publications/[24.01.2019], p. 2.

obligations violations."[21] Because the Guiding Principles are currently the most up-to-date, and are quite effective as for a *soft law* regulation in practical terms, the further part of the study deals with the regulations contained in the Guiding Principles.

The Guiding Principles consist of 31 principles covering the three pillars of the overall framework: states' duty to protect human rights, corporate responsibility to respect human rights, and the need for victims of human rights abuses to have access to remedies, both judicial and non-judicial. This chapter focuses on the core principles of the second pillar. While the Guiding Principles do not list the specific rights and freedoms which enterprises are obliged to respect, Principle 12 indicates *expressis verbis* which international documents are relevant to determine those rights and freedoms. At the same time the Guiding Principles point out that those documents comprise a minimum of rights which enterprises are obliged to respect.

In the first place, the Guiding Principles mention the International Bill of Human Rights, which consists of three different documents with different degrees of legally binding force. The first is the Universal Declaration of Human Rights of 10 December 1948 (hereinafter sometimes "Declaration"). As a UN resolution, the Declaration is of a non-binding nature, but nevertheless it is a milestone document in the history of human rights. The Declaration created common standards of achievements for all people and all nations, and sets out fundamental human rights to be universally protected. The provisions of the UN Declaration of Human Rights have been interpreted by successive European Union governments and by the UN as applying also to corporations.[22] The Declaration is codified in international law through the International Covenant on Economic, Social and Cultural Rights and the International Covenant on Civil and Political Rights, both adopted on 16 December 1966.

In the second place, the Guiding Principles mention the ILO's Declaration on Fundamental Principles and Rights at Work (herein after sometimes "ILO Declaration").[23] According to the ILO Declaration those fundamental principles are:

> the freedom of association and the effective recognition of the right to collective bargaining, the elimination of all forms of forced or compulsory labour, the effective abolition of child labour, and the elimination of discrimination in respect of employment and occupation.

21 E. De Brabandere, Human Rights Obligations and Transnational Corporations: The Limits of Direct Corporate Responsibility, *Human Rights and International Legal Discourse* (2010), Vol. 4, No. 1, p. 78.

22 Kelly, Prosecuting Corporations, p. 345.

23 Adopted in Geneva, 18.6.1998, revised 15.6.2010.

The ILO Declaration covers four main areas for the establishment of a social "floor" in the world of work. These principles and rights have been expressed and developed in the form of specific rights and obligations in conventions recognized as fundamental both within and outside the ILO. Each of these is supported by two ILO conventions, which together make up the eight ILO core labour standards.[24] Like all agreements, the above conventions have to be ratified by states, and not all states have done so. For those that have not, the Declaration makes an important new contribution. It recognizes that the Members of the ILO, even if they have not ratified the conventions in question, have an obligation to respect "in good faith and in accordance with the Constitution of the ILO, the principles concerning the fundamental rights which are the subject of those Conventions."[25] The ILO Declaration refers to, *inter alia*, the OECD Guidelines and EU regulations.[26]

According to the Commentary to the Guiding Principles, depending on the circumstances business enterprises may need to consider additional standards.[27] These additional standards may include the rights of individuals belonging to specific groups or populations that require particular attention in instances where they may suffer from adverse human rights impacts. The Commentary refers to the UN instruments concerning the rights of: indigenous peoples;[28] women;[29] national, ethnic, religious, and linguistic minorities;[30] children;[31] persons with disabilities;[32] and migrant workers and their families.[33] Moreover, according to the Commentary, in situations of an armed conflict enterprises should respect the standards of international humanitarian law (IHL). The International Committee of the Red Cross has published an information brochure called *Business and International Humanitarian Law*, which is intended

24 Convention No. 87 of 9.7.1948; Convention No. 98 of 1.7. 1949; Convention No. 29 of 28.6.1930; Convention No. 105 of 25.6.1957; Convention No. 138 of 26.6.1973; Convention No. 182 of 17.6.1999; Convention No. 100 of 29.6.1951; and Convention No. 111 of 25.6.1958.

25 *ILO Declaration on Fundamental Principles and Rights at Work and its Follow-Up*, adopted by the International Labour Conference at its Eighty-Sixth Session, Geneva, 18 June 1998 (revised 15 June 2010), p. 2.

26 Directive 2014/95/EU of the European Parliament and of the Council of 22.10.2014 amending Directive 2013/34/EU as regards disclosure of non-financial and diversity information by certain large undertakings and groups, *OJ L 330*, 15.11.2014, pp. 1–9.

27 *Guiding Principles on Business and Human Rights*, 2011, p. 14.

28 The United Nations Declaration on the Rights of Indigenous Peoples of 13.9.2007.

29 Convention on the Elimination of All Forms of Discrimination against Women of 18.12.1979, UN Treaty Series, Vol. 1249, p. 13.

30 International Convention on the Elimination of All Forms of Racial Discrimination of 21.12.1965, UN Treaty Series, Vol. 660, p. 195.

31 Convention on the Rights of the Child of 20.11.1989, UN Treaty Series, Vol. 1577, p. 3.

32 Convention on the Rights of Persons with Disabilities of 13.12.2006, UN Treaty Series, Vol. 2515, p. 3.

33 International Convention on the Protection of the Rights of All Migrant Workers and Members of Their Families of 18.12.1990, UN Treaty Series, Vol. 2220, p. 3.

to inform businesses of their obligations and rights under IHL. The brochure explains when IHL is applicable, what the main purpose of this body of law is, and how businesses can conduct themselves in times of an armed conflict so as to avoid violations of IHL.[34] The four Geneva Conventions of 1949 and their Additional Protocols of 1977 constitute the main instruments of IHL. Numerous other treaties address more specific topics related to conflicts, such as the regulation and use of specific weapons. As mentioned earlier, human rights treaties are traditionally understood as only binding on states, while IHL binds both state and non-state actors (e.g. managers and staff of business enterprises) whose activities are closely linked to an armed conflict.[35]

There are no references to the Genocide Convention in the list included in Principle 12 nor in the Commentary to the Guiding Principles. Thus there is an ongoing debate between those who deem that the Genocide Convention should be included in the list of the Guiding Principles (or at least in the Commentary), and those who believe that this is not necessary. While the vast majority of documents indicated in Commentary to the Guiding Principles are devoted to the protection of individuals, this does not really change anything. If corporations are obliged to respect and protect individual human rights, then all the more are they obliged to respect the rights of a given group. Additionally, Principle 11 lays down a general requirement for corporations to respect human rights. This means that the responsibility to respect human rights is a global standard of expected conduct for all corporations – they should avoid infringing on the human rights of others and should address adverse human rights impacts in activities which they are involved in. Corporations are obliged to prevent, mitigate, and where appropriate remedy the infringement of human rights.

Notwithstanding the foregoing, according to Article 4 of the Genocide Convention persons committing genocide or any of the other acts specified in the Convention shall be punished, whether they are constitutionally responsible rulers, public officials, or private individuals. It has been argued that

> [t]his regulation covers individual responsibility, but there is no textual distinction between natural or legal (juridical) in the reference to 'persons'. Also in the preparatory work of the drafters, there is no evidence one way or the other that corporations as such were to be included or excluded from the Genocide Convention's reach.[36]

34 Ten Questions to Philip Spoerri, ICRC Director for International Law and Cooperation, *International Review of the Red Cross* (2012), Vol. 94, No. 887.

35 ICRC, *Business and International Humanitarian Law: An Introduction to the Rights and Obligations of Business Enterprises under International Humanitarian Law* (Geneva 2006), p. 12.

36 Kelly, Prosecuting Corporations, p. 346.

It is easy to imagine that in 1948 and in the period leading up to the approval of the Genocide Convention the position, meaning, and in consequence the responsibility of corporations was not such an important issue as it became later. Regardless of the above, the same principles may be applied to the interpretation of the Genocide Convention as in the case of the European Convention on Human Rights in the scope of its application to legal persons. Both those documents do not contain a definition of "person." From the legal standpoint, there is division of "persons" into *physical* and *legal*. The "plain meaning of words" rule would indicate that those terms cover both natural persons and legal persons. If this rule works in the case of the European Convention it should, or could, also be applied to the Genocide Convention.[37] Contrary to the above documents, Article 1, paragraph 1, of the Inter-American Convention on Human Rights imposes obligations on the states parties to respect and to ensure that all persons can exercise the rights and freedoms recognized in the Convention.[38] However, Article 2, paragraph 2, of this Convention defines the term "person" as meaning "every human being."[39] Similarly, the term "person" was expressly defined by the drafters of the Rome Statute creating the ICC as meaning "natural persons." Thus, while it is possible to take a more restrictive interpretation, since no such specific clarification is included in the Genocide Convention, corporations as legal persons should be deemed to be included under the term "persons" in the Convention. In Lemkin's works we can find descriptions of various types of genocide – political, social, cultural, economic, biological, and physical. He also indicated the methods used to commit genocide, including the destruction of symbols and cultural centres, such as churches and schools. In other words, the general understanding of genocide in Lemkin's output is very wide. The legal definition, however, is rather narrow, and in the years following the adoption of the Genocide Convention, it was interpreted even more narrowly.[40] Nevertheless, both according to Lemkin's intentions and in today's understanding of the duties of business entities, the obligations arising from the Genocide Convention definitely are put on corporations.

The juxtaposition of the above regulations should not arouse any doubts that the Genocide Convention binds corporations. Nevertheless, this raises a factual issue: How could corporations be involved in genocide? In this regard, the Guiding Principles could be helpful. In the above-mentioned second pillar of

37 It should be noted that this is not the only element that decides on the application of the European Convention to legal persons.

38 See P.H. van Kempen, Human Rights and Criminal Justice Applied to Legal Persons. Protection and Liability of Private and Public Juristic Entities under the ICCPR, ECHR, ACHR and AfChHPR, *Electronic Journal of Comparative Law*, (December 2010), Vol. 14.3, www.ejcl.org/143/art143-20.pdf [accessed 29.05.2018], p. 29.

39 Ł.D. Dąbrowski, Entitlement of Legal Entities to Hold Rights under the Inter-American Human Rights Protection System, *International Community Law Review* (2019), Vol. 21, p. 458.

40 A. Applebaum, *Red Famine: Stalin's War on Ukraine* (London 2018), pp. 400, 402.

the Guiding Principles (corporate responsibility), the relevant principle is number 13. This principle states that

> the responsibility to respect human rights requires that business enterprises: a) avoid causing or contributing to adverse human rights impacts through their own activities, and address such impacts when they occur, b) seek to prevent or mitigate adverse human rights impacts that are directly linked to their operations, products or services by their business relationships, even if they have not contributed to those impacts.

The Commentary to this principle clarifies that

> a business enterprise's 'activities' are understood to include both actions and omissions; and its 'business relationships' are understood to include relationships with business partners, entities in its value chain, and any other non-State or State entity directly linked to its business operations, products or services.

From this regulation it follows that

> business may be involved in human rights abuses in three main ways: 1) a company may cause a crime if its actions solely and directly lead to such an abuse, 2) a company may contribute to a crime either by acting in parallel with other entities such that the cumulative effect of their behaviour causes the crime, or by facilitating or motivating the commission of such abuses through a business relationship, 3) a company's operations, products or services may be directly linked to a crime through the company's business relationships, although the company itself did nothing to cause or contribute to the abuse.[41]

These regulations in Principle 13, and the threefold division of different ways in which corporations may participate in human rights abuses, have been formulated in a manner which could be applied to all kinds of human rights abuses on either a national or international level.

In the literature,[42] some helpful criteria to distinguish corporate complicity in international crimes from neutral business activities can be found in the 2008 International Commission of Jurists (ICJ) report on the involvement of corporations in international crimes.[43] According to this report

41 Davis, Preventing, p. 2.

42 W. Kaleck and M. Saage-Maas, Corporate Accountability for Human Rights Violations Amounting to International Crimes, *Journal of International Criminal Justice* (2010), Vol. 8, p. 721.

43 ICJ, *Corporate Complicity & Legal Accountability, Report of the International Commission of Jurists, Expert Legal Panel 011 Corporate Complicity in International Crimes, Vol. 1: Facing the Facts and Charting the Legal Path* (2008), available online at www.icj.org/IMG/Volume_l.pdf [accessed 31.1.2019], p. 9.

> a company should avoid conduct if it: 1) enables the specific abuses to occur, meaning that the abuses would not occur without the contribution of the company, or 2) exacerbates the specific abuses, meaning that the company makes the situation worse, including where without the contribution of the company some of the abuses would have occurred on a smaller scale, or with less frequency, or 3) facilitates the specific abuses, meaning that the company's conduct makes it easier to carry out the abuses or changes the way the abuses are carried out, including the methods used, the timing, or their efficiency.

The above conduct includes both actions and a failure to act, and various forms of participation (e.g. assistance or encouragement). In this respect the ICJ report is quite similar to the Guiding Principles. When a company solely and directly causes a crime it means that a company enables a specific abuse which would not have occurred without the contribution of the company. And a company's contribution may be deemed to make the situation worse if without the facilitation (or motivation) of the company some of the abuses would have occurred on a smaller scale, or with less frequency. These kinds of facilitation may be done by act or omission, and encompass a company's operations, products. or services.

The best way to consider the various forms of participation by corporations in genocide is to examine actual examples. The most uncontested cases of business complicity in genocide are the Jewish, Kurdish, and Darfurian genocides. While the first concerns the horror of the Holocaust and is widely described in the literature, nevertheless it is examined in the next part of the chapter. In the second case, in 1987 and 1988 Saddam Hussein attacked the Kurdish community living in Northern Iraq (the Anfal campaign) using chemical and regular weapons. This resulted in thousands of deaths, disappearances, and the displacement of people. Various national and international businesses were directly complicit in this genocide. In particular, French and German businesses supplied Hussein with the equipment and resources by selling specialized chemical-industry equipment that was particularly useful for producing poison gas.[44] In the case of genocide on the Christian population of Darfur in Sudan, the government's actions led to the massacre of tens of thousands people in the 2003–2005 period and approximately 2 million displaced persons from 1999 to 2006. Mainly Canadian, Swedish, and Chinese corporations were involved in this ethnic cleansing, forced displacement, extrajudicial killings, torture, rape, and physical destruction of civilian homes in their respective oil extraction areas. Most importantly, this complicity materialized through financial and also logistical, material, or infrastructure assistance to the human-rights-abusing troops

44 N. Stel, Business in Genocide: Understanding the How and Why of Corporate Complicity in Genocides, Maastricht School of Management, Working Paper No. 2014/28, www.msm.nl/resources/uploads/2014/09/MSM-WP2014-28.pdf [accessed 28.01.2019], p. 6.

(e.g. servicing disabled military trucks, providing electricity lines to their barracks, and even piping water to the army camps).[45]

With respect to financing, the case of the activities of banks, which in 1994 enabled the carrying out of the campaign of genocide, war crimes, and crimes against humanity in Rwanda, should be noted. Banks allowed the transfer of funds from the Rwanda Central Bank's account to the Swiss account of a South African citizen (a former secretary of the Prime Minister of Rwanda) who was a director of an arms trade company. The funds that were thus transferred were used to purchase, through Zaire, weapons and military equipment that were used to commit crimes against the Tutsi population. Similarly, the activities of banks helped the Argentinian junta and South African apartheid regime. It is deemed that loans provided by banks to those regimes helped implement a policy of growing military expenditures and that the regimes could not have supported their systematic human rights abuses and torture apparatus without the bank loans.[46] In another example, the oil company Shell supported the Nigerian government in its torturing and killing of activists who protested against the environmental damages that Shell's operations caused in the Ogoni Region of Nigeria in the early 1990s. In 1993 and 1994, the Nigerian military was involved in a variety of human rights violations, as well as destroying and looting property – allegedly with the assistance of an oil corporation.[47] It was deemed that the company and its Nigerian subsidiary provided monetary and logistical support to the Nigerian police and bribed witnesses to produce false testimonies.[48]

Another example is the use of corporate property to facilitate killing a local community in Papua New Guinea (PNG). A mining company closed its activities in 1989 due to violent conflicts with local communities. Local people have claimed that at the company's request, the PNG military put down the revolt, and soon thereafter imposed a military blockade on the Bougainville region to secure the mine. Shortly after this incident, a decade-long civil war erupted. The corporation allegedly supported and encouraged PNG's blockade, which prevented medicine, clothing, and other essential items from reaching the people of Bougainville. The PNG government, allegedly using the mining company's helicopters and vehicles, killed several thousand people in its effort to put down the revolt.[49]

The next example of the supposed involvement of mining companies in an infringement of human rights concerns the alleged participation and involvement of a company in crimes committed in the Democratic Republic of the

45 Stel, Business in Genocide, p. 8.

46 Kaleck and Saage-Maas, Corporate Accountability, p. 706.

47 Can companies be involved in genocide, war crimes and crimes against humanity? www.p-plus.nl/resources/articlefiles/Bedrijvenengenocide.pdf [accessed 29.01.2019], p. 2.

48 Kaleck and Saage-Maas, Corporate Accountability, p. 704.

49 Can companies be involved in genocide, war crimes and crimes against humanity? www.p-plus.nl/resources/articlefiles/Bedrijvenengenocide.pdf [accessed 29.01.2019], p. 2.

Congo. In 2004, the town of Kilwa was engulfed by fighting between the Armed Forces of the Democratic Republic and a group of armed rebels. The mining company's staff were charged with facilitating these crimes by providing transportation to the Armed Forces for the operation.[50]

Even if not all of above situations involved genocide per se, they illustrate the ways in which businesses can participate in such violations of human rights. The examples show that the most likely ways for a company to be involved in a genocide are through the provision of: financing, material, infrastructure (providing the necessary means of transportation), human resources (private security groups protecting the company's compounds or assets), equipment, and information to the perpetrator of the genocide, thus enabling and/or exacerbating the genocide.[51] This means that the commission of these offences by a corporation can be categorised at least as complicity in genocide, and maybe even as a conspiracy to commit genocide (Article 3, points b and e, of the Genocide Convention) by contributing, through a business relationship or through its operations, products, or services to actions directly linked to such a crime.

Corporate accountability

Over and above these issues there is the question whether corporations can be held liable under international law. According to Article 6 of the Genocide Convention persons charged with genocide or any of the other acts set out in the Convention should be judged by a competent tribunal of the state in the territory in which the act was committed, or by such an international penal tribunal as may have jurisdiction over the crime and the person.

So far, we have only one permanent criminal court – the ICC in The Hague. According to Article 25 of the Rome Statute of the ICC, the Court may entertain individual criminal responsibility over natural persons. This means that all employees of a corporation could be subject to ICC scrutiny for the corporation's commission of, or complicity in, a genocide.[52] This is possible if the

> alleged illegal conduct is part of a situation of atrocity crimes that has fallen under the jurisdiction of the Court by virtue of a proper referral or investigation, unless such actions fall within the narrow parameters of the relatively small number of situations of atrocity crimes being officially investigated by the ICC at the time.[53]

50 Davis, Preventing Corporate, p. 3.

51 Stel, Business in Genocide, pp. 4, 5.

52 C. Kaeb, The Shifting Sands of Corporate Liability Under International Criminal Law, *Geo. Wash. Int'l L. Rev.* (2016), Vol. 49, p. 377.

53 D. Scheffer, Corporate Liability under the Rome Statute, *Harvard International Law Journal*, (Spring 2016), Vol. 57, Online Symposium, p. 36.

However, holding individual corporate officials and employees criminally liable may not adequately deter certain corporate wrongdoing and harm, and what is more, there may not even be sufficient individual culpability to successfully prosecute anyone individually.[54]

Including corporations within scope of the Rome Statute was specifically considered and rejected during the UN talks in July 1998. Scheffer points out that

> as the court was originally designed to hold natural persons accountable for atrocity crimes, there was too little time to fully consider the proposal. Also, at that time there were an insufficient number of national jurisdictions that held corporations liable under criminal law, as opposed to civil tort liability, which has long been universal.[55]

While a lot has changed since that time, obtaining approval for amendments to the Rome Statute that would extend the ICC's jurisdiction to cover corporations would be extremely difficult to achieve. As Scheffer further points out

> nations with economies that are fuelled by multinational corporations, either as home states or host states, would likely oppose efforts to expose these companies to criminal liability before the ICC. The potential economic cost of a finding of corporate criminal liability, or even the possibility of an ICC investigation in the future, could have devastating impacts on a nation's economy.[56]

In addition to the ICC, and in response to a specific set of mass atrocities and armed conflicts, the international community established the Tribunal for the Former Yugoslavia, the Tribunal for Rwanda, and a series of so-called "hybrid" tribunals in Cambodia, Sierra Leone, East Timor, and Lebanon. Each of these international and ad hoc tribunals functioned under its own founding document. Although there are some similarities between them, the regulations contained in those documents are not identical.[57] Genocide is one of the key crimes subject to prosecution before the Tribunal for the Former Yugoslavia, the Tribunal for Rwanda,[58] and the Special Court for Cambodia, but the statutes creating these organs do not provide for jurisdiction over corporations. The example of the Tribunal for Lebanon presents a different situation. In the *Al-Jadeed* case the Appeals Panel reaffirmed, on 8 March 2016, the existence of corporate criminal liability under international law, and held that legal persons

54 Slye, Corporations, p. 963.
55 Scheffer, Corporate Liability, p. 38.
56 Ibid., p. 38.
57 P.J. Stephens, Collective Criminality and Individual Responsibility: The Constraints of Interpretation, *Fordham Int'l L.J.* (2014), Vol. 37, No. 1, p. 504.
58 See M.A. Drumbl, Restorative Justice and Collective Responsibility: Lessons for and from the Rwandan Genocide, *Contemporary Justice Review* (2002), Vol. 5, No. 1, pp. 5–22.

fall under the jurisdiction of the Special Tribunal for Lebanon (although the specific case ended in a verdict of acquittal).[59] However, there is currently no international court or tribunal that can exercise criminal jurisdiction over transnational business corporations for genocide, as the Special Tribunal for Lebanon was not devoted to this crime.[60]

Regardless of the issue of international jurisdiction, the Genocide Convention actually obliged a competent tribunal of the state in the territory of which an act of genocide was committed to judge such acts of genocide (and acts related to genocide). Therefore, in the first place, companies should be prosecuted for genocide in domestic jurisdictions for violations of domestic law. There is also a view that corporations can be prosecuted domestically for a violation of international law, inasmuch as genocide is a *jus cogens* crime and any court – anywhere in the world – has jurisdiction (universal jurisdiction) over genocide and may hear a case against a company as long as the court has criminal jurisdiction over corporations.[61] It seems that in some countries this solution is possible. In 2000 Canada implemented key provisions of the ICC's Rome Statute to the Canadian Crimes Against Humanity and War Crimes Act. In 2002, provisions were introduced into the Australian Commonwealth Criminal Code for the prosecution of genocide, crimes against humanity, and war crimes. The offences were introduced as a part of Australia's ratification of the Rome Statute of the ICC.[62] These acts, together with domestic law regulations, which provide for responsibility of corporations, would make it possible to prosecute business entities for the above-mentioned crimes. Thus, a domestic prosecution for genocide against a corporation would be possible in Canada and Australia if there is a demonstrable connection between that situation and the respective country. This means that the jurisdictional provisions of the Acts could be employed based on the universal jurisdiction for *jus cogens* crimes like genocide.[63] In 2008 the Norwegian Penal Code incorporated provisions on war crimes, genocide, and crimes against humanity. In this way, there is a possibility for a company to be sanctioned where individuals acting on its behalf of it commit, or are complicit in the commission of, genocide.[64] Criminalization of such corporate actions is possible not only if they were committed on Norwegian territory, but the Norwegian Penal Code also addresses the extraterritorial application of states'

59 Kaeb, The Shifting, p. 370.
60 See Article 2 of the Statute of the Special Tribunal for Lebanon, www.stl-tsl.org/en/documents/statute-of-the-tribunal/223-statute-of-the-special-tribunal-for-lebanon [accessed 13.04.2020].
61 Kelly, Prosecuting Corporations, pp. 364–365.
62 J. Kyriakakis, Australian Prosecution of Corporations for International Crimes: The Potential of the Commonwealth Criminal Code, *Journal of International Criminal Justice* (2007), Vol. 5, p. 814.
63 Kelly, Prosecuting Corporations, pp. 364–365.
64 S. O'Connor, Corporations, International Crimes and National Courts: A Norwegian View, *International Review of the Red Cross*, (Autumn 2012), Vol. 94, No. 887, pp. 1011, 1012.

regulations to acts committed on behalf of an enterprise registered in Norway.[65] A number of other countries, including the Netherlands,[66] United Kingdom, and Poland,[67] have incorporated the offences of genocide, crimes against humanity, and war crimes into their domestic laws on the basis of universal jurisdiction, and also as applicable to legal persons.[68]

In the case of universal jurisdiction, any court, anywhere in the world, has jurisdiction over genocide (committed anywhere in the world) and may hear a case against a company so long as the court has criminal jurisdiction over corporations. However, it has been rightly pointed out that in order

> to investigate the crimes committed on foreign territory, national authorities may have to overcome legal and/or diplomatic hurdles before commencing their investigations, or to obtain the necessary cooperation from the authorities of the foreign states. They may also lack any operational infrastructure on the ground, which is necessary to conduct effective investigations on the territory of a foreign country or to protect potential witnesses or their own investigators.[69]

Nonetheless, a national investigation, despite its many procedural imperfections and difficulties, would constitute an attempt to obviate corporate impunity. This reflects the determination to look for ways to hold companies legally accountable, at least until jurisdiction is extended to international tribunals.

Regardless of whether companies will be judged by national or international courts, the answer to the question posed at the beginning of this chapter – whether corporations can be held liable under international law – is strongly related to the subjective state of mind that must accompany the acts of certain crimes in order to constitute a violation. In the general sense, businesses' involvement in human rights violations may be unintentional; for example, where they result from a lack of understanding of the relevant international human rights standards or of the policies and processes that companies should adopt to meet those standards in practice.[70] The above statement, however, does not apply to genocide. According to Article 2 of the Genocide Convention, a genocide is a mass killing "committed with the intent to destroy, in whole or in part, a national, ethical, racial or religious group."[71] To commit the

65 O'Connor, Corporations, p. 1017.
66 See Kelly, Prosecuting Corporations, pp. 364–365.
67 Due to some limitations in the Act of 28 October 2002, on the Liability of Collective Entities for Acts Prohibited Under Penalty (official Journal 2018 r.no 703, 1277), it seems to be very difficult.
68 See Kyriakakis, Australian Prosecution, p. 819.
69 R. Gallmetzer, Prosecuting Persons Doing Business with Armed Groups in Conflict Areas, *Journal of International Criminal Law* (2010), Vol. 8, p. 948.
70 Davis, Preventing Corporate, p. 6.
71 Stel, Business in Genocide, p. 3.

crime of genocide there must be a specific intent to destroy the population in whole or in part; hence the requirement is raised from a general intent to a specific intent. A mere showing of motive to commit genocide is not enough.[72] The specific intent required for genocide limits the scope of application of international core crimes, at least in practical terms.[73] When we add to this common requirement the fact that in many domestic legal systems only criminal acts of organs (as designated by law or the organizational documents) or representatives (i.e. those that received a delegation of power from an organ) can be imputed to the corporation,[74] the situation is even more complicated.

In most cases, when one seeks to assign responsibility to business leaders or corporate employees, there are two main questions that need to be answered, to wit: (1) Was there any factual link between the provision of materials, goods, or services and the perpetration of an international crime?; and (2) Did the business executives or other corporate employees have at least knowledge that the international crime would be committed by the principal perpetrator[75] by means of using the materials, goods, or services of the company?

After World War II the indictment of 24 former Nazi officials was directed against them both individually and as members of any of the groups or organisations to which they respectively belonged. In three other cases of the so-called "Subsequent Nuremberg Trials" before US military tribunals, high-ranking corporate officers and owners of the IG Farben trust, the Flick trust, and the Krupp firm were indicted for atrocity crimes committed by the SS. Also, in the 1946 Zyklon B case a British military tribunal convicted two businessman for aiding and abetting murder.[76] The Tribunal for Rwanda and the Tribunal for the Former Yugoslavia adopted "joinder" indictments and the concept of "joint criminal enterprise," respectively, to ensure that all individuals involved in the crime perpetrated shared liability for the crime.[77] However, in all the above cases the focus remained on individual criminal accountability: in military cases, the responsibility was imposed on the commanding officer; in corporate cases, the responsibility was imposed on the leading corporate officials. In cases of international corporations, the principles should be reversed – the object of prosecution should be the organization, not the commanding corporate officer(s).[78] In the above-mentioned cases, although the tribunals did not convict corporations but only individuals, they recognized that the standard of knowledge is crucial for the conviction of individual corporate officers. In the

72 Kelly, Prosecuting Corporations, p. 357.
73 Nerlich, Core Crimes, p. 908.
74 C. Kaeb, The Shifting, p. 382.
75 H. Vest, Business Leaders and the Modes of Individual Criminal Responsibility under International Law, *Journal of International Criminal Justice* (2010), Vol. 8, p. 53.
76 Kaleck and Saage-Maas, Corporate Accountability, p. 701.
77 J. Balint, Transitional Justice and State Crime, *Macquarie Law Journal* (2014), Vol. 13, p. 157.
78 Kelly, Prosecuting Corporations, p. 349.

Krupp case, the tribunal recognized that guilt must be personal. In the *Flick* case, the tribunal convicted two civilian industrialists for knowingly using their "influence and money" to further the activities of the SS. In the *Farben* case, pharmaceutical corporate executives were acquitted as there was no evidence that defendants knowingly participated in the planning, preparation, or initiation of a crime. In that case the executives were unaware of the criminal purposes for which the products of the company were being used.[79]

It is surely necessary to agree with Nerlich that the seriousness and magnitude of the crime of genocide requires, at least in practical terms, some involvement of a state or a state-like entity. Thus, under normal circumstances it is unlikely that a transnational business corporation could be held responsible for genocide without the involvement of a state or state-like actor.[80] Without the harnessing of the state and civil institutions, the harm perpetrated would have been of a different dimension.[81] The result in mass atrocities would not be materially possible without people (institutions) who have the capacity to foster public power and have the political institutions and resources to knowingly participate in a program that will result in crimes against humanity and genocide.[82] This means that the specific intent requirement should be interpreted adequately to the specific context of the crime committed. In most cases particular business activities can only be looked at through the prisms of assistance or complicity, especially aiding and abetting, which are most readily transposed to the business case. The crime of aiding and abetting is commonly classified as an accessorial or derivative form of criminal responsibility. Viewed in this way, the accomplice derives his liability from the primary actor with whom he has associated himself.[83] Under customary international law, it is sufficient if a person provides assistance in circumstances wherein they know of the likelihood that their action will assist in the commission of an international crime.[84] A corporation may assist in a genocide by providing a variety of methods; by procuring means (such as weapons); by knowingly aiding and abetting; and by instigation. At least knowledge and approval must be shown in order to bring a case for complicity. In other words, "Did the business entity know or have the possibility to know (i.e. should have known) that its business activities would contribute to carrying out an international crime?" Also, the ICJ in the above-mentioned report indicated that corporate complicity in international crimes takes place when the company or its employees actively wish to enable, exacerbate, or facilitate the gross human rights abuses; or even when, without desiring such an

79 Kelly, Prosecuting Corporations, pp. 352–353.
80 Nerlich, Core Crimes, p. 906.
81 Balint, Transitional, p. 160.
82 D. Irvin-Erickson, Prosecuting Sexual Violence at the Cambodian War Crimes Tribunal: Challenges, Limitations, and Implications, *Human Rights Quarterly* (2018), Vol. 40, No. 3, p. 584.
83 Vest, Business, p. 56.
84 Kyriakakis, Developments, p. 997, 998.

outcome, they know or should have known from all the circumstances of the risk that their conduct will contribute to the human rights abuses, and were wilfully blind to that risk.[85] In particular, the responsibility of corporations for genocide should be based on a legal fiction as regards fulfilment of the special intention. This presumption should be based on recognition that if a corporation participated in the commission of the crime with knowledge (or this knowledge should have been known from all the circumstances) about the intention of the principal offender, it had the same intention as this offender. In other words, criminal liability should be constituted by actions, and not by what states, groups, and/or their leaders say they intend to do through their statements of plans or their policies – it is the act itself that constitutes the intent, not the statement or declaration of that intent.[86] In a general sense anyone caught aiding or abetting genocide should take responsibility in a like manner as the principal offender. In this regard the principle of a "joint criminal enterprise" could be helpful. As Irvin-Erickson noted:

> As legal scholars have recently pointed out, the doctrine of joint criminal enterprise can allow to place greater emphasis on indirect and circumstantial evidence, without having to meet the highly restrictive requirement of showing that a defendant held clear prior intent to commit genocide before he or she acted.[87]

From this point of view corporations could be liable for the crimes of their employees.

Conclusions

As the economic and political power of corporations expands, there is increasing recognition that corporations should take greater responsibility for their actions.[88] The lack of jurisdiction by an international criminal tribunal over corporate crime per se in no way relieves the corporations of their international legal obligations.[89]

> Although corporations do not have formal participatory roles in the creation, shaping, and termination of international law, a significant and growing number of domestic judicial opinions have recognized that corporations can have duties under treaty-based and customary international law, including relevant human rights law, the laws of war, prohibitions of forced

85 ICJ, Corporate Complicity, p. 9.
86 Irvin-Erickson, Prosecuting Sexual Violence, p. 583.
87 Irvin-Erickson, Sixty Years, p. 92.
88 Kelly, Prosecuting Corporations, p. 340.
89 Nerlich, Core Crimes, p. 896.

disappearances, prohibitions of crimes against humanity, slavery, and the prohibition of genocide.[90]

In light of the recent *soft law* regulations, changes in states' law, and judicial developments, it no longer seems to be a matter of *whether* corporations are liable under international law, but rather *how* such liability would be implemented – in other words, what the material elements for liability are and what an effective penalty structure would look like.[91] Nowadays corporations cannot claim that they were unaware that they enabled genocide – corporations must be aware of what they are doing. As Franck notes:

> The intention of the Genocide Convention is to provide both for punishment of individuals who participate in a genocidal enterprise and for the responsibility of corporations which put the machinery and resources of the nation at the disposal of such an enterprise.[92]

But what does it mean to hold a corporation criminally liable? In other words, what penalties are appropriate to sanction a corporation criminally convicted of an international crime? Penalties which should be considered include fines, restraints, structural injunctions, publicity, judicial surveillance and transparency initiatives, equity awards, prohibition from operating in a particular country, and dissolution. Fines are the most common, but can be imposed through civil liability.[93] Some scholars argue that because corporations possess both an individual dimension and an institutional dimension, the accountability process should be integrated and contain both criminal liability for key individuals, and civic liability for key institutions, both state and non-state.[94] In any case, there is a general agreement that monetary sanctions have proven inadequate to control corporate behaviour, and in addition could be viewed as commoditizing moral values, which can have perverse consequences.[95] At the other end of the spectrum is the dissolution of the company, which raises two related questions – which admittedly are based on the grounds of responsibility of states[96] but are appropriate also in the case of business entities – namely: Is it fair that the entire

90 J.J. Paust, Responsibilities of Armed Opposition Groups and Corporations for Violations of International Law and Possible sanctions, inN. Gal-Or, C. Ryngaert, and M. Noortmann (eds.), *Responsibilities of the Non-State Actor in Armed Conflict and the Market Place. Theoretical Considerations and Empirical Findings* (Boston 2015), p. 109.

91 Kaeb, The Shifting, p. 402.

92 See T. Franck, Individual Criminal Liability and Collective Civil Responsibility: Do They Reinforce or Contradict One Another? 6 *Wash. U. Global Stud. L. Rev.* (2007), Vol. 567, pp. 568, 570.

93 Slye, Corporations, pp. 970, 971.

94 Balint, Transitional, pp. 157, 159, 160.

95 C. Kaeb, The Shifting, pp. 373, 390.

96 See Franck, Individual Criminal Liability, pp. 568, 570.

corporation be held accountable for actions initiated by its leaders and executed by its organs? Would such a finding of corporate responsibility not be likely to impose an unfair burden on all its employees, regardless of whether they did, or did not, support or tolerate the acts of the regime that had violated the prohibition against genocide? In other words, the penalties imposed should not affect people who had nothing to do with the crime.[97] And should all kinds of behaviours be attributable to a corporation, or only acts and omissions that are somehow linked to its business activities? In various states, there is a limitation of the liability of legal persons to activities that were undertaken "on account" or "for the benefit" of the company.[98] The above issues raise a further question: Should a company be held responsible for the behaviour of all of its employees, regardless of the "guilt" of specific corporate employees? So far, there are more questions than answers. Some of those questions – e.g. those concerning appropriate penalties – may be considered on a case-by-case basis by the proper court or tribunal. In the case of other issues, more definitive solutions must be found over time. In any case, the interpretation of existing regulations, and the regulations themselves, should evolve over time and adapt and stand up to the new challenges of our times.

Bibliography

Applebaum, A., *Red Famine: Stalin's War on Ukraine*. Anchor Books, London 2018.

Balint, J., Transitional Justice and State Crime, *Macquarie Law Journal*, 13, 2014, 147–163.

Clayton, H., Business and Human Rights: Businesses Doing More Than Domestic Law Requires, *Human Rights Research Journal*, 2, 2011, 1–12.

Dąbrowski, Ł.D., Human Rights Obligations of Enterprises under Public International Law, in M. Sitek, A.F. Uricchio, and I. Florek (eds.), *Human Rights: Between Needs and Possibilities*, 73–89. Alcide de Gasperi University of Euroregional Economy, Józefów, Poland 2017.

Dąbrowski, Ł.D., Entitlement of Legal Entities to Hold Rights under the Inter-American Human Rights Protection System, *International Community Law Review*, 21, 2019, 446–462.

Davis, R., Preventing Corporate Involvement in Mass Atrocity Crimes: Implementing the UN Guiding Principles on Business and Human Rights. Global Centre for the Responsibility to Protect. Policy Brief, March 2016, www.globalr2p.org/publications/.

De Brabandere, E., Human Rights Obligations and Transnational Corporations: The Limits of Direct Corporate Responsibility, *Human Rights and International Legal Discourse*, 4(1), 2010, 66–88.

Drumbl, M.A., Restorative Justice and Collective Responsibility: Lessons for and from the Rwandan Genocide, *Contemporary Justice Review*, 5(1), 2002.

97 J. McMahan, Collective Crime and Collective Punishment, *Crim. Just. Ethics* (2008), Vol. 27, No. 4, pp. 4–12.

98 Nerlich, Core Crimes, p. 902.

Franck, T., Individual Criminal Liability and Collective Civil Responsibility: Do They Reinforce or Contradict One Another? *Washington University Global Studies Law Review*, 567, 2007, 567–573.

Gallmetzer, R., Prosecuting Persons Doing Business with Armed Groups in Conflict Areas, *Journal of International Criminal Law*, 8, 2010.

International Commission of Jurists, Corporate Complicity & Legal Accountability, Report of the International Commission of Jurists, Expert Legal Panel 011 Corporate Complicity in International Crimes, Vol. 1: Facing the Facts and Charting the Legal Path (2008), available online at www.icj.org/IMG/Volume_l.pdf.

International Committee of the Red Cross, *Business and International Humanitarian Law: An Introduction to the Rights and Obligations of Business Enterprises under International Humanitarian Law*, ICRC, Geneva 2006.

Irvin-Erickson, D., Sixty Years of Failing to Prosecute Sexual Crimes: From Raphaël Lemkin at Nuremberg to Lubanga at the International Criminal Court, in M.M. Connellan and C. Fröhlich (eds.), *A Gendered Lens for Genocide Prevention*, 83–109. Palgrave MacMillan, Basingstoke, UK 2017.

Irvin-Erickson, D., Protection from Whom? Tensions, Contradictions, and Potential in the Responsibility to Protect, in E.D. Jacob (ed.), *Rethinking Security in the Twenty-First Century*, 105–123. Palgrave MacMillan, Basingstoke, UK 2017.

Irvin-Erickson, D., Prosecuting Sexual Violence at the Cambodian War Crimes Tribunal: Challenges, Limitations, and Implications, *Human Rights Quarterly*, 40(3) 2018.

Irvin-Erickson, D., Understanding Culture and Conflict in Preventing Genocide, in M. Natarajan (ed.), *International and Transnational Crime and Justice*, 333–338. Cambridge University Press, Cambridge, UK 2019.

Jerbi, S., Assessing the Roles of Multi-stakeholder Initiatives in Advancing the Business and Human Rights Agenda, *International Review of the Red Cross*, 94(887) 2012.

Kaeb, C., The Shifting Sands of Corporate Liability under International Criminal Law, *George Washington International Law Review*, 49, 2016, 351–403.

Kaleck, W., and M. Saage-Maas, Corporate Accountability for Human Rights Violations Amounting to International Crimes, *Journal of International Criminal Justice*, 8, 2010, 699–724.

Kelly, M.J., Prosecuting Corporations for Genocide Under International Law, *Harvard Law & Policy Review*, 6, 2012, 339–367.

Kempen, P.H. van, Human Rights and Criminal Justice Applied to Legal Persons: Protection and Liability of Private and Public Juristic Entities under the ICCPR, ECHR, ACHR and AfChHPR, *Electronic Journal of Comparative Law*, 14(3), 2010, 509–551.

Kyriakakis, J., Australian Prosecution of Corporations for International Crimes: The Potential of the Commonwealth Criminal Code, *Journal of International Criminal Justice*, 5, 2007, 809–826.

Kyriakakis, J., Developments in International Criminal Law and the Case of Business Involvement In International Crimes, *International Review of the Red Cross*, 94(887), 2012, 981–1005.

Lemkin, R., *Totally Unofficial: The Autobiography of Raphael Lemkin*, ed. by Donna-Lee Frieze, Polish edition. Instytut Pileckiego, Poland 2018.

McMahan, J., Collective Crime and Collective Punishment, *Criminal Justice Ethics*, 27 (4) 2008, 4–12.

Moder, K-H., Norms on the Responsibilities of Transnational Corporations and Other Business Enterprises with Regard to Human Rights. Background paper to the FES side event at the 60th session of the UN Commission on Human Rights on 25 March 2005, www.fes-globalization.org/geneva/documents/UN_Norms/25March04_UN-Norms_Background.pdf.

Muijsenbergh, W.H.A.M., and S. van Den Rezai, Corporations and the European Convention on Human Rights, *Pacific McGeorge Global Business & Development Law Journal*, 43, 2012, 43–68.

Naffine, N., International Legal Personality, Collective Entities, and International Crimes, in N. Gal-Or, C. Ryngaert, and M. Noortmann (eds.), *Responsibilities of the Non-State Actor in Armed Conflict and the Market Place: Theoretical Considerations and Empirical Findings*, 79–104. Brill, Boston 2015.

Nerlich, V., Core Crimes and Transnational Business Corporations, *Journal of International Criminal Justice*, 8, (2010), 895–908.

O'Connor, S., Corporations, International Crimes and National Courts: A Norwegian View, *International Review of the Red Cross*, 94(887), 2012, 1007–1025.

Paust, J.J., Responsibilities of Armed Opposition Groups and Corporations for Violations of International Law and Possible sanctions, in N. Gal-Or, C. Ryngaert, and M. Noortmann (eds.), *Responsibilities of the Non-State Actor in Armed* Conflict *and the Market Place: Theoretical Considerations and Empirical Findings*, 105–123. Brill, Boston 2015.

Scheffer, D., Corporate Liability under the Rome Statute, *Harvard International Law Journal*, 57, Spring 2016, Online Symposium, 35–39.

Slye, R.C., Corporations, Veils, and International Criminal Liability, *Brooks Journal of International Law*, 33(3), 2008, 955–973.

Stel, N., Business in Genocide: Understanding the How and Why of Corporate Complicity in Genocides, Maastricht School of Management, Working Paper No. 2014/28, http://web2.msm.nl/RePEc/msm/wpaper/MSM-WP2014-28.pdf [accessed 13.04.2020].

Stephens, P. J., Collective Criminality and Individual Responsibility: The Constraints of Interpretation, 37 *Fordham International Law of Journal*, 501, 2014, 501–547.

Ten questions to Philip Spoerri, ICRC Director for International Law and Cooperation, *International Review of The Red Cross*, 94(887), 2012, 1125–1134.

Vest, H., Business Leaders and the Modes of Individual Criminal Responsibility under International Law, *Journal of International Criminal Justice*, 8, 2010, 851–872.

Part III

Challenges and new developments

7 Probing the boundaries of the Genocide Convention

Children as a protected group

Ruth Amir

Introduction

As Raphael Lemkin noted, genocide by forcible child transfer is an age-old phenomenon that peaked with modernity.[1] The late-fourteenth-century *devshirme* system of the Ottoman Empire targeted Christian boys from the Balkan provinces, converted them to Islam, and enlisted them to serve the Ottoman government. Oliver Cromwell's 1656 program for the removal of Irish children was aimed at bringing them up as Protestants. The Kheokho and San children were forcibly transferred into Boer society as Indigenous labourers to address the shortage of slaves on the frontier during the eighteenth century. In the latter decades of the nineteenth century, Indigenous children in the United States, Canada, and Australia were forcibly removed to residential/boarding schools and foster and adoptive white families, a practice which continued throughout the greater part of the twentieth century.[2] In addition, Ireland's Magdalen Laundries operated from the eighteenth to the late twentieth century as penitentiary institutions for so-called "fallen women." Babies born to these women were forcibly taken for adoption. Similarly, Britain's child migrant program transferred more than 130,000 children from deprived backgrounds to its former colonies, mainly Australia and Canada, between the 1920s and 1970s.

These and similar programs were conveyed as an opportunity for a better life for the children of problematized minority groups. With the growing realization of the qualities of childhood, namely both children's helplessness and their future potential for the state and society, modern states passed various laws for the "protection" of children and even began to intervene in the relations between parents and their children.

The impact of war on children, slavery, and the trafficking of women and children became matters of international concern in the aftermath of the First World War. The Convention to Suppress the Trafficking of Women and

1 Raphael Lemkin and Steven L. Jacobs, *Lemkin on Genocide* (Lexington 2011).
2 The last residential school in Canada closed down in 1996.

Children and the Convention to Suppress Slave Trade and Slavery reflected modern humanitarianism.[3] The League of Nations' earliest involvements in the field included the Rescue Movement established by Armenian individuals and groups, and the American Near East Relief, for the recovery and rehabilitation of women and children forcibly transferred to Muslim households, sweatshops, state factories, farms, or brothels.[4] As Keith Watenpaugh has argued, the League's officials in the field interpreted these forcible child and women transfers as part of the Ottoman Empire's general plan to destroy the Armenian people.[5] The RuSHA case at the Nüremberg International Military Tribunal further affirmed the gravity of forcible child transfers in the eyes of the international community. Both cases paved the way for the protection of children and development of the notion of children's rights as an area of concern for international law.[6]

Article II(e) of the United Nations' Convention on the Prevention and Punishment of Genocide (UNGC) prohibits the act of "[f]orcibly transferring children of the group to another group." This forcible transfer clause (FTC) is the most neglected aspect of the UNGC.[7] The FTC has so far received scant attention by genocide scholars, nor has it been included in an indictment by any international criminal tribunal. Although the Akayesu Chamber of the International Criminal Tribunal for Rwanda (ICTR) and the Preparatory Commission for the International Criminal Court (ICC) outlined the crime's physical elements, some open questions remain.[8]

In recent years, the crime of forcible child transfer has taken a gruesome turn in the form of conscripting and enlisting child soldiers as combatants in hostilities, as well as using them as human shields, suicide bombers, cooks, intelligence collectors, clerks, and sex slaves. So far, the ICC has treated these cases as war crimes regardless of whether the accused was also indicted for genocide. This raises the ever-present inter-temporal legal dilemma, which applies to

3 International Convention for the Suppression of the Traffic in Women and Children (adopted 30 September 1921, entered into force 15 June 1922) 9 LNTS 415; Convention to Suppress the Slave Trade and Slavery (adopted 25 September 1926, entered into force 9 March 1927) 60 LNTS 253.

4 Keith David Watenpaugh, "Between Communal Survival and National Aspiration: The League of Nations and the Practices of Interwar Humanitarianism," in Cyrus Schayegh and Andrew Arsan (eds), *The Routledge Handbook of the History of the Middle East Mandates* (Routledge 2015) 41, 47ff.

5 Watenpaugh (n 4) 47.

6 Keith David Watenpaugh, "The League of Nations' Rescue of Armenian Genocide Survivors and the Making of Modern Humanitarianism, 1920–1927" (2010) 115(5) *American Historical Review* 1315.

7 Convention on the Prevention and Punishment of the Crime of Genocide (adopted 9 December 1948, entered into force 12 January 1951) 78 UNTS 278 (UNGC).

8 *Prosecutor v Akayesu* (Judgment) ICTR-96-4-T, T Ch I (2 September 1998) 509 (Akayesu); "Report of the Preparatory Commission for the International Criminal Court, Addendum Part II Finalized draft text of the Elements of Crimes" PCNICC/2000/1/Add.2 (2 November 2000) 7.

whether crimes of international law are "frozen" in time or are to be interpreted with respect to relevant and applicable legal developments.[9]

Against this backdrop, this chapter examines the applicability of the FTC to the conscription and enlistment of child soldiers. Conscription and enlistment of child soldiers was recognized by the UN Security Council as one of six grave violations against children.[10] This chapter argues, based on an analysis of historical and current forcible child transfer cases, that there is need to extend the protection from forcible transfer granted by the UNGC to children of any identifiable group of persons. Highlighting the gravity of conscription and enlistment of child soldiers when perpetrated with the intent to destroy the group as such in violation of the UNGC Article II(e) is likely to act as a deterrent and contribute to prevention. Moreover, the protracted processes in the ICC in cases involving children call for the establishment of Communications and Rapid Inquiry Procedures under the International Impartial and Independent Mechanisms (IIIMs). Conducting these procedures in a timely manner is especially crucial with respect to child victims.

The first section of this chapter discusses the theory and jurisprudence of the FTC within the UNGC. The second discusses the special protected status of children in international law. The third extracts some forcible child transfer cases and hypothetically applies the FTC. The fourth discusses ICC child soldiers' cases. The chapter concludes with a proposal to amend the UNGC so as to support the recognition of children as such as a protected group.

The FTC: theory and interpretations

The FTC is indeed the most neglected aspect of the UNGC. It was referred to as "enigmatic," purportedly "passed almost as an afterthought," and "a remnant of cultural genocide," excluded from the UNGC by a majority of the drafters' votes.[11] I have argued elsewhere that the FTC is grounded in a mixed consequentialist and deontological ethical reasoning compared to the deontological underpinning of Articles II(a–d) and the UNGC as a whole.[12] Three types of arguments help to unpack the drafters' actual intent to protect children from

9 Leena Grover, "A Call to Arms: Fundamental Dilemmas Confronting the Interpretation of Crimes in the Rome Statute of the International Criminal Court," (2010) *EJIL* 21 543, 579–81.

10 "Children and armed conflict: Report of the Secretary-General" UN DOC A/72/361–S/2018/465 (16 May 2018) https://undocs.org/s/2018/465 [accessed 20 January 2019] (Children and Armed Conflict).

11 William Schabas, *Genocide in International Law: The Crime of Crimes* (Cambridge University Press 2000), 175; Antonio Cassese, *Cassese's International Criminal Law* (Third edn, Oxford University Press 2013), 117.

12 Ruth Amir, "Killing Them Softly: Forcible Transfers of Indigenous Children" (2015) 9(2) *Genocide Studies and Prevention: An International Journal* 41 (Amir 1); Ruth Amir, *Twentieth Century Forcible Child Transfers: Probing the Boundaries of the Genocide Convention* (Lexington 2019), 35–65 (Amir 2).

forcible transfers.[13] First, the FTC grants protection from forcible transfer only to children of the four protected groups. It therefore addresses children as a sub-group of these protected groups, based on an age criterion. Second, in recognizing children's rights to grow up in their family and group, the FTC undertakes a rights-based approach as opposed to the duty-based deontological ethic of Articles II(a-d) and the UNGC as a whole. Finally, recourse to the UNGC *travaux préparatoires* and other supplementary texts and interpretations points to the consequentialist ethical reasoning used by both Raphael Lemkin and the drafters' to justify the inclusion of the FTC in the UNGC.[14] Hence, in his autobiography Lemkin refers to the devastating impact of the Ottoman *devshirme* system on Greece: "Greece … a nation of seven million, would have a population of sixteen million if not for the Greek children who were taken away for four hundred years."[15]

The FTC is commensurable with psychological and other social science research and various instruments of international and municipal law, all of which established children's right not to be separated from their families and kin.[16] International law protecting children mirrors the recognition that a child belongs with his/her family, both during an armed conflict and in peacetime. Effectively, children are already recognized as a special protected group in various international law instruments, such as the Geneva Conventions and protocols, the United Nations Convention on the Rights of the Child (UNCRC), the United Nations Declaration on the Rights of the Child, and the League of Nations Declaration on the Rights of the Child, to name but a few.[17]

13 The United Nations Secretariat, "E/447 Draft Convention for the Prevention and Punishment of Genocide, dated June 26, 1947" in Hirad Abtahi and Philippa Webb (eds), *The Genocide Convention: The Travaux Préparatoires* (Martinus Nijhoff 2008) 214 (E/447 Draft Convention); The United Nations General Assembly Sixth Committee, "UN DOC A/C.6/SR.81, Eighty-First Meeting dated October 22, 1948" in Abtahi and Webb (eds), *The Genocide Convention: The Travaux Préparatoires* 1473; The United Nations General Assembly Sixth Committee, "UN DOC A/C.6/SR.82, Eighty-Second Meeting dated October 23, 1948" in Abtahi and Webb, *The Genocide Convention* 1487.

14 International Military Tribunal, *Trials of War Criminals Before the Nüernberg Military Tribunals Under Control Council Law No. 10; Nüernberg, October 1946–April 1949* (United States Government Printing Office 1949), 674; Sixth Committee "UN DOC A/C.6/SR.82" (n 9) 1487–89.

15 Raphael Lemkin, *Totally Unofficial: The Autobiography of Raphael Lemkin* (Donna-Lee Frieze ed, Yale University Press 2013) 168.

16 John Bowlby, *Attachment and Loss* (Basic 1969); Tara Zahra, *The Lost Children: Reconstructing Europe's Families after World War II* (Harvard University Press 2011) Raphael Lemkin, "Orphans of Living Parents: A Comparative Legal and Sociological View" (1944) 10 Law and Contemporary Problems 834.

17 Sonja C. Grover, *Humanity's Children: ICC Jurisprudence and the Failure to Address the Genocidal Forcible Transfer of Children* (Springer 2012) 17, 171; among the international legal instruments protecting children, such as the League of Nations, Geneva Declaration on the Rights of the Child (adopted 26 September 1924) cl Special Supplement 2143; Declaration on the Rights of the Child (adopted 20 November 1959) G.A.

The Akayesu Chamber furthered our understanding of the elements of the crime of genocide, including those of forcible child transfer.[18] The ICTR Akayesu Chamber was of the opinion that

> as in the case of measures intended to prevent births, the *objective is not only to sanction a direct act of forcible physical transfer, but also to sanction acts of threats or trauma which would lead to the forcible transfer of children from one group to another.*[19]

The Chamber upheld Lemkin and the UNGC drafters' position that forcible child transfer is in essence biological genocide: "there was little difference between the prevention of a birth by abortion and the forcible abduction of a child shortly after its birth."[20]

The concise language of the FTC shuns the temporal dimension of forcible child transfer, which is critical for the protection of children and children's rights. Two interrelated issues arise with respect to the temporal aspects of forcible child transfers. First, the UNGC text does not define until what age a person is considered a child, and second, there is no minimum duration requirement for the transfer to fall within the bounds of the FTC. The former issue is resolved in the Rome Statute with respect to forcible child transfer – but not in the prohibition of conscription and enlistment of child soldiers – which sets the threshold at 15 years. The latter issue – the duration of the transfer and whether to qualify it as genocide; e.g. as indefinite, temporary, or only for the duration of childhood (18 years of age) – has remained open.

Initially, neither the UNGC nor the statutes of various ad hoc tribunals defined until what age a person is considered a child in relation to the FTC. However, these tribunals abided by the UNCRC, which defines a child as "every human being below the age of 18 years unless under the law applicable to the child majority is attained earlier."[21]

Both the UNGC text and the supplementary interpretive materials contain no explicit or implicit minimum duration requirement. In the absence of these, principles of statutory interpretation do not permit us to read into the clause a restrictive term.[22] Legal scholar Gerhard Werle has thus argued that the FTC

Res. 1386 (XIV), 14 U.N. GAOR Supp. (No. 16) 19, U.N. Doc. A/4354; Convention on the Rights of the Child (adopted 20 November 1989, entered into force 2 September 1990) 1577 UNTS 3 (UNCRC); The International Commission of the Red Cross, "The Geneva Conventions of 12 August 1949." www.icrc.org/en/doc/assets/files/publications/icrc-002-0173.pdf [accessed 20 January 2019].

18 *Akayesu* (n 8) 5.

19 *Akayesu* (n 8) ⁋ 509 [emphasis added].

20 "UN DOC A/C.6/SR.82" (n 13) 1496.

21 UNCRC (n 17) 1.

22 Kurt Mundorff. "Other Peoples' Children: A Textual and Contextual Interpretation of the Genocide Convention, Article 2(e)" (2009) 50(1) *Harvard International Law Journal* 61, 90–91.

"encompasses a permanent transfer with the specific intent of destroying the group's existence."[23] He further noted that a duration requirement concurs with the FTC objective to protect the group's biological continuity. Thus, implicit in Werle's interpretation is the proviso that forcible child transfer under the UNGC is dependent on whether or not the (former) child returned and bore children to the group. This proviso suggests that of the five acts enumerated in the UNGC, the FTC is independent of the perpetrators' specific intent (*dolus specialis*). In this, Werle opts for a consequentialist ethic – one that judges the morality of an act by its consequences – rather than the deontological ethic of the UNGC which determines it based on the actor's specific intent. This author argues that considering the malleability and dependency of children as such, a minimum required duration cannot be justified. Furthermore, a duration requirement is highly impractical since determining whether the abducted children returned and bore children to the group involves considerable latency.

The UNGC has two objectives, namely the *prevention of* and *punishment of* genocide. The removal of children from a group during their formative years, even if only for the duration of their childhood, might irrevocably change the child's identity. It might take years to determine whether the forcibly removed child eventually returned to the group and procreated. This not only entails considerable latency in punishment and thwarts prevention, but it is also inconsistent with the UNGC deontological ethical reasoning. Whereas a minimum duration requirement addresses only one tangible aspect of the group's existence – return to the group – it does not address the loss of group identity as a result of the forcible transfer. On these grounds a duration proviso seems unreasonable and is likely to yield absurd consequences.

Two other application-oriented difficulties arise with respect to the FTC. First, the specific intent to destroy the group by forcibly transferring its young was often camouflaged and attempts were made to legitimize the intent by alluding to the perpetrators' benevolent motives. At the Nüremberg International Military Tribunal, Prosecutor Harold Neely argued: "it is no defense for a kidnapper to say he treated his victim well ... This serves to aggravate, not mitigate, the crime."[24] Second, the Akayesu Chamber decided intent can be inferred "either from words or deeds and may be demonstrated by a pattern of purposeful action."[25] This decision was upheld in subsequent case law.[26] Interpreting the FTC, the Akayesu Chamber noted: "[T]he objective is not only to sanction a direct act of forcible physical transfer, but also to sanction acts of

23 Gerhard Werle and Florian Jessberger, *Principles of International Criminal Law* (Third edn, Oxford University Press 2014) 307.
24 International Military Tribunal (n 14) 674.
25 *Akayesu* (n 8) 313.
26 ICTR, *The Prosecutor v. Clément Kayishema and Obed Ruzinanda*, ICTR-95-I-T Ch II, (21 May 1999), 91 (Kayishema and Ruzinanda); ICTR, *The Prosecutor v. Laurent Semanza*, ICTR–97–20–T Ch I, (15 May 2003), ℙ 313 (Semanza).

threats or trauma which would lead to the forcible transfer of children from one group to another."[27]

In outlining the elements of genocide by forcible child transfer and applying the age criterion to determine who is a child, the Preparatory Commission for the ICC charted the elements of genocide via forcible transfers of children:[28]

1. The perpetrator forcibly transferred one or more persons.
2. Such person or persons belonged to a particular national, ethnical, racial or religious group.
3. The perpetrator intended to destroy, in whole or in part, that national, ethnical, racial or religious group, as such.
4. The transfer was from that group to another group.
5. The person or persons were under the age of 18 years.
6. The perpetrator knew, or should have known, that the person or persons were under the age of 18 years.
7. The conduct took place in the context of a manifest pattern of similar conduct directed against that group or was conduct that could itself effect such destruction.

The Preparatory Commission upheld the Akayesu Chamber's position that

> [t]he term 'forcibly' is not restricted to physical force, but may include threat of force or coercion, such as that caused by fear of violence, duress, detention, psychological oppression or abuse of power, against such person or persons or another person, or by taking advantage of a coercive environment.[29]

Children as a protected group

The type of protected groups has been one of the contentious issues surrounding the UNGC. ICTR and ICTY (International Criminal Tribunal for the Former Yugoslavia) case law and is highly instructive regarding our understanding of how to apply the UNGC. The Akayesu Chamber probed whether the list of protected groups is exhaustive, and decided that the groups protected should not be limited to the four enumerated groups. The Chamber held that "*it is particularly important to respect the intention of the drafters of the Genocide Convention, which according to its travaux préparatoires, was patently to ensure the*

27 *Akayesu* (n 8) 509.
28 "Report of the Preparatory Commission for the International Criminal Court Addendum Part II" Finalized draft text of the Elements of Crimes' PCNICC/2000/1/Add.2, (2 November 2000), 7–8 (ICC Preparatory Commission).
29 ICC Preparatory Commission (n 28) 7 fn 5.

protection of any stable and permanent group."[30] This decision was heavily criticized on the grounds that the list was indeed exhaustive and that out of the four groups, three (national, ethnic, and religious) are neither stable nor permanent.[31] Due to the difficulty of fitting diverse victim groups into the types of groups protected by the UNGC, the ICTR in Semanza held that

> the determination of whether a group comes within the sphere of protection … *ought to be assessed on a case-by-case basis by reference to the objective particulars of a given social or historical context, and by the subjective perceptions of the perpetrators.*[32]

While indeed the question of which groups are protected remains unresolved, children as such constitute a clear-cut group. Forcible child transfers target children specifically because of their age-related qualities, such as dependence on adults and malleability, which make them particularly vulnerable to identity destruction. The UN Secretariat Draft Convention acknowledged the key role of children in their group's biological continuity:

> The separation of children from their parents results in forcing upon the former, at an impressionable and receptive age, a culture and mentality different from their parents'. *This process tends to bring about the destruction of the group as a cultural unit in a relatively short time.*
>
> The experts [Henri Donnedieu de Vabres, Vespasian Pella, and Raphael Lemkin] were agreed that this point should be covered by the Convention on genocide, but their agreement did not go further than that.[33]

This consensus by the three international and criminal law experts on the effect of a forcible transfer on children, and its impact on the group's continuity, seems to justify the irregularity of protecting only a sub-group of a protected group. Thus, forcible child transfer was not considered an aggravated circumstance of forcible population transfer, but rather an act of genocide when it is committed with the intent to destroy the group as such.

30 *Akayesu* (n 8) 516 [emphasis added].

31 William A. Schabas, "Groups Protected by the Genocide Convention: Conflicting Interpretations from the International Criminal Tribunal for Rwanda" (2000) 6 *ILSA Journal of International Comparative Law* 382.

32 Semanza (n 26) 317 [emphasis added]; ICTR, *The Prosecutor v. Alfred Musema*, ICTR-96-13-A (27 January 2000) 160–63.

33 E/447 Draft Convention (n 13) 235. This Draft Convention, which is known as the "Secretariat Draft," was prepared upon the instructions of the Economic and Social Council, the Secretary-General, with the assistance of the Division of Human Rights and a group of three experts (Henri Donnedieu de Vabres, Raphael Lemkin, and Vespasian Pella). The experts prepared a Draft Convention that included commentary by the General Secretary and the experts.

The biological impact of forcible child transfers was later emphasized by the US delegate John Maktos, who proposed to include the FTC in the UNGC although it was included in the Secretariat Draft as one of the clauses of cultural genocide. Maktos explained:

> There could be no doubt that a forced transfer of children, committed with the intention of destroying a human group in whole, or at least in part, constituted genocide. The forced transfer of children could be as effective a means of destroying a human group as that of imposing measures intended to prevent births, or inflicting conditions of life likely to cause death.[34]

The US official position as presented by Maktos echoes Lemkin's view that measures to prevent births, forced abortion, forced impregnation, the banning of interracial marriages, and forcible child transfer constitute genocide and fall within Lemkin's definition of genocide. In this definition, genocide is "a coordinated plan of different actions aiming at the destruction of essential foundations of the life of national groups with the aim of annihilating the groups themselves."[35] These practices of biological genocide are aimed at the destruction of the target group's essential foundations and their replacement by those of the perpetrators.[36]

The distinctive qualities of children make them particularly vulnerable to appropriation and their rendering into members of another group. Children conform to the criteria stipulated in *Akayesu* for identifying a group.[37] These are: group membership is not readily challengeable by the members – children cannot deny or renounce their membership; they belong to the group involuntarily, by birth; in a continuous, and often irremediable manner, for as long as they are under 18 years of age. Moreover, the identification of children as group members is determined subjectively by the perpetrators based on the assumption that they inherit their parents' identity and carry it to the future.

The major justification for considering children as such an exclusive protected group is that the protection of children has by now become a peremptory norm of international law, as defined in Article 53 of the Vienna Convention on the

34 United Nations, Economic and Social Council, "UN Doc E/621 Prevention and Punishment of Genocide, Historical Summary, Dated 2 November 1946–20 January 1948," in Abtahi and Webb, *The Genocide Convention* (Vol. 1) (n 13) 1493.

35 Raphael Lemkin, *Axis Rule in Occupied Europe: Laws of Occupation, Analysis of Government, Proposals for Redress* (2nd edn, Lawbook Exchange 2008) 79. For more on Lemkin's notion of genocide, see Amir 2 (n 12) 3–34.

36 Douglas Irvin-Ericson, "Sixty Years of Failing to Prosecute Sexual Crimes: From Raphaël Lemkin at Nuremberg to Lubanga at the International Criminal Court," in Mary Michele Connellan and Christiane Fröhlich (eds), *A Gendered Lens for Genocide Prevention* (Routledge 2018) 89.

37 *Akayesu* (n 8) 516.

Law of Treaties.[38] This norm is both expressed and implied in various international law instruments. Special provisions for the protection of children were created by the League of Nations. These reverberated and complemented the social policies and municipal legislation since the late nineteenth century. The special protected status awarded to children is a part of an individual-based rights approach, awarded irrespective of other identities or group membership of the children.[39] The FTC and the proposed protocol introduced in this chapter provide children with a collective-based right, in order to complement and positively enhance their rights as child members of a group.

The recognition of children as such as a fifth protected group under the UNGC would be commensurable with the special protected status awarded to children. It is needed because historically children of various groups were forcibly transferred to another group with the intent to destroy the group as such. The UNGC grants protection to child members of four groups only, excluding other groups (for example, political, social, socio-economic, gendered). This exclusion leads to consequences which are manifestly absurd, as some transfers are recognized as genocide and others are not, and the type of group and whether or not it constitutes one of the protected groups may be the only significant difference between the cases. The following section applies the physical elements of the crime of genocidal forcible transfers hypothetically to historical cases.

Hypothetical applications of the FTC to historical cases

Hypothetical application of the physical elements of the FTC to the child removal programs of various groups reveals striking similarities across cases and group types, irrespective of the local context and type of group. Forcible child transfers begin with "othering." A group is constructed and problematized, using cultural, biological, ethnic, racial, national, economic, and moral justifications. Quite often, the construction and problematization of a particular group are supported by pseudo-scientific theories. Historically, most forcible child transfers were part of social policies in many states and regulated by special laws.

Child removal policies were undertaken with the proclaimed intent to protect children of particular groups due to some alleged benign or malign impediment of the group. Children became targets of corrective interventions intended to remove them from the purported sources of the problem, mainly their families and groups. Such interventions consisted of destroying the children's particular-

38 United Nations, *Vienna Convention on the Law of Treaties (with annex)*. Concluded at Vienna on 23 May 1969 cl 18,232, 53.

39 See, for example, Protocols I and II Additional to the *Geneva Convention*, the UNGC, UNCRC, and its optional protocol I on child soldiers and the United Nations Convention on the Rights of Children (OPAC 2000), and *Optional Protocol II, on the Sale of Children, Child Prostitution, and Child Pornography*.

collective identity and inculcating them with the perpetrators' ideology. Indigenous people in North America and Australia were categorized and problematized as savages and members of an inferior culture doomed to extinction.[40] Their children's removal was allegedly to save them from the qualities associated with their groups. The removal was authorized by various laws and social policies governing Indigenous people. Children were taken away by force from their families at the age of six years and placed in residential/boarding schools. The children were forbidden to speak their languages or practice their customs or ceremonies, and their circles of kinship were broken.

In Franco's Spain, children of Republicans and other political opposition groups were often arrested together with their mothers, or born in prison, sometimes as a result of rape. The children were taken care of by nuns according to the principles of the FE de las JONS Movement.[41] Francoists believed that the Republicans and all others who opposed the military coup belonged to an inferior race. Psychiatrist Antonio Vallejo Nágera, the director of the Military Psychiatric Services and one of Franco's ideologues, attributed this political difference to an alleged "red" gene responsible for mental pathologies.[42] The removal of the children was to override the effects of this gene. Some children were brought up in orphanages and some were adopted by Franco's supporters – their birth certificates were destroyed and they were given new identities.[43]

In Israel, between 1948 and 1954 children of Yemeni immigrants were separated from their families, sometimes at birth, and taken to childcare institutions and

40 Truth and Reconciliation Commission of Canada, *Honouring the Truth, Reconciling for the Future: Summary of the Final Report of the Truth and Reconciliation Commission of Canada* (TRC Canada 2015); Jeff Benvenuto, Andrew Woolford, and Alexander Hinton Laban, "Introduction" in Jeff Benvenuto, Andrew Woolford, and Alexander Hinton Laban (eds), *Colonial Genocide in Indigenous North America* (Duke University Press 2014) 1; Margaret D. Jacobs, "The Habit of Elimination: Indigenous Child Removal in Settler Colonial Nations in the Twentieth Century" in Woolford, Benvenuto, and Laban Hinton, *Colonial Genocide* 189; Andrew John Woolford, *This Benevolent Experiment: Indigenous Boarding Schools, Genocide, and Redress in Canada and the United States* (University of Nebraska Press 2015); Amir I. (n 12) 41.

41 Ricard Vinyes, "Los Desapariciones Infantiles Durante el Franquismo y sus Consecuencias [The Desparate: Childhood during Francoism and its Consequences]" (2006) 19 *International Journal of Iberian Studies* 53 (Vinyes 1); José Antonio Primo, de Rivera, "Twenty-Six Points Manifesto, November 1934" in (tr), de Rivera, José Antonio Primo (ed), *Selected Writings* (CreateSpace 1934) 132.

42 Antonio Vallejo Nágera, *Eugenesia de la Hispanidad y Regeneración de la Raza* (Editorial española, Burgos 1937) 142 (Vallejo Nágera 1); Antonio Vallejo Nágera, "Psiquismo del Fanatismo Marxista" (1938) 6(1) *Semana Médica Española* 172; Antonio Vallejo Nágera, *Niños y Jóvenes Anormales* (Sociedad de la Educación Atenas, Madrid 1941) (Vallejo Nágera 2); Ricard Vinyes Ribas, "Construyendo a Caín: Diagnosis y Terapia del Disidente: Las Investigaciones Psiquiátricas Militares de Antonio Vallejo Nágera con Presas y Presos Políticos" (2001) 44 *Ayer* 227.

43 Vinyes 1 (n 41).

hospitals due to alleged poor parental practices.[44] Many children who were dispensed to these facilities disappeared. According to state officials most of the children died, although many parents were not notified. Three commissions of inquiry established over the years conceded that there were cases of adoptions without the parents' knowledge or consent. Some of these cases involved identity changes.[45]

Following the Cuban revolution, between December 1960 and October 1962 the United States established Operation Peter Pan in Cuba, which consisted of encouraging the migration of unaccompanied Cuban children to Miami and led to the airlifting of 14,048 children.[46] This child removal program was one of the policies designed to undermine the Cubans' support of Castro and reinstate a regime favourable to the United States' interests. The United States provided visa waivers and provided for the children's stay in institutions and foster care. The propaganda section of the CIA at Quarters Eye disseminated false and vicious rumours about Castro's intention to nationalize Cuban children and denounce parental rights. Yet, it did not intend to destroy the Cuban people.

In these and other cases states used the law and various enforcement organs to discipline the targeted groups.[47] It white-washed this devastating practice under a rhetoric of benevolent motives and the need to correct and redeem children from the destructive influence of their families and groups. In all these cases the transfers resulted in the parents' explicit or implicit loss of custody over the child, and the destruction of the child's identity, and ended effective affiliation with the group from which it was taken.

Table 7.1 presents the cases in terms of time, the victims, and grounds for the transfer. Table 7.2 applies the criteria set by the Preparatory Commission with respect to the elements of the crime. Table 7.3 presents the amenability of the cases to the definition of protected groups.

To recap, most historical forcible child transfers were part of population-engineering policies of states, designed with the objective of, inter alia, dealing with problematized groups. These interventions were presented in progressive terms, mainly to provide these children with "proper" education and values. While these

44 "Report: State Commission of Inquiry in the Matter of the Disappearance of Children of Yemeni Immigrants between 1948–1954; Commission Chairs: Yehuda Cohen; Yaakov Kedmi" Government Printer (Jerusalem, 2001); Boaz Sangero, "Where There Is No Suspicion There Is No Real Investigation: The Report of the Committee of Inquiry into the Disappearance of the Children of Jewish Yemenite Immigrants to Israel in 1948–1954" (2002) 21 *Theory and Criticism* 47; Ruth Amir, *Who Is Afraid of Historical Redress? The Israeli Victim-Perpetrator Dichotomy* (Academic Studies Press 2012).

45 "Report: State Commission of Inquiry" (n 44).

46 Enrique Flores-Galbis, *90 Miles to Havana* (1st edn Roaring Brook Press 2010) 292; Kathlyn Gay, *Leaving Cuba: from Operation Pedro Pan to Elian* (Twenty-First Century Books 2000) 144; Jose G. Perez, "How Washington Uses Emigration as a Weapon against Cuba" in Neville Spencer (ed), *Cuba as Alternative: An Introduction to Cuba's Socialist Revolution* (Resistance Books 2000) 87.

47 For a detailed analysis of the use of law for forcible child transfers in these cases, see Amir 2 (n 12).

Table 7.1 Examples of forcible child transfer cases

Case	*Victim group*	*Subjective type*	*Dominant political doctrine – group's problematization*	*Solution to the "problem" – oppressive state apparatuses*
Australia 1869–1970	Aboriginal people and Torres Strait Islanders	Ethnic/ racial	Uncivilized, savages, Indigenous cultures are inferior and due to be extinct	Civilization, destruction of Indigenous people by breeding out, destruction of Indigenous people's ways of life, communities, and kinship through legislation
Canada 1867–1996	Aboriginal people	Ethnic/ racial	Uncivilized, savages, Indigenous cultures are inferior and due to be extinct	Civilization, destruction of Indigenous people by breeding out, destruction of Indigenous people's ways of life, communities, and kinship through legislation
United States 1860–1978	Indigenous people	Ethnic/ racial	Uncivilized, savages, Indigenous cultures are inferior and due to be extinct	Civilization, destruction of Indigenous people by breeding out, destruction of Indigenous people's ways of life, communities, and kinship through legislation
Spain under Franco 1936–1960	Supporters of the Republic	Racial group, carriers of the "red" gene	Republicans carry the "red" gene, which causes mental pathology. Crooked elements threaten Spain's linearity	Non-judicial killing, imprisonment, legislation
Cuba 1960–1962	National/ political	National/ political	Problematization of Fidel Castro's "communist" regime near US territory. The breaking up of families in order to undermine the Cubans' support of Castro	Use of propaganda and embargo, intended to bring Cubans to near-starvation. Publication of a fake proposed Cuban bill for the nationalization of children. Intended to break up families and social fabric and undermine the Cubans' support of Castro

(*Continued*)

Table 7.1 (Cont.)

Case	*Victim group*	*Subjective type*	*Dominant political doctrine – group's problematization*	*Solution to the "problem" – oppressive state apparatuses*
Israel 1948–1954	Yemeni immigrants, ethnic	Ethnic/ biological	Problematization of the Yemenis' "primitive practices," Arab blood, in need of civilization and assimilation in the Israeli melting pot	Aggressive assimilation, child removal
Democratic Republic of the Congo (DRC) 2002–2003	Ethnic	Ethnic	Defiance of the colonially-constructed ethnic divides	Undermine the national allegiance of the Hema from the DRC to the UPC/ FPLC (Union of Congolese Patriots/ Patriotic Forces for the Liberation of Congo), appropriation of children as sex slaves and child soldiers
Nigeria, Boko Haram 2014–2017	Religious/ ethnic	Religious/ ethnic	Insurgence, establishment of Sharia law, problematization of "infidels"	Appropriating children as soldiers and suicide bombers, enforcing Sharia

interventions carried with them the promise for a better future, in practice they prepared the children for a life of servitude, physical and sometimes sexual abuse, and very basic literacy.[48]

Child soldiers

As previously noted, the recruitment and use of children during armed conflict is one of six grave violations against children identified and condemned by the UN Security

48 Jean Barman, Yvonne Hebert, and Don McCaskill (eds), *Indian Education in Canada* (UBC Press 1986); Amparo Gomez and Antonio Fco Canales, "Children's Education and Mental Health in Spain during and after the Civil War: Psychiatry, Psychology and 'Biological Pedagogy' at the Service of Franco's Regime" (2016) 52(1–2) *Paedagogica Historica* 154; Alice C. Fletcher and United States Office of Education, *Special Report, 1888: Indian Education and Civilization* (Govt. print. off. 1888); Woolford, *This Benevolent Experiment* n 40.

Table 7.2 The physical and mental elements of the crime (Art. 6(e), the Rome Statute)

	Australia	*Canada*	*United States*	*Francoist Spain*	*Cuba*	*Israel*	*DRC*	*Nigeria, Boko Haram*
Number of children	~50,000	~150,000	Over 100,000	~300,000	~10,000	~2,500	~30,000 (in 2003)	~1,500
Forcible transfer? (Physical force, threat, trauma)	+	+	+	+	+	+	+	+
Does the child belong to a group protected under the UNGC?	+	+	+	–	+	+	–	+
Was there a specific intent to destroy?	+	+	+	+	–	–	–	+
Were the children removed from one group to another?	+	+	+	+	+	+	+	+
Persons transferred are under 18 years of age	+	+	+	+	+	+	+	+
The perpetrators knew these persons were under 18 years of age	+	+	+	+	+	+	+	+
Part of a manifest campaign against the group?	+	+	+	+	+	–/+	+	+
Duration of transfer?*	Childhood	Childhood	Childhood	Indefinite	Indefinite	Most indefinite	Until the end of civil war	Until release by the Nigerian Army

* The UNGC, Rome Statute, and case law left open the issue of the duration of the transfer.

Table 7.3 Criteria for protected groups (ICTR–96–4–T *The Prosecutor v Akayesu* §511)

	Australia	*Canada*	*United States*	*Francoist Spain*	*Cuba*	*Israel*	*DRC*	*Nigeria, Boko Haram*
Stable group?	+	+	+	+	+	+	+	+
Group membership unchallengeable by victim?	+	+	+	+	+	+	+	+
Belonging to the group automatically?	+	+	+	+	+	+	+	+
Group membership determined by birth?	+	+	+	+	+	+	+	+
Group membership continuous?	+	+	+	+	+	+	+	+

Council.[49] It is also one of the current forms of forcible child transfer, which might also fall within the boundary of genocide. The UN Secretary-General's 2018 list of shame for the recruitment and use of children includes the armed forces of seven countries (Afghanistan, Myanmar, Somalia, South Sudan, Sudan, Syria, and Yemen).[50] Furthermore, 56 non-state armed groups appear on the 2018 list for the recruitment and use of children (including, among others, the Mai-Mai Nyatura in the DRC, ISIS, Somalia's Al-Shabaab, and the Kachin Independence Army in Myanmar). According to the report, warring parties in 14 countries are guilty of recruiting and using children in conflicts.[51]

Children are conscripted and enlisted in military organizations due to their poor risk assessment and lack of forethought.[52] They are less costly to the organizations than adult recruits and perform various support roles for free. Whereas some children are abducted or forced to join armed groups, becoming a child soldier may seem to some children to be an opportunity to evade a life of poverty and/or ethnic or political persecution.[53]

Ample evidence within clinical and social psychology, as well as public health research, reveals the harms affecting children in war in general and child soldiers

49 Children and armed conflict (n 10).

50 Children and Armed Conflict (n 10).

51 Children and Armed Conflict (n 10) 2.

52 Elisabeth Schauer and Thomas Elbert, "The Psychological Impact of Child Soldiering" in E. Martz (ed.), *Trauma Rehabilitation After War and Conflict* (Springer 2010) 311; Christopher Blattman and Jeannie Annan, "The Consequences of Child Soldiering" (2010) 92 (4) *The Review of Economics and Statistics* 882.

53 Blattman and Annan (n 52).

in particular. Like survivors of forcible child transfers, former child soldiers suffer from post-traumatic stress disorder and other mental harms which tend to be transmitted intergenerationally, such as the severe psychological effects of witnessing or taking part in killing, and the susceptibility to sexual violence and slavery.[54] Whereas the Rome Statute enumerates conscription and enlistment of child soldiers under the age of 15 as a war crime perpetrated by individuals against individuals, it has been argued that under some conditions conscription and enlistment can be considered as genocide.[55] Accordingly, most of the recent literature on child soldiers engages with the harms suffered by children as individuals rather than on the implications on the child's group and society. It is therefore possible, based on the widely researched historical cases, to infer many of the long-term implications on the family, group, and society. Given the incidence of conscription and enlistment in the global south, this impact can be even stronger.

The ICC was criticized for failing to apply the FTC in cases involving the enlistment and conscription of child soldiers, even though they were treated with equal gravity as war crimes. As the United Nations Security Council maintained,

> Preventing violations against children affected by conflict should be a primary concern of the international community. … And yet, as illustrated in the present report, time and again, armed conflict strips away layers of protection afforded by families, society and law and children are victimized as both the targets and the perpetrators of violence.[56]

Hence, the Report acknowledges that children are targeted because of their particular qualities, and alleges that the kidnapping of children by non-state armed organizations "*points to a sustained reliance on children for combat and support duties*."[57]

The Report further acknowledges the targeting of children as *members of a group*. For example, it was found that ISIS abducted children and that "(t)he alleged affiliation of relatives with opposing armed forces or groups was the

54 Cecilia Wainryb, "'And So They Ordered Me to Kill a Person': Conceptualizing the Impacts of Child Soldiering on the Development of Moral Agency" (2011) 54 *Human Development* 273; Child Soldiers International, "How Is Recruiting Children Harmful?" www.child-soldiers.org/how-is-recruiting-children-harmful [accessed 20 January 2019]; Cecilia Wainryb and Patricia K. Kerig, "The Person and the Social Context: Future Directions for Research on the Traumatic Effects of Child Soldiering Around the World" (2013) 22 (8) *Journal of Aggression, Maltreatment & Trauma* 887; Blattman and Annan (n 52); Yael Danieli, *International Handbook of Multigenerational Legacies of Trauma* (Plenum 1998).

55 Sonja Grover, "Child Soldiers as Victims of 'Genocidal Forcible Transfer': Darfur and Syria as Case Examples" (2012) 17 (3) *International Journal of Human Rights* 411; Amir 2 (n 12); Irvin-Ericson, "Sixty Years" (n 36) 83.

56 Children and Armed Conflict (n 10) 3.

57 Children and Armed Conflict (n 10) 2 [emphasis added].

primary reason for abduction."[58] Sonja Grover has criticized the ICC for its failure to address the enlistment and conscription of child soldiers as genocidal forcible child transfers. She has argued that the transfer appropriates children and destroys – often by violence – their loyalties and affiliations and replaces them with allegiance to the perpetrator.[59]

Indeed, the elements of the war crime of enlistment or conscription of child soldiers outlined in Article 8(2)(e)(vii) of the Report of the Preparatory Commission for the ICC share most of the elements of the FTC. The two exceptions are the child's membership in a protected group, and the perpetrator's specific intent to destroy the group in whole or in part. Both crimes are especially designed to target children *as such* and they are transferred from one group to another.

The targeting of children *as such* is clearly evident in the theoretical and empirical realms and is consistent with as well as in the Special Court for Sierra Leone (SCSL) and ICC jurisprudence.[60] Hence, in an *amicus curiae* brief submitted to the Appeals Chamber in the *Sam Hinga Norman* case in response to the fourth "Defence Preliminary Motion Based on the Lack of Jurisdiction" (Child Recruitment),[61] the brief's Statement of Facts maintains that "Children were specifically recruited because rebel and government commanders considered them to be compliant and believed them to be aggressive fighters."[62]

The conscription and enlistment of child soldiers is prohibited and enumerated in the Rome Statute as a war crime. Nonetheless, this prohibition is plagued by the "three-year gap" with respect to the age below which conscription and enlistment are prohibited. Rome Statute Articles 8(b)(xxvi) and 8(e)(vii) pertain respectively to international and non-international armed conflicts and prohibit the conscription and enlistment of children below the age of 15.[63] Article 22(2) of the 1990 African Charter on the Rights and Welfare of the Child provides that "States Parties to the present Charter shall … refrain, in particular, from recruiting any child."[64] Similarly, Article 3(a) of the International Labour Organization Convention Concerning the Prohibition and Immediate Action for the Elimination of the Worst Forms of Child Labour lists "forced or compulsory recruitment of children for use

58 Children and Armed Conflict (n 10) 27.
59 Grover, *Humanity's Children* (n 17).
60 Bernd Beber and Chris Blattman, "The Logic of Child Soldiering," https://chrisblattman.com/documents/research/2011.LogicOfChildSoldiering.pdf [accessed 20 January 2019].
61 *Prosecutor v Sam Hinga Norman* SCSL–2003–08–PT, Amicus Curiae Brief of University of Toronto International Human Rights Clinic and Interested International Human Rights Organizations (31 October 2003) (Amicus Curiae Brief). Sam Hinga Norman died while in custody on 22 February 2007 after the closing arguments and before the verdict.
62 Amicus Curiae Brief (n 61) 5.
63 "Rome Statute of the International Criminal Court" (adopted 17 July 1998, entered into force 1 July 2002) 2187 UNTS 3, Articles 8(b)(xxvi) and 8(e)(vii) (Rome Statute).
64 African Charter of the Rights and Welfare of the Child (adopted on 1 July 1990, entered into force 29 November 1999), Article 22(2).

in armed conflict" as one of the worst forms of child labour.[65] OPAC 2000[66] sets the age threshold at 18, urges non-state actors to avoid recruiting or using children, and requires state parties to take all feasible measures to criminalize such practices.[67] Rome Statute Article 26 excludes the ICC jurisdiction over persons under 18 at the time the alleged crime was committed.[68] Thus, the Rome Statute created a three-year gap in which child soldiers between the ages of 15 and 18 are neither criminally liable nor recognized as victims.[69]

The SCSL was the first international tribunal to try and convict persons for the use of child soldiers (in the AFRC Trial).[70] While the SCSL Statute Article 4(c) prohibits "Conscripting or enlisting children under the age of 15 years *into armed forces or groups or using them to participate actively in hostilities*,"[71] it confers upon the SCSL jurisdiction over people between the ages of 15 and 18. Thus Article 7 states: "The Special Court shall have no jurisdiction over any person who was under the age of 15 at the time of the alleged commission of the crime."[72] Should such persons come before the Court, they "shall be treated with dignity and a sense of worth, taking into account his or her young age *and the desirability of promoting his or her rehabilitation, reintegration into and assumption of a constructive role in society, and in accordance with international human rights standards, in particular the rights of the child*."[73] As in the SCSL, the child soldiers' convictions were apparently examined by the ICC, and as observers within the ICC suggested at the time, these convictions "will have a major impact on upcoming prosecutions at the International Criminal Court."[74]

Apart from the three-year gap, the crime of conscription and enlistment of child soldiers suffers from jurisprudential and evidentiary problems when considered as a war crime. These hurdles are evident in the ICC's first verdict in the matter of Thomas Lubanga Dyilo. On 14 March 2012 Lubanga, a national of the

65 Convention Concerning the Prohibition and Immediate Action for the Elimination of the Worst Forms of Child Labour, (adopted on 17 June 1999, entered into force 19 November 2000), Article 3(A). The Convention may be denounced between 19 November 2020–19 November 2021.

66 The Optional Protocol on the Involvement of Children in Armed Conflict was adopted by the General Assembly on 25 May 2000 and entered into force on 12 February 2002. This is an optional protocol to the UNCRC.

67 As of 2018, 167 out of the 197 UN members have ratified OPAC 2000.

68 Rome Statute (n 56) Article 26.

69 Grover, *Humanity's Children* (n 17).

70 "Agreement between the United Nations and the Government of Sierra Leone on the Establishment of a Special Court for Sierra Leone" (adopted on 16 January 2002); see "Statute of the Special Court for Sierra Leone," pursuant to Security Council resolution 1315 (2000) (adopted on 14 August 2000) (SCSL Statute).

71 SCSL Statute (n 62), Article 4(c) [emphasis added].

72 SCSL Statute (n 62) Article 7 [emphasis added].

73 SCSL Statute (n 62) Article 7.

74 Lisa Clifford, "ICC Examines Child Soldier Convictions," Institute for War and Peace Reporting, 25 June 2007, 118 Africa, Sierra Leone ACR, https://iwpr.net/global-voices/icc-examines-child-soldier-convictions [accessed 20 January 2019].

DRC, was found guilty of conscripting and enlisting child soldiers. Although Lubanga denied he was aware that some of the children conscripted and enlisted to the UPC/FPLC were under 15, he conceded that these children were orphans and argued that they needed protection.[75] The Chamber sided with the prosecution that "the accused agreed with others to gain power in Ituri through the recruitment of 'young persons'."[76] The Office of the Prosecutor (OTP) submitted that "[t]he need for a more substantial army led to increased recruitment of young people – irrespective of their age – by targeting schools and the general public, and through coercive campaigns in the villages."[77] The OTP further alleged that the FPLC recruited children by abduction and exerted pressure on the population during recruitment campaigns.[78]

Evidence suggests that in many cases sexual abuse is intrinsic to the physical act of forcible child transfer.[79] However, as Irvin-Ericson suggested, sexual crimes are often considered as an aspect of organizational anarchy, and are thus cast as "incidental occurrences," which undermines the basis for establishing the defendant's *mens rea* through intent and knowledge.[80] In Lubanga, the prosecution noted that the witnesses "alleged they were beaten, whipped, imprisoned and inadequately fed, and young girls were raped. They were encouraged to drink alcohol and to take drugs, leading to frequent intoxication."[81] The Chamber upheld the OTP argument that "Lubanga either knew that children under 15 years of age were being conscripted or enlisted, or he was at least aware that this was an inevitable consequence of what was occurring."[82] The Chamber in Lubanga held that the protection granted to children

> includes not only protection from violence and fatal or non-fatal injuries during fighting, but also the potentially serious trauma that can accompany recruitment (including separating children from their families, interrupting or disrupting their schooling and exposing them to an environment of violence and fear).[83]

75 *The Prosecutor v. Thomas Lubanga Dyilo*, ICC601/04601/06, Judgment Pursuant to Article 74 of the Statute (14 March 2012), www.icc-cpi.int/iccdocs/doc/doc1379838.pdf [accessed 20 January 2019], ¶ 1277.
76 *Lubanga* (n 74) 22; 38.
77 *Lubanga* (n 74) 26.
78 *Lubanga* (n 74) 30.
79 To name but a few, *TRC Report* (n 40); Australia Human Rights and Equal Opportunity Commission, *Bringing Them Home: Report of the National Inquiry into the Separation of Aboriginal and Torres Strait Islander Children from Their Families* (Human Rights and Equal Opportunity Commission 1997). About sexual violence in Spain see Vinyes 1 (n 41); Ricard Vinyes, Montse Armengou, and Ricard Belis, *Los Niños Perdidos Del Franquismo* [The Forgotten Children of Francoism] (RBA 2005).
80 Irvin-Ericson (n 36) 95.
81 *Lubanga* (n 74) 32.
82 *Lubanga* (n 74) 33.
83 *Lubanga* (n 74) 605.

The Chamber further acknowledged that girls who fell victim to sexual crimes by their commanders or fellow soldiers were stigmatized and found it difficult to reintegrate into their families.[84]

Regrettably, Lubanga's indictment did not include gender-based crimes and sexual violence against children. Thus, Chamber I noted that "many [victims] also alleged they had suffered harm as a result of other crimes, such as sexual violence and torture or other forms of ill treatment, *which are not the subject of charges against the accused.*"[85] Whereas Chamber I engaged quite extensively with this notion, it upheld the Pre-Trial Chamber, which held that "active" is broader than "direct" and also includes "combat-related activities."[86] Yet, the majority of the Trial Chamber did not provide a comprehensive legal definition on what is meant by the "conscripting and enlisting children under the age of 15 and using them *to participate actively* in hostilities," and instead opted for a case-by-case approach.[87] Accordingly, domestic housework performed by many girl soldiers was not considered risky enough to fall within the scope of "active use."

In a dissenting judgement, Judge Odio Benito asserted that excluding sexual violence against children, in the form of sexual slavery and forced marriages of child soldiers,

> would be contrary to the 'object and purpose' of the Rome Statute, contrary to international recognised human rights and discriminatory under Article 21(3), not to define the legal concepts of enlistment, conscription and use to participate actively in the hostilities, independently of the evaluation of the evidence tendered during trial or the scope of the charges brought against the accused.[88]

Because sexual violence was viewed as incidental rather than part of the physical element of conscription and enlistment of child soldiers, or an aggravating factor of Lubanga's crimes, the Appeals Chamber did not find Lubanga liable for reparations in respect of the harm of sexual and gender-based violence.[89]

The ICC *Dominic Ongwen* case highlights the need for prevention, broader protection, and enforcement of the prohibition against the conscription and enlistment of child soldiers. Dominic Ongwen, one of the five leaders of the Lord's Resistance Army (LRA) in Uganda, faces 70 charges, including abductions of children and their use as child soldiers, porters, and sex slaves.[90] On 18 September 2018, Defence Counsel Ayena Odongo noted in his opening

84 *Lubanga* (n 74) 891.
85 *Lubanga* (n 74) 19–20 16 (emphasis added).
86 *Lubanga* (n 74) 283 622.
87 Rome Statute (n 63) § 8(2)(e)(vii).
88 *Lubanga* (n 74) Separate and Dissenting Judgement of Judge Odio Benito 6–8.
89 Irvin-Ericson (n 36) 95ff; *Lubanga ICC-01/04-01/06-3129* (n 74) 77 198.
90 *The Prosecutor v Dominic Ongwen*, ICC-02/04-01/15 (Ongwen).

statement that Ongwen "was just a child when he was abducted, brutalized and made in the bush with no mind of his own." Odongo noted

> the impact on the accused, the spiritualism and mindless brutality on him, the coercive environment bound in torture, [the] spy network woven around him, extreme hunger, the treacherous weather he was made to endure, and the constant reminder that he no longer had parents and a home to return to.[91]

Ongwen was allegedly brutalized and trained in the bush to kill, mutilate, loot, and rape. The defence further argued that

> Children abducted by LRA, the accused inclusive, and used in the war in northern Uganda grew up in one of the most brutal environments, never before known to humanity, with little room for moral development that would enable them to later take independent decisions.[92]

The ICC OTP framed the enlistment and conscription of child soldiers under 15 as war crimes. Indeed, the two distinctive issues of whether the children belong to a protected group and whether the perpetrator acted with the specific intent to destroy the group as such must be established on a case-by-case basis. However, cases such as *Lubanga* and *Ongwen* bear some important implications with respect to the protection of children from forcible transfer. Ongwen's experience as a former victim and current alleged perpetrator suggests that timely interventions are critical for child victims and are conducive to breaking the cycle of violence.

Comparing child soldiers' cases with historical forcible transfers (see Tables 7.1–7.3) points to the similarity of the elements of these crimes. Whereas the proposed recognition of children as such as a protected group draws on hypothetical approaches to historical instances of forcible child transfers, it is important to note the differences between historical and current forcible child transfers. First, historical transfers were practiced by state actors, whereas in current cases both state and non-state actors engage in conscripting and enlisting child soldiers. Nevertheless, UN General Assembly Resolution 60/1 on the Responsibility to Protect and the Optional Protocol to the UNCRC on the involvement of children in armed conflict both establish the responsibility of state parties.[93]

91 *Ongwen* (n 85) Trial Hearing 18 September 2019, 4.
92 *Ongwen* (n 85) 6.
93 "Resolution A/RES/60/1" (Adopted by the UN General Assembly on 16 September 2005); OPAC 2000 (n 39) Articles 4, 6, 7, 8.

Genocidal *mens rea* – the specific intent to destroy the group as such – has yet to be established on a case-by-case basis. Furthermore, it must be proven that the forcible child transfer constitutes part of a wider, general plan to destroy the group or can itself bring about the group's destruction. This may not be the case in Lubanga, but could possibly be established in other cases, such as the Boko Haram kidnappings in Nigeria, the conscription of child soldiers in Sudan, and the destruction of the Yezidis by ISIS.

Conclusions

The spectre of forcible child transfer has taken a malign turn in the form of conscripting and enlisting child soldiers by both state and non-state actors, using the special characteristics of children as such. In view of the recurrent patterns of genocidal forcible child transfers across time and space, the failure to properly address these atrocities as genocide, given that the elements of the crime are established, turns the FTC into a dead letter and undermines the gravity of the crime.

Hypothetical applications of the FTC, as shown in the tables, lead to a result which is manifestly absurd or unreasonable, namely that highly similar cases in terms of the physical and mental elements of the crime have starkly different outcomes, because the UNGC protects children of some groups but not of others from forcible transfer. This makes it increasingly difficult to justify the adherence to the narrow scope of the UNGC with respect to the types of protected groups. This issue cannot be resolved by means of interpretation. Although Article 9 of the Rome Statute allows the ICC some flexibility with respect to the elements of the crimes, this is counterbalanced by Article 22, which explicitly states that "the definition of a crime shall be strictly construed and shall not be extended by analogy."[94]

For nearly two centuries, the protection of children as such has been a consensus issue in municipal and international law. Therefore, this chapter argues for the need to add a protocol to the UNGC to recognize children as such, of any identifiable group of persons, as a fifth protected group.

In addition to expanding the protection granted to children, provisions for prompt action justify the establishment of a Communications Procedure similar to that of the UNCRC Optional Protocol on a Communications Procedure – which entered into force in 2014 – to enable complaints in various forms. A Rapid Inquiry Procedure by an IIIM liaising with the Committee on the Rights of the Child, the ICC OTP and the relevant government is more likely to facilitate timely interventions and interim remedies, such as rehabilitation and humanitarian aid for the victims, than the current procedure of referral to the ICC. Establishing these mechanisms with respect to the conscription and

94 Rome Statute (n 63) Article 9.

recruitment of child soldiers is likely to highlight the gravity of the crime of conscription of child soldiers. However, whether a given case is in violation of the FTC and hence is genocide, or a war crime, will be determined according to the circumstances of each case. The proposed mechanism will hopefully contribute to prevention and early detection and can improve our capacity to deal with violations and contribute to the alleviation of survivors' suffering in a more timely fashion.

8 Interaction between genocide and superior responsibility[1]

Conviction for a special-intent crime without proving special intent?

Michala Chadimová

Introductionm

The treatment of special-intent crimes, such as genocide, is one of the most controversial aspects of superior responsibility. Superior responsibility is often based on omission – the failure to prevent or punish the crimes of subordinates.[2] Thus, for a superior to be held liable under the superior responsibility doctrine, no active conduct on the part of the superior is required. Depending on the circumstances, an omission by a superior in the form of failure to prevent or punish may occur intentionally, although it may also be the result of carelessness.

On the other hand, the crime of genocide refers to specific or special intent: *dolus specialis.*[3] In relationship to genocide, *special intent* means that the perpetrator committed an act while clearly seeking to destroy a particular group, in whole or in part. In applying superior responsibility to the crime of genocide, it is debated whether the superior must himself have had the necessary genocidal intent, or if he must merely have known that his subordinates possessed genocidal intent. In the latter case, a superior could be held liable for genocide committed by his subordinates even if he did not himself have genocidal intent.

This chapter identifies the relationship between the doctrine of superior responsibility and the *mens rea* for genocide. This study will show different approaches demonstrated in the case law of the International Criminal Tribunal for the Former Yugoslavia (ICTY), the International Criminal Tribunal for

1 The present work is an outcome of the project Transitional Justice – Prosecution and Punishment of Crimes of the Past (IGA_PF_2017_016) and International Criminal Responsibility for Special Intent Crimes (IGA_PF_2019_010), supported by the Internal Grant Agency of the Palacky University in Olomouc.

2 As opposed to a superior's responsibility for direct participation in the commission of a crime or ordering the commission of a crime.

3 At the beginning of development of the definition of genocide, no *mens rea* for the crime itself was discussed. However, Lemkin himself anticipated that not only should the principal perpetrators of genocide be held responsible, but also others directly or indirectly involved in its commission. Raphael Lemkin, *Axis Rule in Occupied Europe* (Carnegie Endowment for International Peace, 1944), p. 93.

Rwanda (ICTR) and the Extraordinary Chambers in the Courts of Cambodia (ECCC). First, the author will analyse the case law of the ICTR and point out its rather ambiguous position(s). Subsequently the case law of the ICTY will be discussed. In *Prosecutor v. Stakić* the Trial Chamber (TCH) found that it must be proven that a superior possessed the requisite special intent, whereas the Appeals Chamber (ACH) in the *Brđanin* case found no difficulty in convicting a superior of genocide based on a lower *mens rea*. Lastly, Case 002/02 from the ECCC will be presented as the latest development on the superior responsibility for special-intent crimes.

Furthermore, this work presents the importance of defining the nature of superior responsibility, and shows how a different perception of superior responsibility could resolve the potential legal ambiguity. The author responds to the common criticism of holding a superior responsible for a genocide committed by his subordinates without he himself having had the special intent; i.e. that it weakens the relationship between the principal crime and the superior if the special intent is not required on the part of the superior. The causality requirement will be introduced as a safeguard to the strong connection between the crime committed by subordinates (in this case genocide) and the responsibility of the superior in relation to the crime.

The study answers the question as to whether special intent is required for the superior – a superior who is being held responsible based on his omission/failure to prevent or punish a special-intent crime committed (or about to be committed) by his or her subordinates. This study is especially relevant and applicable in as much as application of the concept of superior responsibility by the International Criminal Court (ICC) has been in a spotlight since the *Bemba* case and also the appearance of the first genocide charges in the *al-Bashir* case. Moreover, superior responsibility in relation to the crime of genocide was recently discussed in Case 002/02 at the ECCC. Superior responsibility and the special intent required in the crime of genocide are well defined by international criminal tribunals and are often the subjects of discussion between academics. However, the unique relationship between superior responsibility and special-intent crimes has not been analysed in a sufficiently comprehensive and complex fashion.[4] Some authors refer to this problem but to a very limited extent.[5] This

4 With some exceptions – see, for example, Patrick Shaun Wood, "Superior responsibility and crimes of specific intent: A disconnect in legal reasoning?" (2013), Univeristy of Pretoria, available online at: https://pdfs.semanticscholar.org/965e/08477a927b76c8a7635d1fa3b7b8d7d0f5f0.pdf; Joshua L. Root, "Some Other Mens Rea? The Nature of Command Responsibility in the Rome Statute" (2013) 23 (119) *Journal of Transnatl. L & Policy*, pp. 119–156.

5 See, for example, William A. Schabas, *Genocide in International Law: The Crimes of Crimes* (Cambridge University Press, 2000), pp. 305 and 312: "Unlike many war crimes, genocide requires the prosecution to establish the highest level of specific intent. But command responsibility is an offence of negligence, and exactly how a specific intent offence can be committed by negligence remains a paradox. [...] [I]t must be wrong in law to consider that genocide

study thus offers a complex analysis of the relationship between superior responsibility and genocide as a special-intent crime, focusing on the concept of superior responsibility and its nature.

Genocide: a special-intent crime

The United Nations (UN) General Assembly first recognized genocide as a crime under international law during its fifty-fifth plenary meeting on 11 December 1946, motivated in large part by Lemkin's lobbying. In its Resolution, genocide was defined as

> a denial of the right of existence of entire human groups, as homicide is the denial of the right to live of individual human beings, such denial of the right of existence shocks the conscience of mankind, results in great losses to humanity in the form of cultural and other contributions represented by these human groups, and is contrary to moral law and to the spirit and aims of the United Nations.[6]

In 1948, genocide was codified as an independent crime in the Convention on the Prevention and Punishment of the Crime of Genocide (Genocide Convention). The crime of genocide is defined in Article II of the Genocide Convention as any of the following acts committed *with intent to destroy, in whole or in part, a national, ethnical, racial or religious group* (emphasis added):

- Killing members of the group;
- Causing serious bodily or mental harm to members of the group;
- Deliberately inflicting on the group conditions of life calculated to bring about its physical destruction in whole or in part;
- Imposing measures intended to prevent births within the group;
- Forcibly transferring children of the group to another group.[7]

Genocide is defined in the Rome Statute of the ICC (Article 6) in the same terms as in the Genocide Convention, as well as in the statutes of other international and hybrid jurisdictions. Article II of the Genocide Convention introduces the special-intent requirement with the wording "with intent to destroy". As such, the crime of genocide has two separate mental elements, namely

may be committed by a commander who is merely negligent." The nexus between superior responsibility and special-intent crimes is also not discussed in the newest contribution on the modes of liability in international criminal law (Miles Jackson, "Command responsibility" in Jereme de Hemptime, Robert Roth, and Elies van Sliedregt (eds.), *Modes of Liability in International Criminal Law*, Cambridge University Press, 2019).

6 UNGA Res 1/96 (11 December 1946) UN Doc A/RES/1/96. This Resolution specifies no *mens rea* requirement.

7 UNGA Res 3/260 (9 December 1948) UN Doc A/RES/3/260, p. 277.

a general one, that could be called "general intent", and an additional special intent embodied in the wording "with the intent to destroy, in whole or in part, a national, ethnical, racial or religious group, as such".[8] A general intent normally relates to all objective elements of a crime (*actus reus*). On the other hand, the "intent to destroy" constitutes an additional subjective requirement that complements the general intent. Two different elements of this special intent can be distinguished. Firstly, it must be shown that the perpetrator wanted to destroy the group as such. Secondly, it must be proven that the perpetrator sought the destruction of the group because of its national, racial, ethnic or religious character.[9]

As the *Akayesu* case was the first case of the ICTR dealing with charges of genocide, it provides a substantial definition of this special intent. The TCH in the *Akayesu* case defined the intent to destroy as "the clear intent to cause the offence"[10] or in other words as the "key element" of an intentional offence which is "characterized by a psychological relationship between the physical result and the mental state of the perpetrator".[11] This special intent is a mental element, and as such it is difficult to determine. In the absence of a confession from the accused, the intent can be inferred from a certain number of presumptions of fact. The TCH found that it is possible to deduce the genocidal intent inherent in a particular act charged from the general context of the perpetration of other culpable acts systematically directed against that same group, whether these acts were committed by the same offender or by others. Other factors, such as the scale of the atrocities committed, their general nature, in a region or a country, or furthermore the fact of deliberately and systematically targeting victims on account of their membership of a particular group, while excluding the members of other groups, can make it possible to infer the genocidal intent of a particular act.[12] The case law of the ICTY further defines the special intent required for the crime of genocide. In the *Mladić* case, the TCH held that the intent may also be inferred from the perpetration of acts which violate, or which the perpetrators themselves consider to violate, the very foundation of a group.[13] The subsequent case law of the ad hoc tribunals further defined the aspect of special intent in relation to the crime of genocide.[14] However, questions remain

8 Otto Triffterer, "Genocide, its particular intent to destroy in whole or in part the group as such" (2001) 14 *Leiden Journal of International Law*, p. 400.

9 Cécile Tournaye, "Genocidal Intent Before the ICTY" (2003) 52 *International and Comparative Law Quarterly* 2 p. 451.

10 Ibid., para. 518.

11 Ibid., para. 518.

12 *Akayesu Case* (Judgment) ICTR-96-4-T (2 September 1998), para. 523.

13 *Mladić Case* (Review of the Indictment) IT-95-5-R61 and IT-95-18-R61 (11 July 1996), para. 94.

14 *Krstić Case* (Judgment) IT-98-33-T (2 August 2001), para. 561, *Jelisić Case* (Judgment) IT-95-10-A (5 July 2001), para. 49. *Tadić Case* (Judgment) IT-94-1-T (7 May 1997), para. 658.

as to the applicability of the requirement of genocidal intent with respect to superiors under the superior responsibility doctrine.

Superior responsibility: general remarks

Superior responsibility is a doctrine of international criminal law addressing the culpability of superiors who fail to prevent or punish international crimes committed by subordinates under their command. This doctrine is remarkable in several aspects, but mainly in criminalizing acts of omission as opposed to ordinary criminal acts involving an affirmative commission. The terms "superior" and "command" have sometimes been used interchangeably as labels for this form of responsibility in international criminal law, but have also sometimes been distinguished in different contexts, in particular to distinguish between a military superior – commander – and a civilian superior. The term "command responsibility" gives a more accurate impression of the origin and purpose of the doctrine, whereas the term "superior responsibility" has become preferred in the last decade because of its neutrality, referring to both civilian and military superiors. Superior responsibility at the ad hoc tribunals, as well as before the ECCC, is understood as de facto superior responsibility and civilian superior responsibility, and the jurisprudence of the tribunals has applied the status of "superior" to those in the military, including paramilitary organizations, as well as civilian organizations. However, Article 28 of the Rome Statute distinguishes between the responsibility of military superiors and other superiors.[15]

Superior responsibility, as developed in the statutes of the ad hoc tribunals, hybrid tribunals and the Rome Statute, has three basic elements. These basic elements are required to establish superior responsibility, and have been clarified by the case law of international criminal tribunals. Although each element differs somewhat between different tribunals, the core of the elements remains the same. A superior may be held criminally responsible for the acts of his subordinates if the following three conditions are met:

1 The existence of a superior–subordinate relationship of effective control between the superior and the alleged principal offender(s);
2 Knowledge of the superior that the crime was about to be, was being, or had been committed; and
3 Failure of the superior to take necessary and reasonable measures to prevent or stop the crime, or to punish the perpetrator(s).

The doctrine of superior responsibility has gained widespread recognition since its application in the *Yamashita* case. In order to deal with the atrocities committed in the former Yugoslavia, the UN Security Council in 1993 created the

15 Unless otherwise specified, the author employs the term "superior responsibility" to denote responsibility attached to all superiors.

ad hoc ICTY. Article 7 of the ICTY Statute deals explicitly with superior responsibility.[16] The elements of superior responsibility were discussed and analysed for the first time by the ICTY, in the *Delalić* case, first by the TCH,[17] and subsequently the findings were confirmed by the ACH.[18] The second ad hoc international criminal tribunal was established in 1994 to deal with the situation in Rwanda, and its Statute also explicitly mentions superior responsibility.[19] The wording for superior responsibility is identical in both statutes. The Statute of the ECCC adopted the wording of the ICTY and ICTR statutes and added an effective control requirement directly into the text.[20]

Negotiations for the establishment of a permanent international court which would be responsible for trying the gravest breaches of international law date back to the 1950s.[21] Nevertheless, the Statute of the ICC was promulgated only in 1998. Superior responsibility can be found under Article 28 of the Statute. This Article sets out the parameters for how the ICC should apply the doctrine of superior responsibility, under which military commanders, persons effectively acting as military commanders, and other superiors are held accountable for the crimes committed by their subordinates. The wording of the ICC

16 "The fact that any of the acts referred to in articles 2 to 5 of the present Statute was committed by a subordinate does not relieve his superior of criminal responsibility if he knew or had reason to know that the subordinate was about to commit such acts or had done so and the superior failed to take the necessary and reasonable measures to prevent such acts or to punish the perpetrators thereof." UNSC, *Statute of the International Criminal Tribunal for the Former Yugoslavia* (adopted 25 May 1993), Resolution 808/1993, 827/1993 and amended by UNSC Resolution 1166/1998, 1329/2000, 114/2002, Art. 7(3).

17 *Delalić Case* (Judgment) IT-96-21-T (16 November 1998), para. 346.

18 Findings confirmed in the *Delalić Case* (Judgment) IT-96-21-A (20 February 2001), paras. 189–198, 225–226, 238–239, 256, 263.

19 "The fact that any of the acts referred to in articles 2 to 4 of the present Statute was committed by a subordinate does not relieve his or her superior of criminal responsibility if he or she knew or had reason to know that the subordinate was about to commit such acts or had done so and the superior failed to take the necessary and reasonable measures to prevent such acts or to punish the perpetrators thereof." UNSC, Statute of the International Criminal Tribunal for Rwanda (adopted 8 November, UNSC), UNSC Resolution 955 (2006) of 8 November 1994 and last amended by Security Council Resolution 1717 (UNSC Resolution 955, 2006) of 13 October 2006, Art. 6(3).

20 "The fact that crimes were committed by a subordinate does not relieve the superior of personal criminal responsibility if the superior had effective superior and control or authority and control over the subordinate, and the superior knew or had reason to know that the subordinate was about to commit such acts or had done so and the superior failed to take the necessary and reasonable measures to prevent such acts or to punish the perpetrators." Law on the Establishment of the Extraordinary Chambers in the Courts of Cambodia for the Prosecution of Crimes Committed During the Period of Democratic Kampuchea (2001) (Cambodia), as amended by NS/RKM/1004/006 (Oct. 27, 2004), Art. 29. The "effective control" requirement had already been established at that time as one of the core requirements of the doctrine by both the ICTY and ICTR case law. See the *Delalić Case*, *supra* note 15, para. 378.

21 Cherif Bassiouni, *International Criminal Law: International Enforcement* (Brill, 2008), pp. 119–120.

Statute differs from the others previously mentioned, mainly in the different *mens rea* requirement for military and for civilian superiors. For a military commander it is required that the accused knew or should have known that the forces were committing or about to commit crimes. On the other hand, for non-military commanders it is required that the accused either knew, or consciously disregarded, information which clearly indicated that subordinates were committing or were about commit illegal acts. This different *mens rea* for civilian superiors requires not only the possession of information regarding the illegal acts, but also that the accused chose not to consider or to act upon it.[22] The last condition for the superior responsibility is the *actus reus* – the superior's failure to act. Under the Rome Statute, it is necessary to prove that the commander failed to fulfil at least one of the duties listed under Article 28. It has to be proven that the commander failed to prevent a crime, failed to repress crimes or failed to submit the matter to the competent authorities for investigation and prosecution.

Unfortunately, Article 28 of the Rome Statute, the statutes of ad hoc and mixed tribunals and Article 86 of Additional Protocol I (AP I) do not provide any express guidance on how to treat special-intent crimes under the concept of superior responsibility.

Case law

International judicial organs in cases involving the superior responsibility doctrine have rendered a significant number of judgments. Nevertheless, a systematic reading of the case law reveals some inconsistencies in the application of the doctrine. The ICTY and ICTR carried out the first significant post-Genocide Convention attempts to punish the perpetrators of genocide, and these tribunals have played a critical role in responding to the crime of genocide. For the first time since Nuremberg, the perpetrators of genocide have been brought before the international community and held accountable for their crimes. Moreover, the ad hoc tribunals have developed a significant body of legal precedent with respect to the crime of genocide, which is now available for future use and application. The latest development is presented in *Case 002/02* rendered by the TCH of the ECCC.

ICTR case law

In the *Akayesu* case, the ICTR had to deal for the very first time with the question of the special intent required for genocide in relation to superior responsibility. Although Akayesu was not convicted in the end under the doctrine of superior responsibility, the TCH made several interesting observations with

22 M. P. W. Brouwers, *The Law of Command Responsibility* (Wolf Legal Publishers, 2012), pp. 8–9.

respect to the doctrine and crime of genocide. The TCH made a distinction between participation in terms of Articles 6(1) and 6(3) of the ICTR Statute, based on the requisite *mens rea*.[23] Article 6(1) governs responsibility for a person who planned, instigated, ordered, committed or otherwise aided and abetted in the planning, preparation or execution of a crime; whereas Article 6(3) applies the doctrine of superior responsibility. In applying Article 6(1) of the Statute, the TCH concluded that the superior "does not need to act knowingly" and it suffices that he had *reason to know* that his subordinates committed the crime (or were about to commit the crime).[24] On the other hand, the TCH held that for conviction under the superior responsibility doctrine set out in Article 6(3), there has to be either "a malicious intent, or the negligence has to be so serious as to be tantamount to acquiescence or even malicious intent".[25] However, the TCH's reasoning is rather confusing. The conclusion of the TCH was reached using the same wording of the Commentary on the Additional Protocols of 8 June 1977 to the Geneva Conventions of 12 August 1949, and Article 86 of AP I,[26] that imposes a responsibility upon the superiors if "they knew, or had information which should have enabled them to conclude in the circumstances at the time". In my opinion, the Commentary on Article 86 of AP I refers to the specification of constructive knowledge (as opposed to the actual knowledge) of the superior. This view is supported by the fact that there was clearly no consensus during the negotiation of the AP on the extent of the term "constructive knowledge". Article 86 of AP I underwent considerable changes during its drafting on the final version. Article 86 of AP I refers to *constructive knowledge* as when a superior "had information which should have enabled them to conclude in the circumstances at the time". This final version was preceded by wording such as "should reasonably have known in the circumstances at the time" or "should have known".[27] In this regard, the Commentary also clarifies that the formulation of constructive knowledge does not mean that it covers all cases of superior's "negligence" but it "must be so serious that it is tantamount to malicious intent".[28] Given the final wording of Article 86(2) of AP I itself and taking account of the circumstance in which the term "malicious intent" is being used in the Commentary, the interpretation of the TCH's conclusions as regards special intent seems to be rather unsupported. Thus, the interpretation of required *mens rea* presented by the TCH in the *Akayesu* case could present limitations on superior responsibility. Moreover, as Akayesu was not convicted for the crime of genocide based on Article 6(3), the conclusion

23 Article 6 of the ICTR Statute encompasses individual criminal responsibility. *Statute of the International Criminal Tribunal for the Former Yugoslavia*, *supra* note 16.

24 *Akayesu Case*, *supra* note 12, para. 479.

25 Ibid., para. 489.

26 Ibid., para. 488.

27 Claude Pilloud (ed.), *Commentary on the Additional Protocols of 8 June 1977 to the Geneva Conventions of 12 August 1949* (ICRC, 1987), p. 1012.

28 Ibid.

behind the first genocide trial at the ICTY remains unclear in a relation to superior's intent.

In the following cases, the *Kayishema* case and the *Musema* case, the application of superior responsibility with respect to the crime of genocide is mixed with direct participation based on Article 6(1).[29] Moreover, the TCH in the *Musema* case refers to the ambiguous findings in the *Akayesu* case.[30] In the cumulative findings, the Court uses argumentation and an evidentiary basis for responsibility under both Article 6(1) and 6(3) of the Statute.[31] For this reason, the findings requiring the special intent are not conclusive and do not serve as a proper argument for requiring a special intent for superior responsibility. The conviction based on both Article 6(1) and also 6(3) of the Statute, while containing evidence providing for a finding of special intent on the part of the accused, cannot be regarded as a requirement of special intent for a conviction for the crime of genocide under the doctrine of superior responsibility.

In the *Ntagerurra et al.* case, in relation to one event, Imanishimwe was found guilty of genocide only on the basis of superior responsibility. The TCH concluded that there was not enough evidence to conclude that Imanishimwe ordered the killing of refugees at the Gashirabwoba football field, but he knew or "should have known" of the killings based on numerous indications, such as the presence of the refugees at the football field, his contact with his subordinate soldiers, and the size of the camp.[32] Nevertheless, the TCH did not explicitly rule on Imanishimwe's state of mind with regard to the killings on the football field. The Chamber limited its findings to his presence on the football field on 11 April 1994 (while the killing occurred on 12 April 1994), his awareness of refugees at the football field, and Imanishimwe's manipulation of the list of refugees and removal of 16 Tutsis and one Hutu from the list. While one could probably infer a genocidal intent based on these factors, the TCH did not explicitly rule on this, and thus it is arguable that a special intent was not required by the TCH in this case.

The change in the ambiguous findings by the Chambers of the ICTR was brought by the *Media* case. In this case, the ACH expressly stated that it is not necessary for the superior to have had the same intent as the perpetrator of the

29 For example, Kayishema was convicted for genocide with cumulative findings on responsibility under Article 6(1) and (3) of the Statute. *Kayishema and Ruzindana Case* (Judgment) ICTR-95-1-T (21 May 1999), paras. 554–596. Musema was convicted for genocide with cumulative findings on responsibility under Article 6(1) and (3) of the Statute. *Musema Case* (Judgment) ICTR-96-13-T (27 January 2000), para. 936.

30 *Musema Case* (Judgment) ICTR-96-13-T (27 January 2000), paras. 130–131.

31 The cumulative convictions under Article 6(1)/7(1) and 6(3)/7(3) were later rejected by the Tribunals. See, for example, *Blaškić Case* (Judgment) IT-95-14-T (3 March 2000), para. 337.

32 The TCH used the "knew or should have known" standard as opposed to "knew or had reason to know" enshrined in Article 6(3) of the ICTR Statute. *Ntagerura Case* (Judgment) ICTR-99-46-T (25 February 2004), paras. 653–657.

criminal act, in the current case direct and public incitement to commit genocide.[33] In the *Bagosora and Nsengiyumva* case, the ACH examined whether the TCH made an error when it did not establish that Nsengiyumva shared his subordinates' intent in relation to the genocide committed by the subordinates.[34] The ACH held that, for a conviction as a superior pursuant to Article 6(3) of the Statute, it is not necessary for an accused to have had the same intent as the perpetrator of the criminal act. The ACH was satisfied if it was proved that the superior knew or had reason to know that the subordinate was about to commit such act or had done so. In this regards, the ACH made a reference to the *Media* case. The ACH concluded that it was not required to establish that Nsengiyumva shared his subordinates' intent to find that he could be held responsible as a superior. As such, the TCH did not err in finding that Nsengiyumva was liable as a superior without considering evidence suggesting that he might not have had such intent.[35]

ICTY case law

Following the ICTR case law, the ICTY entered many convictions on genocide charges. In a relation to nexus between superior responsibility and genocide the most relevant cases are the *Stakić* case, the *Brđanin* case and the *Karadžić* case as those cases draw a line on the genocidal intent requirement for superior responsibility. On the other hand, for example in the *Krstić* case, there is no unambiguous conclusion on the applicability of special intent to superior responsibility. Although Krstić was not held responsible under Article 7(3) of the Statute, the TCH found that he fulfilled the criteria for conviction under superior responsibility for the crime of genocide. However, it stated that it would not enter a conviction under superior responsibility because of the finding of guilt under Article 7(1) of the Statute. While with regard to special intent the TCH found that "his intent to kill the men thus amounts to a genocidal intent to destroy the group in part",[36] it nonetheless also held that the *mens rea* for superior responsibility was proven by evidence showing that he "had to have been aware of the genocidal objectives".[37] This reasoning of the TCH suggests that a specific intent on the part of a superior would not be required for a conviction under Article 7(3) of the Statute.

The *Stakić* case is the first case where the ICTY made a clear conclusion on the applicability of special intent to superior responsibility. In 2002, the TCH considered charges of genocide based on superior responsibility in its Rule 98bis

33 *Media Case* (Judgment) ICTR-99-52 (3 December 2003), para. 865.
34 *Bagosora and Nsengiyumva Case* (Judgment) ICTR-98-41-A (14 December 2011), para. 384.
35 Ibid.
36 *Krstić Case* (Judgment) IT-98-33-T (2 August 2002), para. 652.
37 Ibid., para. 648.

motion of acquittal. The TCH held that it stems from the unique nature of genocide that the *dolus specialis* is required for responsibility under Article 7(3).[38] At the same time, the TCH noted a possible difficulty of proving special intent via acts of omission on the part of civilian leaders. In its judgment the TCH then concluded that it was not proven beyond reasonable doubt that anyone, including any of Stakić's subordinates, had *dolus specialis*, thus Article 7(3) of the Statute was not applicable.[39] Based on this ruling it is not clear whether the superior must himself possess a specific intent and at the same time be aware of the specific intent of his or her subordinates; however, it seems that the TCH required a specific intent on the part of the superior as well as his awareness of the specific intent of his or her subordinates. If the awareness would not be required, the core elements of superior responsibility, with the special nexus between superior and subordinates, would be watered down. The TCH furthermore argued, with regard to joint criminal enterprises (JCEs), that that mode of liability cannot replace a core element of a crime.[40] Moreover, the TCH added that in order to "commit" genocide, the elements of that crime, including *dolus specialis*, must be met. Although this argumentation was used in relation to a JCE, the TCH clearly extended this to superior responsibility.[41]

The TCH in the *Brđanin* case in its decision on motion for acquittal pursuant to Rule 98bis required specific intent for the JCE in its third form (JCE III) but not for superior responsibility in a relation to genocide.[42] Following the appeal against the TCH's decision, the ACH held that a superior does not need to possess special intent, as well as the participant to the JCE III and aider and abettor.[43] The ACH used a comparison to a JCE III and aiding and abetting as the other forms of liability for which a specific intent is not required on the part of the accused. The ACH held that

> the third category of joint criminal enterprise is no different from other forms of criminal liability which do not require proof of intent to commit a crime on the part of an accused before criminal liability can attach. Aiding and abetting, which requires knowledge on the part of the accused and substantial contribution with that knowledge, is but one example. Command responsibility liability, which requires the Prosecution to establish that a Commander knew or had the reason to know of the criminality of subordinates, is another.[44]

38 *Stakić Case* (Decision on Rule 98bis Motion for Judgement of Acquittal) IT-97-24-T (31 October 2002), para. 92.
39 *Stakić Case* (Judgment) IT-97-24-T (31 July 2003), para. 559.
40 Ibid., para. 530.
41 Ibid., para. 559.
42 *Brđanin Case* (Decision on motion for acquittal pursuant to Rule 98 bis) IT-99-36-T (28 November 2003) paras. 30 and 55–57.
43 *Brđanin Case* (Decision on interlocutory appeal) IT-99-36-A (19 March 2004) para. 7.
44 *Brđanin Case* (Decision on interlocutory appeal) IT-99-36-A (19 March 2004) para. 7.

The ACH held that it is critical to distinguish the *mens rea* requirement for the crime of genocide from the mental requirement of the mode of liability by which criminal responsibility is alleged to attach to the accused.[45] Even though the ACH discussed this in relation to the JCE III, the argumentation provided and comparison to superior responsibility suggests that this explanation is clearly applicable to superior responsibility as well. Later on, this conclusion was integrated into the Trial Judgment, which provided further analysis by referring to the previous case law and statutory interpretation of Article 7(3) of the Statute.[46] The TCH referred to the *Ntagerurra et al.* case, stating that "[this] case strongly supports the conclusion that a superior need not possess the specific intent in order to be held liable for genocide pursuant to the doctrine of superior criminal responsibility".[47] However, as analysed above, the *Ntagerurra et al.* case does not in fact provide strong arguments for this conclusion, especially when the findings are compared to the ones in the *Stakić* case.[48] The TCH in the *Brđanin case* explicitly held that the superior must only have known or had reason to know of his or her subordinate's specific intent.[49] The necessity to distinguish between the *mens rea* of subordinates and that of the superior was correctly noted.[50] The TCH stressed that there is no inherent reason why, having verified that it applies to genocide, Article 7(3) should apply to the crime of genocide differently than to any other crime in the Statute.[51]

The findings from the *Brđanin* case were followed in subsequent cases. The special intent was not required in the *Blagojević/Jokić* case with the reference to the *Brđanin* case.[52] The TCH came to the conclusion that:

> the *mens rea* required for superiors to be held responsible for genocide pursuant to Article 7(3) is that superiors knew or had reason to know that their subordinates (1) were about to commit or had committed genocide and (2) that the subordinates possessed the requisite specific intent.[53]

However, from the formulation of TCH it is not clear whether it was only required that the subordinates should have the special intent, or whether it was required that the superior knows about the special intent of his subordinates. However, it is clear that the superior is not required to share such a special intent in order to be responsible on the basis of superior responsibility.

45 Ibid.
46 *Brđanin Case* (Judgment) IT-99-36-T (1 September 2004), para. 720.
47 Ibid., para. 718.
48 Reference made to the Stakić Rule 98bis Decision. *Brđanin Case* (Judgment) IT-99-36-T (1 September 2004), para. 717.
49 Ibid., para. 721.
50 Ibid., para. 720.
51 Ibid.
52 *Blagojević & Jokić Case* (Judgment) IT-02-60-T (17 January 2005), para. 686.
53 Ibid.

In 2016, the TCH found that Karadžić failed in his duty to punish the perpetrators of the killings which occurred prior to the time when he joined the Srebrenica JCE on the evening of 13 July 1995. His genocidal intent was deemed proven based on the events from 13 July 1995 onward, when Karadžić specifically agreed to the killing aspect of the Srebrenica JCE. Thus Karadžić was held responsible under superior responsibility for genocide in relation to crimes committed before he had actually acquired genocidal intent. For the crimes committed after he acquired genocidal intent, he was held responsible under the JCE concept, as his genocidal intent was proven.[54]

ECCC case law

The case law of the ECCC provides the most recent development on the relation between genocide and superior responsibility. In 2018, the TCH in Case 002/02 found Nuon Chea guilty of genocide based on superior responsibility in a relation to the ethnic Cham Muslim minority. The TCH made a clear distinction between *mens rea* requirements for superior responsibility and JCE.

The TCH found that Nuon Chea shared the intent, including the special intent, of the other JCE members to commit the crimes encompassed by the common purpose. However, the TCH expressly stated that it was not possible to identify or infer genocidal intent on the part of Nuon Chea regarding the Cham, nor to find beyond reasonable doubt that he knew that genocide was committed against the Cham.[55] Yet, the evidence supported a finding that Nuon Chea, along with Pol Pot, exercised ultimate decision-making authority to execute the genocidal policy, and convicted him on this charge pursuant to the doctrine of superior responsibility. Thus, Nuon Chea was held responsible for the crime of genocide by killing members of the Cham ethnic and religious group based on his superior responsibility.[56] For the second accused, Khieu Samphan, the TCH concluded that he did not possess the same power within the regime to assist or facilitate the execution of the genocidal policy and declined to convict him for genocide against the Cham.[57]

The TCH also discussed Nuon Chea's state of mind in relation to genocide of Vietnamese. For the crime of genocide by killing members of the Vietnamese ethnic group through a JCE, the TCH required specific intent. The TCH found that Nuon Chea "shared the direct, discriminatory and specific intent of other JCE members" and thus was held responsible for committing genocide the Vietnamese ethnic group through a JCE.[58]

54 *Karadžić Case* (Judgment) IT-95-5/18 (24 March 2016), paras. 5849–5850.

55 *Case 02/002* (Judgment) 002/19-09-2007 (16 November 2018), paras. 4155–4156. See also *Case 02/002* (Summary of the Judgment) 002/19-09-2007 (16 November 2018), para. 50

56 *Case 02/002* (Judgment) 002/19-09-2007 (16 November 2018), para. 4200.

57 Ibid., para 4325

58 Ibid., para, 4161.

The distinction between the mental element's requirement for the JCE and superior responsibility is crucial. It comes with a surprise that the TCH discussed the distinction between Nuon Chea's state of mind in relation to the acts constituting a crime of genocide committed through the JCE and committed by his subordinates. Of even greater surprise is that the TCH came with the determinative demand for the accused's state of mind. The TCH was satisfied with the finding that Nuon Chea at the very least had reason to know that genocide had been, or was about to be, committed against the Cham and thus can be convicted for the crime of genocide based on his superior responsibility even without proving his genocidal intent. The case law of ad hoc tribunals did not provide, with the exception of the *Karadžić* case, the distinction between mental elements for superior and co-perpetrator participating in the JCE. Even though the *Karadžić* case in fact provides factual distinction between the mental elements, the TCH did not expressly state this distinction and did not prove any reasoning. As such, the development in Case 002/02 is a crucial step for applicability of superior responsibility to special-intent crimes. It is regrettable that the TCH did not provide any contextual analysis why the special intent is required on the part of a JCE participant and not required for a superior.

Despite this, the latest development brought by the TCH in Case 002/02 is a plausible step in applicability of superior responsibility to special-intent crimes as not requiring a special intent for the superior and corresponds with the special nature of superior responsibility. It is even more plausible that the TCH made, for the very first, a clear distinction between requirements for mental elements for a superior and for a participant in the JCE.

The nature of the superior responsibility

Irvin-Erickson discusses Lemkin's position on superior responsibility as being two-pronged. Not only can individuals who committed an act be prosecuted individually, but simultaneously the leaders who conducted and orchestrated a series of such acts can be charged for the acts of such individuals. As he further explained:

> Such a position place[s] criminal responsibility with the leaders and elites who set in motion programs of mass atrocities or war crimes, in order to achieve certain ends in a conflict, but who could not be shown to have [directly ordered or caused] each individual act or crime.[59]

This makes it clear that Lemkin had in mind the doctrine of superior responsibility. Unfortunately, Lemkin did not discuss the requisite *mens rea* in a relation

59 Douglas Irvin-Erickson, "Prosecuting Sexual Violence at the Cambodian War Crimes Tribunal: Challenges, Limitations, and Implications" (2018) *Human Rights Quarterly*, p. 576.

to special-intent crimes. Nevertheless, Irvin-Erickson also pointed out in his study on the *Lubanga* case in connection with Lemkin's work that the mental element is often satisfied if it is proven that the defendant "should have known that the crime was going to occur as a result of his or her actions or inactions as a superior in the chain of command".[60] He does, however, make a distinction with regard to sexual crimes, where the ad hoc tribunals have required a superior's direct knowledge of the crime.[61] It may seem that Irvin-Erickson does not find a need to prove special intent on the part of the superior. However, he did not make a distinction between a superior's responsibility in relation to his own participation in the crime (such as a situation when a superior is responsible for aiding and abetting or ordering the crime, etc.) and superior responsibility, which is the subject of this study.

In this chapter I posit that the key point in the question of approaching special-intent crimes through superior responsibility seems to be the nature of superior responsibility itself. At the same time, however, it can be argued that the position of superior responsibility itself is not that clear. When comparing superior responsibility to aiding and abetting, the distinction is made that a superior is being held for his or her own failure(s). This is, however, a conclusion that has not been directly reached by the tribunals. The case law emanating from the aftermath of World War II tends to view superior responsibility as a mode of participation, and the superiors were convicted for their participation in the principal crime committed by their subordinates. This concept was referred to as "acquiescence", and as such, the superiors were held responsible for the crimes committed by subordinates, under the condition that the superiors "had knowledge and had been connected to such criminal acts, either by way of participation or criminal acquiescence".[62] Superior responsibility was understood as a method of participation in the subordinates' crime. In the *Yamashita* case, this responsibility shifted towards forms of strict liability.[63] In either case, the superior was charged and convicted for the principal crime.[64]

60 Ibid., p. 577.

61 Douglas Irvin-Erickson, "Sixty years of failing to prosecute sexual crimes: From Raphael Lemkin at Nuremberg to Lubanga at the International Criminal Court" in Mary Michele Connellan and Christiane Frohlich (eds.), *A Gendered Lens for Genocide Prevention* (Palgrave 2018), pp. 86–87. Similarly, Irvin-Erickson, "Prosecuting Sexual Violence", p. 577.

62 Nuremberg trial of *U.S. v. Wilhelm von Leeb* (the High Command trial), *Trials of War Criminals before the Nuremberg Military Tribunals under Control Council Law No. 10*, Vol. XI (Buffalo: Hein, 1997), p. 555. See also *U.S. v. Wilhelm von List* (the Hostage trial), *Trials of War Criminals before the Nuremberg Military Tribunals under Control Council Law No. 10*, Vol. X, pp. 215–218.

63 United Nations War Crimes Commission, *Law Reports of Trials of War Criminals* (HMSO, 1947), Volume III, pp. 18–22. Maria Prévost, "Race and War Crimes: The 1945 War Crimes Trial of General Tomoyuki Yamashita" (1992) 14(3) *Human Rights Quarterly*, p. 330.

64 Chantal Meloni, "Command Responsibility: Mode of Liability for the Crimes of Subordinates or Separate Offence of the Superior" (2007) *Journal of International Criminal Justice*, p. 623.

Article 86(2) of AP I, as well as the statutes of ad hoc tribunals, are silent as to the nature of superior responsibility. Article 28 of the Rome Statute raises more questions than it answers with respect to the nature of the doctrine.

The ad hoc tribunals' approach

The early case law from the ICTY indicates that superiors were in fact held responsible for the principal crime. This approach has also been given support by the Secretary-General's report relating to the ICTY Statute, which described superior responsibility as "imputed responsibility".[65] In the *Čelebići* case, the TCH held that "[t]he type of individual criminal responsibility for the illegal acts of subordinates ... is commonly referred to as 'command responsibility'".[66] The TCH continued that the fact "[t]hat military commanders and other persons occupying positions of superior authority may be held criminally responsible for the unlawful conduct of their subordinates is a well-established norm of customary and conventional international law".[67] The TCH cited the Secretary-General's report in support of its conclusion. The ACH in the *Čelebići* case also held that where a superior has effective control over his subordinates "he could be held responsible for the commission of the crimes if he failed to exercise such abilities of control".[68] In the *Aleksovski* case, the TCH discussed the distinction between responsibility under Article 7(1) and Article 7(3) of the ICTY Statute. The TCH concluded that "[T]he doctrine of superior responsibility makes a superior responsible not for his acts sanctioned by Article 7(1) of the Statute but for his failure to act." However, it still found that a superior could be "held responsible for the acts of his subordinates" if he did not prevent the perpetration of the crimes of his subordinates or punish them for the crimes.[69]

A turning point can be seen in conclusion of the TCH in the *Halilović* case. In that case the TCH first acknowledged that up to that time the superior had consistently been "responsible for the crimes of his subordinates".[70] However, the TCH reached a different conclusion and held that the superior is "merely responsible for his neglect of duty".[71] The TCH clarified that "a commander is not responsible as though he had committed the crime himself".[72] This was

65 UNSC, Report of the Secretary-General Pursuant to Paragraph 2 of Security Council Resolution 808 (1993) [contains text of the Statute of the International Tribunal for the Prosecution of Persons Responsible for Serious Violations of International Humanitarian Law Committed in the Territory of the Former Yugoslavia since 1991], UNSC S/25,704, 3 May 1993.
66 *Delalić Case*, *supra* note 15, para. 331.
67 Ibid., para. 333.
68 *Delalić Case*, *supra* note 16, para. 198.
69 *Aleksovski Case* (Judgment) IT-95-14/1-T (25 June 1999), para. 67.
70 *Halilović Case* (Judgment) IT-01-48-T (16 November 2005), para. 53
71 Ibid., para. 293.
72 Ibid., para. 54.

followed in the subsequent ICTY case law. In the *Hadžihasanović* case, the TCH followed the findings made in the *Halilović* case, emphasising that superior responsibility "is the corollary of a commander's obligation to act". As such, the TCH argued that superior responsibility is a responsibility for the omission/failure to prevent or punish crimes committed by subordinates, and that the "responsibility is *sui generis* distinct from that defined in Article 7(1) of the Statute".[73]

Another analysis concerning the nature of superior responsibility was provided in the *Orić* case. The TCH in the *Orić* case pointed out that finding a commander

> responsible 'for the acts of his subordinates' [...] does not mean, however, that the superior shares the same responsibility as the subordinate who commits the crime [...], but that the superior bears responsibility for his own omission in failing to act. In this sense, the superior cannot be considered as if he had committed the crime himself, but merely for his neglect of duty.[74]

This is the distinctive element in responsibility under Article 7(1) of the ICTY Statute, and the TCH went on to call superior responsibility under Article 7(3) of the ICTY Statute a responsibility *sui generis.*

The Rome Statute

According to the wording of Article 28 of the Rome Statute, a superior "shall be criminally responsible for crimes within the jurisdiction of the Court" committed by his subordinates "as a result" of his "failure to exercise control properly". From a literal interpretation of this provision it follows that the superior is responsible for the principal crime committed by his subordinates.[75] However, the introductory sentence of Article 28 providing for superior responsibility states that "*[i]n addition to other grounds of criminal responsibility* under this Statute for crimes within the jurisdiction of the Court: (a) A military commander [...]" (emphasis added). This sentence is sometimes interpreted so that it "does not substitute, but supplements all forms of participation as listed in Article 25(3) sub a-f. Article 28 thus extends the scope of individual criminal responsibility for perpetrators in the position of superiors".[76]

73 *Hadžihasanović Case* (Judgment) IT-01-47-T (15 March 2006), para. 75.
74 *Orić Case* (Judgment) IT-03-68-T (30 June 2006), para. 293.
75 Meloni, *supra* note 64, p. 633.
76 Otto Triffterer, "Causality, a Separate Element of the Doctrine of Superior Responsibility as Expressed in Art. 28 Rome Statute" (2002) 15(1) *Leiden Journal of International Law*, pp. 179–186.

The language used in Article 28 seems quite ambiguous. Some consider that what the Rome Statute adopts is a "concept of superior responsibility as a form of liability for omission".[77] It is nevertheless often argued that the literal interpretation of Article 28 indicates that superior responsibility is rather meant to be kind of imputed liability for the base crime resulting from a superior's omission.[78] In the *Bemba* case, the Pre-Trial Chamber (PTCH) concluded that "a superior may be held responsible for prohibited conduct of his subordinates for failing to fulfil his duty".[79] However, the PTCH went on to add that superior responsibility can be better understood "when seen against the principle that criminal responsibility for omissions is incurred only where there exists a legal obligation to act".[80] Later, the TCH expressly stated that "Article 28 provides for a mode of liability, through which superiors may be held criminally responsible for crimes within the jurisdiction of the Court committed by his or her subordinates."[81] The TCH noted the importance of distinguishing the responsibility of a commander under Article 28 and a responsibility of a person who "commits" a crime within the jurisdiction of the Court.[82]

Sui generis omission and the requirement of causality

The nature of superior responsibility has been subjected to many diverse academic discussions. Mettraux argues that a superior is not held responsible for the crimes of subordinates, but is responsible in respect to crimes committed by subordinates based on his own failure to act.[83] Root argues that superior responsibility as enshrined in Article 28 of the Rome Statute should be interpreted as a distinct crime. However, treating superior responsibility as a distinct crime does not seem to be supported by the case law nor consistent with customary international law. In Root's opinion, treating superior responsibility as a mode of liability would "muddy" the heightened *mens rea* of specific intent crimes, or even cause that superior responsibility to not be applied to specific intent crimes.[84] However, I do not agree that treating superior responsibility as a mode of liability would automatically deprive it of being used to establish responsibility for special-intent crimes, as a distinction has to be made between

77 Micaela Frulli, "Exploring the applicability of command responsibility to private military contractors" (2010) 15(3) *Journal of Conflict & Security Law*, p. 452.
78 Barrie Sander, "Unraveling the Confusion Concerning Successor Superior Responsibility in the ICTY Jurisprudence" (2010) 23(1) *Leiden Journal of International Law*, p. 132.
79 *Bemba Case* (Decision Pursuant to Article 61(7)(a) and (b) of the Rome Statute) ICC-01/05-01/08-424 (15 June 2009), para. 405.
80 *Ibid.*
81 *Bemba Case* (Judgment) ICC-01/05-01/08-3343 (21 March 2016), para. 171.
82 Ibid., para. 173.
83 Guénaël Mettraux, *The Law of Command Responsibility* (Oxford University Press, 2009), pp. 37–95.
84 Root, supra note 4, p. 155

the requisite *mens rea* for superiors and that for subordinates. The prevailing academic opinion is that superior responsibility is a *sui generis* form of culpable omission which has no equivalence to any other form of criminal responsibility in either domestic or international criminal law.[85] My suggestion is to treat superior responsibility as a *sui generis* form of responsibility for omission with respect to subordinates' crimes, which would not require a special intent on the part of the superior, but knowledge by the superior about the subordinates' special intentions with regard to special-intent crimes. Nonetheless, some authors argue that there would be too little connection between the conduct of the superior and the conduct of subordinates if the relationship would be limited to the superior's knowledge of his subordinates' intentions.[86] This, however, is where the causality requirement should come into play. The requirement that the conduct of a person charged with a crime must be causally linked to the crime itself is a general and fundamental requirement of criminal law in most national systems.[87] Inasmuch as it is generally accepted that the requirement for justifying criminal punishment by the ICC is higher than for justifying punishment within domestic legal systems, it seems plausible that this principle must apply at the international level as well.[88]

ICTY jurisprudence on the causality requirement

The first ICTY case where the requirement of causality was discussed is the *Delalić* case. Although the TCH arguably opened a door for application of the causality requirement in the "duty to prevent", some authors and subsequent ICTY case law have interpreted the TCH's findings as a denial that the causality requirement covers both types of duties: the duty to punish and the duty to prevent.[89] The TCH pointed out that a superior cannot be held responsible for prior violations committed by subordinates if a causal nexus would be required between such violations and the superior's failure to punish those who committed them.[90] The TCH held that a causal connection cannot possibly exist between an offence committed by a subordinate and the subsequent failure of a superior to punish the perpetrator for that same offence.[91] The Chamber's

85 Kai Ambos, *Treatise on International Criminal Law. Volume I: Foundations and General Part* (Oxford University Press, 2013), pp. 189–197; Meloni, *supra* note 64, pp. 191–207; Mettraux, *supra* note 83, pp. 37–95.

86 For example, Mettraux, *supra* note 83, p. 56.

87 Andrew Ashworth and Jeremy Horder, *Principles of Criminal Law* (Oxford University Press, 2009), p. 124.

88 This is reflected in Article 5 of the Rome Statute, which restricts the Court's mandate to the most serious crimes of concern to the international community as a whole.

89 Erasmus Mayr, "International Criminal Law, Causation and Responsibility" (2014) 14(4/5) *International Criminal Law Review*, p. 863.

90 *Delalić Case*, *supra* note 17, para. 400.

91 Ibid.

main argument was that failure to punish cannot causally influence a crime which has already been committed.[92] In a strict sense this is true, but this view taken by the TCH does not take into account the idea of preventing the commission of future crimes through punishing previous offences. Furthermore, the TCH explained that while a causal connection between the failure of a commander to punish past crimes committed by subordinates and the commission of any such future crimes is not only possible but likely, no such causal link can possibly exist between an offence committed by a subordinate and the subsequent failure of a superior to punish the perpetrator for that same offence.[93] On the other hand, the TCH held that "a necessary causal nexus may be considered to be inherent in the requirement of crimes committed by subordinates and the superiors' failure to take the measures within his power to prevent them".[94] This conclusion reached by the TCH could be seen as an open the door for the application of a causality requirement in the duty to prevent. However, in the same judgment the Chamber stated that it had found no support for the existence of a requirement of proof of causation as a separate element of superior responsibility, and therefore concluded that "causation has not traditionally been postulated as *a condition sine que non* for the imposition a responsibility on superiors for their failure to prevent or punish offences committed by their subordinates".[95] The TCH went on to add, without offering any support for its proposition, that customary international law did not require proof of a causal relationship between the conduct of the accused and the crimes of his subordinates.[96] Controversially, this is regarded by some authors as a rejection of the causality requirement in both types of omission: failure to prevent as well as failure to punish.[97]

The TCH in the *Blaškić* case held that a causal link might be considered inherent in the requirement that the superior failed to prevent the subordinates' crimes.[98] However, the ACH disagreed and found that "the existence of causality between a commander's failure to prevent subordinates' crimes and the occurrence of these crimes is not an element of command responsibility that requires proof by the Prosecution in all circumstances of a case".[99] Even though there is no direct provision on whether the judgment of the ACH is binding, in

92 Mayr, *supra* note 89, p. 863.

93 *Delalić Case*, *supra* note 17, para. 400.

94 Ibid., para. 399.

95 Ibid., para. 398. Cited again in *Kordić & Čerkez Case* (Judgment) IT-95-14/2-A (17. 12. 200), para. 447.

96 The ACH in the Blaškić case noted that the Delalić TCH's finding on that point did not cite any authority for the statement. *Blaškić Case* (Judgment) IT-95-14-A (29 July 2004), para. 76.

97 Christine Bishai, "Superior Responsibility, Inferior Sentencing: Sentencing Practice at the International Criminal Tribunals" (2013) 11 (3) *Journal of International Human Rights*, p. 85.

98 *Blaškić Case*, *supra* note 31, para. 339.

99 *Blaškić Case*, *supra* note 96, para. 77.

the *Aleksovski* case the ACH came to the conclusion that the construction of the Statute requires that the decision of the ACH is binding on the TCH.[100] This means that the conclusion made by the ACH in the *Blaškić* case is binding on all trial chambers. Acknowledging the findings of the ACH in *Blaškić* case, the ACH in the *Kordić & Čerkez* case held that existence of causality between a commander's failure to prevent subordinates' crimes does not have to be proven.[101]

Despite acknowledging the position of the ACH in *Blaškić* case, the TCH in the *Hadžihasanović* case came as close to reintroducing the requirement of causality as the binding jurisprudence of the ACH would allow. The TCH went so far as to state that a causality requirement is necessary to hold a commander responsible as "command responsibility may be imposed only when there is a relevant and significant nexus between the crime and the responsibility of the superior accused of having failed in his duty to prevent".[102]

The ICC's approach

Article 28 of the Rome Statute stipulates that crimes committed by subordinates are a result of the superior's failure to exercise proper control over them.[103] The PTCH II and the TCH III in the *Bemba* case concluded that the causality requirement has to be established between a superior's failure to prevent and the crime. While the PTCH II considered it sufficient to prove that the commander's omission "increased the risk of the commission of the crimes", the TCH III did not elaborate further on the requisite standard. The TCH only held that the causality requirement would be clearly satisfied "when the crimes would not have been committed, in the circumstances in which they were, had the commander exercised control properly, or the commander exercising control properly would have prevented the crimes".[104] The Chamber stressed that this standard is "higher than that required by law".[105] This may suggest that although the Chamber used the "but for test", the "increased risk test" suffices to establish the causality requirement between superior's failure to prevent and the crime.

The causality requirement in the *Bemba* case led to a disagreement among the judges. Two of the three judges issued separate opinions, in which they presented different views on this topic. Judge Steiner expressed her belief that the TCH failed to provide sufficient reasoning in its consideration on the interpretation of the wording "as a result of" and the causality requirement. Judge

100 *Aleksovski Case* (Judgment) IT-95-14/1-A (24 March 2000), paras. 112–113.
101 *Kordić & Čerkez Case* (Judgment) IT-95-14/2-A (17 December 2004), para. 832.
102 *Hadžihasanović & Case, supra* note 73, para. 192.
103 Bert Swart, *The Legacy of the ICTY* (Oxford University Press, 2011), p. 392.
104 *Bemba Case, supra* note 81, para. 213.
105 Ibid., § 213.

Steiner held that a causal link between the commander's failure to exercise control properly and the crimes is required, referring to the analysis of the decision of the PTCH II in the *Bemba* case.[106] Furthermore, she agreed with the conclusion of the PTCH II that "it is only necessary to prove that the commander's omission increased the risk of the commission of the crimes charged in order to hold him criminally responsible under article 28(a) of the Statute".[107] However, she noted that this increased risk test should be applied with a high probability assessment, so that "there is a high probability that, had the commander discharged his duties, the crime would have been prevented or it would have not been committed by the forces in the manner it was committed".[108] Judge Ozaki concluded that a nexus between the commander's failure to exercise control properly and the commission of the crimes is required.[109] He supported this conclusion based on the object and purpose of the Statute. Furthermore, he went on to clarify that the wording of "as a result of" indicates that "the standard adopted [is] more than a merely theoretical nexus to the crimes".[110] Judge Ozaki also favoured an assessment of whether the results were "reasonably foreseeable".[111] The causality requirement was part of the defence appeal.[112] However, the ACH did not address this issue in the Appeal Judgment.[113]

The causality requirement for superior responsibility was also briefly mentioned in the *Ntaganda* case. In its decision on confirmation of charges, the PTCH II held that "[t]he [...] failures of Mr. Ntaganda increased the risk of the commission of crimes by UPC/FPLC members during the time-frame relevant to the charges".[114] However, it is not clear whether this means that the PTCH II requires the causality nexus, in form of the "increased risk test", for the establishment of superior responsibility. The TCH held Ntaganda responsible as a direct perpetrator and indirect perpetrator, omitting findings on his responsibility as a commander under Article 28 of the Statute.[115]

106 *Bemba Case* (Separate Opinion of Judge Sylvia Steiner) ICC-01/05-01/08-3343 (8 June 2018), para. 17.
107 Ibid., para. 23.
108 Ibid., para. 24.
109 *Bemba Case* (Separate Opinion of Judge Kuniko) ICC-01/05-01/08-3343 (8 June 2018), para. 9.
110 Ibid., para. 23.
111 Ibid.
112 *Bemba Case* (Public Redacted Version of Appellant's document in support of the appeal, ICC-01/05-01/0) 38 September 2016, paras. 138–140.
113 *Bemba Case* (Judgment) ICC-01/05-01/08-3636 (8 June 2019), paras. 44–66. *Bemba Case* (Public Redacted Version of Appellant's document in support of the appeal) ICC-01/05-01/03(8 September 2016), paras. 138–140.
114 *Ntaganda Case* (Decision Pursuant to Article 61(7)(a) and (b) of the Rome Statute on the Charges of the Prosecutor Against Bosco Ntaganda) ICC, ICC-01/04-02/06 (9 July 2014), para. 174.
115 *Ntaganda Case* (Judgment) ICC-01/04-02/06 (8 July 2019). See also *Ntaganda Case* (Public redacted version of "Prosecution's Closing Brief") ICC-01/04-02/06 (7 November 2018), paras. 389–413.

Conclusions

The main purpose of this study has been to analyse the *mens rea* requirement for a superior in relation to the crime of genocide committed by subordinates, and determine whether the superior must himself have had genocidal intent. The ICTR and ICTY case law contains multiple convictions of a superior based on Article 6(3)/Article 7(3) of the Statute on the crime of genocide. The early case law suggests (the *Akayesu* case) or openly advocates for (the *Stakić* case) requiring a special intent on a part of the superior in order to be held responsible under the superior responsibility doctrine. However, those findings were disputed by the subsequent cases where the superior's special intent was not regarded as a legal requirement for superior responsibility. It can be argued that in the case law development, the ACH in the *Brđanin* case put forward a precedent that has been followed ever since. In 2018, the TCH in Case 002/02 (ECCC) also held that a superior need not possess specific intent. However, it has never been properly explained why the superior need not possess specific intent. This is clearly not a rhetorical question given the ambiguous findings at the ad hoc tribunals. I agree with the recent case law that does not require a special intent on a part of a superior if he is being held responsible under the superior responsibility doctrine. However, this conclusion deserves more deep analysis and explanation than just referral to a distinction that must be made between *mens rea* for the crime of genocide and the mental requirement of the mode of liability. This argument is correct; however, I believe this needs to be looked at more closely. I suggest that the key issue in the question of treating special-intent crimes within superior responsibility seems to be the nature of superior responsibility itself. The early ICTY case law treated superior responsibility as an imputed liability, holding superiors criminally responsible for the unlawful conduct of their subordinates. This approach was abandoned by the *Haliliović* case, as it was correctly stated that the stronger responsibility is in an omission to prevent or punish crimes committed by subordinates. The language used in Article 28 of the Rome Statute seems quite ambiguous. However, in the *Bemba* case the TCH came to the conclusion that superior responsibility is a mode of liability through which superiors may be held criminally responsible for crimes committed by subordinates. The proposed solution in this work is to treat superior responsibility as a *sui generis* form of culpable omission which has no equivalence with any other criminal responsibility in either domestic or international criminal law. My suggestion is to further treat superior responsibility as a *sui generis* responsibility for omission with respect to subordinates' crimes, which would not require special intent on part of the superior, but knowledge by the superior about subordinates' intentions – i.e. a superior's knowledge about his subordinates' special intent in relation to special-intent crimes.

Furthermore, I do not agree that there would be too little connection between the conduct of the superior and the conduct of subordinates if the relationship would be limited to the superior's knowledge of his subordinates' intentions. This connection should be safeguarded by the requirement of causality: causality between the conduct of the superior and the crimes committed by the subordinates. Causality should be required between the failure of the accused and the commission of crimes by subordinates (with regard to his duty to prevent the crimes), and between his failure and the resulting impunity of the perpetrators (in regard to his duty to punish the crimes). Although the existence of a causality requirement has not found support in the case law of the ad hoc tribunals, the wording of the Rome Statute and the *Bemba* case strongly support the existence of such a requirement in relation to superior responsibility.

Cases

Akayesu Case (Judgment) ICTR-96-4-T (2 September 1998).

Aleksovski Case (Judgment) IT-95-14/1-T (25 June 1999).

Bemba Case (Decision Pursuant to Article 61(7)(a) and (b) of the Rome Statute) ICC-01/05-01/08-424 (15 June 2009).

Bemba Case (Judgment) ICC-01/05-01/08-3343 (21 March 2016).

Blaškić Case (Judgment) IT-95-14 (29 July 2004).

Blaškić Case (Judgment) IT-95-14-T (3 March 2000).

Brđanin Case (Decision on interlocutory appeal – Rule 98bis Appeal Decision) IT-99-36-A (19 March 2004).

Brđanin Case (Judgment) IT-99-36-T (1 September 2004).

Delalić Case (Judgment) IT-96-21-A (20 February 2001)

Delalić Case (Judgment) IT-96-21-T (16 November 1998).

Hadžihasanović Case (Judgment) IT-01-47-T (15 March 2006).

Halilović Case (Judgment) IT-01-48-T (16 November 2005).

Jelisić Case (Judgment) IT-95-10-A (5 July 2001).

Karadžić Case (Judgment) IT-95-5/18 (24 March 2016).

Kordić & Čerkez Case (Judgment) IT-95-14/2-A (17 December 2004).

Krstić Case (Judgment) IT-98-33-T (2 August 2001).

Krstić Case (Judgment) IT-98-33-T (2 August 2002).

Media Case (Judgment) ICTR-99-51-T (28 November 2007).

Mladić Case (Review of the Indictment) IT-95-5-R61 and IT-95-18-R61 (11 July 1996).

Musema Case (Judgment) ICTR-96-13-A (16 November 2001).

Ntagerura Case (Judgment) ICTR-99-46-T (25 February 2004).

Orić Case (Judgment) IT-03-68-T (30 June 2006).

Stakić Case (Decision on Rule 98bis Motion for Judgment of Acquittal) IT-97-24-T (31 October 2002).

Stakić Case (Judgment) IT-97-24-T (31 July 2003).

Tadić Case (Judgment) IT-94-1-T (7 May 1997).

U.S. v. Wilhelm von Leeb (the High Command trial), *Trials of War Criminals before the Nuremberg Military Tribunals under Control Council Law No. 10*, Vol. XI (Buffalo: Hein, 1997), 512–543.

U.S. v. Wilhelm von List (the Hostage trial), *Trials of War Criminals before the Nuremberg Military Tribunals under Control Council Law No. 10*, Vols X and XI, 1271.

Bibliography

Ashworth, Andrew, and Jeremy Horder, *Principles of Criminal Law* (Oxford University Press, 2009).

Bassiouni, Cherif, *International Criminal Law: International Enforcement* (Brill, 2008).

Bishai, Christine, "Superior Responsibility, Inferior Sentencing: Sentencing Practice at the International Criminal Tribunals" (2013) 11 (3) *Journal of International Human Rights*, 83–108.

Brouwers, M. P. W., *The Law of Command Responsibility* (Wolf Legal Publishers, 2012).

Cécile, Tournaye, "Genocidal Intent Before the ICTY" (2003) 52 *International and Comparative Law Quarterly* 2.

Damaska, Mirjan, "The Shadow Side of Command Responsibility" (2001) 49 (455) *American Journal of Comparative Law*, 455–496.

Frulli, Michaela, "Exploring the Applicability of Command Responsibility to Private Military Contractors" (2010) 15 (3) *Journal of Conflict & Security Law*, 435–466.

Irvin-Erickson, Douglas, "Prosecuting Sexual Violence at the Cambodian War Crimes Tribunal: Challenges, Limitations, and Implications" (2018) *Human Rights Quarterly*, 570–590.

Irvin-Erickson, Douglas, "Sixty Years of Failing to Prosecute Sexual Crimes: From Raphael Lemkin at Nuremberg to Lubanga at the International Criminal Court" in Mary Michele Connellan and Christiane Frohlich (eds.), *A Gendered Lens for Genocide Prevention* (Palgrave 2018), 83–109.

Jackson, Miles, 'Command responsibility' in Hemptime, Jereme de, Roth, Robert; Sliedregt, Elies van (eds), *Modes of liability in International Criminal Law* (Cambridge Univeristy Press, 2019).

Law on the Establishment of the Extraordinary Chambers in the Courts of Cambodia for the Prosecution of Crimes Committed During the Period of Democratic Kampuchea (2001) (Cambodia), as amended by NS/RKM/1004/006 (Oct. 27, 2004).

Lemkin, Raphael, *Axis Rule in Occupied Europe* (Washington: Carnegie Endowment for International Peace, Division of International Law, 1944).

Maria, Prévost, "Race and War Crimes: The 1945 War Crimes Trial of General Tomoyuki Yamashita". (1992) 14 (3) *Human Rights Quarterly*, p. 330.

Mayr, Erasmus, "International Criminal Law, Causation and Responsibility"' (2014) 14 (4/5) *International Criminal Law Review*, 855–873.

Meloni, Chantal, "Command Responsibility: Mode of Liability for the Crimes of Subordinates or Separate Offence of the Superior" (2007) *Journal of International Criminal Justice*, 619–637.

Mettraux, Guénaël, *The Law of Command Responsibility* (Oxford University Press, 2009).

Otto, Triffterer, "Genocide, Its Particular Intent to Destroy in Whole or in Part the Group As Such" (2001) 14 *Leiden Journal of International Law*, 399–408.

Pilloud, Claude (ed.), *Commentary on the Additional Protocols of 8 June 1977 to the Geneva Conventions of 12 August 1949* (ICRC, 1987).

Root, Joshua L., "Some Other Mens Rea? The Nature of Command Responsibility in the Rome Statute" (2013) 23 (119) *Journal of Transnational Law & Policy*, 119–156.

Sander, Barrie, "Unraveling the Confusion Concerning Successor Superior Responsibility in the ICTY Jurisprudence" (2010) 23 (1) *Leiden Journal of International Law*, 105–135.

Schabas, William A., *Genocide in International Law: The Crimes of Crimes* (Cambridge University Press, 2000).

Swart, Bert, *The Legacy of the ICTY* (Oxford University Press, 2011).
Triffterer, Otto, "Causality, a Separate Element of the Doctrine of Superior Responsibility as Expressed in Art. 28 Rome Statute" (2002) 15 (1) *Leiden Journal of International Law*, 179–205.
UNGA Res 1/96 (11 December 1946) UN Doc A/RES/1/96.
UNGA Res 3/260 (9 December 1948) UN Doc A/RES/3/260.
United Nations War Crimes Commission, *Law Reports of Trials of War Criminals*, Vol. III (HMSO, 1947).
UNSC, *Statute of the International Criminal Tribunal for the Former Yugoslavia* (adopted 25 May 1993), Resolution 808/1993, 827/1993 and amended by UNSC Resolution 1166/1998, 1329/2000, 114/2002.
UNSC, Resolution 955 (1994) of 8 November 1994 and last amended by Security Council Resolution 1717 (2006) of 13 October 2006.
U.S. v. Wilhelm von Leeb (the High Command/the Hostage trial), *Trials of War Criminals before the Nuremberg Military Tribunals under Control Council Law No. 10*, Vol. XI (Washington, D.C.: U.S. G.P.O., 1949–1953).
U.S. v. Wilhelm von List (the High Command trial), *Trials of War Criminals before the Nuremberg Military Tribunals under Control Council Law No. 10*, Vol X (Washington, D.C.: U.S. G.P.O., 1949–1953).

9 'Kill them all and let God sort them out', or why religiously motivated terrorism should not be confused with the crime of genocide

Milena Ingelevič-Citak and Marcin Marcinko

Introduction

In a speech given in New York City in 1953, Raphael Lemkin referred to the Holodomor perpetrated by the Soviet authorities as the most brutal technique of the long, sustained attack on the Ukrainian nation.[1] According to Lemkin, the Soviet terror aimed at Ukrainians took the form of 'four-pronged genocide', and the Great Famine of 1932–1933 was only one of the stages of destruction of the people of Ukraine.[2] For Lemkin, broadly understood, state terror was carried out in Soviet-controlled lands, and it was germane to the idea of genocide he had developed. Indeed, the notion of 'state terror' (or 'state terrorism'), although not legally defined, generally includes intentional violent actions on the part of state authorities directed against national or other minorities.[3] Under this formula, the crime of genocide would be the most brutal and most serious manifestation of state terror if at the same time it met the legal prerequisites of genocide.

The above qualification, however, may not necessarily refer to actions taken by non-state actors considered to be terrorist organisations. Theoretically, a terrorist organisation could commit the crime of genocide against a particular group treated as a protected group. By way of example, in June 2016 in a report published under the title '"They Came to Destroy": ISIS Crimes Against the Yazidis', the Independent International Commission of Inquiry on the Syrian Arab Republic, based on collected and verified information,[4]

1 See Raphael Lemkin, 'Soviet Genocide in Ukraine' in Roman Serbyn (ed), *In Memoriam Raphael Lemkin (1900–1959)* (Maisternia Knyhy 2009), 31–36.
2 Douglas Irvin-Erickson, *Raphaël Lemkin and the Concept of Genocide* (Penn Press 2016) 54.
3 Ibid., 46.
4 This report is based on 45 interviews with survivors, religious leaders, smugglers, activists, lawyers, medical personnel and journalists. Furthermore, considerable documentary material (including hundreds of statements, photographs, satellite images and reports) was used to corroborate the information collected by the Commission – see United Nations Human Rights Council '"They Came to Destroy": ISIS Crimes Against the Yazidis' (15 June 2016), A/HRC/32/CRP.2, para 4 (UNHRC Report).

presented the dramatic situation of the Yazidis of Sinjar, who fell victim to atrocities perpetrated by an armed non-state actor calling itself the 'Islamic State' (ISIS).[5] ISIS had been charged with and was recognised by the Commission as the perpetrator of genocide on the Yazidis.[6] According to the members of the Commission, 'ISIS has committed, and continues to commit, the crime of genocide (...) against the Yazidis',[7] and this crime 'has not primarily been accomplished through killings, though mass killings of men and women have occurred'.[8] Furthermore, the Commission shared the commonly accepted opinion that 'the Yazidis are (...) referred to as an ethno-religious group',[9] particularly underlining that:

> Little, if any, debate surrounds the Yazidis' identity as a distinct religious group (...). Without exception, diverse members of the Yazidi community interviewed were of the view that the Yazidis constitute a separate religious denomination, with distinct modes of worship.[10]

Acting upon these findings, the Commission stated that considering their religion, Yazidis were deemed a protected group within the meaning of Article II of the 1948 Convention on the Prevention and Punishment of the Crime of Genocide[11] (hereinafter 'Genocide Convention'), inasmuch as public declarations as well as the conduct of ISIS and its fighters, analysed and screened by the Commission, explicitly demonstrated that the intention of ISIS was to exterminate the Yazidis of Sinjar, in whole or in part, which satisfied the definition of the crime of genocide.[12] At the same time, however, the Commission observed

5 As Krzysztof Strachota explains, '[t]he history of the Islamic State is the living history of Sunni radicalism and terrorism. Before June 2014, the organisation known today as the Islamic State was a typical terror organisation, organically linked with al-Qaeda and centred around its founder, the Jordanian Abu Musab al-Zarqawi, who was an outstanding al-Qaeda commander. In the meantime, it changed its name several times: before it became the Islamic State, it was known under such names as the Islamic State of Iraq, then the Islamic State of Syria and Iraq (ISIS, ISIL or Daesh)' (Krzysztof Strachota, 'The Middle East in the Shadow of Islamic State' (2015) 52 *Centre of Eastern Studies 'Point of View'* 1, 8). See also Can Acun, 'Neo al Qaeda: The Islamic State of Iraq and the Sham (ISIS)' (2014) 10 *SETA Perspective* 1, 1–2; Charles Lister, 'Profiling the Islamic State', Brookings Doha Center Analysis Paper, 13/2014, 4–5 www.brookings.edu/wp-content/uploads/2014/12/en_web_lister.pdf [accessed 7 January 2019].

6 While the report analyses a range of international crimes, it specifically seeks to determine whether ISIS has committed the crime of genocide (UNHRC Report (n 4) para 3).

7 Ibid., para 201.

8 Ibid., para 202.

9 Ibid., para 101.

10 Ibid., para 103.

11 Convention on the Prevention and Punishment of the Crime of Genocide, adopted by the General Assembly of the United Nations on 9 December 1948, 278 UNTS 1021.

12 See UNHRC Report (n 4) para 202 *in fine*.

that the notion of 'genocide' in common understanding and public imagination often deviates from the legal definition of the crime:

> The colloquial use of the term "genocide", steeped in images of the Holocaust and the Rwandan genocide, has tended to signify the organised extermination of masses of civilians, regardless of the specific intention behind the killings.[13]

Understood in this way, however, such *notions* of genocide do not satisfy all the legal elements of this crime laid down in international law. As a result of such an approach, certain acts of violence tend to be regarded as acts of genocide, especially when staged by organisations or groups considered as criminal. The foregoing misinterpretations may happen, first of all, in cases of acts of violence committed by terrorist groups who, as a rationale for their criminal activities, put forward the religion of their members. Their terrorist activity is usually aimed at the believers of other religions and, taking into account their extreme cruelty and their intention to inflict as much damage as possible, their acts of terrorism are sometimes mistaken for genocide (e.g. in information campaigns), highlighting the above-mentioned difference between the religion of the terrorists and the religion of their victims. According to the authors of this present chapter, however, this is a far-reaching simplification and confusion of two different forms of criminal violence. The definition of genocide in international law functions as a treaty-based and very specific definition, although in truth its elements leave a wide margin for interpretation, as has been manifested by the case law of the International Criminal Tribunal for the Former Yugoslavia (ICTY) and the International Criminal Tribunal for Rwanda (ICTR). On the other hand, terrorist activity covers a wide spectrum of prohibited acts. Furthermore, acts of terrorism belong to the most grievous crimes of an international nature and terrorists alone are often referred to as the enemies of mankind (*hostes generis humani*), due to their similarity to the sixteenth-century (and subsequent ages of) pirates. Despite the above characterisation, international law still lacks a uniform and universally accepted definition of terrorism.

Since, however, the crime of genocide has been defined in treaty law, it must be determined, and proven, whether acts of terrorism motivated by religion are or may be *ex definitione* deemed to be directed against a protected group – in particular a religious group – and how the motivations of religion-led terrorist organisations should be viewed from the standpoint of the required genocidal intent. Mainly due to this genocidal intent, which constitutes a unique element of genocide (*dolus specialis*), acts of terrorism are difficult to classify as genocidal, and given their heinous nature it therefore seems important to answer the issue of *why* acts of terrorism driven by religion cannot be recognised as genocide. For the purpose of the integrity of this argument and for the sake of proving

13 Ibid., para 13.

the thesis, the above reasoning should be accompanied by a concise description of the characteristics of crimes that, in light of international law, would qualify as acts of terrorism.

How to define terrorism in international law?

The international community is well aware of the dangers that terrorism brings. Although the stakes raised by terrorism are usually national or regional in nature, the impact of terrorist campaigns is often international. Domestic terrorism often has spill-over effects into other countries, and linkages with foreign terrorist groups are not uncommon. Therefore, the drawing up of appropriate conventions that would interpret terrorism as an 'international crime' – prosecuted commonly by all states regardless of the nationality of the perpetrator and the place where the act is committed – has long been the subject of consideration. However, the work on international treaties in this field has constantly come up against obstacles impeding the draft of a single convention wholly regulating the subject. One of these obstacles is the lack of a unified and precise definition of terrorism.[14]

The insistence on a strict definition of the phenomenon in question is connected with difficulties of a political, legal and moral nature. Modern terrorism is far from being uniform and its ideological background is multifarious. Substantial differences exist in, *inter alia*, the underlying ideological and political motivations, world views, religion, principles of the 'philosophy of violence' and the attitude towards violence itself. Few subjects have been treated so extensively and, at the same time, so illogically. The ambiguity and vagueness of the terms lead to discretionary interpretations of terrorism and to conscious and deliberate extensions of the term to activities that have nothing in common with terrorism.[15] Consequently, dozens of definitions of terrorism exist that either reduce it to 'political extremism', 'radicalism' or to the entire spectrum of activities involving the use of force and violation of the rights and freedoms of individuals. According to some other definitions, terrorism consists of unlawful acts of violence that are treated as serious crimes and subject to severe punishment according to domestic criminal codes and penal laws.

While the efforts of states and various international organisations, especially those undertaken after the end of the Cold War, have admittedly resulted in the

14 Marian Flemming, 'Terroryzm polityczny w międzynarodowym prawodawstwie [Political Terrorism in International Legislation]' (1996) 3/4 *Wojskowy Przegląd Prawniczy* 1, 7.

15 For example, for a number of journalists, as well as certain governmental spokespersons and various debaters, the term 'terrorism' is used as a synonym for 'rebellion', 'civil strife', 'insurrection', or 'rural or urban guerrilla war', as well as a dozen other phenomena – including 'genocide' – a fact which has caused a great deal of confusion among the general public as regards the real meaning of the term. The definitions provided by journalists, governmental spokespersons and public debaters often reflect the purely political definition, and, more importantly, tend to be descriptive.

adoption of international treaties – both at the global and regional level – that provide legal grounds for the fight against terrorism, there is no precise, uniform legal definition of terrorism which is digestible for all states. The international anti-terrorist conventions that presently exist and are in force are not uniform; on the one hand one may distinguish between general conventions that focus on complex regulation of the problem in question, and detailed or 'sectoral' conventions that merely address the specific category of acts of terrorism, while on the other hand one may classify the anti-terrorist conventions into universal (with global reach) and regional ones. It is worth emphasising that among the universal anti-terrorist conventions the vast majority are 'sectoral' conventions, while in the case of regional conventions more general ones prevail.[16]

Similarly, there are different approaches to the definition of terrorism in various international treaties. Although regional conventions of a general nature contain very elaborate, even case-by-case definitions of terrorism and terrorist offences, universal 'sectoral' conventions focus exclusively on determination of a specific category of terrorist attacks, completely omitting the general definition of the phenomenon; in certain cases the very word 'terrorism' is not even used. What is more, the categories of prohibited acts, according to 'sectoral' conventions, are usually so extensive that they may also comprise offences difficult to recognise as terrorist. However, they are subject to prosecution and punishment pursuant to such conventions. As an example, the hijacking of a plane by an ordinary criminal, aiming at securing considerable financial gain in the form of a ransom, or the release of his criminal associates in lieu of the life of hostages, is without doubt an act prohibited by the Hague Convention of 1970,[17] although it does not constitute an example of international terrorism.[18]

Due to the complexity of the problem of terrorism and the controversies it generates, and considering the difficulties with its legal definition, international law rather indicates acts that may be referred to as acts of terrorism. So while there is a group of offences recognised as terrorist offences according to treaty law, they are considered offences of serious gravity which cannot be used as justification to enable and enhance a higher effectiveness in counteracting and combating all forms of terrorism. While terrorist offences present 'an evil in itself' (*mala in se*)[19] and consequently may be perceived as separate international offences, what is interesting is that they may be viewed as a category of war crimes or crimes against humanity. Under the circumstances of an armed

16 Zdzisław W. Galicki, 'International Multilateral Treaties and Terrorism' in Kazimierz Lankosz, Michał Chorośnicki and Paweł Czubik (eds), *Walka z terroryzmem w świetle prawa międzynarodowego* [The Fight Against Terrorism in International Law] (Wydawnictwo STO 2004) 12.

17 Convention for the Suppression of Unlawful Seizure of Aircraft, signed at The Hague on 16 December 1970, 860 UNTS 12325.

18 Antonio Cassese, *International Criminal Law* (2nd edn, OUP 2008) 171.

19 See Nicholas N. Kittrie, 'Comments: Panel on Terrorism and Political Crimes in International Law' (1973) 67 *AJIL* 104.

conflict, an act of terrorism may be recognised as a war crime if, generally speaking, it involves an act of violence (or a threat thereof) directed against civilians or other individuals not directly participating in the hostilities and if its primary objective is to intimidate the civilian population.[20] During times of peace, terrorism as a crime against humanity constitutes, in essence, a qualified form of terrorism as a prohibited act. It occurs when an act of terrorism is a part of a massive and systematic attack targeting a civilian population (although terrorist activities as such may be conducted against state representatives or even combatants), and when it additionally takes the specific form of a criminal activity (such as assassination, extermination, causing enormous suffering, grievous bodily injury or physical or mental harm, torture, rape or enforced disappearance).[21]

It must be emphasised that at present there are only rare instances in international law wherein terrorism is regarded as a political offence; it is distinctly stressed, though, that all acts of terrorism, along with the methods and measures used to conduct terrorist activity, ought to be regarded as criminal offences irrespective of where they were committed and by whom. Still, the word 'terrorism' is obviously linked with activity that involves violence and intimidation, mainly directed against innocent persons, for the purpose of forcing governments or society to fulfil political demands made by the perpetrators of such acts. The decisive factor serving as a criterion to evaluate acts of terrorism should be, however, the presence of a criminal intent to perpetrate such an offence rather than the reasons that lead to its actual commitment. The criminal aspect of the discussed problem has been addressed by, among others, the United Nations (UN) General Assembly in paragraph 3 of its Declaration on Measures to Eliminate International Terrorism, contained in the annex to Resolution 49/60 of 9 December 1994. According to the General Assembly, terrorist acts are:

> criminal acts intended or calculated to provoke a state of terror in the general public, a group of persons or particular persons for political purposes [and] are in any circumstance unjustifiable, whatever the considerations of

20 Cassese (n 18) 177. For more on this question, see Roberta Arnold, *The ICC as a New Instrument for Repressing Terrorism* (Transnational Publishers 2004) 66–202; Daniel O'Donnell, 'International Treaties Against Terrorism and the Use of Terrorism during Armed Conflict and by Armed Forces' (2006) 88 *IRRC* 853, 863–870; Hans-Peter Gasser, 'Acts of Terror, "Terrorism" and International Humanitarian Law' (2002) 84 IRRC 547–570; José L. Rodríguez-Villasante y Prieto, 'Terrorist Acts, Armed Conflicts and International Humanitarian Law' in Pablo A. Fernández-Sánchez (ed), *The New Challenges of Humanitarian Law in Armed Conflicts – In Honour of Professor Juan Antonio Carrillo-Salcedo* (Martinus Nijhoff 2005) 13–46.

21 Cassese (n 18) 177. See also Arnold (n 20) 202–275; Michael A. Newton and Michael P. Scharf, 'Terrorism and Crimes Against Humanity' in Leila N. Sadat (ed), *Forging a Convention for Crimes Against Humanity* (CUP 2011) 262–278; Vincent-Joël Proulx, 'Rethinking the Jurisdiction of the International Criminal Court in the Post-September 11th Era: Should Acts of Terrorism Qualify As Crimes Against Humanity?' (2004) 19 *AmUIntlLRev* 1009–1089.

> a political, philosophical, ideological, racial, ethnic, religious or any other nature that may be invoked to justify them.[22]

This approach was reiterated in further Assembly resolutions concerning international terrorism.[23] In a similar manner, the criminal nature of terrorist acts and their objectives is expressed in Article 2(1) of the draft comprehensive convention against international terrorism, which has been prepared by the Ad Hoc Committee on International Terrorism,[24] established by the UN General Assembly in 1996. Although the Committee has not finished its works yet,[25] and the definition of terrorism under Article 2 of the draft convention is purely informal, it contains elements that are already commonly attributed to acts of terrorism. According to Article 2(1), a person commits a terrorist offence if that person – by any means – unlawfully and intentionally causes:

> (a) Death or serious bodily injury to any person; or
> (b) Serious damage to public or private property, including a place of public use, a State or government facility, a public transportation system, an infrastructure facility or the environment; or
> (c) Damage to property, places, facilities, or systems referred to in paragraph 1(b) of this article, resulting or likely to result in major economic loss, when the purpose of the conduct, by its nature or context, is to intimidate a population, or to compel a Government or an international organization to do or abstain from doing any act.[26]

Also, a credible and serious threat of committing an offence as set forth in Article 2(1), an attempt to commit a terrorist offence, as well as other forms of complicity and contribution in order to commit such an offence, is also deemed to be a terrorist offence.[27] Terrorism is still mostly defined by the listing of offences that are incorporated in its scope. This catalogue is obviously not

22 UNGA, Declaration on Measures to Eliminate International Terrorism, UNGA Res 49/60 (9 December 1994), Annex.

23 See, for example: UNGA Res 50/53 (11 December 1995) para 2; UNGA Res 51/210 (17 December 1996) para 2; UNGA Res 54/110 (9 December 1999) para 2; UNGA Res 56/88 (12 December 2001) para 2; UNGA Res 57/27 (19 November 2002) para 2; UNGA Res 60/43 (8 December 2005) para 2; UNGA Res 63/129 (11 December 2008) para 4; UNGA Res 66/105 (9 December 2011) para 4; UNGA Res 69/127 (10 December 2014) para 4; UNGA Res 72/123 (7 December 2017) para 4; UNGA Res 73/211 (20 December 2018) para 4.

24 The text of the draft comprehensive convention – see UNGA 'Report of the Ad Hoc Committee established by General Assembly Resolution 51/210 of 17 December 1996' (28 January – 1 February 2002) 6th Session (2002) UN Doc Supp No 37 (A/57/37, Annex I–III).

25 In fact, the negotiations are deadlocked because of different opinions of states on the final definition of terrorism.

26 Report of the Ad Hoc Committee (n 24) Annex II, Art 2(1).

27 Ibid., Art 2(2–4).

exhaustive and should increase progressively as new detailed conventions are adopted internationally that address specific aspects of terrorist activity. Undoubtedly, a constant characteristic of all offences regarded as terrorist (including those motivated by religion) is to create terror among people or to intimidate a government or an international organisation to further the terrorists' cause.[28]

The notion of 'religious group' in the definition of the crime of genocide and victims of religiously motivated terrorism

In contrast to terrorism, genocide – being an international crime – was defined very precisely. The definition of genocide is included in the Convention on the Prevention and Punishment of the Crime of Genocide of 1948. According to its Article II, genocide encompasses:

> any of the following acts committed with intent to destroy, in whole or in part, a national, ethnical, racial or religious group, as such:
>
> (a) Killing members of the group;
> (b) Causing serious bodily or mental harm to members of the group;
> (c) Deliberately inflicting on the group conditions of life calculated to bring about its physical destruction in whole or in part;
> (d) Imposing measures intended to prevent births within the group;
> (e) Forcibly transferring children of the group to another group.

The above-cited definition has been repeated *expressis verbis* in the statutes of both ad hoc international criminal tribunals – the ICTY[29] and ICTR[30] – as well as in the Rome Statute of the International Criminal Court.[31] It is also accepted by the vast majority of states and confirmed in their internal criminal law regulations. Thus, taking into account this commonly accepted legal definition, the crime of genocide is defined by two characteristic elements:

28 Cf. Art 2(1) of the International Convention for the Suppression of the Financing of Terrorism, adopted by the UN General Assembly on 9 December 1999, UNGA Res 54/109 (9 December 1999), Annex. See also UNSC Res 1566 (8 October 2004) UN Doc S/RES/1566 (2004) para 3.

29 See Art 4 of the Updated Statute of the International Criminal Tribunal for the former Yugoslavia www.icty.org/x/file/Legal%20Library/Statute/statute_sept09_en.pdf [accessed 7 January 2019].

30 See Art 2 of the Statute of the International Criminal Tribunal for Rwanda www.ohchr.org/en/professionalinterest/pages/statuteinternationalcriminaltribunalforrwanda.aspx [accessed 7 January 2019].

31 See Art 6 of the Rome Statute of the International Criminal Court, adopted on 17 July 1998, 2187 UNTS 38544.

1 An objective (material) element – *actus reus* – consisting of the particular prohibited acts enumerated in subparagraphs (a) to (e) of Article II of the Genocide Convention; and
2 A subjective element – *mens rea* – consisting of the special intent to destroy, in whole or in part, a particular protected group enumerated in Article II of the Genocide Convention.[32]

The Genocide Convention specifies four protected groups: national, ethnic, racial or religious. No provision, however, determines the definition and meaning of those groups, which has been left to international jurisprudence and the doctrine of international law.[33] In light of these sources (and particularly in the light of the ICTR jurisdiction), a 'religious group' is a group 'whose members share the same religion, denomination or mode of worship'.[34] It should be underlined that the concept of a 'religious group' must be assessed 'in the light of a particular political, social and cultural context',[35] as well as the historical context.[36] Furthermore, as noted by the ICTY, in order to define each of the protected groups (including a religious group) on the basis of scientifically objective criteria would be 'inconsistent with the object and purpose' of the Genocide Convention.[37]

The treaty definition of genocide refers only to physical destruction of relatively permanent groups whose membership in most cases is somehow 'automatic', irrespective of their will – mostly due to birth. This is what happens in the cases of nationality, ethnic origin and race; only in the case of religious groups is membership based on some sort of choice.[38] However, the above-quoted functional definition of 'religion' proposed by the ICTR, grounded in the objective practices of group members, seems to be rather narrow in light of the broader view in international law of human rights. A definition based on subjective systems of religious beliefs would define a religious group as a group who practice the same religion and share the same creed, beliefs, doctrines or rituals. There is room for controversy over whether atheistic groups would qualify under such a definition. While they hardly are a 'homogeneous group',

32 Cf. *Prosecutor v Goran Jelisić* (Judgement) ICTY-95-10-T (14 December 1999) para 62; *Prosecutor v Radislav Krstić* (Judgement) ICTY-98-33-T (2 August 2001) para 542; *Prosecutor v Vidoje Blagojević and Dragan Jokić* (Judgement) ICTY-02-60-T (17 January 2005) para 640.
33 Michał Matyasik and Przemysław Domagała, *Międzynarodowe trybunały karne oraz inne instrumenty sprawiedliwości tranzytywnej* [International Criminal Tribunals and Other Instruments of Transitional Justice] (Wydawnictwo Difin 2012) 38.
34 See *Prosecutor v Jean-Paul Akayesu* (Judgement) ICTR-96-4-T, T Ch I (2 September 1998) para 515.
35 *Prosecutor v Georges Anderson Nderubumwe Rutaganda* (Judgement and Sentence) ICTR-96-3-T, T Ch I (6 December 1999) para 56.
36 *Krstić* (n 32) para 557.
37 Ibid., para 556.
38 *Akayesu* (n 34) para 511. See also Cassese (n 18) 130.

nonetheless they appear to share a similar belief system. Therefore, the concept of a religious group should have an adequate capacity to also incorporate atheists and non-theists, who may be the target and objective of genocidal attacks due to their own 'beliefs' and functional 'mode of worship' (i.e. by not worshiping at all).[39]

In order to qualify a particular prohibited act as the crime of genocide, it is extremely important to determine the particular positive characteristics of a given group, and not categorise them based on a lack of certain features. As the International Court of Justice (ICJ) stated, '[i]t is a matter of who those people are, not who they are not'.[40] In practice, though, it is not easy to evaluate a specific human group in order to determine whether it qualifies as a protected group. Luckily, the judgments of the ad hoc international criminal tribunals offer aid in this respect, as one may find guidelines useful for the process of assessing whether a given group qualifies as a protected one. The aforementioned tribunals elaborated two concepts in this regard – one objective and the other subjective.

The objective concept was presented in detail by the ICTR in the *Akayesu* case with respect to belonging to a protected tribe. The Tribunal based its decision on tangible signs of belonging to the group and on an objective assessment of the group. The evidence admitted by the Tribunal included testimonies concerning the information contained in identity documents (which were a remnant of the Belgian colonial authority) that identified their holders as members of a tribe (Hutu or Tutsi).[41] The Tribunal found that Tutsi witnesses credibly testified about their ethnic identity and stated that the former Belgian colonisers distinguished them in a similar manner – on the basis of ethnicity.[42] Based on the facts presented during the proceedings, the Tribunal also found that the Tutsi had constituted a stable and permanent ethnic group 'identified as such by all'.[43] Thus, protected groups must be stable and permanent groups, and membership in such groups must be of a continuous and often irremediable character; therefore, they are the opposite of 'mobile' (dynamic) groups (such as political groups), which one joins through an individual voluntary commitment.[44]

As regards the subjective concept, the assessment of the status of belonging to a national, ethnic, racial or religious group is performed from the perspective of individuals who wish to separate such a group from the rest of the community, the most important aspect being the convictions of the genocide

39 David L. Nersessian, *Genocide and Political Groups* (OUP 2010) 24.

40 See *Application of the Convention on the Prevention and Punishment of the Crime of Genocide (Bosnia and Herzegovina v Serbia and Montenegro)* (Judgment) [2007] ICJ Rep 43, para 193.

41 *Akayesu* (n 34) para 702.

42 Ibid., para 172.

43 Ibid., para 702.

44 Ibid., para 511.

perpetrators, who define (i.e. stigmatise) the group which is the victim of their genocidal acts. Stigmatisation means the classification of potential victims based on the assessment of the characteristics of a given group (e.g. black skin, church attendance) and it makes it possible to determine whether a targeted population constitutes a separate national, ethnical, racial or religious group in the eyes of the alleged perpetrators.[45] Importantly, the correct determination of the relevant group as protected and stigmatised by the perpetrator has to be made on a case-by-case basis,[46] consulting both the objective and subjective criteria and applying them to the given situation,[47] and taking into account both the relevant evidence proffered and the political and cultural context.[48]

It is worth noting that in light of the ICTY's judgment in the *Jelisić* case, the above-mentioned stigmatisation may be made by way of positive or negative criteria. A 'positive approach' would consist of the perpetrators of the crime of genocide distinguishing a group by the characteristics which they deem to be peculiar to a national, ethnical, racial or religious group. A 'negative approach' would consist of identifying individuals as not being part of the group to which the perpetrators of the crime of genocide consider that they themselves belong, and which to them displays specific national, ethnical, racial or religious characteristics. Thus, all individuals rejected in this way would – by exclusion – constitute a distinct group.[49] However, the concept of a 'negative' stigmatisation has been rejected both by the ICTY's Appeals Chamber[50] and the ICJ[51] as being inconsistent with the object and the purpose of the Genocide Convention of 1948.

Taking into account the purpose of the Genocide Convention, it is widely acknowledged that the intention to destroy must target at least a 'substantial' part of the group.[52] According to the ad hoc international criminal tribunals, the correct interpretation of the term 'in part' requires the intention to destroy 'a considerable number of individuals who are part of the group'[53] or 'a reasonably significant number, relative to the total of the group as a whole'.[54] However, the part which is targeted must be 'significant enough to have an impact

45 *Jelisić* (n 32) para 70.
46 *Blagojevićand Jokić* (n 32) para 667. Cf. *Krstić* (n 32) para 557.
47 *Prosecutor v. Alfred Musema* (Judgement and Sentence) ICTR-96-13-A, T Ch I (27 January 2000) paras 161, 163.
48 *Rutaganda* (n 35) para 58.
49 *Jelisić* (n 32) para 71.
50 See *Prosecutor v. Milomir Stakić* (Appeals Chamber Judgement) ICTY-97-24-A (22 March 2006) paras 16–28.
51 See *Bosnia and Herzegovina v Serbia and Montenegro* (n 40) paras 193–196.
52 *Jelisić* (n 32) para 82.
53 *Prosecutor v Clément Kayishema and Obed Ruzindana* (Judgement) ICTR-95-1-T, T Ch II (21 May 1999) para 97.
54 *Prosecutor v Duško Sikirica et al.* (Judgement on Defence Motions to Acquit) ICTY-95-8-T (3 September 2001) para 65.

on the group as a whole'.[55] A targeted part of a group could be classed as 'substantial' either because the perpetrators intended to harm a large majority of the group in question, or the most representative members of the targeted community (i.e. the elites).[56] Such 'elites' include political and administrative leaders, religious leaders, academics and intellectuals, business leaders and others – but regardless of the actual number of victims, what counts is the broad intended effect of the action as such, which is an indicator of the crime of genocide. A corroborating argument of the genocidal intent can be the fate of the rest of the group – if a group has its elites exterminated, and at the same time or in the wake of that has a relatively large number of the members of the group killed or subjected to other heinous acts (e.g. deported on a large scale or forced to flee), the cluster of violations must be considered in its entirety in order to interpret the provisions of the Genocide Convention in a spirit consistent with its purpose.[57]

When it comes to terrorist acts, their most characteristic feature is usually the lack of a distinctly defined targeted group. The selection of victims is often casual, and attacks are unfocused and may cover the civilian population en masse, without 'stigmatisation' of its particular members, which leads to a tendency to define terrorism as a 'blind crime'.[58] Obviously, terrorist attacks may be targeted against individuals, representatives of the state (e.g. government members, officials, judges, law enforcement officers) or other persons who are considered by the terrorists as their opponents. However, most frequently purely incidental persons are targeted, unrelated with any group within the meaning of Article II of the Genocide Convention of 1948. Accordingly, acts of terrorism are usually not focused on extermination of a specific group and take the form of indiscriminate attacks.[59]

However, taking into consideration the hatred-driven members of religious terrorist groups against representatives of other religions, it might appear that terrorist organisations that incorporate religious extremists could or should be deemed to be targeting a religious group within the meaning of the Genocide Convention. For example, organisations such as al-Qaeda or certain religious sects could target specific religious groups, such as Christians or Buddhists. Only here the question arises whether the real goal of any such terrorist attack is to destroy in whole or in part a religious group, or rather to make some political and propaganda gains. Actually, the global jihad (a common effort of Muslims) identified with the above-mentioned al-Qaeda, which is not so much an organisation but rather an ideology and a spiritual stance, 'stigmatises' specific groups,

55 *Bosnia and Herzegovina v. Serbia and Montenegro* (n 37) para 198.
56 *Jelisić* (n 32) para 82.
57 Ibid.
58 Cf. Tomasz Aleksandrowicz, *Terroryzm międzynarodowy* [International Terrorism] (Wydawnictwa Akademickie i Profesjonalne 2008) 21.
59 Cf. Arnold (n 20) 288.

ordering their extermination in whole or in part. Jihad protagonists name three enemies whose impact must be defeated in the first instance, namely 'crusaders' (Western Christian societies and Russia), 'Jews' (the State of Israel) and 'minions' (Muslim governments or dictatorships serving or supporting non-Muslims).[60] The only way to defend against these enemies and their never-ending attacks is jihad (a common effort of Muslims) that has to include, inter alia, means of terrorist activity.[61] But are they actually trying to eliminate these groups in whole or in part?

The explanation of who is the enemy of Islam and against whom all attacks must be directed can be found in the fatwas issued by al-Qaeda leaders.[62] One of the most important such fatwas – calling for 'holy war against Jews and crusaders' – was issued in February 1998 by Osama bin Laden and a few other of the most prominent representatives of various radical Islamic groups.[63] Verses from the Quran are quoted therein, as well as statement by prophets and Imams. According to the authors of the fatwa the entire Muslim community is obliged to fight against and defend itself in accordance with the objectives of jihad in the face of 'a crusader-Zionist alliance'.[64] This fight must be in accordance with the words of Allah: 'fight the pagans all together as they fight you all together'[65] and 'fight them until there is no more tumult or oppression, and there prevails justice and faith in God.'[66]

Nevertheless, it does not seem that an opponent as defined above could reasonably be classified into a religious group based on the Genocide Convention. In Islam, unbelievers are divided into 'People of the Book' (i.e. Jews and Christians) and idolaters (polytheists and infidels).[67] The term 'unbelievers' is not sufficiently precise though, and comprises all non-Muslims. Furthermore, in a fatwa issued in 1998 there is a mention of 'minions', which can include Muslims.

60 Wilhelm Dietl et al., *Terroryzm* [Terrorism] (PWN 2009) 122.

61 Ibid., 123.

62 In general, a 'fatwa' is a written legal opinion issued by a qualified Muslim jurist or theologian, or a person of unquestionable authority in the field of Muslim law or theology. It contains reasoning or an indication how to solve a certain problem in compliance with Islamic law. A fatwa is not legally binding: the one who asks for it does not have to follow its recommendations; and the importance of the opinion may depend on the prestige of its author. However, in case of al-Qaeda, its members and advocates consider fatwas issued by its leaders as binding (see Agata Marek, *Islam. Informator dla organizacji pozarządowych* [Islam. Guide for Non-Governmental Organisations] (Vox Humana 2005) 48).

63 'Text of Fatwah Urging Jihad Against Americans' (23 February 1998) www.mideastweb.org/osamabinladen1.htm [accessed 7 January 2019].

64 'The ruling to kill the Americans and their allies – civilians and military – is an individual duty for every Muslim who can do it in any country in which it is possible to do so, in order to liberate the al-Aqsa Mosque and the holy mosque from their grip, and in order for their armies to move out of all the lands of Islam, defeated and unable to threaten any Muslim' (*Text of Fatwah* (n 63)).

65 Ibid.

66 Ibid.

67 Marek (n 62) 51.

Similarly, the term 'crusaders' may not be regarded as sufficiently precise. While in this case religion may seem to be a stigmatising element, it can also include the accepted system of values or the views held by populations. Terrorist attacks conducted by al-Qaeda can therefore be labelled as indiscriminate, and their primary goal is certainly not to destroy, in whole or in part, religious groups as such.

Again, it does not seem plausible that the extermination of a specific protected group (including religious ones) within the meaning of the Genocide Convention would be a leitmotif in the activities of fundamentalist-religious groups or the so-called 'doomsday sects' which are not Islamic. Undoubtedly, the most unsettling characteristic of their activity is the endowment of terrorist acts with a sacramental or transcendental nature, and the elevation of terrorism to a spiritual or eschatological level. In their leaders' eyes, the world is black and white, and each day is a relentless battle between the forces of good, which they represent, and the forces of evil, as represented by the rest of the world.[68] In addition, they are convinced that they are a persecuted and oppressed group of 'chosen ones' who will only be winners in the 'ultimate fight'.[69] The same approach seems to be adopted by various Christian ultra-right movements operating in the USA (inter alia, the Michigan Militia, Aryan Nations, Christian Identity).[70] Members of the aforementioned groups are convinced that through their activity they contribute to the ultimate battle against evil forces, personified by representatives of races other than white; by an omnipotent and sinister government; and by international organisations that attempt to introduce a malevolent 'new world order'.[71]

A definite and express division into 'believers' and 'unbelievers' is reflected in various doomsday cults, among which one can include the Japanese sect Aum Shinrikyo (Supreme Truth), notorious for the deadly Tokyo subway sarin attack it carried out in 1995. It was supposed to be an 'ultimate battle' – the beginning of Armageddon – thus the attack was not directed against a specific group (victims included random subway passengers). What is crucial is that, unlike the majority of traditional cults, the Supreme Truth also proclaimed a fight against the state and its authorities; in 1995 the chief of the National Police Agency was shot to death by its members, and the organisation was also responsible for preparing 'death lists' including names of the most prominent Japanese

68 Marcin Marcinko, 'The Contemporary Face of International Terrorism' (2005) 22 'Pro Memoria' – Information Bulletin of the Auschwitz-Birkenau State Museum 67, 69.

69 Dietl (n 60) 126.

70 Their activity was once limited to acts of violence with racist or religious motivations, directed against individuals, and they used force against the state only when the authorities interfered in the political or religious activity of the cells of a given terrorist grouping. At present, many groups deriving from this trend are manifesting a clear hostility to the government. In the opinion of the followers of these groups, the government is entangled in a wide-ranging conspiracy that threatens the model of life adopted by white Christians (Marcinko (n 68) 69).

71 Ibid.

politicians.[72] Despite its religious character and devastating plans, Supreme Truth was not focused on the destruction of any religious group as such, but rather on the destruction of all persons outside itself.

Thus, it is difficult to assess that in their assumed concept of combat – i.e. 'us versus the rest of the world' – the aforementioned fundamentalist-religious organisations are stigmatising any specific protected groups as categorised in the definition of genocide. It is true that these organisations are striving to inflict as much damage as possible, as well as the maximum number of civilian casualties, but their opponents are understood in too-general terms, without adopting any of the specific criteria used for their choice of victims of criminal acts; for example, in bomb attacks in public places. For religious extremists, people from beyond their group are less valuable. They intentionally describe them in extremely degrading and dehumanised terms, referring to them as infidels or children of Satan. What is more, the foregoing division of the world propagated by the organisations discussed herein, with the 'good ones' being the members of the given organisation and 'evil ones' all the others who do not belong to such organisation, resembles the 'negative approach' connected with interpretation of elements of the crime of genocide, which consists of identifying individuals as *not* being part of the group to which the perpetrators of the crime consider that they themselves belong, and which to them displays specific national, ethnical, racial or religious characteristics. Thereby, all individuals thus rejected could, by their exclusion, be considered to be a distinct group. It is worth recalling though that with regard to genocide, international criminal tribunals and the ICJ have rejected the 'negative approach' as inconsistent with the Genocide Convention. Therefore, acts of terrorism committed by the aforementioned groups would not constitute the crime of genocide because they are indiscriminate and not aimed at specific protected groups in accordance with the Convention.

The genocidal intent of the crime of genocide and the special intent underlying acts of terrorism

As has been mentioned above, in the case of genocide it is not sufficient to simply identify a protected group without having the so-called 'genocidal intent', i.e. the intention to exterminate the protected group in whole or in part. This is the most characteristic trait of genocide, which highlights its peculiarity. This intent amounts to the *dolus specialis* of the crime of genocide; therefore, it excludes other categories of mental elements: recklessness (or *dolus eventualis*) and gross negligence.[73] Importantly, it is this specific intent that distinguishes the crime of genocide from other international crimes and offences.[74] Even if we assume that

72 Dietl (n 60) 242.

73 Cassese (n 18) 137.

74 See *Akayesu* (n 34) para 498; *Kayishema and Ruzindana* (n 53) para 91; *Sikirica et al.* (n 54) para 84.

some terrorist acts can be deemed to be targeted at a protected group (e.g. a religious one), the lack of any such genocidal intent on the part of the terrorists would render their actions incapable of being classified as the crime of genocide.

The genocidal intent must be separate from the general intent to commit one of the prohibited acts enumerated in Article II of the Genocide Convention. This specific intent requires that the perpetrator, by virtue of carrying out one of the above-mentioned prohibited acts, seeks to achieve the destruction, in whole or in part, of a national, ethnical, racial or religious group, as such.[75] Furthermore, it is not sufficient that the perpetrator simply knew that the underlying crime might inevitably or likely result in the destruction of the group – this destruction must be the *aim* of the underlying crime.[76]

For the crime of genocide to occur, the perpetrator must be aware of this crime prior to the commission of the genocidal acts. However, the individual acts themselves do not require premeditation – the only consideration is that the act should be done in furtherance of the genocidal intent.[77] As David Nersessian rightly noted, '[t]his formulation aligns best with the structure of the Convention [of 1948], which penalizes acts committed with a certain mental state, rather than successful results from that conduct'.[78] It should be emphasised, however, that the *dolus specialis* of the crime of genocide cannot be identified with the motivation of the perpetrator:[79] 'the intent to destroy the group as such' should be thus distinguished from the motive, i.e. the incentive, which does not have to be hatred for a given group. The motive may be political, economic, racial or any other, and it may be related to prejudices, revenge or striving to obtain control over specific resources or territory.[80] 'The personal motive of the perpetrator of the crime of genocide may be, for example, to obtain personal economic benefits, or political advantage or some form of power',[81] and even to spread terror. It is important to note, however, that the existence of a personal motive does not preclude the perpetrator from also having the specific intent to commit genocide.[82] The motives of the perpetrators of genocide that prompted them to commit this crime are therefore irrelevant.

75 *Prosecutor v Goran Jelisić* (Appeals Chamber Judgement) ICTY-95-10-A (5 July 2001) para 46. See also *Bosnia and Herzegovina v Serbia and Montenegro* (n 37) para 187.

76 *Blagojević and Jokić* (n 32) para 656. As the ICTY explained: 'Genocidal intent may (…) be manifest in two forms. It may consist of desiring the extermination of a very large number of the members of the group, in which case it would constitute an intention to destroy a group en masse. However, it may also consist of the desired destruction of a more limited number of persons selected for the impact that their disappearance would have upon the survival of the group as such. This would then constitute an intention to destroy the group "selectively".' (*Jelisić* (n 32) para 82).

77 *Kayishema and Ruzindana* (n 53) para 91. See also *Akayesu* (n 34) para 501.

78 Nersessian (n 39) 46.

79 *Jelisić* (Appelas Chamber Judgement) (n 72) para 49.

80 Matyasik and Domagała (n 30) 38.

81 *Jelisić* (AC Judgement) (n 75) para 49.

82 Ibid.

However, the motive of the perpetrator may serve as further evidence of genocidal intent.[83] In cases of genocide, courts and tribunals extremely rarely deal with direct evidence of a genocidal intent; therefore, it is difficult to show that the perpetrator was guided by this intent, unless he confesses to aiming to commit genocide. In most cases the genocidal intent must be inferred from a certain number of presumptions of fact.[84] The factors taken into consideration by the courts and tribunals are, for example, the number of victims, the previous methods and pattern of conduct of the perpetrator, and his statements and deeds.[85] A general political doctrine that gave rise to the crime of genocide is relevant, as well as the repetition of destructive and discriminatory acts; the scale and nature of the atrocities committed; the discriminatory targeting of the members or property of one group to the exclusion of others; methodical or systematic planning of killings; the weapons employed; and the extent of injury inflicted.[86] Acts of so-called 'cultural genocide' and other forms of conduct that violate (either in reality or only in the eyes of the perpetrators) the very foundation of the group or its roots are also relevant.[87] Ultimately, all these factors and facts can be of great importance in the evidentiary proceedings, and although they do not constitute legal elements of genocide per se, they can help in proving (or confirming) that in a given case there was indeed a genocidal intent.[88]

In the case of terrorism, determination of the motive of operation of terrorists allows us to distinguish terrorism as a manifestation of 'collective' criminality from other offences (such as murders, kidnapping, bomb attacks), which tend to be regarded as 'individual' criminal acts. Acts of terrorism are usually committed by groups or organisations, or single perpetrators acting on their behalf or otherwise associated with them. Surely an act of terrorism, e.g. a bomb attack, can also be committed by an individual who does not belong to any such organisation or group. The act, however, would only be regarded as terrorist if individuals were directed by an ideology or a set of rules (e.g. religious), personally identifying themselves with a group or organisation whose objective is to commit the aforesaid acts. Thus in such a case the criminal activity is not undertaken for personal reasons (e.g. for revenge, for profit, holding a grudge, or because of hatred); it may be based on political, ideological or religious motives, or something similar. Motive is, therefore, a factor that transforms the criminal act undertaken by an individual into an act of terrorism.[89]

83 Nersessian (n 39) 35.
84 *Akayesu* (n 34) para 523.
85 Cf. *Jelisić* (n 32) para 73.
86 Nersessian (n 39) 34–35. See also *Jelisić* (n 32) para 73; *Kayishema and Ruzindana* (n 53) paras 94, 531, 533–536, 542; *Musema* (n 47) paras 928, 930–931.
87 Nersessian (n 39) 35. See also *Krstić* (n 32) paras 480, 595–597.
88 Cf. Cassese (n 18) 142.
89 Ibid., 167–168.

In order to effectively prosecute and punish perpetrators of terrorist acts, the motivation underlying their acts must not be treated as a justification of their conduct or circumstances that exclude unlawfulness; if acts of terrorism are to be regarded as crimes, the assessment criteria applied to weigh any such acts ought to include criminal intent to commit a crime, not the underlying reasons behind the crime. As stated above, in international law attention is seldom paid to the political nature of terrorism; what is rather underlined is that all acts of terrorism ought to be considered as criminal offences regardless of by whom, where and for what reasons they were committed. This implies that under no circumstances should terrorism be justified by political, philosophical, ideological, racial, ethnic, religious or similar reasons. The political, ideological or any other goal must never be used to rationalise means based on terror and intimidation, and consequently it must not be assumed that condemnation of acts of terrorism would depend on subjective criteria such as views, the origin of a perpetrator or the motives that lie at the heart of action. For example, 'although most people acknowledge the legitimacy of the Palestinians' claims to self-determination, they do not automatically consider the use of suicide bombings as legitimate'.[90]

However, while the mere motive to undertake a terrorist activity is not sufficient to recognise a prohibited act as a terrorist act, the specificity of a terrorist offence means that in the case of terrorism it is impossible not to consider the goal that terrorists intend to achieve, which in turn may result from the motives underlying their criminal activity. In the above-mentioned definitions of terrorism – including the definition formulated by the UN Security Council in Resolution 1566 (2004)[91] – acts of terrorism are:

> criminal acts, including against civilians, committed with the intent to cause death or serious bodily injury, or taking of hostages, with the purpose to provoke a state of terror in the general public or in a group of persons or particular persons, intimidate a population or compel a government or an international organization to do or to abstain from doing any act.[92]

Thus, the purpose of terrorist acts may be '*either* spreading terror among the population *or* compelling a government or an international organization to perform or abstain from performing an act'.[93] A third possible objective might be to destabilise or destroy the political, constitutional, economic or social structures of a given state[94].

90 Arnold (n 20) 4–5.
91 UNSC Res 1566 (8 October 2004) UN Doc S/RES/1566 (2004).
92 Ibid., para 3.
93 Cassese (n 18) 166.
94 Ibid. Cf. Sebastian Wojciechowski and Adrian K. Siadkowski, *Understanding Contemporary Terrorism and Counterterrorism* (Academy of Business 2014) 33.

However, given the content of the various definitions of terrorism (including the definition of the Security Council), it seems that the overriding objective of terrorists is always to force a public (or private) institution to behave in a particular way. According to Antonio Cassese:

> [t]he spreading of deep fear or anxiety is only a *means* for compelling a government or another institution to do (or not to do) something; it is never an end in itself. Also, the destabilization of the political structure of a state is a means of making the incumbent government take a certain course of action.[95]

In some instances, terrorists do not clearly formulate their goal(s), neither before nor after committing a terrorist act. However, it is difficult to assume that murders, kidnappings or bombings are committed for the very fact of committing them, because in fact they are aimed at inducing a public or private entity to do or refrain from doing something.[96]

Ultimately, every form of terrorism 'always pursues one primary and essential purpose, that of coercing a public authority (…) or a transnational private organization (…) to take (or refrain from taking) a specific action or a certain policy'.[97] This purpose can be achieved by terrorists in two ways: first, by spreading fear or anxiety among civilians (e.g. by kidnapping or hijacking civilians, or by bombings in public places or in public transport) – the aim of terrorists is to induce the intimidated population to exert pressure on the authorities and force them to undertake a certain behaviour;[98] second, by engaging in criminal activity directed against public institutions (these could be bomb attacks or threats of such attacks against government buildings, military headquarters, the premises of parliament, embassy buildings, etc.) or against political leaders or leading representatives of public authorities or private entities (e.g. the head of state, a member of the government, chairman of a political party, ambassador, general manager of a bank, president of a commercial corporation), thus exerting pressure directly on public or private entities.[99]

From the legal standpoint, an act of terrorism understood as an offence consists of two subjective elements (*mens rea*) – mental, i.e. the 'general' element of an individual's intention to commit the offence, which is a necessary element of many offences, including kidnapping, hijacking, bomb attacks, etc. (*dolus generalis*); and a 'special' intent which requires that a public or private entity be forced to take or refrain from taking a specific action (*dolus specialis*).[100] Thus

95 Cassese (n 18) 167.
96 Ibid.
97 Ibid.
98 Cf. Wojciechowski and Siadkowski (n 94) 36.
99 Cassese (n 18) 167.
100 Ibid., 168.

an act of terrorism is characterised by a unique special intent different from genocidal intent, and it is this very difference that precludes the possibility to classify acts of terrorism as acts that constitute the crime of genocide. If, for example, the crime of genocide involves extermination of members of a specific group, it requires both a direct intent to commit murder (excluding thereby recklessness and negligence) as well as an intent to commit genocide, while acts of terrorism, which may incidentally contribute to the execution of a genocidal plan, are not perceived as genocide unless special genocidal intent was present on the side of a perpetrator. In addition, a specific feature of terrorism is an incidental selection of victims, who in fact are the means to achieve a goal other than destruction or annihilation, in whole or in part, of a national, ethnic, racial or religious group.[101] As interestingly pointed out by Brian M. Jenkins, terrorism is theatre, with the directors being terrorists, the audience the society or government, and victims as the actors; therefore, the victims' role is instrumental (usually without any links to terrorist goals) and is staged to produce an adequate response from the audience. In other words, in contrast to the crime of genocide, terrorism is intended for those who watch, not for those who have become victims.[102]

Conclusions

In light of the above legal analysis, it seems that the only element linking the crime of genocide and acts of terrorism is their criminal nature and the fact that they cannot find any justification, regardless of the motives and purposes of their perpetrators. However, the legal classification of both criminal phenomena is not so similar. Genocide is an international crime and as such is defined in international treaty law and in the statutes of international courts and tribunals. In the case of terrorism, there is no universal and commonly accepted definition of this phenomenon, as so far it has not been decided to recognise acts of terrorism as international crimes, although they are undoubtedly treated as serious offences of an international nature.

The lack of a uniform legal definition of terrorism means that terrorist acts are sometimes treated as certain forms of war crimes or crimes against humanity if the acts meet the legal requirements of these crimes. However the specific elements of the crime of genocide, and in particular the so-called 'genocidal intent', mean that acts of terrorism cannot be 'matched' to the definition of the crime of genocide. Even the presence of an element that at first glance could seem to be a link between terrorism and genocide, namely 'religion', does not change this. In light of Article II of the Genocide Convention, one of the protected groups is a religious

101 Cf. Arnold (n 20) 300.

102 See Brian M. Jenkins, 'International Terrorism: A New Mode of Conflict' in David Carlton and Carlo Schaerf (eds), *International Terrorism and World Security* (Croom Helm 1976) 16.

group, while one of the forms of terrorism is religiously motivated terrorism, which is thus directed against the followers of other religions. In the light of the definition of the crime of genocide, this religious group should be defined positively, i.e. the characteristics of this group which distinguish it from other groups should be taken into account, and perpetrators attacking members of this group may be of any religion (they may even be followers of the same religion). On the other hand, in the case of terrorist groups, religion is a feature distinguishing the members of many of these groups from the rest of the world – religious terrorists target all who do not share their faith and religious values, and therefore the attacks of these terrorist groups are indiscriminate, without stigmatising specific religious groups.

In addition, in acts of terrorism one cannot find the key element constituting the essence of the crime of genocide – a genocidal intent. The perpetrators of genocide act with the explicit intent of destroying, in whole or in part, a national, ethnical, racial or religious group, as such. The destruction of a given group is therefore the driving force behind the perpetrators of genocide, although their motives may be varied. However, in the case of terrorism, victims caused by terrorist attacks are not an end in itself – these victims are treated instrumentally by terrorists, because the main intention of terrorist acts – regardless of their form – is usually to compel a government, an international organisation or a private entity to perform or abstain from performing a specific action. Obviously, terrorist groups whose members are considered religious extremists (e.g. ISIS) may commit the crime of genocide against a specific religious group (e.g. the Yazidis of Sinjar), but this proves that every case of violence directed at a specific community should be assessed from the perspective of legal regulations, and it is only then that one can definitively confirm whether a given case constitutes the crime of genocide or an act of terrorism.

10 Blurring the distinction between ethnic cleansing and genocide

Tamas Vince Adany[1]

Introduction

Compared to the long history of international law, which encompasses several millennia, the direct responsibility of individuals for international crimes is a relatively new idea within this normative system. It is therefore hardly surprising that the respective crimes also have a far shorter history, and instead of millennia of development, the legal concepts have evolved only in the past several decades. Thus certain differences between these new legal terms and their social adoption and recognition can also be expected. Nevertheless, the discussion on the proper use of the phrases "genocide" and "ethnic cleansing" highlight a startling divide between the necessarily strict interpretation of criminal law terms in the legal discourse, and the phrases used to describe similarly heinous atrocities in non-legal social sciences and in the general public discourse. For criminal law procedures, the term "ethnic cleansing" is hardly adopted at all. For the general public and non-legal academic discourse, "genocide" and "ethnic cleansing" sometimes even seem interchangeable,[2] while some scholars draw attention to the limitations of both terms.[3]

The first difficulty in resolving this divide lies in the different sources for the two respective terms, which leads to an inevitable methodological disagreement. Genocide, simplified at this point as the destruction of a specific

1 The author wishes to express his gratitude to the organizers and all the participants of the December 2018 Conference on Genocide – Marking 70 Years of the Genocide Convention in Kraków and also to Erkan Akdogan for their valuable comments on some ideas expressed in this chapter. Any errors in the arguments are those of the author alone.

2 Micol Sirkin, "Expanding the Crime of Genocide to Include Ethnic Cleansing: A Return to Established Principles in Light of Contemporary Interpretations Comment" *Seattle University Law Review* 489. Jobair Alam, "The Rohingya of Myanmar: Theoretical Significance of the Minority Status" (2018) 19 *Asian Ethnicity* 180. For other examples, see Robert M. Hayden, "Schindler's Fate: Genocide, Ethnic Cleansing, and Population Transfers" (1996) 55 *Slavic Review* 727, p. 731 *et seq.*

3 Antonio Ferrara, "Beyond Genocide and Ethnic Cleansing: Demographic Surgery as a New Way to Understand Mass Violence" (2015) 17 *Journal of Genocide Research* 1.

group of people, is a phenomenon that was present throughout human history, while the term itself was coined by Raphael Lemkin only in the middle of the twentieth century. The concept of genocide as we know it today was finalised by an international treaty-making procedure and a resulting convention in 1948. The legal definition was implemented in national legal systems,[4] and it became a legal cornerstone which solidified a legal method for its interpretation. For this legal interpretation it is less relevant that Lemkin briefly considered using *ethnos* (nation)[5] instead of *gens*,[6] since this "ethnocide" never became a legally-defined term.[7] Nevertheless, some fifty years later violent practices erupted to create ethnically homogeneous areas,[8] and the resulting atrocities against ethnic groups led to the appearance of a new phrase in the popular language of international politics: "ethnic cleansing." It is much harder to pinpoint the exact origin of this phrase,[9] partly because, unlike genocide, this label was first used by the perpetrators themselves.[10] Generally it refers to a set of practices meant to create an ethnically homogeneous territory, usually by forceful means. The diversity of the practices employed makes it extremely hard to define concisely. As an early commentator noted:

> At one end [ethnic cleansing] is virtually indistinguishable from forced emigration and population exchange while at the other it merges with deportation and genocide. At the most general level, however, ethnic cleansing can be understood as the expulsion of a population from a given territory.[11]

4 See, for example, Tamás Hoffmann's chapter in the present volume.

5 See Raphael Lemkin, *Axis Rule in Occupied Europe: Laws of Occupation – Analysis of Government – Proposals for Redress* (Carnegie Endowment for International Peace 1944), p. 80 note 1.

6 Tanya Elder, "What You See before Your Eyes: Documenting Raphael Lemkin's Life by Exploring His Archival Papers, 1900–1959" (2005) 7 *Journal of Genocide Research* 469, note 3. See also Rony Blum and others, "'Ethnic Cleansing' Bleaches the Atrocities of Genocide" (2008) 18 *European Journal of Public Health* 204; Elihu Richter and Gregory Stanton, "Response to Hayden: Comment on 'Ethnic Cleansing' and 'Genocide'" (2008) 18 *European Journal of Public Health* 210.

7 Although it still appears in academic discourse; see Brian Glyn Williams, "Hidden Ethnocide in the Soviet Muslim Borderlands: The Ethnic Cleansing of the Crimean Tatars" (2002) 4 *Journal of Genocide Research* 357.

8 Interim Report S/35374. See the speech of UN Special Rappoerteur Tadeusz Mazowiecki at the 50th session of the Commission on Human Rights, Geneva, 28 February 1994. Cited in Drazen Petrovic, "Ethnic Cleansing – An Attempt at Methodology" (1994) 5 *European Journal of International Law* 342, p. 349.

9 Carrie Booth Walling, "The History and Politics of Ethnic Cleansing" (2000) 4 *The International Journal of Human Rights*, p. 48; Petrovic, op.cit. p. 343; William A. Schabas, *Genocide in International Law: The Crime of Crimes* (Cambridge University Press 2000), p. 190.

10 Schabas, p. 192.

11 Andrew Bell-Fialkoff, "A Brief History of Ethnic Cleansing" (1993) 72 *Foreign Affairs* 110.

Notably, unlike "genocide" "ethnic cleansing" is not a legal term,[12] and as of late 2019 it still lacks a definition in a legally binding international instrument. Several United Nations (UN) bodies have offered working definitions,[13] but none of these were embodied in a binding source of international law. Formally, resolutions of the General Assembly are mere recommendations for states, and thus fail to pass the threshold of *nullum crimen sine lege*, a basic tenet of every fair criminal trial.[14] This Latin maxim translates into the modern-day prohibition of punishment for conduct that was not rendered an offence punishable by law at the time of its commission.[15] The applicable law can be part of either a national or an international legal instrument, but must be enacted *before* the commission of the act. As a human rights norm, this principle allows for no legally recognised exceptions, so the lack of a legally binding definition for an offence effectively precludes any criminal law procedure with respect thereto.

Consequently, in a fair trial, a classification of a practice as ethnic cleansing cannot in itself constitute the sufficient legal grounds to connect the facts of the case to the appropriate legal sanctions. Whenever the factual background of a case justifies its categorisation as ethnic cleansing, a relevant criminal law category must be identified that offers another, legally pertinent, fitting description of the same practice. These legal categories should not only address the individual criminal acts that altogether comprise ethnic cleansing, but they must also cover the link connecting those acts into a single atrocity. Considering the gravity of the offence of ethnic cleansing, the entirety of such practices can be duly treated only at the level of international crimes, i.e. either as genocide or crimes against humanity.[16]

In terms of the present discussion, the most important differences between the two crimes concern the mental elements of crimes against humanity (knowledge of a systematic or widespread attack on the civil population) and genocide (the intent to destroy the group itself). This different intent is persistently cited as the reason to conclude that ethnic cleansing is not genocide, but rather a crime against humanity.[17]

12 Schabas, p. 112; Lieberman.

13 Raphael Lemkin, "Les Actes Constituant Un Danger General (Interétatique) Consideres Comme Delites Des Droit Des Gens – Rapport spécial présenté à la 5me Conférence pour l'unification du droit pénal à Madrid, 14-20 oct. 1933" (A. Pedone, 1933).

14 No punishment without law, ICTY (IT-98-33) *Prosecutor v. Radislav Krstić* Trial Chamber Judgment, 2 August 2001 (hereinafter: Krstić Trial Judgment) para. 580.

15 See Universal Declaration of Human Rights Article 11(2); International Covenant of Civil and Political Rights, Article 15;

16 Another option – if the ethnic cleansing happens within an armed conflict – may be war crimes. Due to such a conditional application of this legal category no further examination is offered in this chapter on its classification as a war crime. Although ethnic cleansing commonly happens in an armed conflict, this should not be understood as a necessary element of the criminal law categories encompassing ethnic cleansing.

17 For example, Krstić Trial Judgment, para. 494.

Destruction of a group, as an element of the concept of genocide, had been already part of Raphael Lemkin's 1933 original proposal at the Madrid Conference.[18] His later publications also focused on *extermination/annihilation* of a group.[19] However, he described the methods of destruction in a broader sense than the final legal text adopted by the states in the 1948 Genocide Convention. For an assessment of ethnic cleansing as genocide it is of some importance that under the 1944 "Axis rule," Lemkin reasoned that deprivation of one's livelihood would endanger the survival of the group as such.

> The destruction of the foundations of the economic existence of a national group necessarily brings about a crippling of its development, even a retrogression. The lowering of the standards of living creates difficulties in fulfilling cultural-spiritual requirements. Furthermore, a daily fight literally for bread and for physical survival may handicap thinking in both general and national terms.[20]

After the war, when Lemkin worked as one of three UN experts on the draft of the Genocide Convention, he still promoted his broader definition, but the other two experts took a more conservative stance. Due to fears of "reconstituting a former protection of minorities [...] under cover of the term genocide" they deliberately excluded not just most of the Lemkinian concept of cultural genocide, but also the "forced expulsion from the group's homeland, an act known more recently known as ethnic cleansing."[21] What Lemkin described as "economic genocide" was transformed into the genocidal conduct of "imposing life conditions calculated to bring about the destruction of the group."

Although some of Lemkin's key ideas were turned down in the drafting process, there was still a proposal during the state-level negotiations from the Syrian government to insert a sixth criminal conduct to genocide, namely "measures intended to oblige members of a group to abandon their homes in order to escape the threat of subsequent ill-treatment."[22] In supporting this proposal, the representative from Yugoslavia added "genocide could be committed by forcing members of a group to abandon their homes."[23] A clear

18 Raphael Lemkin, "Les Actes Constituant Un Danger General (Interétatique) Consideres Comme Delites Des Droit Des Gens" (1933).: "les actions exterminatrices dirigées contre les collectivités ethniques, confessionnelles ou sociales quels qu'en soient les motifs (politiques, religieux, etc.); tels p. ex. massacres, pogromes, actions entreprises on vue de ruiner l'existence économique des membres d'une collectivité etc."

19 Raphael Lemkin, "Genocide" (1946) 15 *American Scholar* 227.

20 Lemkin, *Axis Rule in Occupied Europe*, p. 86.

21 Schabas, p. 178.

22 A/C.6/SR.82. p. 183.

23 Schabas, p. 184.

majority of the representatives voted against this proposal, albeit for different reasons. Most argued that it would give the concept of genocide "an indefinite scope"[24]; or that it would "go too far" without even a threat of genocide;[25] and some proposed that it should be sent to the Third Committee as it is, by virtue of the displaced people, a social affair.[26]

Consequently, the physical destruction of a protected group became the predominant, but still not exclusive, method of committing genocide. Nevertheless, the UN General Assembly (UNGA) rightly called the crime of genocide the "denial of the right of existence of entire human groups."[27]

Why ethnic cleansing is different from genocide

When ethnic cleansing emerged as a burning issue in the 1990s, attempts were made to comprehend it in a legal procedure through two established criminal law concepts: crimes against humanity or genocide. In terms of sentencing, the two crimes show no significant differences.[28] The stigmatising effect of genocide is arguably more profound,[29] which can also be relevant in terms of the preventive function of criminal law.[30] Still, there are far less judgments from international tribunals convicting persons for genocide than those related to crimes against humanity. One significant reason for this scarcity of international genocide judgments is the colloquially recognised restrictive nature of the legal definition of genocide.[31] This restrictive nature again relates to the *nullum crimen* principle: a fair criminal trial cannot be based on an extensive interpretation of the legally-prescribed elements of a crime.

From a legal/technical perspective, this latter feature explains the debated relationship between ethnic cleansing and genocide. Early in the discussion it seemed that ethnic cleansing would be accepted within the concept of genocide. A resolution of the UNGA from December 1992 declared that the UNGA was gravely "concerned about [...] the abhorrent policy of 'ethnic

24 A/C.6/SR.82 Comment by Kaeckenbeek (Belgium) p. 184.
25 A/C.6/SR.82 Comment by Sundaram (India) p. 184.
26 A/C.6/SR.82 Comments by Fitzmaurice (UK) p. 185; Raafat (Egypt); Abdoh (Iran) p. 186.
27 UNGA Res. No. 96 (I).
28 The actual sentences seem factually to depend more on other factors. For more details, see Mark B. Harmon and Fergal Gaynor, "Ordinary Sentences for Extraordinary Crimes" (2007) 5 *Journal of International Criminal Justice* 683, p. 690.
29 David L. Nersessian, "Comparative Approaches to Punishing Hate: The Intersection of Genocide and Crimes against Humanity" (2007) 43 *Stanford Journal of International Law* 221, p. 262; Patricia M. Wald, "Genocide and Crimes against Humanity" (2007) 6 *Washington University Global Studies Law Review*, p. 629; Manashaw, p. 530.
30 Nersessian.
31 See, for example, Wald; Akhavan.

cleansing', which is a form of genocide."[32] The use of this wording could have been seen as settling the legal categorisation of ethnic cleansing if the resolutions of the General Assembly were legally binding on states. However, even if without such legal force the political support for the resolution can be traced from the voting records. The resolution was accepted without any states opposing by casting a vote against it, but the number of abstentions were relatively large (57, compared to 102 in favour). Abstaining countries included four permanent members of the UNSC;[33] all the founding members of the EU; traditional human rights strongholds like Canada, Finland, Japan, Norway, and Sweden; and major developing states like India or Brazil, etc.[34] Still, a year later two other UNGA resolutions reiterated the statement,[35] and this time both were accepted without vote; i.e. unanimously.

This issue is also echoed in the academic discourse. Most authors today would agree that some forms of ethnic cleansing may be tantamount to genocide, or at least some of its elements.[36] For some scholars, it seems obvious that ethnic cleansing, like genocide, results in the disappearance of an ethnic group and the creation of an ethnically homogeneous territory; therefore, it meets the requirements of genocide under the law.[37] A result, however, is not an element of the crime of genocide; therefore, it is not surprising that many other scholars propose an interpretation of genocide that does not include ethnic cleansing. William Schabas argued in his seminal book that

32 UNGA A/RES/47/121 p. 2.

33 In spite of its subsequent reluctance "to use the g-word" – for example, in the case of Rwanda (see Samantha Power, "Bystanders to Genocide" in *The Atlantic*, September 2001) – only the USA supported the resolution.

34 Voting records are available at https://digitallibrary.un.org/record/282898?ln=en (November 2019).

35 A/RES/48/143.

36 *Decision on the Prosecution's Application for a Warrant of Arrest against Omar Hassan Ahmad Al-Bashir* (Pre-Trial Chamber I), No. ICC-02/05-01/09-3, See, for example, Leibermann Maja Munivrana Vajda, "Ethnic Cleansing as Genocide – Assessing the Croatian Genocide Case before the ICJ" *International Criminal Law Review* 147, p. 151 *et seq.*; H. Zeynep Bulutgil, "Social Cleavages, Wartime Experience, and Ethnic Cleansing in Europe" (2015) 52 *Journal of Peace Research* 577.

37 See, for example, Linnea D. Manashaw, "Genocide and Ethnic Cleansing: Why the Distinction – A Discussion in the Context of Atrocities Occurring in Sudan Comment" *California Western International Law Journal* 303; Sirkin; Jennifer Jackson Preece, "Ethnic Cleansing as an Instrument of Nation-State Creation: Changing State Practices and Evolving Legal Norms" (1998) 20 *Human Rights Quarterly* 817, p. 836. Some authors argue it justifies a broad interpretation of the intent: Milena Sterio, "The Karadzic Genocide Conviction: Inferences, Intent, and the Necessity to Redefine Genocide" *Emory International Law Review* 271, p. 295.

> it is incorrect to assert that ethnic cleansing is a form of genocide, or even that in some cases, ethnic cleansing amounts to genocide. Both, of course, may share the same goal, which is to eliminate the persecuted group from a given area. While the material acts performed to commit the crimes may often resemble each other, they have two quite different specific intents. One is intended to displace a population, the other to destroy it. The issue is one of intent and it is logically inconceivable that the two agendas coexist.[38]

International tribunals have generally followed this latter approach. Most judicial panels have understood the two phrases as referring to two distinct practices, since ethnic cleansing, understood as the *forcible removal* of an ethnic group from its habitation, is not equal to the *physical destruction* of the same group, and the genocidal intent typically also remains questionable.[39]

Relying on the aforementioned UNGA resolutions, whenever the International Court of Justice (ICJ) has been faced with a dispute over genocide in a contentious procedure, the initiating state has made an express reference to ethnic cleansing as a form of genocide. In its application Bosnia and Herzegovina submitted to the Court "that in fact 'ethnic cleansing' is really a euphemism for acts of genocide within the meaning of the Genocide Convention."[40] The Serbian Counter-Memorial rebutted this assertion by admitting that "Ethnic cleansing is a loathsome unlawful policy. But if the goal of that policy is to repulse by force, including killings and torture, members of an ethnic or religious group from a certain territory, this excludes 'the intent to destroy, in

38 Schabas.

39 European Court of Human Rights *Jorgic v. Germany (Application no. 74,613/01) Judgment 12 July 2007*, para. 45, citing the ICJ: "'Neither the intent, as a matter of policy, to render an area "ethnically homogeneous", nor the operations that may be carried out to implement such policy, can *as such* be designated as genocide: the intent that characterizes genocide is "to destroy, in whole or in part" a particular group, and deportation or displacement of the members of a group, even if effected by force, is not necessarily equivalent to destruction of that group, nor is such destruction an automatic consequence of the displacement. This is not to say that acts described as "ethnic cleansing" may never constitute genocide, if they are such as to be characterized as, for example, "deliberately inflicting on the group conditions of life calculated to bring about its physical destruction in whole or in part", contrary to Article II, paragraph (c), of the Convention, provided such action is carried out with the necessary specific intent (*dolus specialis*), that is to say with a view to the destruction of the group, as distinct from its removal from the region. As the ICTY has observed, while "there are obvious similarities between a genocidal policy and the policy commonly known as 'ethnic cleansing' (*Krstić*, IT-98-33-T, Trial Chamber Judgment, 2 August 2001, para. 562), yet "[a] clear distinction must be drawn between physical destruction and mere dissolution of a group. The expulsion of a group or part of a group does not in itself suffice for genocide."'"

40 Application Instituting Proceedings Filed in the Registry of the Court on 20 March 1993 Application of the Convention on the Prevention and Punishment of the Crime of Genocide (ICJ *Bosnia and Herzegovina v. Yugoslavia (Serbia and Montenegro)*, hereinafter: Bosnian Genocide Case) para. 20.

whole or in part, a national, ethnical, racial or religious group, as such. Or, at least, it does not imply the existence of such an intent.'"[41]

Following the jurisprudence of the International Criminal Tribunal for the Former Yugoslavia (ICTY),[42] the judgment of the ICJ maintained that physical destruction of the group and its "mere dissolution" are two distinct acts: the former is genocide, the latter is ethnic cleansing. More importantly, the Court seemed to imply that there is an inextricable difference between the required genocidal intent and the purpose of ethnic cleansing. Based upon the different intent of the perpetrators, the relevant paragraph of the judgment declares that neither "the intent [...] to render an area 'ethnically homogeneous', nor the operations that may be carried out to implement such policy, can as such be designated as genocide." Nonetheless, an important finding of the Court clarifies that dogmatically it is not impossible that an act of ethnic cleansing may be tantamount to genocide: "This is not to say that acts described as 'ethnic cleansing' may never constitute genocide"[43] – in this case the relevant genocidal act would most likely be "deliberately inflicting on the group conditions of life calculated to bring about its physical destruction in whole or in part." The fact that the Court also found that ethnic cleansing can be a sign of genocidal intent could lead to certain interpretation discrepancies: ethnic cleansing can be an *actus reus* of genocide or it can sometimes be proof of the genocidal intent. In his dissenting opinion, Judge Al-Khasawneh argues that the "jurisprudence of the international criminal tribunals on this point is less amenable to artificial distinctions between the intent relevant to genocide and that relevant to ethnic cleansing than the Court."[44] The present author agrees with this dissent – i.e. that the harsh distinction between destruction and dissolution of the *group* is indeed artificial, or even arbitrary, while an important statement accepted by the ICJ majority mitigates the confusion[45] about the role ethnic cleansing plays in genocide litigation. This laconic line states that "in the context of the Convention, the term 'ethnic cleansing' has no legal significance *of its own*."[46] Therefore in this judgment the ICJ based its arguments on an understanding that ethnic cleansing is a factual description and not a legal category. Consequently, the Court did not exclude ethnic cleansing from forming a part of genocide, but understandably refused to differ from the conventional definition of the crime of crimes. The conclusion should be that ethnic cleansing may be suitable

41 Serbian Counter-Memorial (Bosnian Genocide Case) p. 7 para. 1.1.3.5.

42 For more details, see below. The references in the ICJ Judgment are: Krstić, IT-98-33-T, Trial Chamber Judgment, 2 August 2001, para. 562; Stakić, IT-97-24-T, Trial Chamber Judgment, 31 July 2003, para. 519.

43 ICJ Bosnian Genocide Judgment of 26 February 2007, pp. 122–123 para. 190.

44 He adds, in line with the Krstić Judgment, that "ethnic cleansing may be relied on as evidence of the mens rea of genocide."

45 As Judge ad hoc Mahiou formulated it in his dissent: "there gradually ceases to be a frontier with genocide itself; it is at once the warning signal, the means and the purpose."

46 ICJ Bosnian Genocide Judgment of 26 February 2007, p. 123 para. 190 (emphasis added).

to constitute any or all elements of genocide, but such a finding is definitely not automatic.

While the intention of the Court could have been to avoid creating a place in international law for the notion of ethnic cleansing, the above-cited paragraph of the judgment was heavily relied on by both parties in a later dispute between Croatia and Serbia. Still, the Court found no reason to depart from its previous position and decided to focus on the circumstances of the forced displacements. If the circumstances supported that they had been intentionally calculated to bring about the physical destruction of the group, then that particular ethnic cleansing would have been genocide. The ICJ found that this was not the case, and again the intent seemed more important for its finding than the physical act of violence, despite the fact that both the ICJ and the ICTY found that indiscriminate shelling[47] of civilian areas did actually take place. While artillery fire on civilian targets seems generally suitable for achieving the physical destruction of a significant part of the group, the majority of the ICJ ruled that the shelling was used only to expel a substantial part of the population,[48] without the actual intent of placing them in conditions to bring about their physical destruction.[49] While a part of the target group was indeed destroyed, the Court this time focused on the impact of the *actus reus* on the entirety of the protected group.

Based on the above interpretation, it seems that international law today argues that ethnic cleansing is not genocide[50] because the victim population and members thereof have a bitter choice: "move or die";[51] while in cases of genocide the victims typically do not have this choice. In the following section, this chapter looks for the proper label for an atrocity when such a choice prima facie exists, albeit limited to options which all lead to an inevitable, but not imminent, destruction of a group in the foreseeable future. The hypothesis that such an overlap[52] exists between genocide and ethnic cleansing is based on the assumption that survival of the members of a group does not equate to the survival of the group itself.[53]

47 ICJ Application of the Convention on the Prevention and Punishment of the Crime of Genocide (*Croatia v. Serbia*) (hereinafter: ICJ Croatian Genocide Case) Judgment of 3 February 2015 paras. 466 and 479–480; for more details, see also ICTY (IT-06-90) *The Prosecutor v. Ante Gotovina et al.* Appeal Judgment of 16 November 2012 para. 25.

48 ICJ Croatian Genocide Judgment of 3 February 2015 para. 466.

49 Ibid., para. 479–480.

50 In addition to the ICJ, the ECHR also reached similar conclusions in *Jorgic v. Germany* §45.

51 Andrew Bell-Fialkoff, "A Brief History of Ethnic Cleansing" (1993) 72 *Foreign Affairs*, p. 110. William A. Schabas, "'Ethnic Cleansing' and Genocide: Similarities and Distinctions" (2003) 3 *European Yearbook of Minority Issues Online* 109, p. 118. Note also the finding that "despite the attempts by the VRS to make it look like a voluntary movement, the Bosnian Muslims of Srebrenica were not exercising a genuine choice to go, but *reacted reflexively to a certainty that their survival depended on their flight.*" Krstić Trial Judgment, para. 530 (emphasis added).

52 Which the ICJ Judgment does not preclude. See supra, note 43.

53 Lemkin, *Axis Rule*, p. 79.

Ethnic cleansing between genocide and crimes against humanity: the practice of international criminal tribunals

As stated above, the conceptual differences between the legal notions of genocide and crimes against humanity are well established, both in the case law of international tribunals as well as in the supporting literature.[54] The core difference is the special genocidal intent;[55] i.e. that the purpose of the perpetrator is to destroy the protected group.[56] It is essential to note again that it is this intent, and not the achieved result, that is a fundamental element of the crime of genocide.[57] While certain mental elements are also required to find crimes against humanity, the most important distinguishing factor in those crimes much rather lies within the systematic or widespread nature of the offence.[58] The purpose of the perpetrators of crimes against humanity is not necessarily an essential part of the legally required elements of those crimes,[59] even if the objectives of an ethnic cleanser are usually also identifiable. Drazen Petrovic, one of the first authors on a methodological approach toward ethnic cleansing, discussed the goals of such practice on both the local and global levels. He argues that the goals are (locally) to terrorise the target group in order to obtain control of an area, and (globally) to irreversibly change the demographic structure of an area by the creation of ethnically homogeneous regions.[60] He also claims that a third goal can be the extermination of certain groups of people from a particular territory.

Since the perpetrator does not intend to cause the brutal and imminent *destruction* of the victim group, but is satisfied with the brutal and imminent *removal* of the group from a given territory, the above-discussed mental element of the crime of genocide in such cases is well-nigh impossible to prove.[61] As was noted by the ICJ in the genocide cases, forcible removal of a group from a territory does not necessarily equal its destruction: as cynical and evil as it may sound, in the perpetrators' minds the victims maintain a right to exist – only elsewhere. This does not make ethnic cleansing more legitimate or less heinous: it remains a crime under international law. The fact that the legal concept of

54 Patricia M. Wald, "Genocide and Crimes against Humanity" (2007) 6 *Washington University Global Studies Law Review*.

55 Petrovic, p. 17. Also in ICTY (IT-95-16) *Prosecutor v. Zoran Kupreskic et al.* Trial Judgment of 14 January 2000, para. 636; ICTR (IT-97-23) *Prosecutor v. Jean Kambanda* Trial Judgment of 4 September 1998, para. 16; ICTY (IT-99-36) *Prosecutor v. Radoslav Brdanin* Trial Chamber Judgment of 1 September 2004 (hereinafter Brdanin Trial Judgment) para. 699.

56 Krstić Trial Judgment para. 571.

57 See David L. Nersessian, "Comparative Approaches to Punishing Hate: The Intersection of Genocide and Crimes against Humanity" (2007) 43 *Stanford Journal of International Law* 221, pp. 246–247. Brdanin Trial Chamber para. 697.

58 See, for example, Wald, p. 630.

59 Rome Statute Art. 7(1) has some forms of special mental elements, like: persecution, enforced disappearances of persons, etc.

60 Petrovic, p. 351.

61 Ibid.

genocide prima facie does not cover *every* ethnic cleansing means only that the legal category of crimes against humanity must also be examined to identify the proper legal framework.

This finding also does not mean that "crimes against humanity" and "ethnic cleansing" are two synonymous terms for the same phenomenon: as "ethnic cleansing" is a non-legal term, such an equation can hardly be correct. The correct conclusion is that certain forms of crimes against humanity and ethnic cleansing actually do overlap. It was also shown above that the ICJ left open the door for an interpretation of ethnic cleansing as genocide.[62] Acts of ethnic cleansing are essentially stuck at the border between genocide and crimes against humanity. In order to identify the elements laying the foundations for judicial findings, a court-by-court method should be applied, as the elements of crimes against humanity have changed considerably since its first appearance in positive law, which happened in the London Agreement of 1945.

International military tribunals

Although the jurisprudence of the International Military Tribunals (IMTs) has been essential to contemporary international criminal law, it is hardly indicative of the legal classification of ethnic cleansing. An important reason for this is that public conscience of the period was shocked by and focused on the *destructive* nature of genocide[63] as "an old practice in its modern development" rather than the forced and mass displacement of entire peoples. Establishing an ethnically homogeneous area was not the only goal of the atrocities, but such a territory was achieved by the destruction of a selected part of the population. The pre-war policy of forced emigration of the Jews from Germany, which would be understood today as ethnic cleansing, was therefore later superseded by the more destructive genocidal practices, as shown for example by the well-known Nazi policies of the *Endlösung*,[64] reflected also in the Eichmann case[65] or by the SS reports submitted as evidence in the *Einsatzgruppen* case.[66] The IMT cases suggest that the intent to destroy was stronger than the intent to expel the population from occupied territories.

The overlap between crimes against humanity and genocide in the immediate post-war practice is further strengthened by the relative uncertainty of the legal terminology of that time. Differentiation between crimes against humanity and genocide was only evolving along with the definitions themselves. The judgment in the trial of the major war criminals at the IMT in Nuremberg carefully

62 See supra, note 43.

63 Kristina Hon, "Bringing Cultural Genocide in by the Backdoor: Victim Participation at the ICC Comment" Seton Hall Law Review 359, p. 364.

64 Christopher Browning, *The Origins of the Final Solution* (University of Nebraska Press – Yad Vashem Institute 2004), pp. 1, 18–19, 35.

65 Schabas, *Genocide in International Law*, p. 200.

66 *Ohlendorf et al.* (Einsatzgruppen Case), USA MT IX, Judgment (08-04-1948)(E) p. 424.

avoided using the new name for the crime of genocide, since the judges delivered their judgment two years prior to the finalisation of the Genocide Convention. Instead, the genocidal acts and policies that urged Lemkin to propose this new term were treated in the judgment as the crime against humanity of persecution. Subsequent Nuremberg judgments under Control Council Law No. 10 were bolder, and at several times they used the term "genocide,"[67] but not as a *sui generis* charge. Due to this factual and normative mixture of genocide and crimes against humanity, the search for legal classification of ethnic cleansing must focus on more recent jurisprudence.

The Tokyo trials draw attention to yet another important element of ethnic cleansing: it designates the targeted ethnic group as "the enemy" as such, so that it must be cleansed from a territory. The resulting unlawful and indiscriminate violence in an armed conflict can also be treated as a war crime, instead of the more serious crimes against humanity or genocide. Although certain practices matching today's ethnic cleansing concept were not alien to the war in the Far East, the Tokyo Tribunal addressed them mostly as war crimes. In the early 1930s the Japanese Kwantung Army murdered 2,700 civilians in Manchuria for allegedly supporting the units of the Chinese volunteer army. A report from the later prime minister, Kuniaki Koiso, then Chief of Staff of the Kwantung Army to the Japanese War Ministry, explained these killings by an escalating ethnic struggle: "Racial struggle between Japanese and Chinese is to be expected. Therefore, we must never hesitate to wield military power in case of necessity."[68] "This practice continued throughout the China War; the worst example of it probably being the massacre of the inhabitants of Nanking in December 1937."[69] The treatment of this practice as war crimes may be explained by the design of the Japanese Government not to apply the laws of war in the operations in Manchuria, which they dubbed as an "incident."[70] Subsequent practice, however, suggests that the sheer scale and the discriminatory nature of ethnic cleansing makes it a more serious crime.

UN ad hoc tribunals

From the outset the practice of the UN ad hoc tribunals faced the many political and legal challenges. One of the biggest legal tasks was to adapt the IMTs' legacy to the major developments in the positive laws of humanity, namely

67 "Even when Germany was retreating on all fronts, many troops sorely needed on the battlefield were diverted on this insane mission of extermination. In defiance of military and economic logic, incalculable manpower was killed off, property of every description was destroyed – all remained unconsidered as against this insanity to genocide." *Ohlendorf et al.* (Einsatzgruppen Case), USA MT IX, Judgment (08-04-1948)(E) p. 451.

68 International Military Tribunal for the Far East, Judgment of 4 November 1948, p. 49603.

69 For more details, see ibid., p. 49605.

70 "It was officially decided in 1938 to continue to call the war in China an 'Incident' and to continue for that reason to refuse to apply the rules of war to the conflict." Ibid., p. 49602.

international human rights law and international humanitarian law. The development of the notions behind crimes against humanity fit into this pattern, and the text of the respective statutes evolved considerably through the jurisprudence of the tribunals. As one focal point of this evolution, international media coverage started to use the phrase "ethnic cleansing" from the early 1990s to describe the events in the former Yugoslavia and subsequently in various ongoing African conflicts.

Following the traditions of the post-war tribunals, Article 5 of the ICTY Statute defined crimes against humanity as a set of criminal actions directed against any civilian population.[71] While this list lacked any explicit reference to ethnicity, nonetheless there were several crimes which were of particular relevance for the evaluation of ethnic cleansing. Deportation[72] and persecution[73] were clearly key punitive elements of that practice, leading to forcible removal from a territory and mass deprivations of human rights based on certain protected characteristics. These characteristics were listed and included political, racial, or religious grounds. Crimes against humanity as they were defined by the Statute of the International Criminal Tribunal for Rwanda (ICTR) differed in two major aspects from those of the ICTY. First, there was no connection to an armed conflict, but an attack of a widespread or systematic nature on the civilian population was required. Second, a discriminatory element was added to the general requirements of crimes against humanity, whereas the attack on the population derived from national, political, *ethnic*, racial, or religious grounds.

Against this statutory background both tribunals treated cases involving atrocities that the general media reported as "ethnic cleansing" even though the legal classification was always different. As the ICTY Trial Chamber observed, "the so-called 'ethnic cleansing', [...] although it is not a term of art, is particularly germane to the work of this Tribunal."[74] Both tribunals carefully avoided promoting ethnic cleansing as a legal category, but could not and did not recede from addressing that practice. Judges found appropriate legal categories in two basic manners: *first*, by means of identifying distinctive elements for the respective crimes against humanity, namely deportation/forcible transfer and persecution; and *second* by examining, in appropriate instances, the shared purpose of the perpetrators as part of the applicable mode of liability.

The first relevant crime against humanity to be examined here is deportation or forcible transfer. The difference between these two acts is the existence or

71 This statutory definition still linked crimes against humanity to an armed conflict, which was factually true in the former Yugoslavia, but such a condition was omitted from later texts. The Statute of the ICTR proved to be more influential in this regard via the establishment of the threshold of a "systematic or widespread" nature of the attack on the civil population.

72 Art. 5 (d).

73 Art. 5 (h).

74 Kupreskic Trial Judgment, para. 606.

lack of a cross-border element.[75] The common aspect in both cases is displacement, which is not necessarily unlawful in and of itself.[76] As some defence counsels argued,[77] it may be demanded by humanitarian considerations, maybe even by an international humanitarian law obligation.[78] However, for both crimes "the absence of genuine choice [on the part of the victims] makes displacement unlawful."[79] This "genuine choice" should not be equated with consent. Also, displacement is not temporary: the intent is to displace on a permanent basis.[80] Deportation is "an open-conduct crime. In other words, the perpetrator may commit several different conducts which can amount to 'expulsion or other coercive acts', so as to force the victim to leave the area where he or she is lawfully present."[81]

Persecution is much akin to genocide, although it is a far less restrictive crime. Like genocide, the "ultimate victim [...] is the group, although its destruction necessarily requires the commission of crimes against its members, that is, against individuals belonging to that group."[82] The victims of persecution are also singled out because of their membership in a particular group, which leads to the specific mental element.[83] In the *Kordic and Cerkez* Trial Judgment, the ICTY further clarified the discriminatory intent behind persecution: "[T]he acts of the accused must have been aimed at singling out and attacking certain individuals on discriminatory grounds," with the aim of "removal of those persons from the society in which they live alongside the perpetrators, or eventually even from humanity itself."[84] This closing remark – the removal from humanity – implies that although persecution is aimed at a serious deprivation of human rights, or, in the form of an ethnic cleansing aimed at removal, it may also be tantamount to actual physical destruction.

Although persecution is a more open crime than either genocide or deportation,[85] the acts constituting persecution are nevertheless measured against

75 ICTY (IT-97-24-A) *Prosecutor v. Milomir Stakić* Trial Chamber Judgment of 31 July 2003, para. 671.
76 See e.g., ICTY *Prosecutor v. Jovica Stanišić & Franko Simatović* (IT-03-69) Trial Judgment paras. 993–995; Krstić Trial Judgment paras. 524–527.
77 See supra, note 75.
78 Article 49 of the 4th Geneva Convention 1949. See also Jean-Marie Henckaerts and Louise Doswald-Beck, "Customary International Humanitarian Law" Cambridge University Press-ICRC Geneva, 2005, Rule 129 p. 457 *et seq.*
79 Krnojelac Appeal Judgment, para. 229. *Simatović et al.* Trial Judgment 993–994.
80 *Simatović et al.* Trial Judgment 995.
81 ICC-01/09-01/11-373 *Ruto et al. Decision on the Confirmation of Charges Pursuant to Article 61(7)(a) and (b) of the Rome Statute* para. 244.
82 *ICTY Prosecutor v. Dusko Sikirica, Damir Dosen, Dragan Kolundzija*, Case No. IT-95-8-T, Judgment on Defence Motion to Acquit, 3 September 2001 ("Sikirica Rule 98bis Decision"), para. 89.
83 See, for example, the Kupreskic Trial Judgment, paras. 636 & 751.
84 *Kordic and Cerkez* trial, para. 214. See also the Kupreskic Trial Judgment, para. 634.
85 See: *Kordic and Cerkez* para. 191–192; Kupreskic Trial, paras. 597–598.

strict standards. The underlying acts must infringe on a fundamental right and must be of a gravity comparable to other crimes against humanity,[86] but these acts alone, without any distinguishing criteria, are not necessarily crimes under international law.[87] The acts, taken together, must pass the threshold of an international crime. As the ICTR formulated in the *Nahimana* case: "underlying acts of persecution can be considered together. It is the cumulative effect of all the underlying acts of the crime of persecution which must reach a level of gravity equivalent to that for other crimes against humanity."[88]

Deportation, forcible transfer, and the openly defined *actus reus* of persecution together broadly encompass the versatile set of actions establishing an ethnic cleansing.[89] At the same time, the similarly open mental element of this latter crime makes the label of persecution less fitting to ethnic cleansing. Persecution is a discriminatory crime, and does not require an intent to destroy, but the intent to expel is also missing from its elements. In situations of ethnic cleansing this gap may cause important supporters of – or even the very masterminds of – ethnic cleansing to avoid criminal justice, if they themselves do not commit the acts of persecution,[90] but "only" create the fateful common design thereof.

The underlying acts creating the coercive force to expel the selected population varied from killing, torture, beatings, and rape to arson and destruction of property and places of religion. Such atrocities could take place at a number of indeterminate locations: in private homes, military barracks, police stations, internment camps, or even UN safe zones. This variety of acts and locations carries with it the inherent danger that the acts are treated as independent human rights violations or war crimes. Nevertheless, in spite of the diverse acts, the common purpose behind ethnic cleansing remained clearly identifiable and established the link among the distinct elements, particularly in the Bosnian conflict. For the ethnic Serb perpetrators, strong evidence of such a plan was a statement from the leader of the Bosnian Serb State, Radovan Karadzic, where he articulated six strategic goals of the Serbian People of Bosnia and Herzegovina. The first of these was the "separation from the other two national communities – separation of states"; the other goals focused on certain territorial demands (corridors to other Serb territories or to the sea). Seizure and control

86 Popovic Appeal 762.

87 *Nahimana et al.* Appeal Judgment, para. 985; Brdanin Appeal Judgment, para. 296; *Kvočka et al.* Appeal Judgment, para. 323; Popovic 738.

88 Nahimana, Appeal 987.

89 Deportation may even be understood as a form of persecution. See the Kupreskic Trial, para. 605; *Krnojelac Appeal* (IT-97-25) paras. 217–222; *Stanišić & Simatović* (IT-03-69) Trial Judgment para. 970.

90 ICTY, *Prosecutor v. Radoslav Brdanin*, IT-99-36-A, Appeals Chamber, Judgment, 3 April 2007, paras. 407–409. See also Vincent Chetail, "Is There Any Blood on My Hands: Deportation as a Crime of International Law Hague International Tribunals: International Criminal Courts and Tribunals" *Leiden Journal of International Law* 917.

of the territory "entailed the permanent removal of a significant part of the non-Serb population."[91] A similar policy was found by the ICTY in the Lasva Valley atrocities, where the Croatian community of Herzeg-Bosna launched systematic attacks on the local Muslim population.[92] The common plan in this case was proven retrospectively, by events leading to the ethnic violence[93] and by the impact of the attacks.[94]

The diverse acts which can constitute ethnic cleansing must thus be coordinated according to a common plan or policy: the perpetrators act in relative concert to advance that design. In the *Tadic Appeal* Judgment, the judges observed such a "shared intention on the part of a group to forcibly remove members of one ethnicity from their town, village or region (to effect "ethnic cleansing") with the consequence that, in the course of doing so, one or more of the victims is shot and killed."[95] Technically, this "shared intention" is not an element of the relevant crime, but is subsumed in the so-called "mode of liability". The physical and mental elements of the crime are required conditions for a judge to find that *a crime has been committed*, while the "mode of liability" is the required link *to connect the crime to the perpetrator.*[96] When there is more than one perpetrator – which is rather common in international criminal law[97] – this link may reflect certain differences, but the perpetrators still act together to further a "common criminal purpose." In interpreting the post-war tribunals' case law, the Appeals Chamber in *Tadic* found that in those cases "offences perpetrated by any of [the perpetrators] may entail the criminal liability of all the members of the group."

This led to a new form of criminality,[98] subsequently referred to as an extended form of joint criminal enterprise, or JCE III. This mode of liability later became highly contested, both in the international criminal legal practice and in the literature alike.[99] The same appeal judgment in *Tadic* defined it by establishing within the group of perpetrators "a common design to pursue one course of conduct where one of the perpetrators commits an act

91 Brdanin Trial Judgment, paras. 77.
92 Blaskic Trial Judgment para. 343–350.
93 Ibid.
94 Ibid., para. 634.
95 *Tadic Appeal* Judgment para. 204.
96 See, for example, ICTY *Prosecutor v Radoslav Brdanin Decision on Interlocutory Appeal*, 19 March 2004 paras. 5–6.
97 See Giulia Bigi, "Joint Criminal Enterprise in the Jurisprudence of the International Criminal Tribunal for the Former Yugoslavia and the Prosecution of Senior Political and Military Leaders The Krajišnik Case" (2010) 14 *Max Planck Yearbook of United Nations Law Online* 51, p. 53.
98 Although primarily developed by the ICTY, it was also applied at the ICTR. See *Ntakirutimana et al.* (ICTR-96-17) paras. 463–469.
99 See Andrés Pérez, "Here to Stay? Extended Liability for Joint Criminal Enterprise as a Tool for Prosecuting Mass SGBV Crimes," ASIL Insights, 12 June 2015; Kevin Jon Heller, "The ECCC Issues a Landmark Decision on JCE III" opinioiuris.org, 23 May 2010.

which, while outside the common design, was nevertheless a natural and foreseeable consequence of the effecting of that common purpose."[100] The judges went on to offer an explanation: "[M]urder may not have been explicitly acknowledged to be part of the common design, it was nevertheless foreseeable that the forcible removal of civilians at gunpoint might well result in the deaths of one or more of those civilians."[101] If these conditions are met, the perpetrators share criminal responsibility also for reasonably foreseeable acts which fall outside the range of their original plan. An appeals chamber of the ICTY even reached the conclusion from this form of liability that someone may become criminally liable for a genocide that he personally did not intend to commit,[102] although the reference cited in support of this conclusion reads: "in the case of participation in a joint criminal enterprise, i.e. as a co-perpetrator, the requisite *mens rea* is intent to pursue a common purpose."[103]

Having established the role of a common plan behind ethnic cleansing, the next issue to be addressed is the difference between this common plan and the specific genocidal intent. Raphael Lemkin gave a name to the previously nameless crime, and in doing so he pushed genocide into the spotlight; and together with the existence of international criminal tribunals the culture of impunity ceased to be universal. Therefore, today it is not reasonable to believe that any persons organising a genocide would document or even publish their genocidal plans.[104] Even policies for ethnic cleansing are highly unlikely to be published. After the "war on terror" became part of the international political parlance, the target group would most likely be addressed as "terrorists." Obviously, genocide could never be legitimised, not even by the target population's involvement in an armed conflict or terrorist activities. The rhetorical change shows, however, that reserving the crime of genocide solely to instances where a stated public policy of physical destruction exists would soon render null the protection this term can offer for the victim groups.

The resulting foreseeable lack of documentary or physical evidence would mean that proving intent would probably require inductive or deductive methods, and while result is not an element of the crime, the actual impact on the target group may become an important factor in the judicial assessment of intent.[105] However, this actual impact cannot be assessed properly without defining the target group. The first aspect of such a definition is the assumption that while the suffering is borne by the members of the group, the group as

100 *Tadic Appeal* Judgment.
101 Ibid.
102 Brdjanin, Interlocutory Appeal, paras. 5–6.
103 Vasiljevic, Appeal Judgment, para. 102.
104 Ibid., p. 357.
105 ICJ Croatian Genocide Judgment paras. 479–480; see also, for example, the Rohingya example in MacLean, p. 91.

such is also the victim of genocide.[106] The perpetrator seeks and intends the destruction of the group, although not necessarily in its entirety.[107] Targeting a substantial part of the group is sufficient to establish genocide if other elements of the crime also exist. This "substantial part" can be defined, inter alia, by using a geographical perspective; i.e. when the perpetrators focus on a territorially-selected segment of the group.[108] The defence in *Krstić* argued that defining an artificial group by limiting the geographical area would contradict the concept of genocide. The Chamber agreed that the group itself cannot be defined solely on the basis of its geographical location, because that is "not a criterion contemplated by the Convention."[109] On the other hand, considering the formula "part of a group," the Court ruled that "the intent to eradicate a group within a limited geographical area such as the region of a country or even a municipality may be characterised as genocide."[110]

Genocide, therefore, is possible against national, racial, religious, or ethnic groups living within a designated geographical area. Without a documented genocidal intent the result in such a case is the same as in the case of an "ethnic cleansing" – an ethnically homogeneous area, where a part of the previous dwellers have fled and another part have been destroyed.[111] Therefore, without questioning that the delimitation between genocide and crimes against humanity is the requisite intent, the proximity of genocide and ethnic cleansing remains palpable.[112] The difference between the contents of the two terms seems to be a matter of proportion.

Furthermore, the time factor of the intent adds to the already complex relationship between ethnic cleansing and genocide. The genocidal intent need not be long-standing or premeditated.[113] It is therefore possible that a common

106 See A. Dirk Moses on "groupism" in A. Dirk Moses, "Raphael Lemkin, Culture, and the Concept of Genocide," in Donald Bloxham and A. Dirk Moses (eds), *The Oxford Handbook of Genocide Studies* (2010); also the Krstić Trial Judgment para. 552; Akayesu Trial Judgment, para. 522; Kayishema; and Ruzindana Trial Judgment, para. 99.

107 Krstić Trial Judgment para. 590: "the perpetrators of genocide need not seek to destroy the entire group protected by the Convention, they must view the part of the group they wish to destroy as a distinct entity which must be eliminated as such."

108 Ibid.: "the physical destruction may target only a part of the geographically limited part of the larger group because the perpetrators of the genocide regard the intended destruction as sufficient to annihilate the group as a distinct entity in the geographic area at issue. In this regard, it is important to bear in mind the total context in which the physical destruction is carried out."

109 Krstić Trial Judgment paras. 558–559.

110 Krstić Trial Judgment paras. 589–595. According to early commentators (Robinson, Drost) cited by the judges, it may be "a region or even a local community if the number of persons targeted was substantial." See also "Report of the Commission of Experts, UN Doc. S/1994/674" para. 94.

111 See Krstić Trial Judgment 595.

112 See, for example, Benjamin Lieberman, "Ethnic Cleansing versus Genocide?" in Donald Bloxham and A. Dirk Moses (eds), *The Oxford Handbook of Genocide Studies* (2010); Sirkin.

113 Krstić Trial Judgment, para. 572; Jelisic Appeal Judgment para. 48: a plan is not required.

plan had been established to create an ethnically homogeneous area by means of deportation and persecutions, but at some points the perpetrators opted for the physical destruction of the group, at least partially. This suggests that the aim of ethnic cleansing and genocidal intent are in a dynamic relationship: ethnic cleansing may be a herald of genocide.[114] The somewhat obsolete JCE III responsibility added further complexity by making it possible to find responsibility even if the intent of several perpetrators changed, but the result finally achieved would have already been reasonably foreseeable according to the original plan: an intent to forward the common plan may be sufficient to find someone criminally liable for genocide.[115] The Chamber in *Krstić* acknowledged a progressively developing convergence between the concepts of ethnic cleansing and genocide in international customary law.[116] However, the majority of the judges remained doubtful about the actual results of that progress at the time of the judgment, and therefore based their findings on the more restrictive interpretation of genocide.

If it is accepted that genocide can be committed against a part of the targeted group living in a sufficiently large area, the actual methods used for the destruction of the group are also relevant from the perspective of ethnic cleansing. Contrary to the original ideas of Raphael Lemkin, cultural genocide was rejected in the final text of the Convention, with the exception of the forcible removal of children from the group. Therefore today an "enterprise attacking only the cultural or sociological characteristics of a human group in order to annihilate these elements – which give that group its own identity distinct from the rest of the community – would not fall under the definition of genocide."[117] A forced assimilation or dissolution of a group is therefore not genocide, but this observation does not define what are those elements which only "give to that group its identity" (cultural genocide)[118] and what are those which are necessary for the survival of the group itself (e.g. economic genocide).[119]

Access to a specific territory may be regarded under both headings: living in a territory may be part of the identity of a group, or it might be essential for its survival. While it is physically possible for the members of the group to earn a living elsewhere, it also seems reasonable to accept that mass displacement is

114 Schabas, *Genocide in International Law*.
115 Supra, see notes 97–98.
116 Krstic Trial Judgment, para. 580, notes this ongoing development (see also para. 571), whereas ethnic cleansing under resolutions specifically referred to at the time of the Judgment notes only physical or biological destruction. Para. 571 reads: "Some legal commentators further contend that genocide embraces those acts whose foreseeable or probable consequence is the total or partial destruction of the group without any necessity of showing that destruction was the goal of the act."
117 Krstić Trial Judgment 580.
118 Lemkin, *Axis Rule*, p. 83.
119 Ibid.

different from mere suppression of a culture, a language, or a religion.[120] The writings of Lemkin make it clear that he associated destruction with the "crippling" of the group.[121]

None of the above answer the question whether deprivation from access to a territory can be a form of the physical destruction required by the legal concept of genocide. To approve such an interpretation, it must be shown *first* that living on a territory can be a part of the group's identity; and *second* that the deprivation from access to the territory will result in the group's destruction.

The special role of a territory as an identity element is supported by, for example, UNGA Resolution 61/295 issued under the United Nations Declaration on the Rights of Indigenous Peoples. This Declaration has recognised on multiple occasions the connection between an indigenous group and the territories which they traditionally owned. The text does not make any explicit reference to either ethnic cleansing or genocide;[122] however, some inferences can be made from the prohibition of deportation and forcible transfer.[123] Article 26 of the Declaration recognises an explicit right of indigenous people to the "the lands, territories and resources which they have traditionally owned, occupied or otherwise used or acquired." The special link to a territory requires a closer examination in future cases where indigenous people are targeted by ethnic violence, and Lemkin's original ideas on cultural genocide may gain new support in this respect.[124]

Case law also incorporates a connection between the group's survival and its access to its territory, but with a reservation of causality. Genocide may also incapacitate the group from returning to its previous location. Such a result was found in case of the Srebrenica genocide, and this result was in turn used as evidence of the genocidal intent:

> The strategic location of the enclave, situated between two Serb territories, may explain why the Bosnian Serb forces did not limit themselves to expelling the Bosnian Muslim population. By killing all the military aged men, the Bosnian Serb forces effectively destroyed the community of the Bosnian Muslims in Srebrenica as such and eliminated all likelihood that it could "ever re-establish itself on that territory".[125]

The remaining issue is therefore whether a group can be destroyed by forcible removal from its territories. Nothing in the preparatory works or in the case law

120 Ferrara, p. 2.
121 Lemkin, "Genocide" (1946); see also Moses.
122 UNGA Resolution 61/295 Article 8.
123 UNGA Resolution 61/295 Article 10.
124 For more details, see Damien Short, "Cultural Genocide and Indigenous Peoples: A Sociological Approach" (2010) 14 *The International Journal of Human Rights* 833.
125 Krstić Trial Judgment, para. 597.

suggests that the destruction of a group which is the victim of genocide must be immediate. The Trial Chamber in *Akayeshu* ruled

> that the expression deliberately inflicting on the group conditions of life calculated to bring about its physical destruction in whole or in part, should be construed as the methods of destruction by which the perpetrator does not immediately kill the members of the group, but which, ultimately, seek their physical destruction.[126]

It therefore seems more likely that the causality between the genocidal act and the intended destruction of the victim group must be direct, but not imminent.[127] A direct link would mean that even absent any third-party intervention or *deus ex machina*, the perpetrators' actions would result in the elimination of the group as such. But genocide can also be committed through the slow death of the group.[128] Ethnic cleansing can be designed to achieve such ends, although it poses difficulties in proving that such a result was the "calculation" of the perpetrators.[129] By coercive means, a smaller part of the group is destroyed locally, which places their survival in a position without any genuine choice. If they stay, their destruction would be immediate. If they leave, the group will lose its identity. This could very well happen if, for example, a religious minority is deprived of access to holy places; or if a linguistic minority is forced to flee to a country where a one-language policy is in force. In cases like this, forcible removal from the territory physically eliminates the group in the targeted area as well, as it destroys the group itself within one or two generations.

Conclusions

The works of Raphael Lemkin did not reflect on "ethnic cleansing" under this heading as such, but his writings strongly suggest that he included the distinctive elements of such a policy in his definition of genocide. These are the very elements that were persistently removed from his original concept in the treaty-making procedure. The final, restrictive version of genocide became part of international law in 1948 and is therefore the foundation for any legal argument. In criminal law an extensive interpretation is less than welcome. The gravity of the offence requires a very careful approach, even in a mere academic examination. While there is a temptation to use "genocide" in a broader sense to offer wider protection for the victims, the term should

126 Akayesu, Trial Judgment, paras. 505–506.
127 Lemkin, *Axis Rule*, p. 79.
128 Ibid. See also Payam Akhavan, "The Crime of Genocide in the ICTR Jurisprudence" (2005) 3 *Journal of International Criminal Justice* 989, p. 1004.
129 William A. Schabas, "'Ethnic Cleansing' and Genocide."

be reserved for the most serious acts. "A strong case can be made that the reckless use of the term 'genocide' is dangerous."[130] The above arguments are therefore not meant to present a case for a re-conceptualisation of the legal definition of genocide.

At the same time, however, a total rejection of ethnic cleansing as a form of genocide would be a mistake and stand in contradiction to the intent of Lemkin. He

> did not define genocide as the attempted extermination of an entire group. Lemkin, who lost 49 members of his family, including his parents, to the Final Solution, knew that if extermination were the threshold for a response, action would inevitably come too late.[131]

Several authors argue that ethnic cleansing is a forerunner of a genocide to come. After the Wannsee Conference decided on the details of the Final Solution, the violence against European Jews rose to a new, horrible level. The difference between the pogroms and the *Kristallnacht* marked – when compared to the horror of the concentration camps – a change in the aim of the perpetrators, but it may or may not be the pattern for future events in different cultural settings.

At the same time, fixing a rigid, restrictive concept of genocide and then stretching it to encompass any mass violence is equally wrong. In light of Lemkin's writings, an outright rejection of new forms of genocide, where the physical destruction is not as prevalent as it had been in the twentieth century, as well as accepting that any mass atrocity is genocide, would both indeed lead to strange results. As A. Dirk Moses wrote, it would suggest

> that Lemkin did not properly understand genocide, despite the fact that he invented the term and went to great trouble to explain its meaning. Instead, most scholars presume to instruct Lemkin, retrospectively, about his concept, although they are in fact proposing a different concept, usually mass murder.[132]

Today there seems to be increasing agreement among academics that certain forms of ethnic cleansing fall within a grey zone[133] between crimes against humanity and genocide. If it is accepted that genocide can be committed without the physical *and* imminent annihilation of the victim group, it becomes

130 Robert M. Hayden, "'Ethnic Cleansing' and 'Genocide'" (2007) 17 *European Journal of Public Health* 546.

131 See Samantha Power, "It's Not Enough to Call It Genocide", *Time*, 4 October 2004.

132 A. Dirk Moses, "Raphael Lemkin, Culture, and the Concept of Genocide," in Donald Bloxham and A. Dirk Moses (eds), *The Oxford Handbook of Genocide Studies* (2010).

133 See, for example, Hon, p. 375.

obvious that mass forced removal of people from their homes may easily destroy the group locally. The International Criminal Court Pre-Trial Chamber in *Al-Bashir* noted that

> the practice of ethnic cleansing – which usually amounts to the crime against humanity of persecution [...] may result in genocide if it brings about the commission of the objective elements of genocide provided for in article 6 of the Statute and the Elements of Crimes with the dolus specialus/specific intent to destroy in whole or in part the targeted group.[134]

In this grey zone there are already policies of ethnic cleansing that should be classified as genocide. The simplicity of the arguments presented in the separate opinion of Judge Lauterpacht in the Bosnian Genocide Case at the ICJ is indeed convincing:

> [I]t is difficult to regard the Serbian acts as other than acts of genocide in that they clearly fall within categories (a), (b) and (c) of the definition of genocide quoted above; they are clearly directed against an ethnical or religious group as such, and they are intended to destroy that group, if not in whole certainly in part, to the extent necessary to ensure that that group no longer occupies the parts of Bosnia-Herzegovina coveted by the Serbs.

In simpler terms: if the act is genocidal, the intent is genocidal, and the victim group is protected by the Convention – then why should it not be called a genocide?

The hesitation to admit the existence of such a grey zone or an actual overlap may be due to several different reasons. To balance the arguments based on the *travaux préparatoires* of the Genocide Convention, it should be noted that during the creation of the Genocide Convention forced population transfers were taking place in European and other Allied countries in surprisingly large proportions. The end of World War II was followed by mass, forced expulsions of populations (often sharing the ethnicity of former Axis countries, which were perceived to be responsible for the Holocaust).[135] The Soviet authorities alone effectively cleansed large areas they had obtained from Poland, Hungary, and Romania as well as their own former territories, like the Crimean Peninsula – and a significant part of the deported persons

134 ICC-02/05-01/09 *The Prosecutor v Omar Hassan Al-Bashir*, Decision on the Prosecution's Application for a Warrant of Arrest against Omar Hassan Ahmad Al-Bashir, 4 March 2009, Para. 145.

135 Liebermann; Hayden, p. 728.

died in gulags located in or around Siberia.[136] Hundreds of thousands of civilians were selected from "working age" men and women – so tragically echoing the later Srebrenica genocide committed against men of "military age" (while both terms generally defined the mating age for human beings). The reluctance toward group rights thus did not prevent policies based on collective guilt, but this was never a monopoly of autocratic or totalitarian regimes.[137] It would have been a political impossibility in the late 1940s to include these acts within the same legal categorisation as the Holocaust.

Contemporary advocacy groups also argue that

> the term to be used [in public discourse] is determined by willingness to take action to stop the killing. When the terms 'ethnic cleansing' or 'crimes against humanity' were used, it indicated unwillingness to take forceful action to stop the crimes. These weak words have never motivated the use of force.[138]

However, calling an atrocity a genocide does not guarantee intervention, either.[139]

Admitting that an ethnic cleansing which resulted in a genocide *was* actually genocide itself would help to avoid an implicit, sordid dilemma for future judges. If ethnic cleansing practices must be separated from the subsequent genocide, who will be able to name the last victim of the ethnic cleansing and identify the first victim of the genocide?

136 See Tamas Stark, "Genocide or Genocidal Massacre? The Case of Hungarian Prisoners in Soviet Custody" 1(3) Human Rights Review, p. 109; Milada Polisenska, "Legal, Diplomatic and Moral Aspects of Deportation of Czechoslovaks to the Soviet Gulag," in Peter Bolcha and Rowland M. Brucken (eds.), *Proceedings of the Interdisciplinary Conference on Human Rights*. Praha: Anglo-Americká Univerzita. Vermont: Norwich University (2019), p. 101.

137 Liebermann.

138 *"Persecution, Forced Displacement, and Genocide of Rohingya, Kachin, Shan, Karen and Other Minorities of Myanmar."* Testimony of Dr. Gregory H. Stanton to the Permanent People's Tribunal Kuala Lumpur, Malaysia 18 September 2017.

139 Rebecca Hamilton, "The G-Word Paradox: Why Calling an Atrocity a 'Genocide' Is Rarely a Game-Changer," at www.foreignpolicy.com 22 March 2016.

11 Genocide and culture

Revisiting their relationship 70 years after the Genocide Convention

Marco Odello

Introduction

The present chapter starts from the assumption that the definition of genocide in the 1948 Convention on the Prevention and Punishment of the Crime of Genocide (Genocide Convention)[1] was the product of a specific historical, political, and ideological context; and that the text of the Convention was limited in some dimensions by several factors that influenced the choices made by states at the time. This issue has been well described by Bilsky and Klagsbrun as the 'inherent tension between law and history.'[2]

Since the adoption of the 1948 Genocide Convention, actions and crimes that have led to different instances of genocide have not ceased. Furthermore, there has been an increasing use of different methods by actors who have perpetrated genocidal actions, and these deserve particular attention in order to understand whether the original definition adopted by the 1948 Genocide Convention may provide for new or different ways of interpretation of the crime and its components. The aim of this chapter is to explore in particular the link between genocide and culture, including the destruction of cultural heritage, property, and other cultural expressions, such as languages and traditions. These cultural expressions have different definitions,[3] such as: (1) 'cultural heritage,' which includes the legacy of physical artefacts and intangible attributes of a group or society that are inherited from previous generations, maintained in the present, and bestowed for the benefit of future generations;[4] (2) 'tangible heritage,' which includes buildings, historic places, monuments, artefacts, etc. which are considered worthy of preservation for the future; and (3) 'intangible heritage,' defined as 'the practices, representations, expressions, knowledge, skills – as well

1 UN General Assembly, *Convention on the Prevention and Punishment of the Crime of Genocide*, 9 December 1948, United Nations, Treaty Series, Vol. 78, p. 277.

2 Leora Bilsky & Rachel Klagsbrun, 'The Return of Cultural Genocide?' (2018) 29(2) *European Journal of International Law* 373–396, 375.

3 See Janet Blake, *International Cultural Heritage Law* (Oxford: Oxford University Press, 2015).

4 UNESCO, *Convention Concerning the Protection of the World Cultural and Natural Heritage*, Paris, 16 November 1972, Article 1.

as the instruments, objects, artefacts and cultural spaces associated therewith – that communities, groups and, in some cases, individuals recognize as part of their cultural heritage.'[5] These include objects significant to the archaeology, architecture, science, or technology of a specific culture.

This chapter takes into account three main issues:

1 The discussion on genocide that led to the adoption of its international legal definition in 1948;
2 The developments in international law related to human rights, and cultural rights in particular, that came after the adoption of the Genocide Convention;
3 The role of international criminal jurisdictions in addressing actions against cultural heritage and goods.

This study is premised on a cohesive view of the relationship between different areas of international law and some of their sub-categories, such as international human rights law, international humanitarian law (IHL), and international criminal law. These areas of international law have emerged and developed over time in different – but often related – contexts, and with very similar purposes, such as the protection of human dignity and providing protection for the victims of certain acts. Often the developments in one area have influenced new developments in other areas. For instance, the violations of IHL during the Second World War led to the development of a new area of international criminal law, as the crimes committed against individuals in armed conflicts increased the support for the adoption of the 1949 Geneva Conventions and their 1977 Additional Protocols.

The present chapter looks at the development of cultural rights in international law, and how there is a growing need for their more explicit protection when they are targeted, whether in situations of peace or during armed conflicts. In both cases it is relevant to consider how recent developments in international criminal law have included more and better references to the protection of cultural property, and how useful it would be to have a more comprehensive approach to the protection of cultural goods and heritage. The purpose of this analysis is also to avoid an 'anachronism' in international law, an idea developed by Reisman with particular reference to human rights and sovereignty, as

> [a]nachronism can only be avoided in legal decision by systematic actualization, which considers inherited norms in the context of changed constitutive normative systems and makes sensitive assessments of the relative weight each is to be given and the various intensities with which each is demanded.[6]

5 UNESCO, *Convention for the Safeguarding of the Intangible Cultural Heritage*, Paris, 17 October 2003, Article 2.

6 W. Michael Reisman, 'Sovereignty and Human Rights in Contemporary International Law' (1990) 84 *Am. J. Int'l L.* 866–876, 874.

Also, this evolutionary approach to interpretation can be found in the 1969 Vienna Convention on the Law of Treaties (VCLT),[7] which in Article 31(3)(c) refers to 'any relevant rules of international law applicable in the relations between the parties' as a way to determine the meaning of the obligations under a treaty. This method provides for a more teleological interpretation of treaties; one that would better secure the application of the 'object and purpose' of treaties, as defined by Article 31(1) of the 1969 VCLT. It is clear that this interpretation should not exceed the meaning and purposes of the treaty, as Fitzmaurice explained that

> [t]his, of course, however excellent, is not law but sociology; and although the aim is said to be "in support of the search for the genuine shared expectations of the parties," it would in many cases have – and is perhaps subconsciously designed to have – quite a different effect, namely, in the guise of interpretation, to substitute the will of the adjudicator for that of the parties.[8]

However, inasmuch we are dealing with human rights protection, it would be appropriate to take into consideration the approach to interpretation provided by Article 29 of the American Convention of Human Rights;[9] i.e. that the interpretation of international instruments should be done in the light of the legal framework at the time of interpretation,[10] based on the International Court of Justice's Advisory Opinion in the *Namibia* case.[11] Also, the *pro homine* interpretation, which has been affirmed repeatedly by the Interamerican Court,[12] provides a teleological approach in favour of a better protection of human rights, which can help in the discussion in this chapter.[13]

7 United Nations, *Vienna Convention on the Law of Treaties*, 23 May 1969, United Nations, Treaty Series, Vol. 1155, p. 331.

8 Gerald Fitzmaurice, 'Vae Victis or Woe to the Negotiator? Your Treaty of Our Interpretation of It' (review essay) (1971) 65 *AJIL* 358–373, 372.

9 Organization of American States (OAS), *American Convention on Human Rights, 'Pact of San Jose', Costa Rica*, 22 November 1969, available at: www.refworld.org/docid/3ae6b36510.html [accessed 10 November 2019].

10 IA Court H.R., *Interpretation of the American Declaration of the Rights and Duties of Man within the Frame-work of Article 64 of the American Convention on Human Rights*, Advisory Opinion OC-10/89, 14 July 1989, Series A No. 10, para. 37.

11 *Legal Consequences for States of the Continued Presence of South Africa in Namibia (South West Africa) not-withstanding Security Council Resolution 276 (1970)*, Advisory Opinion [1971] ICJ Rep 16.

12 IA Court H.R., *Case of Ricardo Canese v. Paraguay*, Merits, Reparations, and Costs, Judgment of 31 August 2004, Series C No. 111, para. 181.

13 For a full discussion on this matter, see Lucas Lixinski, 'Treaty Interpretation by the Inter-American Court of Human Rights: Expansionism at the Service of the Unity of International Law' (2010) 21(3) *EJIL* 585–604.

The original proposals regarding the definition of genocide by Lemkin,[14] who supported a broader concept of genocide, should be reconsidered in light of the developments that have taken place in the last 70 years. Both human rights protection and international criminal law cases seem to support a renewed approach to the concept of genocide that could take into account the original proposed definition. Also, the development of group rights in relation to minorities and indigenous people, and the definition of culture (which is elaborated below) seem to support a more coherent approach that links acts against culture to international crimes that may affect humanity more generally, and specific groups in particular.

The purpose of this chapter is not to read into the definition of genocide what was not expressly included by states in 1948. Rather, it attempts to justify the possible inclusion of certain acts that did not receive sufficient attention at the time – for different reasons that will be explained – but which have become more relevant during the past 70 years, due to the evolution of international rules and principles that cannot be set aside in the process of interpretation of legal rules in contemporary scenarios. One of these is certainly the concept of culture, its definition, and its relevance for nations, minorities, and groups in international law.

Definition of genocide in the 1948 Convention and the historical and political background

The adoption of the 1948 Genocide Convention was based on a series of historical and political factors which both influenced and distorted the original proposals that were formulated by Raphael Lemkin. The original draft, based on the scripts of Lemkin, who wrote on this subject in the period between the two world wars, has received renewed attention in academic writings on genocide.[15] The time and the context in which the Genocide Convention was adopted were not propitious for a definition of genocide that could include the destruction of culture in the form of cultural objects, artefacts, and expressions; i.e. the so-called 'cultural genocide,' which has been defined as 'the purposeful weakening and ultimate

14 Raphael Lemkin, *Axis Rule in Occupied Europe: Laws of Occupation, Analysis of Government, Proposals for Redress* (Washington, DC: Carnegie Endowment for International Peace, 1944) 79–95.

15 See, among others, Douglas Irvin-Erickson, *Raphael Lemkin and the Concept of Genocide* (Philadelphia, PA: University of Pennsylvania Press, 2017) 19–41; A. Dirk Moses, 'Raphael Lemkin, Culture, and the Concept of Genocide', in Donald Bloxham and A. Dirk Moses (eds), *The Oxford Handbook of Genocide Studies* (Oxford: Oxford University Press, 2010) 19–41 Chapter 1; Dominik J. Schaller and Jürgen Zimmerer (eds), *The Origins of Genocide: Raphael Lemkin as a Historian of Mass Violence* (London/New York, NY: Routledge, 2009); Anton Weiss-Wendt, 'Hostage of Politics: Raphael Lemkin on "Soviet Genocide"' (2005) 7(4) *Journal of Genocide Research* 551–59.

destruction of cultural values and practices of feared out-groups.'[16] However, the renewed attention to Lemkin's writings and the relevance of international legal developments concerning the protection of culture may provide grounds for a more comprehensive understanding of the concept of genocide in its original formulation and its relationship to culture.[17] This issue is going to be addressed by, initially, looking at the original formulations of the crime of genocide and the position of those states which rejected a broad concept of genocide in relation to cultural destruction. Later, the concept of culture and its development and meaning in international law will be discussed to bring together the arguments related to the role of culture in the context of genocide.

Definition of genocide: from broad to narrow

The definition of genocide provided in Article 2 of the 1948 Genocide Convention reads as follows:

> In the present Convention, genocide means any of the following acts committed with intent to destroy, in whole or in part, a national, ethnical, racial or religious group, as such:
>
> (a) Killing members of the group;
> (b) Causing serious bodily or mental harm to members of the group;
> (c) Deliberately inflicting on the group conditions of life calculated to bring about its physical destruction in whole or in part;
> (d) Imposing measures intended to prevent births within the group;
> (e) Forcibly transferring children of the group to another group.

It is important to keep in mind the links between the acts and the intention. The 'special purpose'[18] required for genocide means that it is essential to demonstrate a specific intent on the part of the perpetrators to destroy a protected

16 Lawrence Davidson, *Cultural Genocide* (New Brunswick, NJ: Rutgers University Press, 2012) 18–19.

17 Leora Bilsky and Rachel Klagsbrun, 'The Return of Cultural Genocide?' (2018) 29(2) *European Journal of International Law* 373–396; Jeffrey S. Bachman (ed.), *Cultural Genocide: Law, Politics, and Global Manifestations* (London/New York, NY: Routledge, 2019).

18 ICTY, *Prosecutor v. Goran Jelisić* (Judgment) IT-95-10-T 14 December 1999, paras 66–108; Geert-Jan Alexander Knoops, 'Mens Rea and Genocide', in *Mens Rea at the International Criminal Court* (Leiden: Martinus Nijhoff, 2016) 93–110; Devrim Aydin, 'The Interpretation of Genocidal Intent under the Genocide Convention and the Jurisprudence of International Courts' (2014) 78(5) *The Journal of Criminal Law* 423–441; William A. Schabas, 'The Mental Element or Mens Rea of Genocide', in *Genocide in International Law: The Crime of Crimes*, 2nd ed. (Cambridge: Cambridge University Press, 2009) 241–306.

group.[19] In some cases, the destruction of culture has been used as evidence of this specific mental intent,[20] as will be further discussed below.[21] However, the question is whether the destruction of culture could be included in the list of acts that aim at the destruction of the group; i.e. as an *actus reus*.

What is more relevant for the present analysis is that the definition of genocide was – during the negotiations leading to the adoption of the text of Genocide Convention – narrowed down from the original broader proposal formulated by Lemkin, which was as follows: 'By genocide we mean the destruction of a nation or of an ethnic group,'[22] and this action is pursued through 'a coordinated plan of different actions aiming at the destruction of essential foundation of the life of national groups, with the aim of annihilating the groups themselves.'[23] These actions include plans which would pursue the

> disintegration of the political and social institutions, of culture, language, national feelings, religion, and the economic existence of national groups, and the destruction of the personal security, liberty, health, dignity, and even the lives of the individuals belonging to such groups.[24]

This definition looks comparable to the 1948 Convention insofar as it shows that the requirement of a special intent was an original component of Lemkin's definition. However, the difference between Lemkin's proposal and the Convention becomes clear when one considers the *acts* which could constitute genocide, as Lemkin's proposal included a wide variety of actions, without a defined catalogue. The 1948 Convention included the list of acts which qualified as genocide in Article 2, and they must be accompanied by the special intent that aims at the destruction of a group. However, the list of acts in the Genocide Convention may be subject to interpretation in order to clarify the meaning of certain acts.

Reasons behind the restriction of the actus reus

The text of the 1948 Convention clearly limited the type of acts that were targeting groups through specific actions against individuals, and by doing so affected the survival of the group. This may be linked to two main reasons: the interests of some states at the time of the negotiations and the concept of

19 ICTR, *Prosecutor v. Jean-Paul Akayesu* (Judgment) ICTR-96-4-T, 2 September 1998, para. 485.
20 ICTY, *Prosecutor v. Krstić* (Trial Judgment) IT-98-33-T, 2 August 2001, para. 580.
21 See the sections 'International criminal law and culture-related crimes' and 'Destruction of culture and genocide' below.
22 Lemkin, *Axis Rule in Occupied Europe*, 79.
23 Ibid.
24 Ibid.

human rights that was emerging in international law at the same time, as the Universal Declaration of Human Rights (UDHR)[25] was adopted the day after the adoption of the Genocide Convention at the same UN General Assembly meeting in Paris in December 1948.

STATES' INTEREST RELATED TO MINORITIES AND COLONIAL TERRITORIES

The drafting process of the 1948 Convention included a debate on the possible inclusion of acts aiming at the destruction of cultural elements of a group as part of the definition of genocide. Article 1(2) of the draft proposal, presented by the UN Secretary-General, mentioned a series of acts constituting genocide, and in its subsection 3 it referred to:

> Destroying the specific characteristics of the group by: (a) forced transfer of children to another human group; or (b) forced and systematic exile of individuals representing the culture of a group; or (c) prohibition of the use of the national language even in private intercourse; or (d) systematic destruction of books printed in the national language or of religious works or prohibition of new publications; or (e) systematic destruction of historical or religious monuments or their diversion to alien uses, destruction or dispersion of documents and objects of historical, artistic, or religious value and of objects used in religious worship.[26]

The debate over these aspects involved the representatives of those states which formed an ad hoc committee, including China, France, Lebanon, Poland, the Soviet Union, the USA, and Venezuela. This committee drafted a second version of the Convention where the cultural dimensions of genocide were moved to a separate article, allegedly to allow more debate and possible reservations by delegations. The new article recited:

> In this Convention genocide also means any deliberate act committed with the intent to destroy the language, religion, or culture of a national, racial or religious group on grounds of the national or racial origin or the religious belief of its members such as:
>
> 1. Prohibiting the use of the language of the group in daily intercourse or in schools, or the printing and circulation of publications in the language of the group;

25 UN General Assembly, *Universal Declaration of Human Rights*, 10 December 1948, 217 A (III).

26 *Draft Convention on the Crime of Genocide prepared by the Secretary-General of the United Nations*, 26 June 1947, UN Doc E/447 in Hirad Abtahi & Philippa Webb (eds), *The Genocide Convention: The Travaux Préparatoires* (Leiden: Martinus Nijhoff, 2008) 229.

2. Destroying, or preventing the use of libraries, museums, schools, historical monuments, place of worship or other cultural institutions and objects of the groups.[27]

The subsequent debate pitted the positions of France and the USA against those of the Soviet Union and Venezuela. The US delegation declared that

> the decision to make genocide a new international crime was extremely serious, and the United States believed that the crime should be limited to barbarous acts committed against individuals, which, in the eyes of the public, constituted the basic concept of genocide.[28]

On the contrary, the Soviet Union expressed the idea that 'the concept of genocide must also cover measures and actions aimed against the use of the national language or against national culture.'[29]

This initial debate on the relevance of culture shows that groups may be identified by certain cultural elements and that the destruction of the group may involve not only the physical destruction of individuals. This argument becomes particularly relevant in the contemporary debate on the protection of culture and related rights, as will be discussed later.

However, the drafting process was steered by the interests of states that feared possible negative repercussions connected to various policies they pursued in relation to national minorities and colonial territories under their jurisdiction. The UN Trusteeship Council, which dealt with the mandate system, expressed the idea that indigenous tribal structures were an obstacle to the development of indigenous peoples, and the representative of New Zealand pointed out the possible contradiction within the UN if provisions related to cultural traditions were included in the Genocide Convention.[30] The Canadian delegation declared more openly, at the end of the debate, that 'according to instructions from External Affairs, the Canadian delegate had only one important task, namely to eliminate the concept of cultural genocide from the Convention.'[31] This position was certainly based on the Canadian government's policies towards the

27 *Second Draft Genocide Convention, Prepared by the Ad Hoc Committee of the Economic and Social Council, meeting between 5 April 1948 and 10 May 1948*, UN Doc. E/AC.25/SR.1.

28 Ad Hoc Committee on Genocide, *Summary Record of the Fourteenth Meeting*, Lake Success, New York, Wednesday, 21 April 1948, UN Doc. E/AC.25/SR.14, in Abtahi & Webb, *Genocide Convention*, 890.

29 Ad Hoc Committee on Genocide, 'Basic principles of a Convention on Genocide, Submitted by Delegation of the Union of Soviet Socialist Republics on 5 April 1948', UN Doc. E/AC.25/7, in Abtahi & Webb, *Genocide Convention*, 697.

30 UN Doc. A/C.6/SR.83, 25 October 1948, 201, in Abtahi & Webb, *Genocide Convention*, 1499–1519.

31 *Progress Reports on Work of the Canadian Delegation in Paris*, 1 November 1948, NAC RG 25, Vol. 3699, File 5475- DG-2-40.

indigenous populations in Canada,[32] which included, for instance, the destruction of family and cultural links by the creation of residential schools for indigenous children.[33] Children were separated from their families and sent to faraway schools where they would be educated either in English or in French, with the purpose of assimilation (at the time called 'civilisation') of the indigenous groups within the Canadian society. Only in the 1990s was this matter properly investigated[34] and acknowledged by the Government of Canada, followed by the granting of compensation to the victims of the policy.[35]

At the end of the drafting process of the Genocide Convention, the only provision that went to the UN General Assembly was Article 2 in its present wording. This definition lists the acts constituting genocide without any explicit reference to cultural elements. The main emphasis in the definition, and its interpretation so far, focuses on the physical destruction of individuals within the group that would lead to the extermination of the group.

However, there are exceptions to this narrow interpretation. For instance, the provision related to the forceful transfer of children from one group to another does not mean their physical destruction. It is noteworthy that only two states at the time – the Netherlands and Belgium – pointed out that the provision 'did not necessarily mean the physical destruction of a group.'[36] This is quite an interesting exception, because the idea that genocide involves only acts that directly imply the physical annihilation of a group seems to be undermined by this observation. The inclusion of the provision concerning the forcible transfer of children from one group to another could be read as a possible reference to cultural destruction, but this was not explicitly mentioned in the text, as it could have opened up a debate over which acts could have a cultural dimension and which would not.[37] Cultural genocide would mean that some acts can destroy a group if its identity, in cultural terms, is destroyed without the actual killing of the individuals forming that group. This view may bring into the picture the interpretation of 'mental harm' in Article 2(b) of the Genocide Convention. This issue will be discussed below in the context of human rights and their cultural dimension and in relation to the definition of culture in international law.

32 Canada, *An Act to encourage the gradual Civilization of the Indian Tribes in this Province, and to amend the Laws respecting Indians*, S.C. 1857, c 26.

33 Canada, *An Act to amend and consolidate the laws respecting Indians*, S.C. 1876, c 18.

34 The Royal Commission on Aboriginal Peoples was a Canadian Royal Commission established in 1991 to address many issues related to Aboriginal status. The final report was published in 1996.

35 See Canada's Truth and Reconciliation Commission, *Final Report of the Truth and Reconciliation Commission of Canada, Volume 1: Summary* (Toronto: James Lorimer & Company, 2015).

36 Eighty-first Meeting, held at the Palais de Chaillot, Paris, on Friday, 22 October 1948, Continuation of the consideration of the draft convention on genocide, UN Doc. A/C.6/SR.82, in Abtahi & Webb, *Genocide Convention*, 1495.

37 Elisa Nović, *The Concept of Cultural Genocide: An International Law Perspective* (Oxford: Oxford University Press, 2016) 27.

THE LIBERAL CONCEPT OF HUMAN RIGHTS

An element that should be considered in relation to the failure to include issues concerning cultural genocide in the 1948 Genocide Convention relates to the concept and idea of international human rights. During the drafting process of the Genocide Convention, it was pointed out that 'an undue extension of the notion of genocide [...] amounted to reconstituting the former protection of minorities – which was based on other conceptions – under cover of the term genocide.'[38] Some delegations, such as the USA and France, supported this position, suggesting that the protection of different types of minorities should be included in a different document.[39] Furthermore, the prohibition of interference in domestic matters under Article 2(7) of the UN Charter[40] – which was linked to the concepts of sovereignty and domestic jurisdiction – was particularly relevant at that time[41] and diminished the interest of states in possible forms of intervention concerning the internal matters of other states.

However, the protection of minorities was not included in the UDHR. In the end the approach that prevailed in the UDHR was essentially aimed at the protection of *individual* human rights, based on the illuminist and personalist political and philosophical approaches of constitutional rights and civil liberties derived from USA constitutional rights[42] and the 1789 French Declaration of the rights of men.[43] This same concept would later pervade the definition contained in the 1966 Covenant on Civil and Political Rights (ICCPR)[44] in relation to minorities and groups. Article 27 of the ICCPR affirms that:

38 Draft Convention on the Crime of Genocide prepared by the Secretary-General of the United Nations, 26 June 1947, UN Doc E/447 in Abtahi & Webb, *Genocide Convention*, 234.

39 ECOSOC, UN Doc. E/623 (30 January 1948) paras 11–13. For more details, see Andreas S. Kolb, *The UN Security Council Members' Responsibility to Protect: A Legal Analysis* (Berlin: Springer, Max-Plank Institute 2018) 213–217.

40 United Nations, *Charter of the United Nations*, 24 October 1945, 1 UNTS XVI.

41 See Maziar Jamnejad & Michael Wood, 'The Principle of Non-intervention' (2009) 22(2) *Leiden Journal of International Law* 345–381; see also UN General Assembly, *Declaration on the Inadmissibility of Intervention in the Domestic Affairs of States and the Protection of Their Independence and Sovereignty*, 21 December 1965, A/RES/2131(XX); UN General Assembly, *Declaration on Principles of International Law concerning Friendly Relations and Cooperation among States in accordance with the Charter of the United Nations*, 24 October 1970, A/RES/2625(XXV).

42 *The Constitution of the United States of America: Analysis and Interpretation, Centennial Edition, Interim Edition: Analysis of Cases Decided by the Supreme Court of the United States to 26 June 2013* (Washington, DC: U.S. Government Printing Office, 2013), 1043–2275.

43 France, *Declaration of the Right of Man and the Citizen*, approved by the National Assembly of France, 26 August 1789, available at: www.refworld.org/docid/3ae6b52410.html [accessed 30 November 2019].

44 UN General Assembly, *International Covenant on Civil and Political Rights*, 16 December 1966, United Nations, Treaty Series, Vol. 999, 171.

> In those States in which ethnic, religious or linguistic minorities exist, persons belonging to such minorities shall not be denied the right, in community with the other members of their group, to enjoy their own culture, to profess and practise their own religion, or to use their own language.

Note that the protection seems to be provided to 'persons' rather than to the group as such. However, this view has been challenged,[45] and the developments in international law – particularly in relation to the protection of collective rights[46] – demonstrate an increasing use of this concept to support a new approach to the possible links between culture and genocide, which is examined in more detail below.

Human rights: from individual to collective rights

As mentioned above, the drafting process of the 1948 Convention was influenced by the view that crimes committed against individuals prevailed over the protection of groups as such. Although the definition of genocide focuses on the destruction of specified groups, at the same time it then seems to restrict it to violence and acts against individuals. The question arises: does this definition raise potential issues of interpretation of the concept of genocide, in light of the aims and purposes of the crime?

It is undeniable that human groups are formed by individuals. However, the question is whether the group is something more than or different from the collection of individuals that form it. The answer depends on how groups are identified and how human aggregations are perceived. This analysis is developed

45 See: Peter Jones, 'Human Rights and Collective Self-Determination', in Adam Etinson (ed.), *Human Rights: Moral or Political?* (Oxford: Oxford University Press, 2016) 441–459; Dwight Newman, *Community and Collective Rights: A Theoretical Framework for Rights held by Groups* (Oxford: Hart, 2011); Koen De Feyter & George Pavlakos (eds), *The Tension Between Group Rights and Human Rights: A Multidisciplinary Approach* (Oxford: Hart, 2008); Will Kymlicka, *Liberalism, Community and Culture* (Oxford: Clarendon, 1989); James Crawford, 'The Rights of Peoples: Some Conclusions, in James Crawford (ed.), *The Rights of Peoples* (Oxford: Clarendon, 1988) 159–175.

46 See UN General Assembly, *International Covenant on Civil and Political Rights*, 16 December 1966, United Nations, Treaty Series, Vol. 999, p. 171, Articles 1(1), and 1(2) (common to the United Nations International Covenants on Human Rights) regarding the right to self-determination of peoples and their rights to property, natural resources, and wealth and their development; ILO, *Indigenous and Tribal Peoples Convention*, C169, 27 June 1989, Article 23(1); UN General Assembly, *United Nations Declaration on the Rights of Indigenous Peoples*, UN Doc. A/RES/61/295, 2 October 2007; UN Committee on Economic, Social and Cultural Rights, General Comment No. 21, UN Doc E/C.12/GC/21, 21 December 2009, para. 9; UN, *Draft Declaration on the rights of peasants and other persons working in rural areas presented by the chairperson-rapporteur of the working group*, UN Doc. A/HRC/WG.15/4/2, 6 March 2017, Article 1.

mostly by anthropological and sociological studies,[47] which have only partially been taken into account in the legal debates.[48] One of the main issues here is whether the individual is an entity in itself, or whether the individual is also defined as part of one of more groups. This element is an essential characteristic of the crime of genocide, as the individuals are targeted as 'members of the group' rather than as individuals per se. Therefore, the fact that an individual is seen or perceived as connected to a group constitutes the crucial difference. As the Greek philosopher Aristotle said in his *Politics*, 'man is a social animal.'[49] This means that individuals tend to aggregate and fit into societies and aggregations of different types, such as families; tribes; ideological, religious, and economic organisations; and other groups. Aristotle also later said that 'society is something that precedes the individual',[50] supporting in a way the idea that groups determine the nature and functions of individuals.

Without entering into a detailed analysis of these issues, which would go beyond the limits of this chapter, the discussion brings into the picture the question of the *identity* of individuals and groups, and the role of collective rights[51] that have become particularly relevant in the debate concerning the definition of the rights of minorities and indigenous groups.[52] In this section, the focus will be on these two last groups in relation to the concepts of identity and culture, as this relationship can provide more elements to the discussion on the protection of cultural elements of groups in the context of genocide.

Cultural rights and groups

The two 1966 Covenants on Civil and Political Rights and on Economic, Social and Cultural Rights were shaped by ideological counter-positions of the Cold War. They kept the cultural elements in a negligible position[53] compared to

47 See Anthony P. Cohen, *Self Consciousness: An Alternative Anthropology of Identity* (London: Routledge, 1994).

48 See Dan Danielsen & Karen Engle (eds), *After Identity: A Reader in Law and Culture* (New York, NY: Routledge, 1995); Jane K. Cowan, Marie-Bénédicte Dembour, & Richard A. Wilson (eds), *Culture and Rights: Anthropological Perspectives* (Cambridge: Cambridge University Press, 2001).

49 Aristotle, *Aristotle in 23 Volumes*, translated by H. Rackham (Cambridge, MA: Harvard University Press; London: William Heinemann Ltd., 1944), Vol. 21, 'Politics', 1.1253a.

50 Ibid.

51 Douglas Sanders, 'Collective Rights', (1991) 13 *Hum Rts Q*, pp. 368–386.

52 Joshua Castellino (ed.), *Global Minority Rights* (Abingdon/New York, NY: Routledge, 2016); Patrick Thornberry, *Indigenous Peoples and Human Rights* (Manchester: Manchester University Press, 2013); James Summers, *Peoples and International Law*, 2nd rev. ed. (Leiden: Brill, 2014); Gaetano Pentassuglia, *Minority Groups and Judicial Discourse in International Law: A Comparative Perspective* (Leiden/Boston, MA: Martinus Nijhoff, 2009); Alexandra Xanthaki, *Indigenous Rights and United Nations Standards: Self-Determination, Culture and Land* (Cambridge: Cambridge University Press, 2007).

53 Elsa Stamatopoulou, *Cultural Rights in International Law: Article 27 of the Universal Declaration of Human Rights and Beyond* (Leiden: Martinus Nijhoff, 2007) 4–6.

other individual rights, such as freedom of expression and right to life. For a long time, the meaning of *cultural rights* has been narrowly interpreted in the framework of international human rights, covering mainly matters such as education, arts, and intellectual property. It was only with the end of the Cold War that the debate over cultural rights gained traction and provided more insights on the meaning of *culture* and the relevance of related rights, not only for individuals but also for groups. New initiatives and approaches developed after the Vienna Declaration in 1992, which stated that all human rights are 'indivisible, interdependent, and interrelated.'[54] Two main developments should be mentioned in this regard: the international actions of indigenous peoples' groups on the occasion of the 1992 celebrations of the 'discovery' of the Americas, and UNESCO's work towards a definition of culture in the context of human rights. These activities have contributed to the new considerations concerning the role of groups and their rights in the context of protection of cultural expressions under international law. The definition of cultural rights, in its new and wider perspective, implies a proper consideration of collective rights, and in particular the relevance of identity and its cultural dimension.[55]

Identity, culture and human rights

'Identity' has become an essential focus to understand the development of cultural rights as an element that contributes to defining a collective bond. *Identity* has different meanings, which are relevant both for individuals and for groups. In the present analysis, *identity* refers to some common shared links among individuals within a community, which define those individuals as part of a group. Debates on identity also refer to possible multiple identities or shared identities, as individuals can be part of one group and share some common elements with other groups. For instance, individuals can share common nationality but different religious beliefs, or a common citizenship but a different linguistic or ethnic affiliation. This makes the recognition and definition of identity a complex issue both for individuals and for groups, particularly in relation to the possible legal protection of the rights connected to the concept of identity. This debate brings to the forefront the foundation of international human rights, particularly in relation to individual and group rights and the role of cultural relativism in the conception of fundamental rights.

Inasmuch as human rights developed from an individualist approach to human beings – conceived as 'individuals' or 'persons'; the idea that groups may have rights as groups has been particularly challenging. However, it is

54 UN General Assembly, *Vienna Declaration and Programme of Action*, 12 July 1993, UN Doc. A/CONF.157/23, para. 5.

55 Janne Mende, *A Human Right to Culture and Identity: The Ambivalence of Group Rights* (London/New York, NY: Rowman & Littlefield, 2018); Yvonne Donders, *Towards a Right to Cultural Identity?* (Antwerp/Oxford: Intersentia, 2002).

difficult to deny that many of the acts that have been identified in history as possible acts of genocide were based on the idea of targeting a 'group' as such, rather than the individuals in the group per se. The fact that individuals were the object of specific criminal acts, like deportation or extermination, was a consequence of the existence of, or the affiliation of the individual to, a particular 'group,' defined according to different criteria and usually developed by the perpetrators. Examples include the massacres of Armenians, Jews, Roma people, intellectuals, political dissidents, indigenous communities, and Tutsis.

Therefore, identity becomes a relevant element in the construction and identification of target groups that fall within the definition of genocide within the 1948 Convention. As the UNESCO Universal Declaration on Cultural Diversity has affirmed:

> culture should be regarded as the set of distinctive spiritual, material, intellectual and emotional features of society or a social group, and it encompasses, in addition to art and literature, lifestyles, ways of living together, value systems, traditions and beliefs.

Further it adds that 'culture is at the heart of contemporary debates about identity, social cohesion, and the development of a knowledge-based economy.'[56]

These statements clearly link the ways of life, as a set of features that define certain groups, to the concept of the identity of those groups. It is thus of crucial importance to understand how the concept of culture has developed and its meaning in international law, and to identify what measures and protections can be provided, including in the case of international crimes, like genocide.

The protection of culture in international law

Culture and cultural goods can describe a variety of elements, both material and immaterial. The international protection of cultural goods was initially developed in the context of IHL within the Hague Conventions of 1899[57] and 1907[58] and the Roerich Pact of 1935.[59] Also, the 1949 Geneva Conventions include the protection of cultural goods, which may have an historical, archaeological, religious, or artistic value. The main document in IHL related to the

56 UN Educational, Scientific and Cultural Organisation (UNESCO), UNESCO Universal Declaration on Cultural Diversity, 2 November 2001, available at: www.refworld.org/docid/435cbcd64.html [accessed 13 April 2020].

57 *Convention (II) with Respect to the Laws and Customs of War on Land*, The Hague, 29 July 1899, Arts. 23, 25, 27, 28.

58 *Convention (IV) Respecting the Laws and Customs of War on Land*, The Hague, 18 October 1907, Arts. 23(g), 25, 27, 28.

59 OAS, *Treaty on the Protection of Artistic and Scientific Institutions and Historic Monuments*, Washington DC, 15 April 1935, 167 LNTS 289.

protection of cultural property is the UNESCO 1954 Convention,[60] and its two Protocols,[61] which in its Article 1(a) included not only monuments but also

> movable or immovable property of great importance to the cultural heritage of every people, such as monuments of architecture, art or history, whether religious or secular; archaeological sites; groups of buildings which, as a whole, are of historical or artistic interest; works of art; manuscripts, books and other objects of artistic, historical or archaeological interest; as well as scientific collections and important collections of books or archives or of reproductions of the property defined above.

However, in all the above-mentioned documents, the protection refers to the civilian nature of cultural buildings or artefacts, and does not refer to other types of cultural expressions. Due to the fact that these are treaties related to IHL, they apply only in the case of armed conflict,[62] and not in peacetime. Therefore, the destruction of cultural goods outside an armed conflict does not fall within these provisions, limiting the scope of protection of cultural goods under IHL to the context of armed conflict. However, this protection is enhanced by the provisions in the 1999 Second Protocol[63] related to the criminal prosecution – including forms of international judicial cooperation – of those who commit acts against cultural property in the context of armed conflicts. The usefulness of these elements will be taken into account later when dealing with the prosecution of crimes against culture in the context of international criminal law.

A wider concept of culture

A different concept of culture, including a wider notion of cultural expressions, has emerged in the context of international human rights law. Also, in this case UNESCO has contributed to exploring the meaning of culture and its relevance in the context of human rights. The Preamble to the 1954 UNESCO Convention on the Protection of Cultural Property in case of armed conflict recognises that 'damage to cultural property belonging to any people whatsoever means

60 UN Educational, Scientific and Cultural Organisation (UNESCO), *Convention for the Protection of Cultural Property in the Event of Armed Conflict*, 14 May 1954.

61 *Protocol to the Convention for the Protection of Cultural Property in the Event of Armed conflict 1954*, The Hague, 14 May 1954; *Second Protocol to the Hague Convention of 1954 for the Protection of Cultural Property in the Event of Armed Conflict 1999*, The Hague, 26 March 1999.

62 Hirad Abtahi, 'The Protection of Cultural Property in Times of Armed Conflict: The Practice of the International Criminal Tribunal for the Former Yugoslavia' (2001) 14 *Harv. Hum. Rts. J.* 1–32.

63 *Second Protocol to the Hague Convention of 1954 for the Protection of Cultural Property in the Event of Armed Conflict*, The Hague, 26 March 1999, Arts. 15–21.

damage to the cultural heritage of all mankind, since each people makes its contribution to the culture of the world', and that 'the preservation of the cultural heritage is of great importance for all peoples of the world and that it is important that this heritage should receive international protection.' The question is whether these important considerations should also be taken into account in contexts that fall outside the occurrence of an armed conflict.

This problem is linked to the clarification of the meaning of *culture*, *cultural goods*, and *expressions of culture*. This is also a terminological issue, as it is important to identify what may constitute the object of protection within the notion of cultural rights.

The wider concept of culture has been defined over time in different UNESCO documents,[64] in particular in the 2003 Convention for the Safeguarding of the Intangible Cultural Heritage[65] and the 2005 Convention on the Protection and Promotion of the Diversity of Cultural Expressions,[66] which in Article 1 declares that:

> [c]ulture takes diverse forms across time and space. This diversity is embodied in the uniqueness and plurality of the identities of the groups and societies making up humankind. As a source of exchange, innovation and creativity, cultural diversity is as necessary for humankind as biodiversity is for nature. In this sense, it is the common heritage of humanity and should be recognized and affirmed for the benefit of present and future generations.

Authors who support the concept of cultural genocide refer to the link between groups and their identity,[67] and argue that the destruction of a group would be perpetrated not only by killing of its individual members, but also by the destruction of fundamental cultural elements that define that group. It is therefore useful at this stage to consider the evolution of the protection of cultural goods and expressions, both tangible and intangible, which can be linked to the prosecution of international crimes and the growth of international criminal law.

64 Jiri Toman, *The Protection of Cultural Property in the Event of Armed Conflict* (Aldershot: Dartmouth and UNESCO, 1996) 258–259.

65 Paris, 17 October 2003, available at: http://portal.unesco.org/en/ev.php-URL_ID=17716&URL_DO=DO_TOPIC&URL_SECTION=201.html [accessed 23 November 2019].

66 UNESCO, *Preliminary Draft Convention on the Protection and Promotion of the Diversity of Cultural Expressions*, 20 October 2005, 33 C/23; Annex V, available at: www.refworld.org/docid/435cbdac4.html [accessed 22 September 2019]; www.unesco.org/new/en/culture/themes/cultural-diversity/cultural-expressions/the-convention/convention-text/.

67 Lindsey Kingston, 'The Destruction of Identity: Cultural Genocide and Indigenous Peoples' (2015) 14(1) *Journal of Human Rights* 63–83; David B. MacDonald, *Identity Politics in the Age of Genocide: The Holocaust and Historical Representation* (London/New York, NY: Routledge, 2008) 1–12.

International criminal law and culture-related crimes

The evolution of the concept of culture can be useful to understand the possible implications for the enhanced approach to the protection of culture under international law. Initial attempts for the protection of culture,[68] and later the failed prosecution of perpetrators[69] for crimes against culture, emerged after the First World War as a reaction to widespread instances of severe damage, like the destruction of Louvain University's library and Reims Cathedral.[70] More effective prosecution took place in the Nuremberg International Military Tribunal, including the prosecution of Rosenberg for the role he played in the confiscation of cultural and artistic artefacts in occupied territories. It is relevant to note that the US prosecutor referred to '[T]he forcing of this treasure-house by a horde of vandals bent on systematically removing to the Reich these treasures which are, in a sense, the heritage of all of us.'[71] This conviction constituted an important source of support for the future development of the idea of crimes against humanity, and possibly genocide as well, as is discussed below. With the development of international criminal tribunals, new cases have led to further attention being paid to crimes related to the destruction and targeting of culture.[72] They are essentially limited to situations of armed conflict, but they may provide interesting elements of reflection for the purpose of this work.

The Statute and practice of the International Criminal Tribunal for the Former Yugoslavia (ICTY)[73] and of the International Criminal Court (ICC) are the main focus of this analysis. For instance, the 2001 ICTY *Blaskic* case[74] considered that the destruction of cultural objects might fit into crimes against humanity outside the context of an armed conflict.[75] In the *Krstić* case, the ICTY considered that attacks against cultural and religious symbols can be used as evidence of an intent to destroy a group, because

68 *International Declaration Concerning the Laws and Customs of War*, 27 August 1874, not ratified, (1907) Vol. 1(supp.) *American Journal of International Law* 96.

69 John Horne & Alan Kramer, *German Atrocities, 1914: A History of Denial* (New Haven, CT: Yale University Press, 2001) Appendix, 448–50.

70 Paul Clemen, *Protection of Art during War* (Leipzig: E.A. Seemann, 1919).

71 Count Three (War Crimes), Part E (Plunder of Public and Private Property), Indictment, in *Trial of the Major War Criminals before the International Military Tribunal*, Nuremberg, 14 November 1945–1 October 1946, (42 vols, Nuremberg: [s.n.], 1947–1949), Vol. IV, 81.

72 ICTY, *Prosecutor v. Tihomir Blaskic* (Trial Judgement), IT-95-14-T, 3 March 2000, paras. 159–185; *Prosecutor v. Stanilav Galic* (Trial Judgement and Opinion), IT-98-29-T, 5 December 2003, para. 45; *Prosecutor v. Dragomir Milosevic* (Trial Judgment), IT-98-29/1-T, 12 December 2007, paras. 939–940; *Prosecutor v. Milan Martic* (Judgment), IT-95-11-T, 12 June 2007, para. 67.

73 Micaela Frulli, 'Advancing the Protection of Cultural Property through the Implementation of Individual Criminal Responsibility: The Case-Law of the International Criminal Tribunal for the former Yugoslavia' (2005) 15 *Italian Yearbook of International Law* 195.

74 ICTY, *Prosecutor v. Tihomir Blaskic* (Trial Judgement), IT-95-14-T, 3 March 2000.

75 Idem, para. 71.

> where there is physical or biological destruction there are often simultaneous attacks on cultural and religious property and symbols of the targeted group as well, attacks which may legitimately be considered as evidence of an intent to physically destroy the group.[76]

The main cases that deserve attention are *Jokič*[77] and *Strugar*[78] in the ICTY, and *Al Mahadi*[79] in the ICC. The two cases in the ICTY dealt with the bombardment of the old town of Dubrovnik[80] during the armed conflict in Yugoslavia. In *Jokič* the ICTY, referring to war crimes defined in Article 3(d) of its Statute,[81] considered that '[t]he shelling attack on the Old Town [Dubrovnik] was an attack not only against the history and heritage of the region, but also against the cultural heritage of humankind.'[82] In the same way, in *Strugar* the Court declared that with regard to the 'seriousness of the offence of damage to cultural property (Article 3 (d)), the Chamber observes that such property is, by definition, of "great importance to the cultural heritage of every people."'[83] Therefore, 'the offences under Articles 3(b) and 3(d) of the Statute are serious violations of international humanitarian law.'[84] It also confirmed its previous decision in *Tadič*[85] that the rules concerning the protection of cultural property under the 1954 Convention can be considered customary law, and therefore applicable both in international and non-international armed conflicts.[86]

A further step in this evolution can be perceived in the ICC's ruling in the 2016 *Al Mahadi* case.[87] This was the first case where the main issue under consideration was the destruction of valuable cultural buildings and historical mosques in Timbuktu, Mali by an armed group that considered these buildings as examples of idolatry. The fact that the case was dealing with the destruction of cultural buildings, not necessarily linked to other war crimes related to civilian victims and individuals, shows the increasing attention being devoted to these types of crimes under international criminal law. The ICC considered that the

76 ICTY, *Prosecutor v. Krstić*, (Trial Judgment), IT-98-33-T, 2 August 2001, para. 580.
77 ICTY, *Prosecutor v. Miodrag Jokič* (Sentencing Judgement), IT-01-42/1-S, 18 March 2004.
78 ICTY, *Prosecutor v. Pavle Strugar* (Trial Judgment), IT-01-42-T, 31 January 2005.
79 ICC, *Prosecutor v. Ahmad Al Faqi Al Mahdi*, ICC-01/12-01/15, Judgment & Sentence, 27 September 2016.
80 See Clémentine Bories, *Les bombardements serbes sur la vieille ville de Dubrovnik: La protection internationale des biens culturels* (Paris: Pedone, 2005) 41–47.
81 UN Security Council, *Statute of the International Criminal Tribunal for the Former Yugoslavia (as amended on 17 May 2002)*, SC Resolution 827, 25 May 1993.
82 ICTY, *Prosecutor v. Miodrag Jokič* (Sentencing Judgement), IT-01-42/1-S, 18 March 2004, para. 51.
83 *Strugar*, para. 232.
84 *Strugar*, para. 232.
85 ICTY, *Prosecutor v. Dusko Tadič aka 'Dule' (Decision on the Defence Motion for Interlocutory Appeal on Jurisdiction)*, IT-94-1, 2 October 1995, para 98.
86 *Strugar*, para. 229.
87 Above, n. 77.

attack against the monuments were particularly serious, as the buildings were included in the UNESCO World Heritage list.[88] The ICC also cited the UNESCO Constitution,[89] as the affected 'buildings reflect their special importance to international cultural heritage,' noting that

> the wide diffusion of culture, and the education of humanity for justice and liberty and peace are indispensable to the dignity of man and constitute a sacred duty which all the nations must fulfil in a spirit of mutual assistance and concern.

This was emphasised when the ICC said that the attack against the 'monuments appears to be of particular gravity as their destruction does not only affect the direct victims of the crimes, namely the faithful and inhabitants of Timbuktu, but also people throughout Mali and the international community.'[90] Despite the strong support for the protection of cultural heritage, the ICC considered that 'Mr Al Mahdi is not charged with crimes against persons but with a crime against property. In the view of the Chamber, even if inherently grave, crimes against property are generally of lesser gravity than crimes against persons.'[91] This may challenge the idea that crimes committed against culture could be included in the concept of genocide. However, it should be emphasised that cultural objects and buildings are recognised as fundamental values for the international community, which require particular protection.

A different approach might be used in trying to protect cultural expressions. In fact, the cases that have been discussed so far refer to situations of armed conflict and to attacks against buildings with special cultural value.

Culture, crimes against humanity, and genocide

The assumption that *genocide* always and only implies the physical destruction of a group and its individuals is certainly not supported by the very wording of the 1948 Convention. Lemkin's definition stated that

> genocide does not necessarily mean the immediate destruction of a nation [...]. It is intended rather to signify a coordinated plan of different actions aiming at the destruction of essential foundations of the life of national

88 *Al Mahadi*, para 40.

89 Constitution of the United Nations Educational, Scientific and Cultural Organization, adopted in London on 16 November 1945, available at http://portal.unesco.org/en/ev.php-URL_ID=15244&URL_DO=DO_TOPIC&URL_SECTION=201.html [accessed 21 October 2019].

90 *Al Mahadi*, para. 80.

91 *Al Mahadi*, para. 77.

> groups [...]. Genocide is directed against the national group as an entity, and the actions involved are directed against individuals, not in their individual capacity, but as members of the national group.[92]

It is not impossible to find a way to include acts which are not aimed at the physical destruction of a group within the definition of genocide in the Genocide Convention. A relevant example is provided by the *Akayesu* case, where the International Criminal Tribunal for Rwanda included rape and sexual violence in the definition of genocide. The Tribunal affirmed that rape and other forms of sexual violence

> certainly constitute infliction of serious physical and mental harm on the victims and are even, according to the Chamber, one of the worst ways of inflicting harm on the victim as he or she suffers both physical and mental harm [...]. Sexual violence was an integral part of the process of destruction, specifically targeting Tutsi women and specifically contributing to their destruction and to the destruction of the Tutsi group as a whole.[93]

The definition of genocide in the 1948 Convention contains no reference to rape and sexual violence. However, in interpreting Article 2(b) concerning 'serious bodily or mental harm to members of the group,' acts of sexual violence could be prosecuted as acts of genocide as a form of bodily and mental harm. If we accept, as the wording of Article 2(b) suggests, that 'mental harm' may be the result of certain acts, without necessarily and directly affecting the integrity of the body, those forms of violence that create and cause mental harm may fall within the definition of genocide. The same concept of harm has been used in the definition of victims of human rights abuses.[94] The Committee against Torture defines victims as persons who individually or collectively suffered harm, including physical or mental injury, emotional suffering, economic loss, or substantial impairment of their fundamental rights.[95] This has been explained in the following terms: 'When a group with its own cultural identity is destroyed, its survivors lose their cultural heritage and may even lose their intergenerational connections.'[96] This means that the destruction of culture can lead to 'genocide as social death' and the 'harm' would consist in 'destroying the "national pattern" of the oppressed group and replacing it with the national pattern of the oppressor.'[97]

92 Lemkin, *Axis Rule in Occupied Europe*, 79.

93 ICTR, *Prosecutor v. Jean-Paul Akayesu*, Judgment, Case No. ICTR-96-4-T, 2 September 1998, para 731.

94 See Larry May, *Crimes Against Humanity: A Normative Account* (New York, NY: Cambridge University Press, 2005) 80–95.

95 Committee Against Torture, *Implementation of Article 14 by States Parties*, General Comment No. 3, 2012.

96 Claudia Card, 'Genocide and Social Death' (2003) 18(1) *Hypatia*, 63–79, 73.

97 Mohammed Abed, 'Clarifying the Concept of Genocide' (2006) 37(3–4) *Metaphilosophy*, 37, p. 312.

The question here is whether the destruction of culture would be better defined as a crime against humanity rather than genocide. Crimes against humanity are acts that are deliberately committed as part of a widespread or systematic attack directed against any civilian or an identifiable part of a civilian population. Crimes against humanity are not codified in an international convention,[98] although there is an international effort to clarify their content.[99]

Unlike war crimes, crimes against humanity can be committed both in times of peace or of armed conflict. They must be part of either a government policy or of a widespread practice of atrocities tolerated or condoned by a government or a de facto authority. Massacres, dehumanisation, ethnic cleansing, deportations, unethical human experimentation, extrajudicial punishments (including summary executions), forced disappearances, military use of children, enslavement, torture, rape, and other human rights abuses may reach the threshold of crimes against humanity if they are part of a widespread or systematic practice. The acts must be accompanied by the element of persecution, which are acts 'of a physical, economic, or judicial nature that violate an individual's basic or fundamental rights,'[100] and they must reflect a widespread and systematic attack[101] against a civilian population with 'clear evidence of the discriminatory intent,' based on Article 5(h) of the ICTY Statute.

This view was confirmed in *Kordic*, where the ICTY affirmed that persecution 'took the form of the most extreme expression of persecution, i.e., of attacking towns and villages with the concomitant destruction and plunder, killing, injuring and detaining Bosnian Muslims.'[102]

In contrast to genocide, crimes against humanity do not need to target a specific group. Instead, the victim of the attack can be any civilian population, regardless of its affiliation or identity. The relevant factor is that 'humanity is harmed when these crimes are perpetrated.'[103]

98 May, *Crimes Against Humanity*; M. Cherif Bassiouni, *Crimes Against Humanity in International Criminal Law*, 2nd rev. ed. (The Hague/London/Boston: Kluwer Law International, 1999), pp. 62–88; William Schabas, *Unimaginable Atrocities: Justice, Politics, and Rights at the War Crimes Tribunals* (Oxford: Oxford University Press, 2012), pp. 51–53.

99 *Draft Code of Crimes Against the Peace and Security of Mankind*, 1996, 51 UN GAOR Supp. (No. 10) at 14, UN Doc. A/CN.4/L.532, corr.1, corr.3 (1996); Rome Statute of the International Criminal Court, Rome 17 July 1998, United Nations, Treaty Series, Vol. 2187, No. 38,544, Art. 7.

100 ICTY, *Prosecutor v. Zoran Kupreškić et al.* (Trial Judgment), No. IT-95-16-T (14 January 2000), para. 616.

101 UN Security Council, *Statute of the International Criminal Tribunal for Rwanda (as last amended on 13 October 2006)*, 8 November 1994, available at: www.refworld.org/docid/3ae6b3952c.html [accessed 1 December 2019], Art. 3; UN General Assembly, *Rome Statute of the International Criminal Court (last amended 2010)*, 17 July 1998, ISBN No. 92-9227-227-6, available at: www.refworld.org/docid/3ae6b3a84.html [accessed 1 December 2019], Statute, Art. 7.

102 ICTY, *Prosecutor v. Dario Kordic, Mario Cerkez* (Trial Judgment), IT-95-14/2-T, 26 February 2001, para. 827.

103 May, *Crimes Against Humanity*, 82.

This difference becomes an essential element in relation to the 'purpose' or 'intent' of the destruction of cultural elements of a group. If the destruction of culture is not linked to the annihilation of a group, but may be defined as 'persecution,'[104] then acts against culture could be defined as crimes against humanity due to the fact that the victims of the destruction of important cultural expressions and artefacts are not only the individuals and groups who are directly affected, but humanity as a whole, based on the idea that there are expressions of culture that benefit all humanity. As Larry May states: '[I]n some sense, humanity is harmed when those crimes are perpetrated.'[105]

Therefore, these crimes could be recognised as a form of crimes against humanity, going beyond the causal link with the war crimes definition, as they may happen during peacetime, and as independent acts of crimes against humanity. In particular, certain monuments and specific areas are defined as World Heritage, which are places that are important to, and belong to, everyone in the world, regardless of where they are located. They are an irreplaceable legacy that the global community has decided to protect for the future. The question is whether the destruction of cultural monuments, artefacts, etc., but also traditions, languages, and legal systems can be seen as values that shape the identity of a group, turning attacks and destruction that affect those cultural elements into an international criminal act.

Destruction of culture and genocide

In the *Krstić* case, the ICTY discussed the issue of cultural destruction and genocide.[106] The ICTY recalled that genocide fits into Article 6(c) of the Nuremberg Tribunal Statute,[107] which defines crimes of persecution that are 'not limited to the physical destruction of the group but covered all acts designed to destroy the social and/or cultural bases of a group.'[108] The *Greifelt* case recognised acts which 'were carried out as part of a systematic program of genocide, aimed at the destruction of foreign nations and ethnic groups, in part by murderous extermination, and in part by elimination and suppression of national characteristics'[109] as war crimes and crimes against

104 Israel, District Court of Jerusalem, Criminal Case No. 40/61, 11 December 1961, para. 55; ICTR, *Prosecutor v. Clément Kayishema and Obed Ruzindana*, (Judgment) Case No. ICTR-95-1-T, 21 May 1999, para. 578; Judgment, para. 717.

105 May, *Crimes Against Humanity*, 82.

106 *Krstić*, paras 539–599.

107 United Nations, *Charter of the International Military Tribunal – Annex to the Agreement for the prosecution and punishment of the major war criminals of the European Axis ('London Agreement')*, 8 August 1945, available at: www.refworld.org/docid/3ae6b39614.html [accessed 30 November 2019].

108 *Krstić*, para. 575.

109 United Nations War Crimes Commission, 'Trial of Ulrich Greifelt and others', *Law Reports of Trials of War Criminals*, Vol. XIII, London, United Nations War Crimes Commission, 1949, case No. 73, 2.

humanity.[110] As the Israeli Supreme Court affirmed in the *Eichmann* case, the Nazi plan was 'to oust [Jews] from the economic and cultural life of the State.'[111] Similarly, the Polish Supreme National Tribunal in three relevant cases – *Amon Goeth*,[112] *Rudolf Hoess*,[113] and *Arthur Greiser*[114] – also referred to 'the biological and cultural extermination of subjugated nations'[115] and the 'genocidal attacks on Polish culture and learning.'[116] In the *Goeth* case,

> the Prosecution endeavoured to do much more than establish only the physical and biological aspects and elements of the crime of genocide [...] in establishing before the Supreme National Tribunal also other components of this new type of crime, such as its economic, social and cultural connotations.[117]

However, this broader interpretation has been excluded by the International Law Commission (ILC) in the following terms:

> As clearly shown by the preparatory work for the Convention, the destruction in question is the material destruction of a group either by physical or by biological means, not the destruction of the national, linguistic, religious, cultural or other identity of a particular group. The national or religious element and the racial or ethnic element are not taken into consideration in the definition of the word "destruction", which must be taken only in its material sense, its physical or biological sense.[118]

Despite the significant reservations of the ILC, in its subsequent comments it does not clarify the meaning of 'mental harm' and how it relates to the physical or biological destruction of the group. Similarly, when the ILC comments on

110 Idem, 40–42.
111 Israel, District Court of Jerusalem, Criminal Case No. 40/61, 11 December 1961, para. 56.
112 United Nations War Crimes Commission, 'Trial of Hauptsturmfuhrer Amon Leopold Goeth', *Law Reports of Trials of War Criminals*, Vol. VII, London, United Nations War Crimes Commission, 1948, case No. 37, 1–10.
113 United Nations War Crimes Commission, 'Trial of Obersturmbannfuhrer Rudolf Franz Ferdinand Hoess', *Law Reports of Trials of War Criminals*, Vol. VII, London, United Nations War Crimes Commission, 1948, case No. 38, 11–26.
114 Supreme National Tribunal of Poland, 'Trial of Gauleiter Artur Greiser', case No. 74, 21 June to 7 July 1946, 70–117, available at www.worldcourts.com/imt/eng/decisions/1946.07.07_Poland_v_Greiser.pdf [accessed 22 November 2019].
115 'Trial of Obersturmbannfuhrer Rudolf Franz Ferdinand Hoess', above, 24.
116 'Trial of Gauleiter Artur Greiser', above, 112.
117 'Trial of Hauptsturmfuhrer Amon Leopold Goeth', above, 8.
118 Draft Code of Crimes Against the Peace and Security of Mankind, *Yearbook of the International Law Commission*, 1996, Vol. II(2), para.50; UN Doc. A/CN.4/L.532, corr.1, corr.3 (1996), 30–31.

the forcible transfer of children, it is not clear how this act would physically or biologically lead to the extermination of the group.

The ICTY recognises that there have been some different approaches in interpreting the meaning of 'destruction of a group.' It mentions the link between ethnic cleansing[119] and genocide,[120] but more importantly the German Federal Constitutional Court in 2000 affirmed that:

> [T]he statutory definition of genocide defends a supra-individual object of legal protection, i.e. the social existence of the group [...] the intent to destroy the group [...] extends beyond physical and biological extermination [...] The text of the law does not therefore compel the interpretation that the culprit's intent must be to exterminate physically at least a substantial number of the members of the group.[121]

This interpretation seems more adequate to the spirit, aims, and purposes of the Genocide Convention, as it takes into account the rules of interpretation of the VCLT. Article 31 provides that:

> A treaty shall be interpreted in good faith in accordance with the ordinary meaning to be given to the terms of the treaty in their context and in the light of its object and purpose.

The restrictive interpretation of the term 'genocide,' limiting it to the physical and biological destruction of the group, is essentially based on Article 32 of the VCLT that refers to 'supplementary means of interpretation, including the preparatory work of the treaty,' which should be used 'to determine the meaning when the interpretation according to article 31:

(a) Leaves the meaning ambiguous or obscure; or
(b) Leads to a result which is manifestly absurd or unreasonable.'

Therefore, it seems that the use of 'supplementary' means of interpretation were used to overcome the rules set up in Article 31, which is neither the logical nor the right way to proceed.

Conclusions

Despite the traditional view that 'genocide' only implies the physical or biological destruction of a group, there is an increasing literature in genocide

119 For a different opinion, see Schabas, *Genocide in International Law*, 200.
120 UN Doc. AG/Res/47/121 (18 December 1992).
121 Germany, Federal Constitutional Court, 2 BvR 1290/99, 12 December 2000, para. (III)(4)(a)(aa).

studies that would support a wider consideration of acts, including the so-called 'cultural genocide.' It is true that the destruction of culture, both material and immaterial, is not explicitly included among the acts foreseen by the 1948 Convention. However, there is no doubt that the above arguments, which are based on Lemkin's original thoughts on the concept of genocide, are quite attractive and certainly it is difficult to deny that the destruction of a group's identity by targeting cultural goods and expressions may be part of a method of annihilation of the group.

The analysis in the present chapter has shown that culture, in its different forms, can be considered a component of the identity of a group. Hence it would be suitable to consider the following options when acts target or destroy cultural goods and expressions.

The first option is to see the destruction of culture as a crime against humanity that could be perpetrated not only in war but also in times of peace. The main international protection of culture comes from the 1954 Convention and from IHL. However, considering the fact that the destruction of culture can be committed in peacetime, it would be appropriate to classify the destruction of the culture of a group or nation which would affect humanity as a whole and the common heritage of mankind as an international crime.

The second option would consider the targeting of cultural elements of a group not only as evidence of a genocidal intent on the part of the perpetrators, but also as acts that aim at the destruction of a group. This seems to be the most suitable way to link culture and genocide in line with the text of the 1948 Genocide Convention.

Article 2(b) of the Genocide Convention refers to acts that cause either 'bodily' or 'mental harm,' and the two conditions are not necessarily interlinked. The question is whether the destruction of culture, in its different forms and expressions – i.e. acts against the identity of a group – can reach the threshold of serious harm that would qualify them as genocidal acts, and not merely as acts which are evidence of an intent to commit genocide. This does not mean, as Fitzmaurice warned, to do sociology rather than law. The law is often interpreted and developed thanks to contributions that may come from other disciplines. For instance, it would be difficult to define torture without medical and psychological inputs.

As international criminal tribunals have recognised the importance of prosecuting individuals responsible for the destruction of cultural heritage in the event of armed conflict, the question which remains is whether the destruction of cultural elements – in many cases intangible, such as language, traditions, and social structures – may inflict such harmful consequences to nations, groups, and minorities that it would endanger their survival and lead to the destruction of their identity and therefore their survival as a distinctive group.

If so, the qualification of such destruction as genocide would seem to be in line with the original concept of genocide coined by Lemkin, and supported by the aims and purposes of the Genocide Convention, including its literal interpretation based on the developments concerning the value and relevance of culture in international law. This view is also supported by the finding in recent studies that 'acts of cultural genocide seem as just as likely to lead to the destruction of groups as those acts currently listed in the genocide statute that involve killing people, and hence just as significant.'[122]

122 Larry May, *Genocide: A Normative Account* (Cambridge: Cambridge University Press, 2010) 104.

12 Social media incitement to genocide

ECHR countries' perspective

Piotr Łubiński

Introduction

We can observe a revolution in communication within the last decade. One of the most significant aspects of it is the phenomenon of social media. Social media has become an excellent channel to mobilize support, disseminate narratives, wage information operations, or even coordinate military operations in the real world,[1] and has become one of the most powerful tools for coordinating nearly all of the world's political movements. The content on social media can be distributed by means and methods which avoid control or censorship, or even quality control. This leads to an increasing number of problems related to its mass use, particularly in cases when it is used to fuel social unrest. There is no recent or ongoing conflict which is not partly at least a result of the mass use of social media. The "Arab Spring", or the more current "*Mouvement des gilets*" in France, were powered by the use of social media to organize a massive group of protesters. As a result, larger, more loosely connected groups could conduct coordinated actions that were previously reserved for formal organizations.[2] Social media has also been used to support military operations.[3]

An intrinsic element of the mass use of social media is its vulnerability to manipulation(s). These popular movements are difficult to control, in particular with respect to ensuring that the content distributed amongst followers on the internet is accurate.[4] In recent years social media has not only become a channel for social unrest and data manipulation, but also constitutes a useful channel for spreading hate speech that may amount to behaviour known in the

1 Beata Biały, Social Media: From Social Exchange to Battlefield, *Cyber Defense Review*, Vol. 2(2) (Summer 2017), p. 75.

2 Clay Shirky, The Political Power of Social Media Technology, the Public Sphere, and Political Change, *Foreign Affairs*, Vol. 90, 2011, p. 35.

3 Biały, p. 75.

4 Matthew Mastromauro, Pre-trial Prejudice 2.0: How YouTube Generated News Coverage Is Set to Complicate the Concepts of Pre-trial Prejudice Doctrine and Endanger Sixth Amendment Fair Trial Rights, *Journal of High Technology Law*, Vol. 289, 2010, p. 291.

legal doctrine as "incitement to genocide". Within the last few years there have been at least two widely discussed examples of using social media with genocidal intent. The first was the case of ISIS and the Yazidi, and the second the case of the Rohingya population in Myanmar.

This article analyses the use of social media by ISIS (or Daesh) against the Yazidi population. In the Yazidi case I try to address the more general question of whether social media activity may, under certain circumstances, fall within the scope of incitement to genocide. This general issue is separated into several elements. It begins by presenting the scale and nature of ISIS activity in social media. Next, overlapping notions and legal regulations are examined, bearing in mind, for example, that the same content may constitute hate speech, incitement to terrorism, and/or incitement to genocide. Subsequently, some concepts in the jurisprudence on incitement will be applied to the new media, particularly from the perspective of the media cases adjudicated by the International Criminal Tribunal for Rwanda (ICTR) and International Criminal Tribunal for the Former Yugoslavia (ICTY) as well as the European Court of Human Rights (ECtHR).

Finally, the question of the criminal responsibility of persons engaged in ISIS's social media activities will be addressed, with particular attention to the internet genocide inciters supporting ISIS cause in European Convention on Human Rights (ECHR) countries.

Prevention of genocide: the legal framework

The Convention on the Prevention and Punishment of the Crime of Genocide of 1948 (Genocide Convention) provides in Article 1 for general obligations on state parties, declaring that "genocide, whether committed in time of peace or in time of war, is a crime under international law which they undertake to prevent and to punish". It creates the *hostis humani generi* character of the crime. It was also confirmed by the ICTR in the case of *Prosecutor v. Ntuyahaga* that universal jurisdiction exists for the crime of genocide. Thus the Convention puts on all state parties a legal obligation to combat genocide in all possible forms. Article 2 defines genocide as:

> [A]ny of the following acts committed with intent to destroy, in whole or in part, a national, ethnical, racial or religious group, as such: (a) Killing members of the group; (b) Causing serious bodily or mental harm to members of the group; (c) Deliberately inflicting on the group conditions of life calculated to bring about its physical destruction in whole or in part; (d) Imposing measures intended to prevent births within the group; (e) Forcibly transferring children of the group to another group.

In August 2014 the Yazidi population suffered from acts proscribed by points (a), (b), (c), (d) and (e) of Article 2.[5]

The main question addressed in this chapter is: which acts referred to in Article 2 are punishable? Should just physical extermination be punished? Or should other forms – including incitement to genocide as foreseen in the Article 3 (c) *Direct and public incitement to commit genocide*[6] – which are conducted and executed in the social media realm be punishable? This issue raises important questions as to whether mere social media activity can be considered as acts prohibited by international law, especially taking into consideration the nature and scale of the ISIS internet operation.

Incitement to commit genocide: general remarks

Lemkin's views on incitement and propaganda

When creating the concept of genocide, Raphael Lemkin was fully aware of the notion of incitement. As Irvin-Erickson has noted in his excellent book on Lemkin, in 1932 in the early years of his career Lemkin was collaborating with Professor Emil Rappaport on a new Polish criminal code. Lemkin was an author of, inter alia, Article 113, which criminalized incitement to aggressive war. His position corresponds with a 1927 Hersch Lauterpacht essay declaring that prohibitions on propaganda to incite war could be enshrined in national laws. In his further elaborations Irvin-Erickson mistakenly states that the Lemkin legacy led to the first criminal code which outlawed propaganda to incite violence.[7] It only outlawed incitement to wage an aggressive war.

Lemkin was bitterly aware of the nature of hateful propaganda. It was during the time of the Madrid conference in 1933 that Ukrainians were facing a Soviet-induced Holodomor (great famine; see Chapter 2). In his article "Soviet genocide in the Ukraine", published in 1953, Lemkin stated in a very direct way that genocide had taken place there. He was also greatly aware of the nature of Nazi propaganda at the time of the Holodomor. Later, his ideas were presented in the trials held by the International Military Tribunal at Nuremberg in 1946. The sentencing of *Der Stürmer* editor Julius Streicher and Hans Fritzsche, Reich Minister of Public Enlightenment and Propaganda, showed to the world the true nature of Goebbels' Nazi propaganda, with its hateful incitement of Germans to actively persecute and murder their Jewish neighbours.

5 Human Rights Council Report, Thirty-Second Session on Human Rights Situations That Require the Council's Attention, "They came to destroy": ISIS Crimes Against the Yazidis, A/HRC/32/CRP.2, 15 June 2016, pp. 21–28.

6 1948 Convention for the Prevention and Punishment of the Crime of Genocide, opened for signature 9 December 1948, Art. II, 78 UNTS 277 (entered into force 12 January 1951).

7 Douglas Irvin-Erickson, *Raphaël Lemkin and the Concept of Genocide*, University of Pennsylvania Press, 2017, p. 41 (footnote 3).

Lemkin's approach is reflected in Article 3 of the Genocide Convention, which prohibits direct and public incitement to genocide as well as all forms of complicity.[8] In order to maintain the preventive character of the prohibition of genocide, this inchoate crime concept – i.e. of direct and public incitement – became a punishable offence.[9]

Incitement to genocide and freedom of speech under international criminal tribunals and the ECHR

When discussing the issue of incitement in the new media age one may argue that it is protected by freedom of speech and that everything is blurred and it is very difficult to govern, and that for the sake of protecting a cornerstone of democracy, we should take a more lenient approach.

Freedom of speech is indeed truly one of the most fundamental rights in a democratic society. However, it is not unlimited. A lack of limits on freedom of speech easily leads to violation of the rights of others. Freedom of speech has been meticulously shaped by international law and courts. The International Covenant on Civil and Political Rights provides that "Any propaganda for war shall be prohibited by law" and "Any advocacy of national, racial or religious hatred that constitutes incitement to discrimination, hostility or violence shall be prohibited by law."[10]

Similar language is used in the International Convention on the Elimination of All Forms of Racial Discrimination. Article 4(a) declares that state parties

> [s]hall declare as an offence punishable by law all dissemination of ideas based on racial superiority or hatred, incitement to racial discrimination, as well as all acts of violence or incitement to such acts against any race or group of persons of another colour or ethnic origin and the provision of any assistance to racist activities, including the financing thereof.

The European Convention of Human Rights also protects freedom of expression. In the *Handyside* case the Court, then referred to as "the Commission", explained righteously that this right may be "favourably received or regarded as inoffensive or as a matter of indifference, but also [...] those that offend, shock or disturb".[11] But freedom of expression is not unlimited. Article 10.2 of the ECHR provides that

8 Convention on the Prevention and Punishment of the Crime of Genocide, United Nations, *Treaty Series*, Vol. 78, p. 277. https://treaties.un.org/doc/publication/unts/volume%2078/volume-78-i-1021-english.pdf/

9 William Schabas, *The UN International Criminal Tribunals: The Former Yugoslavia, Rwanda and Sierra Leone*. Cambridge: Cambridge University Press, 2006 p.181

10 International Covenant on Civil and Political Rights 1966, 999 UNTS 171, (1966) 6 ILM 368; available at: https://treaties.un.org/doc/publication/unts/volume%20999/volume-999-i-14668-english.pdf.

11 *Handyside v UK* (1976) Series A No 24, para 49.

> the exercise of these freedoms [...] may be subject to such formalities, conditions, restrictions or penalties as are prescribed by law and are necessary in a democratic society, [...] for the prevention of disorder or crime.[12]

In this regard two values must be balanced: freedom of speech and the prevention of genocide as broadly construed. The prevention of genocide, or specifically the exclusion of incitement to genocide from the protections of freedom of speech, should be interpreted in conjunction with Article 17 of the ECHR, which says that groups and individuals should not "engage in any activity or perform any act aimed at the destruction of any of the rights and freedoms set forth herein or at their limitation to a greater extent than is provided for in the Convention". The Court has applied Article 17 in cases of Holocaust revisionism and forms of anti-Semitism.[13]

The ECtHR has several times strongly opposed incitement to violence. In *Hizb ut-Tahrir and Others v. Germany*, the ECtHR referred to the ban on activities of an Islamist association for advocating the use of violence (active jihad, suicide attacks in Israel) in order to destroy Israel. The association was calling for the banishment or killing of Israeli inhabitants and for the overthrow of the governments of the Israeli state. In the Court's view, the association's approach, by "employing this right for ends which are clearly contrary to the values of the Convention, notably the commitment to the peaceful settlement of international conflicts and to the sanctity of human life"[14] was not nor should be protected by the Convention.

The Court's finding was confirmed in the case of *Kasymakhunov and Saybatalov v. Russia*.[15] The applicant was convicted for spreading the ideology of Hizb ut-Tahrir al-Islami, banned as a terrorist organisation in Russia, and for

12 Article 10 reads in full: "1. Everyone has the right to freedom of expression. This right shall include freedom to hold opinions and to receive and impart information and ideas without interference by public authority and regardless of frontiers. This Article shall not prevent States from requiring the licensing of broadcasting, television or cinema enterprises. 2. The exercise of these freedoms, since it carries with it duties and responsibilities, may be subject to such formalities, conditions, restrictions or penalties as are prescribed by law and are necessary in a democratic society, in the interests of national security, territorial integrity or public safety, for the prevention of disorder or crime, for the protection of health or morals, for the protection of the reputation or rights of others, for preventing the disclosure of information received in confidence, or for maintaining the authority and impartiality of the judiciary." Council of Europe, *European Convention for the Protection of Human Rights and Fundamental Freedoms, as amended by Protocols Nos. 11 and 14*, 4 November 1950, ETS 5, available at: www.echr.coe.int/Documents/Convention_ENG.pdf [accessed 11 July 2019].

13 Antoine Buyse, Dangerous Expressions: The ECHR, Violence and Free Speech, *International and Comparative Law Quarterly*, Vol. 63(2), April 2014, p. 494.

14 Case of *Hizb Ut-Tahrir and others v. Germany* (App No 31098/08, 12 June 2012) para 74, available at: http://hudoc.echr.coe.int/eng?i=001-111532 [accessed 10.07.2019].

15 Case of *Kasymakhunov and Saybatalov v. Russia* (Applications No 26261/05 and 26377/06), available at: http://hudoc.echr.coe.int/eng?i=001-117127 [accessed 10.07.2019].

recruiting new members. The organization was glorifying warfare and Islamic rule based on the Sharia (religious law). According to the ECtHR, the dissemination of these kinds of political ideas fell within the scope of the Article 17 prohibition.

A very similar line was confirmed in the ECtHR decision in *Belkacem v. Belgium*.[16] In this case the Court declared that the applicant's claim that he was unjustly sentenced to a fine and prison was inadmissible. The applicant, the leader and spokesperson of the organisation Sharia4Belgium, was sentenced for incitement to discrimination, hatred, and violence on account of remarks he made in YouTube videos concerning non-Muslim groups. In the Court's view, the hateful attack was incompatible with the values of tolerance, social peace, and non-discrimination.[17] Moreover, in the Court's opinion his remarks advocating jihad and defending Sharia and calling for violence to establish it could be regarded as "hate speech".[18]

In the light of the judgments of international courts as well as the opinions of a number of legal scholars, incitement to genocide is prohibited. It is prohibited not only in ICTR judgments but also constitutes an *ius cogens* norm.[19]

This approach is supported by the ECHR, which prohibits the abuse of rights and freedoms. The ECtHR has in several cases admitted that freedom of expression is not unlimited and that Article 17 provides a reasonable tool for fighting against the abuse of basic freedoms. The ECtHR has mostly dealt with hate speech, but referring to *argumentum a maiori ad minus* has clearly indicated that incitement to genocide is a form of hate speech and is not protected by the freedom of expression under the ECHR.

Incitement to genocide and genocide: a causal link

The issue of incitement raises a question regarding causality of the crime. Should incitement be punishable only when the incited crime took place? This is of particular importance when we are speaking about social media. Very often, due to the nature of incitement in cyberspace there is little or no territorial link with a crime in question. But from the perspective of crime prevention, the simple fact of incitement should be punished.

16 Press Release – Registrar of the Court ECHR 253 (2017) 20.07.2017, available at: https://hudoc.echr.coe.int/app/conversion/pdf?library=ECHR&id=003-5795519-7372789&filename=Decision%20Belkacem%20v.%20Belgium%20-%20hate%20speech%20by%20the%20leader%20of%20a%20radical%20Salafist%20organisation.pdf.

17 Ibid.

18 For more, see Guide on Article 17 of the Convention – Prohibition of Abuse of Rights, March 2019, available at: www.echr.coe.int/Documents/Guide_Art_17_ENG.pdf [accessed 10.07.2019].

19 More on Report of the International Law Commission Sixty-Sixth Session (5 May–6 June and 7 July–8 August 2014) (A/69/10) vide Tladi annex, available at: https://legal.un.org/docs/?path=./ilc/reports/2014/english/annex.pdf&lang=EFSRAC.

This line of reasoning has been confirmed by international courts prohibiting public and direct incitement towards genocide. As was pointed out in the *Akayesu* case, the incitement to commit genocide should be punished whether or not it was successful.[20] A similar reasoning was confirmed in the *Nahimana* case, where the Court ruled that no causal link between the words and the act was necessary for the crime of incitement to have occurred.[21] It underlined that there is no need for evidence that genocide was committed as a result of the incitement.[22]

The legal nature of incitement to genocide was confirmed by the *Media Case* Appeals Chamber.[23] Incitement crimes are known as "inchoate" offenses. In other words, the crime is committed when the words are uttered in the proper context. There need be no results in terms of violence.[24] Causation is not an element of the crime of incitement to genocide.[25]

Incitement to genocide: direct and public

In order to fulfil the liability requirements of the Genocide Convention one has to have a specific intent to cause genocide, and the incitement must be *direct* and *public*.[26] As regards the term "incitement", according to the Cambridge dictionary it means "to encourage someone to do or feel something unpleasant or violent".[27] The meaning of the term "incitement" was explained in the *Kajelijeli* judgment as follows:

> In the common law jurisdictions, incitement to commit a crime is defined as encouraging or persuading another to commit the crime, including by

20 Wibke Kristin Timmerman, The Relationship between Hate Propaganda and Incitement to Genocide: A New Trend in International Law Towards Criminalization of Hate Propaganda? *Leiden Journal of International Law*, Vol. 18, 2005, p. 267.

21 Ibid., p. 267.

22 *Nahimana et. al.* (ICTR-99-52-T) in Schabas, p. 181.

23 Shannon Fyfe, Tracking Hate Speech Acts as Incitement to Genocide in International Criminal Law, *Leiden Journal of International Law*, Vol. 30(2), 2017, p. 538.

24 Elizabeth M. Renieris, Combatting Incitement to Terrorism on the Internet: Comparative Approaches in the United States and the United Kingdom and the Need for International Solution, *11 Vand J. Ent. & Tech. L.* 673, 682 (2009) (with reference to incitement to terrorism); Susan Benesch, Vile Crime or Inalienable Right: Defining Incitement to Genocide, *48 Va. J. Int'l L.* 485, 494 (2008) (with reference to incitement to genocide).

25 For more on that see Gregory S. Gordon, *Atrocity Speech Law: Foundation, Fragmentation Fruition*, Oxford University Press, 2017 (noting that causation is not a required element and specifying that "to make out a prima facie case, the prosecutor need not prove the incitement resulted in genocide"); and Gregory S. Gordon, "Freedom of Expression, Hate Speech, and Incitement to Terrorism and Genocide: Resonances and Tensions," in Anne F. Bayefsky and Laurie R. Blank (eds), *Incitement to Terrorism*, Brill Nijhoff, 2018, p. 16.

26 Benesch, p. 493.

27 Collins Cobuild online dictionary https://dictionary.cambridge.org/pl/dictionary/english/incite.

> use of threats or other forms of pressure, whether or not the crime is actually committed. [...] Civil law systems punish direct and public incitement assuming the form of provocation, which is defined as an act intended directly to provoke another to commit a crime or a misdemeanour through speeches, shouting or threats, or any other means of audio-visual communication.[28]

The meaning of the term "direct and public" was later developed by the international criminal courts, particularly by the ICTR and ICTY. In the *Akayesu* case, the Court stated that:

> The 'direct' element of incitement implies that the incitement assumes a direct form and specifically provokes another to engage in a criminal act, and that more than mere vague or indirect suggestion goes to constitute direct incitement.[29]

Furthermore, in the *Nyiramasuhuko* case the Court stated:

> 'Direct' incitement to commit genocide requires that the speech is a direct appeal to commit an act referred to in Article 2 (2) of the Statute. It must be more than a vague or indirect suggestion, and an accused cannot be held accountable for this crime based on hate speech that does not directly call for the commission of genocide. However, even when a speech contains no explicit appeal to commit genocide, it may still constitute direct incitement to commit genocide in a particular context, so long as the speech is not considered ambiguous within that context. In order to determine the speech's true meaning, it may be helpful to examine how it was understood by the intended audience. In the context of Rwanda, the culture and nuances of the Kinyarwanda language should be considered when determining what constitutes direct incitement to commit genocide.[30]

The public element was deliberated upon in the *Kajelijeli* case, where the Court stated that:

28 The *Prosecutor v Kajelijeli* Judgment, 1 December 2003, para. 850, available at: https://unictr.irmct.org/sites/unictr.org/files/case-documents/ictr-98-44a/trial-judgements/en/031201.pdf; see also footnote 1060 of the case and reference to Ashworth, *Principles of Criminal Law*, p. 462, cited in Akayesu, Judgment (TC), para. 555.

29 The *Prosecutor v Akayesu*, Judgment (ICTR-96-4-T) 1998, para. 557, in Schabas, p. 182, available at: https://unictr.irmct.org/sites/unictr.org/files/case-documents/ictr-96-4/trial-judgments/en/980902.pdf.

30 *The Prosecutor v. Pauline Nyiramasuhuko et al.*, Trial Judgment, 24 June 2011, para. 5986, available at: https://unictr.irmct.org/sites/unictr.org/files/case-documents/ictr-98-42/trial-judgments/en/110624.pdf.

> The 'public' element of incitement to commit genocide is appreciated by looking at the circumstances of the incitement – such as where the incitement occurred and whether or not the audience was select or limited. As in Akayesu the call, for criminal action, to a number of individuals in a public place or to members of the general public at large by such means as the mass media, for example radio or television.[31]

The nature and scope of public incitement was also clarified in the *Nyiramasuhuko* case, as follows:

> In discussing the 'public' element of this crime, the Appeals Chamber has noted that 'all convictions before the Tribunal for direct and public incitement to commit genocide involve speeches made to large, fully public assemblies, messages disseminated by the media, and communications made through a public address system over a broad public area'.
>
> Moreover, the Appeals Chamber has taken into account the travaux préparatoires of the Genocide Convention, which confirm that 'public' incitement to genocide pertains to mass communications. Conversely, the travaux préparatoires indicate that 'private' incitement – understood as more subtle forms of communication such as conversations, private meetings, or messages – was specifically removed from the Convention.[32]

This last sentence seems to be of particular importance. Current online communication is often not private or "subtle"; i.e. resulting in "private incitement". Social media posts, shares, and likes can reach thousands or even millions of people, not to mention the almost unlimited number of followers on a platform such as Twitter or Facebook. Seen in this perspective, information provided through social media channels can certainly be considered as "direct and public".

Incitement to genocide and hate speech

There is a distinction between hate speech and incitement to genocide. This was noted in the *Media Case* by the ICTR.[33] At the same time, incitement to

31 *The Prosecutor v Kajelijeli* Judgment, 1 December 2003, para. 850; and *The Prosecutor v Akayesu* Judgment 2 September 1998, para. 851, available at: https://unictr.irmct.org/sites/unictr.org/files/case-documents/ictr-98-44a/trial-judgments/en/031201.pdf.

32 *The Prosecutor v. Pauline Nyiramasuhuko et al.*, Trial Judgment, 24 June 2011, para. 5986, available at: https://unictr.irmct.org/sites/unictr.org/files/case-documents/ictr-98-42/trial-judgements/en/110624.pdf.

33 *The Prosecutor v Nahimana et al.*, ICTR-99-52-A, A Ch (28 November 2007), para 986.

genocide certainly often overlaps with hate speech. Since the same wording may be attributed to both forms of offensive language, here I refer to the broadly discussed Susan Benesch test, proposed in her article "Vile Crime or Inalienable Right: Defining Incitement to Genocide". According to Benesch, hate speech may be considered as an incitement to genocide when:

1 The speech (was) understood by the audience as a call to genocide;
2 The speaker has authority or influence over the audience and the audience has the capacity to commit genocide.

She also poses additional questions:

3 Have the victims-to-be already suffered an outbreak of recent violence?
4 Were contrasting views still available at the time of the speech? Was it still safe to express them publicly?
5 Did the speaker describe the victims-to-be as subhuman, or accuse them of plotting genocide of their own?
6 Had the audience received similar messages before the speech?[34]

All these elements provide a solid ground to consider certain acts of speech not only as hate speech, but also – or maybe first and foremost – as incitement to genocide. However, one comment needs to be made. Benesch's conditions were crafted to be applied to the traditional media environment. For this reason some modifications may be proposed. For example point 2 – "The speaker has authority or influence over the audience and the audience has the capacity to commit genocide" – is based on the history of popular and influential singer Simon Bikindi, whose talent, popularity, and recognition were used by the Hutu genocidal enterprise.[35] In modern days, especially in the realm of social media, this issue of authority or influence on the audience may have a different meaning. It is not necessarily the result of mass popularity of a singer such as Simon Bikindi, but rather may arise because of a personal individual connection between incit*ee* and the incit*or*, who may be someone not influential like Bikindi but known only as an influencer on a particular forum. All the other Benesch points can be easily adapted to the reality of the social media environment.

Genocide incitement techniques

Using traditional, conventional words, Shannon Fyfe made several observations regarding verbal oppression as an example of genocide incitement techniques.[36]

34 Benesch, p. 498.
35 *The Prosecutor v Simon Bikindi*, ICTR-01-72-A, available at: https://unictr.irmct.org/sites/unictr.org/files/cases/ictr-01-72/public-information/en/profile-bikindi.pdf.
36 Fyfe, p. 531.

Also, Richter points out in a more detailed way different forms of incitement techniques:

1 Dehumanization – a method used by perpetrators to evoke feelings of loathing, contempt, and revulsion.[37]
2 Demonization – blaming the target for the perpetrators' personal misfortunes or those of his/her group and/or provoking feelings of fear towards a specific group.
3 Delegitimization – denying the existence or history of the other group, and/or accusing the target of extreme criminal acts.
4 Disinformation – presenting false or partial information with the intent to malign.
5 Denial – negating historical facts or denying past atrocities.
6 Threats – statements of intent to inflict pain, injury, damage, or other hostile action on groups or individuals.
7 Glorification[38] of terror by invoking well-known perpetrators of genocidal violence as role models (such as memorializing the "martyrs" or financial compensation for families of "martyrs" or terrorists).[39]

Both offenses – incitement to genocide or hate crimes – employ a technique known as "accusation in a mirror", which occurs when the perpetrator of the crime tries to accuse the victims of the very thing that the perpetrator is doing. This insidious technique was used to great effect in the Rwandan

37 "Dehumanization: After all, what does it take to treat fellow human beings as though they are not human beings? And the answer is this: dehumanization technique. In genocidal Rwanda, extremist Hutus routinely dehumanized Tutsis by referring to them in their incitement as snakes, cockroaches, and rats. Similarly, consider *Der Stuermer*, which was the viciously anti-Semitic paper edited by Julius Streicher. Based on the content of his newspaper, Streicher was prosecuted for crimes against humanity and found guilty at Nuremberg. The Palestinian Authority's outlets – and even children's shows and school curricula – have long called Jews snakes, monkeys, and pigs and called for the annihilation of Israel." Gordon, Freedom of Expression, p. 20.

38 "Glorification [...] Both incitement to genocide and terrorism tend to glorify past violence. For example, glorification of terrorism is currently taking place in the Palestinian Authority (PA). A recent example would be Jabril Raboul, a PA official, possibly a successor to PA leader Mahmoud Abbas. In 2015, he called a shooting attack in Beer-sheba that killed two and injured eleven an act of heroism. This incitement technique has resonances with the Rwandan Genocide. In addressing the population on Radio Television Libre des Mille Collines, RTLM, the infamous 'Radio Machete', announcer Georges Ruggiu congratulated the 'valiant combatants' who engaged in a 'battle' against innocent Tutsi civilians. This was a glorification of genocidal violence." Gordon, Freedom of Expression, p. 18.

39 See Elihu D. Richter, Incitement, Genocide, Genocidal Terror, and the Upstream Role of Indoctrination: Can Epidemiologic Models Predict and Prevent? *Public Health Reviews*, December 2018, p. 14, available at: https://link.springer.com/article/10.1186/s40985-018-0106-7.

Genocide.[40] For example, in an infamous speech in the lead-up to the Rwandan Genocide, Hutu extremist politician Leon Mugesera declared:

> These people called '*inyenzi*' [which means "cockroaches", thus also representing dehumanization] are now on their way to attack us. I am telling you, and I am not lying, it is they who want to exterminate us. They only want to exterminate us. They have no other aim. Are we really going to wait until they come to exterminate us?[41]

This speech was delivered by a person whose organization was planning genocide. So this is a classic "accusation in a mirror". This method can easily be discovered in ISIS's direct and public incitements to genocide, examined below.

Social media activity of ISIS: global and European aspects

There are a number of organizations which use social media for propaganda, recruitment, fundraising, data mining, and – what is most important – for indoctrination and incitement to criminal acts.[42] Al-Shabaab used Twitter during its attacks on a shopping mall in Nairobi in 2013. Lashkar-e-Taiba even coordinated its operation in Mumbai using data from Google Earth and other apps to hit the most crowded places.[43] A number of other examples are also well known.

There are several ways of exploiting social media to support military objectives. Tomas Elkjer Nissen identifies six of them: intelligence collection; (geo-) targeting; cyber operations; command and control; defence; and psychological warfare (informing and influencing).[44] This chapter analyses the most prominent, the so-called PSYOPS element.

In its psychological warfare ISIS has constructed a "state of the art" social media presence. It has underlined the notion of "information warfare" on several occasions. For example, Abu Hamza al-Muhajir, formerly War Minister and Prime Minister in the Islamic State of Iraq, contended that: "The Messenger of Allah (peace be upon Him) used to employ the most influential type of media

40 See Kenneth L. Marcus, Accusation in a Mirror, 43 *Loy. U. Chi. L.J.* 357, 358 (2012) ("In other words, AiM [Accusation in a Mirror] is a rhetorical practice in which one falsely accuses one's enemies of conducting, plotting, or desiring to commit precisely the same transgressions that one plans to commit against them.").

41 *Mugesera v. Canada* [2005] 2 s.c.R. 100, 2005 scc 40 app. ill, |i8. Cited in Gordon, Freedom of Expression.

42 Alexander Tsesis, Terrorist Speech on Social Media, *Vanderbilt Law Review*, Vol. 70, 2017, p. 655.

43 James P. Farwell, The Media Strategy of ISIS, *Survival, Global Politics and Strategy*, Vol. 56(6), 2014.

44 Tomas Elkjer Nissen, Social Media as a Tool of Hybrid Warfare, NATO Strategic Communications Centre of Excellence, 2016, p. 11, cited in Biały, p. 76.

in His time that had the greatest impact on the spirits of His enemies, which is poetry."[45] Using Twitter,[46] Facebook, and Snapchat it managed to influence thousands of followers.[47] At the peak of its activity, ISIS and its supporters were producing 90,000 tweets and other social media responses every day.[48] Their social media activity was linked with so-called anonymous sharing portals such as JustPaste.it, Sendvid.com, and Dump.to, which protect user anonymity.[49] ISIS achieved mastery in publicly presenting its actions, with its heinous acts meticulously directed, staged, and streamed all around the world.

ISIS used social media to try and achieve several goals. Its strategy was presented in a document called "Media Operative, You Are a Mujahid, Too", which was published online by ISIS in April 2016 on the its official propaganda channel on the social platform Telegram.[50] ISIS directly empowered its followers, saying "that participant[s] in the production and delivery" of propaganda should be regarded as one of ISIS' "media mujahidin".[51] This particular notion is of great importance. It makes it possible to classify ISIS social media followers not as bystanders, but as conscious individuals fully aware of their role in the military and genocidal efforts of ISIS.

There is no doubt that an intentional concept of incitement through social media was spread by ISIS. Winter quotes *Media Operative*, which says, "Inciting others to join the *jihad* is tantamount to engaging in the *jihad* oneself, as is steering others towards it and opening their eyes to it. The one who incites is a *mujahid* in the way of Allah the Almighty".[52]

Regardless of whether it was fully intentional or not, it certainly created a grey area of complicity. Especially from the ISIS perspective, the social media mujahidin operation was highly successful because it blurred the line between curious onlookers, supporters, and members of ISIS.[53]

ISIS not only mastered its propaganda, it also created a tailored narrative – both a positive and negative one. The positive one was oriented toward creating

45 Charlie Winter, Media Jihad: The Islamic State's Doctrine for Information Warfare, ICSR King's College London, available at: https://icsr.info/wp-content/uploads/2017/02/ICSR-Report-Media-Jihad-The-Islamic-State%E2%80%99s-Doctrine-for-Information-Warfare.pdf (12.04.2019), p. 12.

46 Tsesis, p. 655.

47 Joseph Shaheen, Network of Terror: How Daesh Uses Adaptive Social Networks to Spread its Message, NATO Strategic Communications Centre of Excellence, 2015, available at: www.stratcomcoe.org/network-terror-how-daesh-uses-adaptive-social-networks-spread-its-message.

48 Ahmad Shehabat and Teodor Mitew, Black-boxing the Black Flag: Anonymous Sharing Platforms and ISIS Content Distribution Tactics, *Perspectives on Terrorism*, Vol. 12(1), 2018, p. 83.

49 Ibid., p. 81.

50 Winter, p. 8.

51 Ibid., p. 9.

52 Ibid., p. 14.

53 Ibid., p. 9.

an alternative to the existing status quo.[54] Not only did it involve breaking "crusaders'" dirty deals, such as the Sykes–Picot agreement or fighting post-colonial injustice, but also spreading the Truth.[55] This positive message was strengthened by images of ISIS warriors in long lines of Hilux pickups sporting heavy equipment and weaponry, which were meant to convince jihadists to join the cause. As regards how successful it was, the numbers speak for themselves – by the end of 2016 ISIS managed to recruit over 30,000 fighters.[56] Thousands of Western European ISIS followers were encouraged by social media. It is assumed that nearly 5,000 ISIS fighters were recruited from Europe alone.[57] ISIS's positive narrative was definitely successful in building support and recruiting new members.[58]

The negative narrative was much more straightforward. The message was clear: there is a need to kill all opponents and enemies of holy jihad. Taking into consideration the size of the conquered territory, the mere killing of civilians, journalists, and opponents[59] was not enough. To subdue such a large Iraqi and Syrian territory required visual manifestations of its gory action, beheadings, and executions. The aim was clear – intimidation. The same role was played by the corporal punishments, imposed during public events with the aim to spread terror amongst the civilian population,[60] punishments which were also streamed live through various platforms.

All this – namely propaganda and its own story-telling – was streamed and published in social media and in traditional media outlets. Media supporting ISIS were not only located in the Middle East but also in Europe. Media such as Amaq News Agency, the Al-Bayan radio station, and the Halumu and Nashir news outlets serve as good examples.[61]

54 Ibid., p. 15.

55 Opposition to the colonial rule can be found in other sources; for example, a video streamed by ISIS, "There is No Life Without Jihad", featuring testimonials from self-identified Britons and Australians rejecting the current borders of the Middle East as drawn up by the foreign powers after the First World War. For more on this, see Farwell, p. 50.

56 Thomas Zeitzoff, How Social Media Is Changing Conflict, *Journal of Conflict Resolution*, Vol. 61(9), 2017, 1970–1991.

57 Radicalisation Awareness Network, Responses to Returnees: Foreign Terrorist Fighters and Their Families, July 2017, available at: https://ec.europa.eu/home-affairs/sites/homeaffairs/files/ran_br_a4_m10_en.pdf p. 6 [accessed 20.10.2019].

58 Farwell, p. 50.

59 Human Rights Council Report, Twenty-Seventh Session on Human Rights Situations That Require the Council's Attention (A/HRC/27/CRP.3) on the Syrian Arab Republic, *Rule of Terror: Living under ISIS in Syria*, pt. 19. p. 4, available at: www.ohchr.org/Documents/HRBodies/HRCouncil/CoISyria/HRC_CRP_ISIS_14Nov2014.doc [accessed 20.10.2019].

60 Ibid., p. 4.

61 In 2018, according to a Europol press release, the European Union, Canada and United States conducted a successful joint operation against the Amaq News Agency media outlet affiliated with ISIS. The operation was coordinated by the European Union Internet Referral Unit within the European Counter Terrorism Centre at Europol and involved authorities from Belgium, Bulgaria, Canada, France, the Netherlands, Romania, the United Kingdom and the United States. A seizure of digital evidence and ISIS servers took place on April 25 and 26, which helped identify both the administrators of ISIS websites and "potentially radicalized individuals on European soil and beyond", the agency said. Available at: www.europol.europa.eu/newsroom/news/islamic-state-propaganda-machine-hit-law-enforcement-in-coordinated-takedown-action [accessed 29.03.2019].

A pivotal element hooking ISIS social media and media outlet activities involved the anonymous sharing portals such as JustPaste.it.[62] This platform activity also garnered broad attention amongst government and intelligence bodies. It is/was owned by a Polish citizen, Mariusz Żurawek.[63] In 2014 ISIS began using this website to disseminate its online videos, images of beheadings, and what is particularly important, its digital edition of the ISIS online magazine *Dabiq*.[64] As Shehabat and Mitew assert, during the site's peak 70 per cent of its website content was ISIS.[65] So while formally the website was neutral, it was used to carry out the massive dissemination of ISIS content.

ISIS propaganda as "direct and public" incitement to genocide in traditional and social media

Nowadays it is rather difficult to distinguish between traditional and social media. They are highly interconnected. One of the most "popular" propaganda ISIS magazines, *Dabiq*, was published in PDF format and then disseminated through several information channels and methods. Its popularity was particularly enhanced using social media platforms. The question to be discussed here is whether ISIS propaganda and social media activity can or should be considered as "direct and public" indictment to genocide.

ISIS's origins can be traced back to Jordanian jihadist Abu Mus'ab al-Zarqawi. In the late 1990s, he travelled to Afghanistan, where he met the leaders of al-Qaeda. After the US invasion, al-Zarqawi fled to Iraq, where he became a well-known jihadist commander. His trademark was attacks against non-combatants, particularly targeting Shia places of worship.[66] Organizations under the command of Abu Omar al-Baghdadi also continued attacks against other religious groups, such as the Yazidis. An auger of the future ISIS attitude toward the Yazidis was the joint car bomb attacks which killed nearly 800 Yazidis in northern Iraq in 2007.[67] ISIS is/was an organization which identifies with a movement in Islamic political thought known as Jihadi-Salafism. Adherence to this ideology was explicitly advanced several times; for example, when ISIS leader Abu 'Umar al-Baghdadi appealed "to all Sunnis, and to the

62 O. Wasiuta, S. Wasiuta, P. Mazur, Państwo Islamskie ISIS: nowa twarz ekstremizmu - The Islamic State ISIS: a new face of extremism, Difin, Warszawa p. 182, 2018.

63 His biography is available at www.linkedin.com/in/zurawek/?originalSubdomain=pl.

64 Shehabat and Mitew, p. 88.

65 Ibid., p. 91.

66 National Center of Excellence for Islamic Studies, University of Melbourne, *ISIS (Islamic State of Iraq and Syria): Origins, Ideology, and Responses by Mainstream Muslim Scholars – A Resource for Community Leaders*, 2016, p. 1, available at: https://static1.squarespace.com/static/55120ecae4b01593abadc441/t/58fe89feff7c5003d9acbd86/1493076481168/ISIS_Origins%2C-Ideology%2C-and-Responses-by-Mainstream-Muslim-Scholars.pdf.

67 Ibid., p. 2.

young men of Jihadi-Salafism (*al-Salafiyya al-Jihadiyya*)".[68] According to Bunzel, Salafism offers fertile ground for the elimination of different forms of idolatry (*shirk*) and affirming God's Oneness (*tawhid*). As a part of Salafi propaganda/beliefs they consider themselves to be the only true Muslims, and find those who practice a so-called "major idolatry" to be outside Islam. ISIS was particularly hostile toward Yazidis, as they were perceived to be worshipping stones, saints, tombs, etc., and are considered apostates and deserters of the true religion.[69] ISIS's justification for the persecution of Yazidis was thus of a religious character.

ISIS ideology was spread through a blend of traditional and social media comments and also involved the use of video clips and movies. Before Tikrit was captured in 2014, ISIS released a movie, called *New*, which was disseminated both conventionally and unconventionally. Apart from the mass killing of Iraqi soldiers it also pictures the destruction of Shia mosques and religious objects.[70]

Direct and public incitement to Yazidi genocide may be found in *Dabiq*. An article entitled "The Revival of Slavery Before the Hour"[71] fulfilled several of the above-mentioned Richter categories. The article calls the enemy "Satanist and devil worshipers", which constitutes dehumanization (1); delegitimization (3); and disinformation (4).[72] It also contains direct and public threats (6) against the Yazidis. By stating that "Unlike the Jews and the Christians, there was no room for the jizyah payment [a tax to be paid to avoid conversion or death]", it was calling for the direct killing of Yazidi males, while another paragraph called for the enslavement of Yazidi females. This call for enslavement and calling persons spoils of war objectified and dehumanized Yazidi women (1).

> After capture, the Yazidi women and children were then divided according to the Shariah amongst the fighters of the Islamic State who participated in the Sinjar operations, after one fifth of the slaves were transferred to the Islamic State's authority to be divided as khums [spoils of war].[73]

It is difficult to precisely determine the number of social media tweets, links, and other data related to the dissemination of propaganda on the various forums. However, just one website – JustPaste.it – which harboured the full panoply of ISIS content (from incitement to pictures of hundreds of executions

68 Cole Bunzel, From Paper State to Caliphate: The Ideology of the Islamic State. Brookings Project on U.S. Relations with the Islamic World Analysis, Paper No. 19, 2015, p. 7.

69 Bunzel, p. 8.

70 G. Klein, Propaganda Daesh, Akademia Sztuki Wojennej-Academy of National Defence, Przegląd Strategiczny – Strategic Review 2016 nr 9, Warszawa, p. 187, 2016.

71 *Dabiq*, The Revival of Slavery Before the Hour, Issue 4, 2014, pp. 14–16, available at https://clarionproject.org/docs/islamic-state-isis-magazine-Issue-4-the-failed-crusade.pdf [accessed 03.07.2019].

72 Ibid., p. 14.

73 Ibid., p. 15.

of Yazidi men and boys) in 2014 had about 2.5 million unique users a month, which works out to about 6 million sessions every month.[74] This clearly made the ISIS propaganda very public. Furthermore, the ISIS incitement was direct and the audience grasped the meaning.[75]

The penalization of ISIS-related incitement

The penalization of incitement refers to the general criminalization concept based on the 1948 Convention on the Prevention and Punishment of the Crime of Genocide. Genocide, and the prohibition of genocide, have obtained an *ius cogens* character. The preventive nature of the prohibition of genocide requires punishing all the acts foreseen by Article 3 of the Convention.

Penalization of incitement requires a mental element. That is, a person convicted of direct and public incitement to commit genocide must have had the intent to cause the destruction, in whole or in part, of a national, ethnical, racial, or religious group. This intent fulfils the *mens rea* requirement of *dolus specialis.*[76] According to Gordon, in cases of incitement to genocide the mental element (*mens rea*) is of a dual nature: the first is the intent to incite, and the second the intent to commit the genocide itself.[77] However, taking into consideration the already-discussed issue of causation in cases of the crime of genocide, even incitement without the (personal) intent to commit the genocide gives grounds for penalization. In this regard the decisive factor is that the intended recipients of the message belonged to the general public, which requires an appeal to an indeterminate group of people (a fact that is indisputable in the social media and internet environment). As for the *mens rea*, the perpetrator must act with the intent to directly and publicly incite others to commit genocide, which presupposes genocidal intent on his/her part.[78]

The ICTR held that the crime is inchoate in nature, meaning that it is punishable even if no act of genocide resulted therefrom. So from the penalization perspective, a conviction for direct and public incitement to commit genocide does not require proof of a link between the incitement and any subsequent crime (a causal link). According to Peterson and Timmermann, this goes beyond what the drafters of the Genocide Convention could agree on. The Convention's *travaux préparatoires* demonstrate that the initial proposition that incitement to genocide should be criminalized regardless of whether or not it

74 Carmen Fishwick, How a Polish Student's Website Became an Isis Propaganda Tool, The Guardian, August 15, 2014, available at: www.theguardian.com/world/2014/aug/15/-sp-polish-man-website-isis-propaganda-tool.

75 Gordon, p. 16.

76 Fyfe, p. 536.

77 Gordon, p. 16.

78 Ines Peterson, International Criminal Liability for Incitement and Hate Speech, in Martin Böse, Michael Bohlander, André Klip, and Otto Lagodny, *Justice Without Borders: Essays in Honour of Wolfgang Schomburg*, Brill/Nijhoff, 2018, p. 337.

was successful was eventually dropped.[79] However, in light of the rulings of international criminal courts regarding the development and prevention of genocide, this strict approach taken by the Convention drafters no longer holds. Not to mention that this book is devoted to Raphael Lemkin, the founder of the concept of genocide. His works had a great impact on the mindset of the Polish delegation (Juliusz Katz-Suchy, Manfred Lachs, Aleksander Bramnson, and Aleksander Rudziński). During the Sixth Committee meeting, the Polish delegation insisted that a vital element in incitement is the creation of "an atmosphere favourable to the perpetration of the crime".[80] And penalization of even an unsuccessful incitement clearly prevents the creation of such an atmosphere. This position was surprisingly supported by the Soviets,[81] who felt that the "repression of genocide should include prohibition of incitement to racial hatred as well as various preparatory or preliminary acts, such as study and research aimed at developing techniques of genocide".[82]

The language of ISIS propaganda is clear. Its very strong wording, calling for the extermination of Yazidis, leaves little room for reasonable doubts. Such wording makes it possible to attribute to ISIS the mental element of a culprit, which is relevant to the requisite *mens rea*. Article 30 of the International Criminal Court Statute provides that

> [f]or the purposes of this article, a person has intent where: (a) In relation to conduct, that person means to engage in the conduct; (b) In relation to a consequence, that person means to cause that consequence or is aware that it will occur in the ordinary course of events. […] For the purposes of this article, 'knowledge' means awareness that a circumstance exists or a consequence will occur in the ordinary course of events. 'Know' and 'knowingly' shall be construed accordingly.[83]

This fulfils what is known under civil law as *dolus directus* (the perpetrator foresees the harmful consequences of the criminal act and wants to bring about those consequences), and *dolus indirectus* (the perpetrator foresees certain additional consequences of the criminal act as a likelihood or merely a possibility and brings about those consequences even though that is not what he wanted or desired to bring about), with the exception of *dolus eventualis*.[84]

79 Ibid., p. 337.

80 *Akayesu*, *supra* note 68, para. 557, in Timmerman, p. 269.

81 Taking into consideration the nature and scope of Soviet-era propaganda.

82 William Schabas, *Genocide in International Law: The Crime of Crimes*, 2nd edition, Cambridge University Press, 2009, p. 72.

83 Rome Statute of the International Criminal Court 17 July 1998, 2187 UNTS 90 (last amended 2010).

84 Johan Van der Vyver, The International Criminal Court and the Concept of Mens Rea in International Criminal Law, *University of Miami International & Comparative Law Review*, Vol. 12, 2004, pp. 63–64, Emory Public Law Research Paper.

These words cover the situation, as noted by the ICTR in *Nahimana*, where explicit calls for violence were made by the accused, as members of the Coalition pour la Defense de la Republique (CDR) were chanting "*tubatsembatsembe*" (or "let's exterminate them").[85] Thus the similar appeals made by ISIS should not only be prohibited, but also criminalized.

Other social media activity: copy-pasting, sharing, or liking as a form of incitement

Posting by a user means creating a story, making a comment, linking a content, or simply putting a picture online. Usually, the legal status of the post is similar amongst different social media platforms. The social media user is the owner of the content (he/she can remove it at will). From the criminal law point of view, the posting of specific content is attributable to the physical person. Unless a post is posted by computers or bots, this requires a mental element which can be further penalized. Amongst volunteers joining ISIS there were a significant number of females (around 550). Many unsuccessful ISIS brides were caught because of posting their willingness to make *hijra*[86] on their social media accounts.[87]

All forms of communicating via social media seem to satisfy the mental element of the crime, whether it is sharing, liking, or following. In all these forms the user publicly announces his or her views or beliefs. Liking ISIS content that will be visible to an unspecified group of people is very public. Not only so-called Facebook friends, but also the poster's friends' friends can see his likes, comment on them, or share them. This basically means that content containing a hateful comment or an incitement to genocide is broadcast to the public in a way which is not much different from, for example, radio or TV. Thus such action satisfies the requirements of public and direct action as foreseen by Article 2 of the Genocide Convention.

Naturally the question of criminal responsibility of the social media platforms themselves as an accomplice to genocide is also very interesting. However, it is beyond the scope of this chapter.

These forms of sharing views can be analysed using the already-mentioned Benesch test. It is possible to imagine that a person of great influence – a Simon Bikindi-type personality – shares or likes posts or movies with a genocidal

85 Timmerman, p. 269.
86 "Hijra" is an Arabic word meaning "emigration", evoking the Prophet Muhammad's escape from Mecca to Medina. Abdullah Azzam defined "hijra" as departing from a land of fear to a land of safety, a definition he later amplified to include the act of leaving one's land and family to take up jihad in the name of establishing an "Islamic State". For more on it see Anita Perešin, Fatal Attraction: Western Muslimas and ISIS, *Perspectives on Terrorism*, Vol. 9(3), 2015, p. 34, Footnote 4, SN 2334–3745, available at: www.researchgate.net/publication/301748250_Fatal_Attraction_Western_Muslimas_and_ISIS.
87 Perešin, p. 22.

content. In such a scenario it would seem to be reasonable to consider such actions as an intentional form of incitement to genocide, punishable under international and/or domestic law.

Currently, instead of a person of great influence we simply have influencers. This category of persons mirrors the category recognized by the ICTR. As a result, in my opinion a person does not need to be particularly famous (i.e. a Simon Bikindi type of popularity). It is enough if he or she has an impact on the lives of followers. In such a case one may be not only an *internet mujahidin*, but also an inciter to genocide, and as such responsible for violation of the 1948 Genocide Convention.

Conclusions

While it is obvious that the world has changed, in the realm of communication we are facing a real revolution. A vital element of this revolution is social media, which was born out of the desire for free and undisturbed communication. However, the lack of control over social media has become its greatest sin. Persons who operate without any real control create space for hate speech and other forms of lawlessness. The lack of a truly efficient means of legal procedure against lawbreakers has created unprecedented safe havens for any person who wishes to use social media not as a peaceful Mr Jekyll in Hyde Park but as nasty Mr Hyde.

There are, however, legal means to prosecute incitement to genocide committed on social media, or more generally in cyberspace. As was discussed above, incitement on the internet may fulfil all the requirements provided by the Genocide Convention, relevant treaties, and customary law. The major challenges are still the uncontrolled nature of Facebook and other social media platforms. The complex jurisdictional issues, combined with a lack of domestic regulation of social media, result in unprecedented impunity. However, the existing domestic legal mechanisms may, with the support of universal jurisdiction, provide a solution.

Incitement with the use of social media will be most likely a growing phenomenon. There is a definite need for stricter policies. There is a need to provide a relevant, cross-culture-sensitive protection, based on local legal regimes, in order to protect against incitement to genocide. Pressure has to be put on communication platform operators worldwide, such as Facebook or Twitter, and local ones such as JustPaste.it. A lack of efficient prevention may lead to further degeneration of freedom of speech (and its limits). Subsequently genocides may be sparked and orchestrated using social media.

As author I have made all efforts to prove in this chapter that all the elements of incitement to genocide, such as incitement per se, *direct* and *public*, and with a *special intent* may be fulfilled in cases of inciting genocide by using the social media realm.

Index

For Product Safety Concerns and Information please contact our EU
representative GPSR@taylorandfrancis.com
Taylor & Francis Verlag GmbH, Kaufingerstraße 24, 80331 München, Germany

www.ingramcontent.com/pod-product-compliance
Ingram Content Group UK Ltd.
Pitfield, Milton Keynes, MK11 3LW, UK
UKHW020016200926
475702UK00014B/1922
9780367504984